Rising Expectations
India's Transformation

Rising Expectations
India's Transformation

Uma Narula

ATLANTIC
PUBLISHERS & DISTRIBUTORS (P) LTD

Published by

ATLANTIC

PUBLISHERS & DISTRIBUTORS (P) LTD

7/22, Ansari Road, Darya Ganj,
New Delhi-110002
Phones : +91-11-23273880, 23275880, 23280451
Fax : +91-11-23285873
Web : www.atlanticbooks.com
E-mail : info@atlanticbooks.com

Branch Office
5, Nallathambi Street, Wallajah Road,
Chennai-600002
Phones : +91-44-64611085, 32413319
E-mail : chennai@atlanticbooks.com

ISBN 978-81-269-1222-3

Printed in India at Nice Printing Press, A-33/3A, Site-IV, Industrial Area, Sahibabad, Ghaziabad, U.P.

Dedicated to

Tara with her Indian roots
And those of her generation
Who would create a transformed India

Acknowledgements

My acknowledgements are due to ordinary people from high and low end who shared their stories, their frustrations, and their hopes and expectations for a transformed India. My thanks are also due to those at the helm of affairs—both in public and private sectors—who have committed themselves to motivate people and raise their aspirations to achieve growth and economic boom for India; make every effort to accelerate the pace of transformation that will empower the people of India for a better tomorrow.

I owe my acknowledgements to the editorial and production team at the Atlantic Publishers and Distributors (P) Ltd. who so diligently and efficiently produced the book. I admire their patience to check and re-check my suggestions to produce the book. My thanks are due to Manish Kumar, MD, Atlantic Publishers, who endorsed my attempt to produce the transformation story of India and agreed that its publication will be relevant to the times. I am grateful to him that the book has shaped well and will give amazing insights to the readers.

Uma Narula

Preface

Rising Expectations: India's Transformation is the third book in the globalization series. Its focus of study is the story of India's transformation through globalization since 1990s.

It is heartening to note that changing emerging practices brought about by globalization in domains like social, cultural, political, public administration, and business enterprises tend to empower people. People's empowerment creates global empowerment through changing communication practices.

Indian economic scenario began to change in various domains with the introduction of globalization efforts in 1991. The book highlights how and why globalization started in India. Globalization is an ongoing process. It did create challenges for India from various perspectives and it continues to face more and more challenges as the process, the structure, the dimensions and face of globalization change vis-à-vis India. And that is the transformation story of India—the road to growth—the focal point of this study.

The book studies globalization story of India not only as a road to growth but as an ongoing big shift in policies and programmes that brought the transformation leading to global integration and people empowerment through emerging communication practices.

Transformation of India through business expansion, products and services, and economic practices for creating economic growth, prosperity and boom, financial and human capital development, infrastructure development and wider connectivity through development of telecommunication since 90s have put India on the road to growth.

The multiple domains in which India has changed tremendously include on the one hand, economy, business, technology, computerization, telecommunication, education, public health, consumerism, leisure and entertainment, human rights, family and social growth, etc. On the other hand, the governance and politics, terrorism-violence-war, etc. have also changed India. The changes in these multiple domains are multi-directional, encompassing economic, political, social, cultural and religious aspects.

Rising expectations of its people and the world expectations from India have all been transforming India towards higher levels of modernity, economic growth and prosperity and globalization. It is an interesting story of the success of globalization process leading to rising expectations in a developing country like India which is transforming itself through global empowerment and people empowerment at home on many fronts and aspiring to be a super achiever and a global power to reckon with.

It is a challenge that India is making earnest endeavours to transform a developing country of more than one billion people into a developed nation and global leader by 2020 despite severe constraints like scarcity of resources, illiteracy, poverty and problems in implementation of plans and policies.

The main focus of the book is India's transformation story at these levels. This transformation is ongoing. The book seeks to address ensuing transformation challenges that India is facing now and is likely to face in future to ensure its presence in the global scene as a global power and more so trying to transform this world into a better place for its own people.

Globalized outsourcing was the start of India's transformation story as it sailed through with government and private efforts, policies, planning and actions. Besides people's endeavours, efforts at national and international level were significant and essential for the ensuing transformation to take place. This was the first significant contributory factor for economic boom. This also highlights the significance of interdependency loop for global participation in India's development projects through foreign funds. This has been another contributory factor for India's economic boom and rising expectations.

Transformation was set in through rising expectations of economic gain achieved by means of these practices. In the later ongoing stages, the process of transformation is being accelerated by exposure to more and more of emerging best practices in various domains. India is treading on its transformation journey by choosing the best practices which are facilitating its progress in various walks of life.

The changing political and social practices have contributed to India's economic growth, prosperity and boom and these all added to India's rising expectations, growth story and transformation journey; but these are not being addressed in this book for fear of losing sight of the main focus of economic transformation.

Over the past 18 years, India has moved from a largely impoverished, underdeveloped country to a bustling, innovative, fast-changing society. This book shows how and why this could be possible. There are vast changes that have recently taken place to turn this once sleeping giant into one of the world leaders in the realms of entrepreneurship, private participation, science and technology, etc.

After travelling many countries—both developed and developing—I travelled back to India. When I stepped out of the airport going to Delhi Metro, I witnessed significant improvements on its roads, highways and the airport itself. There were more regulated traffic, well-lit roads without any garbage on them. But there was little change in terms of prosperity or economic growth. Even there is no safety in travelling during late night. Cases of heinous murders and looting of passengers, particularly foreigners are frequent in India even in the capital of the country. How would airport, police and tourist authorities respond to it?

I am amazed to see the transformation that India has undergone since 90s, and the rising expectations of people from the transformation and globalization.

But the biggest questions are: How do we face these challenges? Do we have strategies to achieve these through cooperation and collaboration of public and private sector?

The content of the book about configurations of transformation of India is presented through issues related to anecdotes, events, news in the media and formal and informal discussions and conversations with people and their critical thinking. These are interwoven. Events—both at home and global level—shape them. The changing events in India inspired me to research and probe into this aspect of globalization story and pen down those thoughts. The dreams and aspirations, the hopes and despairs, fears and anxieties of people around goaded me to think about transformation taking place around us. I believe that India matters as never before to the future of the world. These created the background, and the urge to write about ongoing transformation journey of India.

The book attempts to analyse the amazing excitement about India's rise, and deep concerns over the serious challenges that India faces. It studies in detail India's incredible metamorphosis and grim vision, its possibilities and perils, and stories and opinions of people. This change may be interpreted variably by informed and not-so-informed readers.

It is not possible to capture in one book, the totality of India's rising expectations, its transformation and the challenges when the country is changing at a pace of historic velocity. Therefore, I have focused on economic transformation—an important aspect of this change.

Organization of the Book

The book comprises nine chapters. Each chapter deals with different aspects of the story of India's economic transformation. Chapter 1 gives the conceptual framework for the book and the relevance of key concepts of globalization to transformation.

Chapter 2 highlights the background to India's global participation, rising expectations, thus providing a detail to this journey to transformation.

Chapter 3 focuses on global structure of business expansion. It gives a snapshot of Indian companies highlighting their foray into expanding products and services, new technologies and multiple geographies. Randomly selected, a few big companies, medium to small upcoming companies in various domains, give glimpses of the entrepreneurship, progress, global participation and acceptance, collaboration and joint ventures, highlighting their current business product focus, collaboration and joint ventures with other global partners, the book concentrates on all these and underlines the significance of global technologies and global participation which have been the major drive behind India's transformation.

Chapter 4 studies the development of that physical infrastructure which is an integral component of global transformation dimension leading to transforming India. As we began our journey to the road to growth and transformation, we soon realized the importance of world class physical infrastructure and hence, attention was paid to the development thereof—from power plants, highways and expressways, rails and airlines—to new ports and shipbuilding, telecommunication, and safe drinking water, etc. including space research and defence infrastructure. We also need other supporting infrastructure of tourism, and entertainment economy. A boost in energy sector covering power, oil, petrol and gas—is the driving force for infrastructure development contributing to India's transformation and economic growth.

Chapter 5 deals with the three major factors, important for human development infrastructure in India, viz. healthy work force, soundly educated human resource with wider horizon and creativity, skills and training, matching the changing employment scenario and creating employability. The way India's businesses are expanding and its economy is burgeoning, it can achieve optimum employment if it targets at creating employability. This assumes greater importance in the present environment of economic slowdown. The book throws light on these aspects in the context of changing scenario.

Chapter 6 discusses development of capital for economic growth. The capital flow—both from domestic and foreign resources—is important for India. Capital is indispensible to expand businesses, develop infrastructure and achieve transformation in various domains. Equally important is to be selective about the channels of capital as well as its management for optimum utilization and benefits.

Chapter 7 focuses on connectivity, highlighting the rising expectations of people in India as the three components of connectivity—telephone, computer and television—are making tremendous progress worldwide and in India as well. They are playing an important role in bringing about changes in life.

Chapter 8 deals with the transformation challenges that India has been facing since 90s when the economic liberalization policies were initiated. India efficiently handled the challenges to create niche and opportunities for itself through focus on business expansions in key areas of products and services in different global markets. It faced the challenges of raising people's expectations and aspirations for economic growth by motivating them and getting social and political consensus. It also confronted the task of adopting latest technology to achieve economic growth. From 2000 onward it has shifted its attention to the development of physical and human infrastructure, bringing further expansion of businesses through new models, and transforming rural base to enhance its global power image. It envisions that future challenges creating transformation revolution will improve the quality of life of majority of people in India, particularly those living in rural and remote areas.

Chapter 9 reflects the global financial crisis. It discusses global meltdown and its impact on Indian financial scenario. It also studies the risk management in the emerging situation.

The book will be of immense value to the students, teachers, and researchers of Economics. Those who have an urge to know about the changes that have occurred in Indian economic scenario in the wake of globalization will find it interesting and inculcating.

Uma Narula

Contents

PART I

Globalization: Key Concepts

1

We feel it is important to offer even the most informed readers the foundations and tools to understand the global economy and globalization process. In this context, the three tiers of conceptual framework of globalization with the key concepts of globalization process and global economy, global communications, global business markets, emergent society and emergent markets, and emerging global practices in the context of global empowerment and people empowerment are the key concepts that we highlight.

Conceptual Framework of Globalization

The conceptual framework of globalization is defined in three tiers. The first tier defines the concepts of global structure, dimension of global transformation, and transformation challenges relevant for ongoing process of globalization. The second tier defines the supporting concepts and models of loop model, interdependency model, learned dependency model, business models for special segments and globalization model. Supporting concepts and models are essential and important for the first tier concepts as well as for the ongoing globalization processes to work effectively.

Global Structure: The focus of global structure is on business expansions in key areas of products and services and different geo-markets and expansion and development of new business models as applied to expansion and development of new products and services and markets in new geographies.

Globalization is further structured through the development of human, intellectual and financial capitals.

Appropriate human manpower is essential for globalization and its success. It is developed relevant to the demands of global markets through creative education system, development of talents and skills of the workforce through education and training programs. Different countries would be approaching and participating in global markets through different business models, with different characteristics and demographics of its people, and with varied cultural practices. The development of human capital in every country should be relevant from these perspectives for providing productive employment to the people both in national contexts for entering the global markets and in global contexts for participating in the globalization process. Thus, development of human capital depends on the planning, policies and actions of the countries.

Intellectual capital is developed through technological innovations as well as initiating innovative applications of the existing products. The intellectual capital is also boosted by the growing rate of applications and adoption of existing technologies also such as wider use of cell phone, computers and Internet, television and video, etc. Different countries also use these medium in varied and many times in novel ways through newer applications which further enhances the intellectual capital.

Development of financial capitals is also necessary and important for globalization process. This can be done by developing indigenous natural resources of steel, cement, food crops and oil refineries, etc. through its own resources, through collaboration and joint ventures and through outside mergers and acquisitions. This can be both for domestic consumption as well as to earn export revenues. Financial capital is also raised through manufactured products and outsourcing services to other countries by importing products and services. Financial capital can be further enhanced by encouraging foreign direct investments (FDI) through foreign institutions in stock markets, bonds, mutual funds, insurance and pension funds, etc. Foreign investors also invest foreign capital when they collaborate with domestic enterprises such as in retail, telecommunications, steel, cement, oil, food crops research and drugs/pharmaceutical research, etc. These financial investments in emerging markets are negotiated through the policies of particular countries. Thus, both export and import revenues boost financial capitals and benefiting the participating countries.

Dimension of Global Transformation: It focuses on (i) connectivity through telecommunication, media channels, various means of transport, travel and tourism; and (ii) creating awareness, education, entertainment and consumer consumption and consumerism through these channels. Thus, transformation would depend on economic growth and boom through connectivity, creative educational system, entertainment economy and consumerism.

Infrastructure development is second dimension of global transformation. Development of physical infrastructure of roads, expressways, bridges, dams, airports, dry ports, and means of transportation such as rails, buses, metros, airlines, etc. and zonal planning of cities. Besides, this infrastructure needs to be developed for providing safe water for drinking and substantial water for other needs and farm irrigation, sanitation and power both in rural and urban areas. Development of healthcare infrastructure and infrastructure for school and higher education system both for urban and rural areas are necessary conditions for transformation of any country.

The positive rate of transformation that will occur in this regard will depend on particular country's participation in globalization process through its planning, policies and action implementation.

Transformation Challenges: These are posed both by global structure and by the abovementioned two dimensions of global transformation. The transformation challenges will be both from internal and external factors.

The three transformation challenges impacted by internal national factors will be as follows:

Political consensus is important for transformation policies and programs such as development of infrastructure, inviting foreign investments and collaborations, taking outsourcing with specific countries. The consensus will be taken in the context of economic growth, policies, plans and targets and most important in implementation of these. This is most challenging particularly in a democracy when global concerns or interests are associated with the national interests.

Overpopulation and density of living space with minimum basic needs, inequitable economic growth and benefits, minimizing absolute and relative poverty and limitation of physical, human and financial resources to achieve the targeted economic growth is the second transformation challenge.

The resulting economic boom and combined with young demographics and exposure to global life styles and availability of consumer products and services may create consumerism. The increase in disposable income for the younger generation may develop certain changing societal values that may not commensurate with traditional values and life style of people. This will be the third challenge which the society will face, will undergo change through push and pull process when undergoing transformation through globalization process.

The tensions between the globalization system and the ancient forces of culture, geo, tradition and community is challenging.

The four transformation challenges impacted by external global factors are: the external factors of external threat of terrorism combined with internal subversions, political conflicts with neighbors and associated countries, economic conflicts with global business enterprises, religious and social tensions create challenges for countries and societies which are trying to transform themselves for higher economic growth.

Thus, both internal national factors and external global factors pose transformation challenges while participating in the globalization process.

Models for Empowerment

The four new models for global and people empowerment are significant and are discussed as we move on in the text. (i) Loop model that interconnect people and governance.

(ii) Interdependency model with three Is of interdependency loop in its wider connotation, when viewed positively is inter-reliance, inter-collaboration and inter-operability. (iii) Learned dependency model suggesting that such practices of depending on government would disempower people and people must wean from it and focus on self-reliance both in national and global contexts. (iv) Business models for special segments consumer markets such as rural markets, co-creation business model for poor and bottom of the pyramid model; and microfinance practices to empower people.

Loop Model: What is also of utmost importance in this loop is the good governance and the political will to empower people. Thus, it is a circular loop for empowerment. The essential nodes in this loop are people, businesses, governance, and political will. All nodes are important and facilitate each other, therefore, for effective empowerment, it is important that they should be in tandem with each other and are on good wavelength for understanding. The forces that can pull them apart or bring them close are 'Learned dependency' and market forces. This is the primary empowerment loop.

Interdependency Loops: Being in the 'Global Interdependency Loop' empowers people. Global interdependency in this loop is mutual dependency of developed and developing nations, developed or emerging markets on the basis of mutual strengths. It is more like collaborative efforts of being dependent. It empowers people more and more as they use mutual and collective powers and resources of many nations to raise, discuss and find solutions and act on global issues. *Such global issues concerns and impacts all in the loop and even those on the periphery of the loop. Such is the power of globalization of 2000 decades.*

The three Is of interdependency loop, interactions, and information and information flow are essential for emerging communication practices in Globulation, Glocalization and Globalism contexts.

Today, there is no weak or strong partner in the global interdependency loop. Anybody is dominant player according to its strengths. *Collaboration is the business model for globalization. The very notion of superpower will undergo a change as nations become more interdependent.*

Globalization is a full wider circle enclosing many countries, individuals who want to be pulled to it and be enclosed within this circle. There may be some who are at the periphery by current circumstance and eventually may be pulled in. The global players are in the global network and are interconnected to others as dyad, clusters and bridges, etc.

To be in the global interdependency loop, one must have the requisite information and that is essential. But more significant is how it flows and to whom it flows; whether it is vertical, horizontal or circular among countries sharing interests on different fronts. Even it is equally significant if the information flow is vertical, horizontal or circular among different segments of a population within a country.

Interaction among people, different societies and among countries creates circular communications to bring convergence of ideas, products and services and mutual understanding among all the players in these contexts to deliver them according to the specific demands.

Interdependency loop in its wider connotation, when viewed positively is inter-reliance, inter-collaboration and inter-operability. But when looked at from negative point of view, this is real interdependency where it becomes survival issue bringing some negative post issues effects. USA is dependent on Middle-Eastern oil countries for oil, and these countries are dependent for petrol dollar earnings. Both of them get into real interdependency loop. As we have observed such dependency have been causing hostilities, wars, untold hardships and coercion to take each other to ransom to reduce prices or make more profits.

The interdependency of developed, developing and emerging markets is not for economic subjugation but for mutual economic benefits and prosperity. Your best talents, best skills are in demand and sought for whichever country you may belong to. The flow of funds globally, flow of talents and skills globally and flow of businesses globally cannot only interconnect economy but boost economy worldwide.

1950s experienced another form of globalization through the development models such as dominant paradigm, interdependency model, dependency model. The earlier interdependency model in 60s advocated a global perspective for development. Developed countries wanted to be the dominating power both in business and values through ideological domination and ideological aggression. Ideological domination was conveyed through commercial communication networks, transnational marketing corporations. The ideological aggression resulted when the transnational corporations penetrated the political sphere via their control over modern technology, education and by their own ideological and economic logic. Their agendas were that the worldwide hierarchy of power and values should organize developing countries.

This interdependent approach implied that developing countries must develop in the context of political and economic realities of the developed countries. The offshoot of this was the dependency model where developing countries are faced with the problem of underdevelopment due to dependency created by the imposition of economic and political realities of the developed countries. Dominating powers controlled the mass media channels and its contents, created consumerism bias, aggravated dependency that unleashed frustration among the low earning level population and led to collective aggressiveness as an escape valve.

Globalization Model: The globalization model has five significant components: globalism, glocalization and globulation, iconoclasm, outsourcing and in-forming.

Globalism: Globalism discourse is based on three levels—values, knowledge and interests. The focus is on global understanding and global consciousness. It is awareness that local events have global consequences and understanding of global impact.

Globalism suggests a global culture of standardization of food, clothes, music, TV, films, business styles. The divergent values and norms merge. It is not true that these processes lead to global integration. The same processes propelling globalization can integrate as well as disintegrate it. Disintegration occurs when the value system that dominates globalization is refused. In a way this also protects weaker units. Interdependence does not merge nations into larger units. Global transactions can create more co-operation, competition as well as conflicts.

Globulation and Glocalization: These are significant for its operation, sustainability and impacts. Globulation is revolution from beyond. That is the global markets will force upon us the business practices and disciplines which we cannot generate internally. Glocalization is localizing the global trends. Glocalization is merging local and global trends. This model operates in two ways: one is adapting and fitting global trends to local ways such as fitting global business practices to local business cultures. Second, local trends are changed into global trends, such as business practices are changed to global practices of doing business.

Iconoclasm: The iconoclasm of globalization refers to rapidly developing process of complex interconnection among the societies, cultures, institutions, and individuals worldwide. It is a process which involves compression of time and space, shrinking distances through a dramatic reduction in time either physical or representational—to cross them, so making the world seem smaller and bringing human beings closer to one another. It is also a process that stretches social relationships from local contexts to global contexts.

The iconoclastic implications of the concept of globalization are that it challenges the familiar ways of describing the world. It threatens to destroy the images of the world cherished in so many intellectual and critical traditions, displacing or forcing re-examination of certain givens of social and cultural analysis.

The iconoclasm of globalization lies in the implicit demand to re-envisage the world that arises once the nature of the complex global interconnectedness and the process of time-space compression and action at distance are recognized. Re-envisioning is disturbing and inevitably involves the destruction of shibboleths, many of which may be linked to political and moral commitments. But re-envisioning is not the same as revisionism.

Outsourcing and Offshore Business Models: They are now open to new combinations of outsourcing, service providers, and offshoring. The outcomes of such business models are: globalization, global delivery models, multi-country supplier and delivery models, hub-and-spoke model in globalization of services, captive centers model, small and medium enterprises using offshoring. There are product development and design facilities offshoring model.

The developed countries are outsourcing their various business processes to developing countries because of cheaper costs and thus earn more profit. The capabilities, which are outsourced offshore, have moved from IT-centric functions into business processes. The complexity of these capabilities continues to climb with functions such as patent research, drug research and development, legal services and equity research beginning to emerge as the high-end of offshore outsourcing. There are services such as data entry, technical support and financial analytics, which require vastly different skill sets.

Educated English speaking younger age manpower, IT-centric trained personnel, low labor costs, growing infrastructure, suitability of time zones and willingness of business and the government to regulate, facilitate outsourcing to developing countries. Broad categories like people skills and availability; business environment, and financial structure facilitate it further. Apart from cyber security, other issues that are critical to growth of IT are infrastructure and human resources, e.g. India has depth and breadth of technologically skilled labor, available at a low cost; English language skills that facilitate communications with the developed English-speaking countries; an improving telecommunications infrastructure and extensive IT experience.

Different developing countries have different outsourcing strengths such as India has more IT-centric, software development strengths. China has manufacturing strength both garments and hardware mechanical devices. Stiff competition is growing-up among countries with high or low strengths as outsourcing product and services scope is widening.

Increasing acceptance for offshoring is a foregone conclusion for multinational corporations that must keep pace with global competition, global supply and global delivery models. The role of offshore outsourcing will continue to grow in importance as offshoring moves to a corporate "must have" and as companies develop more sophisticated global delivery models across IT and multiple business processes.

A 'second wave' seems to be coming in offshoring of business processes in which English language fluency will not be a decisive factor. These will be expertise-driven jobs, requiring mainly the ability to analyze and solve complex problems.

For example, these workers may be involved in bio-informatics, or risk analytics for insurance, or scenario management in sell-side equity research, and then, someone in the US can wrap the English language around their work.

Some businesses are offshoring product development and design facilities. The problem with it is that technology will leak out to local competitors. For companies that rely on cutting-edge innovation, protecting intellectual property is critical especially as local competitors are also going up the technology ladder.

There is outgrowing trend of reverse outsourcing also. Bharti Telecommunication, India's premier telecom has outsourced its maintenance of its telecom infrastructure to IBM and Siemens who have set up business facilities in India (Gurgaon) to service it. This trend is likely to grow worldwide.

Both outsourcing and offshoring factors are interlinked to the economies of the developed world. There is interconnecting of markets and knowledge. The convergence of technology and events allowed India, China and many other countries to become part of the global supply chain for services and manufacturing. Such globalization has its challenges though no doubt creating global prosperity and economic growth for themselves.

In-forming: It is the web search through search engines Yahoo, Google, Microsoft. These do not push their products and services on their customers but build collaborative systems that enable customers to pull on their own and then respond to what they pull.

Internet adds to information, knowledge and instant messages and connectivity. It provides forum, enables consumers to gather around a topic that are meaningful to them in ways that are impractical and impossible offline. The in-informing makes the world transparent.

Globalization Process and Global Economy

The term globalization is linked to a variety of different perspectives and ideas about what globalization is and how it affects people and communities around the world. Globalization currently defined is a process that creates connectivity and convergence. It is understood from four contexts. One is cultural convergence. Second is political context, which is concerned about free flow of information. Third is economic context focusing on capitalism, consumerism, transnationalism and globalization of western economic values. Fourth is media context focusing on media contribution to all the above-mentioned three contexts.

These days there is no way any economy can escape the rapid process of integrating with the world economy. Globalization is a vehicle for progress that we cannot ignore. However, what we have quickly learned from globalization trend is that the economic fate of a country is not solely in its own hands. In the globalize world, events in one corner of the world can have immense effect on the fortunes of others in faraway corners and not at all involved with the events. Many of the institutions that affect the global economy can be difficult to understand, historically as well as functionally. In addition there are new terms that are being thrown around in the corporate world and in the development sector that can be confusing and somewhat ambiguous.

Globalization is not just phenomena, nor passing trend but an international system here to stay. It is the integration of technology, information and capital across national borders that are creating a single global market place and society. This new system is influencing the domestic policies, market forces, and international relations of virtually every country. One cannot understand the morning news; the investments market trends unless one is into the system. Integration is the key to globalization.

In the contexts of 'thinking global' four factors are significant for globalization to occur and to let it sustain and have impact on nation-states, businesses, companies and individuals. These are technology, finance, information and information flow, and decision-making. These four factors have changed how we communicate, how we see the world and how we invest.

In today's globalization system, it does not matter where you are and who you are but what you are that matters the most and on that depends the choices you make for prosperity in this system. Therefore, it is not whether we globalize that matters but how we globalize is important and significant.

Global Communications

Global communication is imperative these days to connect to people globally not only on just one-on-one basis but across many countries because of growing needs and demands on many fronts, viz. political, economic, socio-cultural, technology, etc. A network of communication across countries, inter-country and cross-country leads to globalization. An interesting example is holding summits. Globalization follows a circular model of communication.

Globalization is the major focus of international communication in this era. The social process of globalization is the basic context in international communication.

Globalization is being approached from diverse perspectives of political, economics and trade, migration, infotainment and communication.

In 2000 decade the focus of global communication is with multi-stakeholders both in the developed and developing world and with both high and low economies. This multilevel communication is to develop global solidarity and a global platform for various issues such from oil and energy related issues, population control, health care and disease control and find cure for HIV/AIDS epidemics, environmental issues, as human rights and poverty eradication, etc. since problems and hazards of these issues in one country affect worldwide. The solutions for these problematic issues also lie in worldwide collaborative efforts. On the other hand, business expansion globally through diverse products and services, expertise and diverse geographies impact and challenge both the national as well as the global economies.

Global communication has five major focuses. One, global communication for conflict resolution and peace processes. This deals with war, political and military conflicts, and terrorism in national territory affecting the international interests and peace. People's interactions from diverse point of views create political and military conflicts and terrorism. Second, focus is on development of developing countries and dealing with issues of development in the world at large such as issues of environment pollution, health, education, poverty, population, etc. People's exposure to different lands and communities through mass media or interpersonal communication creates desire for different lifestyles and for better ways of living and amenities; and therefore need for development. The interactions, exposures bring people's interests, talents closer and they together search for technological innovations to benefit humanity.

Third is technological focus. This focuses on scientific and technological breakthroughs in various aspects of people's lives and thus creating the world community. The recent technologies of computers and computer chips, Internet, cellular phones, mobile communication and satellites have brought humanity closer to each other thus breaking the geographical, cultural, and language barriers. The communication revolution through these technologies has brought the consumers in direct contact with evolving tastes all over the world. The information age has created information societies and knowledge economy. The technological innovations create economic visions and in turn pose economic challenges for people. Fourth focus deals with the global economic challenges and visions that the global communication through information age and knowledge economy has created. The fifth focus—the cultural perspective focusing on inter-cultural and cross-cultural communications is significant in dealing with the above four mentioned focuses in creating a global community.

This is the core of global communication. The theory and practice of these five focuses for global communication lead to theory and practice of globalization.

(*Handbook of Communications Perspectives...*, 2006 by author)

Economic Context of Globalization highlights that global communication industries study ways of customizing or innovating products suitable within geo-linguistic or geo-political regions. The local level producers are drawn on the global codes and conventions. There is exposure to different lifestyles of the world people.

The enhanced and diversified trade and commerce markets usher countries into new economy. Unequal center and periphery relationships, hegemony vs. rivalry, upper and lower class structures, and uneven cyclical developments affect world economy.

The ideological categories and labels offer ideological self-satisfaction but impede and obscure the analysis of material real world, economic development, and real rather than ideal alternative choices it offers yesterday, today, and tomorrow.

There are three major trends that are shaping the future of the world. First, there is wide proliferation of the modern information and communication technologies. Second, there is increasing democratization of the social systems around the world. The third trend is the intensifying global expansion of mainly western-based corporations.

Thus, the convergence of these trends—communication technologies, political, and economic liberalization has transformed the way we live and communicate.

Global Capitalism: In the past decade, the rise of market capitalism around the world has contributed to the new economy boom. It has created millions of jobs around the world. It has transferred trillions from rich countries to poor nations, developed to developing countries through equity, investments and commercial loans. Foreign direct investment has soared in these countries to create better economy. It has helped people topple dictators by making information freely available in once sheltered societies.

Internet is poised to narrow the commercial and cultural gulf separating the rich nations from poor even further in the decades to come. So many poor countries are forging ahead in the boom. There are poor, strife-ridden countries, they neglect investment in its own people and have poor economic policies. In such countries the direct foreign investments have brought foreign exchange and more jobs for people.

As impact of global capitalism multinationals are facing a new era of accountability in the third world. Now the people's voices are heard globally and echo around the world through myriad websites. Issues are more contentious where investment is concerned. Sorting out the issues gets complex. The developing nations need revenues for development.

For instance, local people often do not clamor for foreign oil or mining companies to pull out. What they really want is more equitable share in the revenues and job opportunities. If they do not get the economic benefits as well as bear the environment consequences also, they are not happy (World Bank study).

The result is shaping up of corporate responsibilities. Multinationals are hiring human rights advisers, drafting and enforcing codes of conducts, appointing monitors and improving operating practices. They are developing global standards of conduct. They are putting local people on board of directors and urging governments to adhere to international practices.

Global Business Markets

Tapscott (2006) argues that in context of globalization, mass collaboration changes everything. Due to changes in technologies, demographics, business, the economy and the world, we are entering a new world where masses can participate in the economy now as never before through the process of globalization. New forms of collaboration are changing the ways how goods and services are invented, produced, marketed and distributed. They are creating news stories, sequencing the human genome, remixing their favorite music, designing software, finding cures for diseases, editing school texts, inventing cosmetics, building motorcycles, etc. Mass collaboration is based on four powerful new ideas: Being open, peering, sharing and acting globally. These are very different from the hierarchical, close, secretive and insular multinationals.

New low cost collaborative infrastructure from Internet telephony to open source software to global outsourcing platforms allow masses to co-create products and access markets and give rise to new capabilities and business models to empower people and businesses and economy as well. There will be recurrent need to reconfigure people and capabilities to serve ever-changing markets which also means for people to constantly changing and renewing their career.

Through Internet masses can produce content goods and services. Internet is not just about websites, it is changing the innovation, corporation and every industry. A new generation of Internet will highlight how collaboration and communication technologies are democratizing the creation of value.

Wikinomics (2006) sheds light on the many faces of business collaboration and presents a powerful new strategy for business leaders in the world where customers, employees, and low cost producers are seizing the control. Knowledge creation turbocharged to engage the ideas and energy of customers, suppliers and producers in mass collaboration. 'Creative commons' can be a boon and not threat to business.

Collaboration externally with customers, suppliers and business partners and internally across business and organizational boundaries is critical. One of the most profound shifts transforming business and society in the early 21st century is the rapid emergence of open and collaborative innovation models that are driving the change. Fueled by the global adoption of the Internet, which has enabled new forms of collaboration and spawned new forms of communities, we are entering a second bigger wave of Internet. Companies gain efficiencies by a unique blend of peer interaction, creative modeling and collaboration.

Changes of great magnitude have occurred before. In fact human societies are punctuated by periods of great change through disruptive technologies of printing press, telephone, automobile, railways, etc. These have made people to think and behave differently and give rise to new social order and institutions. And change the culture and economy. Today in the New Web, people, knowledge, objects, devices and intelligent agents are converging very quickly and with intensity and a hyper competitive global economy is reshaping enterprises. Technology, demographics and global economics are converging for business revolution.

Emerging Markets: Emergent Society

The success story of outsourcing to developing countries and emerging markets of BRIC (Brazil, Russia, India, and China) does highlight the advantages of advance computerization and telecommunication and economic impact of globalization resulting in economic growth and prosperity. These empower people. But at the same time these very factors are challenging for both outsourced and outsourcing countries. These challenges can empower or disempower the people.

Emerging societies along with emerging markets is necessary for sustainable globalization. We need sustainable community depending on sustainable culture and environment for sustainable globalization. Globalization will be sustainable depending upon how well each of us manages the filters to protect our culture and environment.

There is growing awareness among the leaders of the world that both emerging markets and emerging societies are necessary to succeed in globalization system.

The emerging societies are characterized by pushing to be in the global limelight by being innovative, creative, outsourcing their ideas, services and skills and higher exposure to multimedia channels on one hand; and on the other hand people in these societies demand change in life styles, consumerism, and more disposable incomes. These societies adjust their skills with modern demands to succeed in the global system.

There is flow of global funding and capital, and investments in the emerging markets to promote global and world class experience for emerging societies. The foreign investments may be to develop infrastructures, develop businesses, and commitment to diffuse update technology. The developed markets invest the funds for both capital and product profitability. The model of interdependency loop is also operable in this context. Thus, the major stakes for the emerging societies to prosper is through optimum utilization of their skills and human resources and also enjoy the consumerism thus promoted.

Emerging Globalization Practices

Many communication practices are emerging continuously in globulation, glocalization and globalism contexts. Such practices are search for best practices to deliver the products, ideas and services to the majority of the people in a country, in many countries and within the globalization framework. These emerging practices seek to empower people in various domains of lifestyle, business, finances, professions on one hand and on the other hand empower the political leadership, government and administration of particular country to deal with changing scenarios. Together, we expect global empowerment of people, businesses and governments, since all being in the interdependency loop. The empowerment of people through changed practices leads to global empowerment.

Globalization forces continue to grow, bringing with them successes as well as discontents. Our interests are to assess the changing communication practices' impacts at global level on society, attitudinal and behavioral changes, capacity strengthening, leadership and decision-making both potential and in real time. We think of individual empowerment, and a country's empowerment through global empowerment and vice versa.

Thus, many new practices emerge and we endeavor to communicate our willingness to be in the globalization race through practicing them.

For instance, globalizations, technology and economic liberalization have tremendously changed the business practices worldwide. The emerging economies are booming because of these three factors. Business practices have to keep pace with the rapid technological change to be successful. Best practices of yesterday may not serve the consumers of today; therefore the practices are on a continuum of change. The three models of globalism, glocalization and outsourcing in the context of globalization may profile business practices differently.

Narula (2008a) advocates that the demands of 'globulation', will force upon us the business practices and disciplines which we cannot generate internally. It will make us change many of the practices to fit in these changing scenarios. On the second count, in the domestic scenario, many of the old practices become redundant; new glocalized practices emerge to fit the changing scenario. The 'glocalization' suggests adoption and influence of local cultural practices, local talents and also localizing the global trends. Since divergent values and norms merge as many countries and ethnic cultural groups interact both personally and through media; 'globalism' occurs which suggests a global culture of standardization of food, clothes, music, TV, films, and business styles. The challenge of iconoclasm for globalization is through globalization convergence of social institutions and the process by which social institutions become adopted on a global scale; and the process by which a business or company becomes international or starts operating at an international level. The concepts of glocalization and globalism are important and significant for emerging social practices.

Many practices in varied domains focus to bring about global empowerment and people empowerment. These two concepts of are significant for globalization. In these contexts, Narula (2008a) advocates that global empowerment comes from economic growth, economic prosperity, developing human resources and the development of society in general and for globalization roles. Highlighting what practices enhance global empowerment, such as, when technology bridges the digital divide between developed and developing nations by interdependency loop; when technology, political and social will bridges the digital divide between various segments of society—rural and urban, between higher and low socio-economic strata and between higher and lower educated. The later sets the stage for people empowerment which leads to enhanced global empowerment. Thus, information, ICTs and various digital divide bridges, and technology bridges contribute to global empowerment and enhance these experiences. The efforts to seek the best practices of the current times would facilitate development and global empowerment.

Narula (2008b) what creates people's empowerment in the context of local and wider global issues? In wider term, people may get empowered if they can accept the challenges of iconoclasm of globalization and globulation; democracy of communications and flow of information around the world. The loop model is conducive to bring effective people empowerment if its essential nodes of people, businesses, governance, and political will are in tandem with each other. They can facilitate empowerment of different segments of people such as women, poor, rural and urban marginalized and digitally divided, educated and skilled, etc. Further empowerment comes when particular concerns such as health, education, employment, and economic gains are addressed. These result both from emerging local practices and when these practices are oriented and emerge due to global influences.

The changing practices communicated in the right perspective would empower people, government, NGOs, and global forces to envision and invent better future. Best, next and emerging communication practices do bind us all in the interdependency loop of people, societies, cultures and businesses. In such scenario what will empower people most will be the democracy of communications around the world.

India's transformation story is researched and presented in the conceptual framework of the above-mentioned key concepts.

We look forward to global trends and visions for emerging people, emerging markets and emerging technologies.

Backdrop to Globalization in India

2

The greatest power to change is through ideas.
Ideas are expressed through success stories
spinning fantastic futures and visions.

India is witnessing one of the most far reaching transformations of this century. Over a billion people are seeking salvation within the framework of an open economy and an open society committed to fully respecting fundamental human freedoms and the rule of law. As a result of economic reforms initiated in the early 90s, India is experiencing an explosion of creativity and entrepreneurial spirit that has unleashed an economic boom.

The process of globalization that started in 90s decades has been an ongoing process that has been encashing on gradual progress made during those years. To participate in globalization was a hard decision with many ifs and buts, political and social blockages. Those were challenging. Once the decision was taken, there is no looking back and the transformation is progressive towards overall economic growth and prosperity with consequential human and social growth. Connectivity and transformation are the key words that pose challenges for India's globalization and these were/are the challenges that nation, society and people faced and are facing. Equally challenging is effectively managing the burgeoning globalization.

We, in India did not make much progress in globalization of businesses till 90s. The economic reforms of 90s onwards created better ambiance for globalization. More important was the better information flow. Till 90s the information flow about business information, government rules, economy, etc. were not accessible, transparent, accountable to foreign business parties from home and abroad due to bureaucratic snags and inefficient and lackadaisical attitudes and that did encourage doing business in India to a certain extent.

Globalization Convergence: How this is applied to Indian situations and change over. Four types of convergence occur to create globalization. These convergences focus on connectivity for globalization. First, is the convergence with the new fields with new processes for modernization and development. Second, convergence is the development of business personnel infrastructure to deal with globalization and development of new set of business practices and skills. Third, convergence is giving access to billions of people from many developing countries to converge with the new fields with new processes. Fourth, convergence is in the contexts of political, cultural, social, economic and media practices.

In India first convergence happened when new fields in business enterprises, technology, education with new processes for modernization and development by media exposure and literacy on one hand and industrialization and urbanization on the other hand were initiated.

Second convergence occurred (though the global forces may be there) with the emergence of large cadre of managers, innovators, business consultants, business schools, designers, IT specialists, CEO, and workers to get comfortable with the new system, and developing the horizontal collaboration and value creation processes and habits that could take advantage of this new playing field. In short, the convergence of these global forces begets the convergence of new set of business practices and skills, and then these two begin to mutually reinforce each other.

Third convergence gave access to people from so many countries in China, India, Eastern Europe, Latin America, Russia and Central Asia (in collaborating horizontally) in 90s to join the free-market game when their economic and political systems opened up. Billions of people converged with the new fields with new processes.

Fourth convergence focuses on cultural resources and practices, political context, which is concerned about free flow of information, economic context focusing on capitalism, consumerism, transnationalism, and globalization of western economic values, and the media context focusing on media contribution to all the above-mentioned contexts.

Friedman (2000) suggests that eight habits of highly effective countries can help their populations participate in globalization successfully and effectively: (i) How wired is your country by Internet, telecommunications and other technologies. (ii) How fast is your country in picking new global trends and practices? (iii) How much does your country weigh, i.e. the substitution effect whereby knowledge and information technologies are increasingly substituted by creation of products in economic value. (iv) Does your country dare to be open. Keeping your economy as open as possible will give multiple benefits in globalization system. Knowledge is the key to economic growth in this era and if you close your economy to best brains in the world or best technology in the world you are liable to fall behind fast. (v) How good is your country at making friends? In a global economy you cannot survive in certain industries unless you compete on a global basis and for that you need alliances. The sheer amount of scientific and technical knowledge needed to develop certain complex products need the pooled resources of several companies. The only way these companies can recover their costs for research and development is by selling worldwide and not just in their small domestic market. This also needs alliances. Thus for economic security you need alliances in international economic realm. We need more partners and alliances for the national security also and for countering the terrorism which crosses all borders. These transnational issues can be more threatening.

Further, (vi) How good is your country in managing globalization. Management and leadership matter to attract other countries to be interested in investing in your resources and businesses and doing business with you. The other countries would be assessing how your management and leadership, both political and business understand the four democratizations and know how to take advantage of them. Can they synthesize six different dimensions of politics, technology, finance, culture, national security and ecology at the same time and can they do information arbitrage. (vii) How good is your country's brand? In today's globalize world it is important that the powerful country and powerful company need to have 'strong brand' as well as strong brand image for product and services to attract consumers and investors. When both of these are satisfied, they associate with the brand and country and are willing to pay even a premium price. To build brand equity, the company needs to distinguish its products and services from others in the market and align with marketing and advertising to deliver what it says about products. (viii) As more and more people start to realize that their country can go for prosperity and they see through exposure to technology how people live in style and prosperity. They are going to ask why their government has not chosen policies for prosperity. People's demands and willingness to participate in implementation of such policies can push them for global products and services.

Emerging Concerns: Globalization Participation

India's globalization started with economic reforms and opening the economy to market forces; but it soon dawned that India would follow global models of collaboration, co-operation, glocalization and interdependency to face challenges of globalization. It would play upon its strengths of educated and English speaking professional talents and low cost labor. On one hand, there was progressive need to develop the skilled manpower, develop more and more of its strengths to keep ahead in the globalization race, and demand and supply. India wanted to be the dominant player and superpower.

On the other hand it realized, it needs to improve and create globalization of its infrastructure to invite people from around the world to do business with India successfully as well as they needed global expertise for its infrastructure development to be world class. And that is the road to growth for the nation and its people in global as well domestic contexts. Global empowerment as well people empowerment is targeted through such growth.

Good infrastructure development is essential both for global and domestic development and gives connectivity to people. Connectivity and transformation are the key words. Connectivity through better means of transporting people and goods, roads, highways, expressways, railways, airlines, airports, etc. Connecting people through better telecommunication systems. Such connectivity transforms nations and people's lifestyles. But to facilitate such transformation the other kind of infrastructure development, that is power generation is needed. We need power plants, fuel—oil, gas, coal or other kind. Either these are to be developed in-country or bought from other countries; and water resources both for human, industrial, and agriculture consumption need to be developed. The focus has to be on products and services in agriculture, industrial and service sectors.

India has been fast realizing that globalization demands as well facilitate infrastructure development through joint ventures, collaboration and co-operation in businesses, technical expertise, financial and capital flows and investments and above all manpower use and that road to growth is through optimum infrastructure development. Interdependency loop is operative in all these areas.

The story of India's transformation will be through infrastructure development of roads, highways, expressways, railways, airlines, airports, etc., energy power plants (fuel—oil, gas, coal or other kind), water and food; and connectivity through telecommunications.

Transformation of India through infrastructure development heading towards modernity and globalization has been of concern. The equal concern was emerging that India's growth story needs focus on the human side also where rural, urban, and urban communities need priority on the globalization scale to reap gains of globalization to balance the development. India would face transformation and globalization challenges from these two perspectives. It is an interesting story of globalization process and success story of developing country of India and the rising expectations; transforming through globalization on many fronts and aspiring to be a super achiever and a global power to reckon with.

The globalization story of India is not only a road to growth but an ongoing big shift to transformation for global and people empowerment through emerging communication practices.

Indian mind set is transforming through socio-economic changes towards modernity and globalization. The cultural ways of Indians are changing fast since India is in the midst of social revolution—through economic reforms and communication revolutions worldwide. This human drama unfolds everyday and at every step of our existence—sometimes very visible and sometimes subtle. Mindset is changing in multi-domains and multi-directions in the specific domains. People try to cope with the changing situations through visions and ideology, performance and reality.

The multiple domains in which India has changed are, on one hand, economy, business, technology, computerization, telecommunication, education, public health, consumerism, leisure and entertainment, civil rights, family and social growth. On the other hand, the other domains and issues of governance and politics, terrorism-violence-war have changed India. The change in these multiple domains is in multi-directions such as economic, political, social, cultural and religious. Changing India in these multiple domains has changed the Indian mindset and the change is tremendous.

What is important is how the change both in positive and negative directions is coordinated between governance and people; and how such change impact the mindset.

India aspires to be the global dominant player and superpower. What motivates its people to aspire for being the dominant player in international and national contexts?

India is emerging as a confident nation and is being recognized in several dimensions and is likely to be a dominant player in the international arena from various perspectives in the future. Indians want to be entrepreneurs in multi-domains, bold and risk taking. They are challengers as well as accept the challenges in the international markets. They do want to strive for global empowerment as well give empowerment to its people by handling those challenges. People are certainly confident of moving ahead despite the odds of not so stable, educated and forward looking polity, widespread corruption and bureaucratic hassles, low literacy, overpopulation and poverty and above all development of people not in commensuration with the money and efforts of governance is the major concern.

India is making progress, juxtaposed with lower costs, improved scale of operations, investments in technology, and in technical and skilled manpower required. Moreover, intellectual capital and cost efficiency has put India on the global map. It is focusing on healthcare, education and poverty related solutions, etc. in the national front to give empowerment to its people.

Such evolution has not been totally private effort. Government has also leveled the playing field. It initiated economic reforms by opening the economy to market forces, encouraged manufacturing, lowered inflation, and allowed foreign exchange inflows to cut down the prime lending bank rates. Government has invested in highways, railways, airports, ports and other related infrastructure, technology development, talent and skills development through educational and training programs and gradually allowing foreign capital investments, collaborations, and joint ventures.

Narula (2006a) discussing about economic scenario in India, viz. realities and visions presents how achievement can occur if there is efficiency in economic management through instrumental economic reforms and liberalization, planning strategies for direction and pace for economy, remedies for structural and resource backwardness and functional welfare model for all. She states categorically that this requires involved efforts of the governance and people. It is important how people and governance communicate their visions (economic, developmental) to each other. The visions can be made successful by efforts of governance and people, economists and businesses.

The two configurations: visions and ideology, performance and reality in social and economic contexts are significant for changing India and its people.

India's grand visions many times degenerate into weak, difficult-to-implement macro-level maneuvers that are often without perspective. India acts as an asymmetrical (mistaken often as pluralistic), dissension-filled society of divisions and dichotomies. Hence, what is planned is not realized. Whether society succeeds or not is a big question mark.

In India, when we build one Sardar Sarovar Dam, thousands pour out to galvanize public opinion, right or wrong, in their favor. But when China decides to build the world's biggest dam—the Three Gorges—nobody gets to know how many get displaced and hopefully rehabilitated. Whether the executive and political talent of China is individually as good as ours may be questioned, but collectively, it is an unbeatable delivery machine.

India must focus on development of three kinds of capital: human capital, intellectual capital and financial capital to be the global player. Further it must focus on the architectures of law, technology and leadership which are important for globalization. Legal architecture means new laws, regulations and taxing and spending. Technology changes include different directions in research and design. The architectures of technology shape opportunities. Leadership changes involve new thinking by those who hold institutional power, but also new leadership from below, facilitated by more advanced media of the era. Entrepreneurial leadership focuses on risk taking and risk reducing. Strong leaders in various domains move the nation to globalization. Such leaders are government and political leaders, business leaders and social leaders. Technology leaders can also help to think forward. Their innovations always bring the future into being. Political reform change in law is more susceptible.

Development of Capitals

Development of Human Capital: India needs to find ways to harness the full creative capability of its inhabitants across all industries, occupations, classes and geo-regions. This would give India an advantage in the global creative economy and provide the world with a large-scale model for how development of human capabilities is the most effective route to true economic development and people empowerment.

Moreover, to be a real dominant player, people have to match the quality, organization, competition, straightforwardness and honesty in dealings with non-material aspects of social and cultural life, and in polity. They must practice these values first at the national level and thence on project the same in international dealings. Development of its people both in material and non-material aspects is a big challenge for being dominant player.

Secondly, Participatory Development and Good Governance (PDGG) model should be the focus. The focus is on strengthening the partnership approach to participatory development and good governance. This has radical implication for world economy. The emphasis is on micro level action contexts, local resistance to change, community participation, and empowerment of people. Economic and political liberalism is necessary for PDGG model. It is necessary that there should be vital connection between open, democratic, and accountable political systems.

Anti-corruption strategies should strengthen social, business, and monetary institutions. Both government and people can bring integrity in public life. In addition to reforming the government, we must recognize the powerful influence of public scrutiny and participation. Therefore, all strategies must begin with a commitment to build economies and societies that are open, transparent, and ultimately accountable.

Development of Intellectual Capital: Therefore, for successful applications of technologies in various domains, it is important as well as imperative to consider perspectives of government, people and media community. In India, the government may have planned pro-social objectives of media channels in pluralistic society. It may encourage updated technologies for businesses and various management outputs by imports and exports and by development and research of indigenous technologies and by democratization of technologies. Government should be able to provide efficient, accessible, reliable and credible technologies. Social technology approach is necessary from people's perspective to assimilate the particular technology in their lifestyle, to improve work ethics and skills, and for self-reliance and development. Media community perspective creates awareness, information, knowledge and motivation to diffuse innovative technologies in their lifestyles.

An important part of India's innovation system is the diffusion of modern and more efficient technologies in all sectors of the economy. Same may be true of China and other emerging markets.

Development of Financial Capital: Equally important has been to develop financial capital in India for economic growth. The focus has been on inviting foreign investments in businesses through collaborations, in both physical and human infrastructure and funds in stock markets. Government did open its economy gradually and cautiously to foreign investments. This led to globalization of investments and businesses in various sectors. Opening of economic policies, economic reforms and creating better bureaucratic and political ambiance for facilitating such investments helped financial development. The Indian government's decision to allow Foreign Direct Investment (FDI) in various domains in business, technologies and socials is expected to elevate Indian developments to international standards.

Economic Situation Analysis: India

A situation analysis of the economic scenario in India gives us insights into current economic strengths and weaknesses of Indian society.

Strengths

- The vast number of manpower can be strength if they are handled efficiently through education, skill development and employment.
- Indian businesses take initiatives for growth both nationally and internationally.

- Science and technology initiatives are developing for global markets, such as satellites launching, computer software and hardware development, telecommunication development and development of high grade pharmaceutical products, etc.
- Government does plan for development though it is ideological.
- The constraints to economy are controllable.

Weaknesses

- Political instability, corruption, and criminality in politics can be major weakness. India needs political cleansing to get rid of irresponsible and unprincipled politics playing with peoples' mandate. Political corruption, low respect for laws, rules and regulations presents wrong role models to people.
- Economic instability, economic crisis, and recession can lead to low economic growth. Economic cleansing is needed for wholesome development of economy of the masses. Checking corruption at all levels, black economy, and economic offences and focusing on consistent economic policies can facilitate this.
- Weak welfare model particularly total neglect of the absolute poor in real terms.
- Majority of the people cannot afford basic minimum needs and services.
- The need is to redefine employment policies and monitoring them overtime. Low employment is created by unskilled manpower, skills not matching the job market demands, and lack of upgrading of skills to match the jobs. Further, either the manpower demand forecasts are unrealistic or if they happen to be realistic demand forecasts, they are ignored and not implemented.
- Manpower forecasts must be matched by developing educational courses, skills and training programs. Job opportunities need to be created particularly for rural areas and for absolute poor.

- We need to invest more and wisely in education and employment generation.
- Low work ethics is problematic for high employment rate, productivity and prosperity. It affects economic efficiency.
- Low grade infrastructure and bottlenecks of roads, airports, railways, bridges, transport, electricity, power, sanitation, safe drinking water, and telecommunication, etc. can affect economic growth.
- Ineffective laws, rules and regulations affect self-discipline of the people and nurture corruption at all levels.
- Overpopulation and urbanization when not handled efficiently become problematic.

Opportunities

External

- Compete in the nuclear power development, oil and gas development, steel and mining, telecommunication, etc. with other nations.
- Global provider for computer software development.
- Outsourcing and offshoring through BPO, KPOs, RIM and collaborative business models with the global partners can help develop the economy. Compete in highly competitive diversified businesses.

Future

- Infrastructure improvement can boost trade, industrial growth, and foreign investment.
- Skilled manpower is asset to the nation. Higher skills lead to higher earning, more purchasing power, and better quality of life.
- Government will have higher revenue if taxes are not evaded, and black economy is under control. Higher revenue can be spent on development projects and making life more affordable for people.
- Focus on creating opportunities for non-agro rural jobs, rural markets for customize and innovative products can

check urban migration of rural people and check negatives of urbanization. Develop agriculture through modernized farming practices and safeguards for farmers' interests.

- Overpopulation can be a national economic asset if it is self-disciplined, skilled, and have higher work ethics. These create more productivity and prosperity and therefore higher economic growth for the nation.
- Economic choices will be socially relevant.

Threats

External

- Political uncertainty and low political consensus on salient issues can threat economic growth both internally and externally.
- Poor infrastructure will withhold external investors to invest in Indian financial institutions. Country's infrastructure development is needed urgently otherwise international credibility and connectivity will suffer.
- India will be a poor and weak nation due to low economic growth. The economies of people will suffer and so do their quality of life.
- If 'absolute poor' are not handled properly and given a status; they will perpetuate poverty and will be a drain on the nation's economy. Thirty-six per cent of the population is absolute poor.
- If social opportunities of health, education, and employment are created but not implemented as planned and financed; they can pose a big threat to the nation.

Future

- Periodic monitoring and evaluation of development projects related to health, education, and employment is essential for proper implementation. Further action plans must be refocused according to monitoring and evaluation.
- Globalization of businesses and development projects and upgrading of manpower skills in globalization contexts can boost economy and quality of life for people.

The future scenario identified in 'opportunities and threats' pose challenges for India to be the global dominant player. In 1991, the government introduced economic reforms and liberalization policies but there was lack of initiative towards a radical change in social policies including basic education, health and creating more skilled labor.

Secondly, the pragmatics of Indian economy are to deal with the issues of urbanization and overpopulation and to provide the masses with basic minimum needs of food, safe drinking water, sanitation and other civic amenities, clothing, shelter, education, employment, and purchasing power parity. Economic stability, political stability and effective laws, rules and regulations and functional welfare models as social insurance are necessary to deal with these issues. On the other hand, India expands the businesses, its products and services in the context of technology and globalization to improve the economy culminating in better quality of life for its people.

Pragmatics of Indian Economy

The internal and external factors affect the economic growth and stability of the country. Governance and people both must meet challenges for creating economic growth and prosperity for people.

The pragmatics of Indian society is impacted by both internal and external factors. The salient internal economic issues are basic minimum needs for people, overpopulation, urbanization, effective laws, corruption, black economy and tax evasion, government subsidies, price rise of commodities, crime, social insurance, employment, equality and poverty, and other diverse issues of privatization, market forces and technology, political stability and strong political leadership. Further, it is salient how in turn these affect the economic growth and stability.

The external factors are foreign investment, international trade and competition, international aid and the challenges of globalization. Foreign investors are cautious about political stability and consistent economic policies of a country to invest in its markets. Over and above, they are much concerned about how the bureaucracy efficiently handles the clearing of plans and projects and rules and regulations for efficient investment and working in the country. This applies for both the foreign investors and their domestic counterpart/s with which they collaborate.

Governance and people both must meet challenges of economic reforms in India to fulfil the visions of economic prosperity of country and its people. These are created by both the internal and external factors of pragmatics of Indian economy. If the governance wants economic growth and prosperity for its people; it must reform the way businesses are done both nationally and internationally, the consistent economic policies, policies conducive to the good of all segments of the society, spending resources for updating and developing technology, developing human resources and over and above the speed and efficiency of functioning in these areas.

The main challenge is to provide economic and social opportunities to people by streamlining economic policies. For this, it is important and necessary to develop and streamline skills and resources, develop opportunities and strengths of people and economy, and work out to improve on weaknesses, and threats and vulnerabilities of people and economy. These three challenges are interdependent. To achieve this, it will be necessary and imperative to make economies open, transparent and accountable. These three basic challenges call for the other three challenges such as: national efforts, citizens' efforts and international efforts to handle the basic challenges efficiently.

India's biggest challenge is that India's economic growth and innovations are mostly concentrated on handful of regions. Virtually all significant technological innovations came from five city regions Bombay, Bangalore, Hyderabad, Delhi NCR, and Pune. Outside these, other creative centers, large sections of India's population live hand to mouth existence. There is divide between creative haves and creative have-nots. Still there is great tradition of creativity to build on. India has long valued the development of talent across multiple dimensions.

India needs to find ways to harness the full creative capability of its inhabitants across all industries, occupations, classes and geo regions.

This would give India an advantage in the global creative economy and provide the world with a large-scale model for how development of human capabilities is the most effective route to true economic development.

India's future could depend on the strength of its 'creative economy'. India's future depends crucially on its ability to compete fully in the creative economy—not just in technology and software, but across design and entrepreneurship, arts, culture and entertainment; and the knowledge based professions of medicine, finance and law. While it's creative assets outstrip those of China and other emerging competitors still India must address several challenges to increase its international competitiveness (Martin Kenney, 2006). Indian economy and the global economy as a whole is undergoing fundamental structural changes.

Projections: Indian Economy

According to the Organization for Economic Cooperation and Development's (OECD) first economic survey of India released in New Delhi on 9 October 2007, India's economic growth can reach a sustainable 10 per cent in 2011 and equitably distributed across the country if the government pursues ambitious and wide-ranging economic reforms.

The report also added that India is now the third largest economy after US and China in terms of real prices and purchasing power.

According to the survey the government should continue its program of increased discipline in public spending, focusing more on the poor. More publicly-owned firms should be privatized to improve productivity and profitability. Infrastructure development should keep pace with demand. It further recommended reducing tax exemptions to allow more money to be transferred to fund public services in urban areas.

The IMF has projected eight per cent GDP growth for India in the medium term but said the country would require policies to foster improvements in labor market conditions for better job creation and in the financial sector for sustaining investment efficiency.

The International Monetary Fund (IMF) projection has come at a time when the Planning Commission has proposed nine per cent Gross Domestic Product (GDP) growth rate in the 11th Plan (2007-12).

IMF working paper on 'wild or tamed: India's potential growth' suggested that "The recent shift to a more investment-led growth pattern, along with strong productivity gains, seem to have raised India's medium-term potential growth to around eight per cent." Referring to the downside risks, it pointed out, the pace of investment could decline as well, to the extent it is underpinned by cyclical forces. Based on the experiences of the fast-growing Asian economies, even productivity gains, which are pushing up India's growth, could become volatile, adversely impacting India's growth story. India would need continued improvement in economic policies to deal with the problems emanating from volatility in productivity gains. It said the country's investment efficiency is at a high level of 35 per cent of GDP over the medium term, comparable to the Asian countries just before the crisis, and maintenance of this rate would need meeting some challenges.

According to the Asian Development Bank (ADB), Asia's developing economies, the fastest growing nations in the world, will expand 8.3% in 2007 higher than the previous forecast of 7.6%. The ADB forecasts growth of 8.2% in 2008, up from an earlier prediction of 7.7%. The region grew 8.5% in 2006. Growth in Asia (excluding Japan) in 2007 will be largely led by rapid expansion in China and India, with a 55% share in the regional GDP.

Growth in China has been estimated at 11.2% in 2007, up from an earlier forecast of 10%, and at 10.8% in 2008. India's economy will move up 8.5% in 2007, up from the previous estimate of 8%, and will expand another 8.5% in 2008.

There is also the possibility of a downward revision in 2008 estimates due to a credit crunch in the West. However, Asia's strong position will enable it to withstand external shocks, like a recession in the United States, the main market for its export-led economies.

A recession resulting from recent losses in the U.S. subprime mortgage sector, or any such event, could possibly prune growth to a range of 6-7% from a prediction of 8.2% in 2008.

International ratings agency Standard and Poor's (S&P) said, India's economic expansion is being driven by strong local demand, and a moderation in growth in the current fiscal year was a 'soft landing'. Despite adverse global developments, it forecasts that the Indian economy would grow 8.6 per cent in the fiscal year ending in March 2008, slower than 9.4 per cent in 2006/07 but a notch higher than the central bank's forecast of 8.5 per cent.

"Overall, while global developments have made the environment more risky, the strength of domestic demand is expected to keep the Indian economy on a relatively high growth trajectory," S&P said in a report. In the calendar year 2007 and 2008, S&P expects the economy to grow 9 per cent and 8.8 per cent respectively.

The ratings agency said Indian interest rates were clearly peaking. The central bank has raised its main short-term lending rate five times since last June, with the last increase taking effect in March, to cool demand pressures in the world's fastest growing major economy after China (Oct. 2007).

The Planning Commission of India estimates economic growth at 8.5-9% in FY08 albeit a deceleration in industrial growth in July 2007.

Deputy Chairman of the commission Montek Singh Ahluwalia termed the slow growth in the second quarter as "moderation" rather than a slowdown. According to him it is an outcome of successful macro economic management which reflects non-inflationary potential of the economy along with sustained growth.

Gross domestic product rose 9.3% in April-June 2007. Industrial growth contracted 7.1% in April-July 2007 from 13.2% in April-July 2006. The deceleration in growth is a result of high interest rates, which adversely affected consumers spending on household items and automobiles, leading to slowdown in the manufacturing sector.

Indian Economy: The forecast by the Prime Minister's Economic Advisory Council, headed by former Reserve Bank governor C. Rangarajan is that Indian economy is riding an investment boom, the Indian economy will grow 9% in the current fiscal 2007-08 on top of last year's 9.4% growth and price rise will be contained at 4%.

The panel says, the economy's managers will have to make some tough choices like curbing the inflow of external debt, allowing the rupee to appreciate further and removing 'administrative and procedural impediments' to acquisitions abroad. The panel has made some oblique criticism of the present accounting practice in public finance which understates the combined fiscal deficit of the Centre and the States by around 2% of the gross domestic product.

The panel's prognosis is more bullish than that of RBI, which has pegged the FY08 growth at 8-8.5%. It sees the external environment as still being benign and expects sustained investment to keep growth booming. The need to curb capital inflows comes from the mismatch between the current account deficit, which is seen at $17.4 billion and surpluses on the capital account (nearly $58 billion).

The excess inflow of foreign capital can make the rupee far too strong; managing this would mean jacking up money supply which could harden inflation and eventually interest rates. A sensible policy response is to allow all these three things to happen in moderate doses and to discourage external borrowing for rupee expenditure.

The council is not in favor of disrupting foreign equity investments. "Equity investment by its very nature is high risk and policy continuity is an essential element to initiate and maintain such flows. They cannot be turned on and off at will. However, on the debt side, there are some areas that can do with some scrutiny," it said. The panel suggested three instruments to face the strong capital flow: allowing the rupee to appreciate, sterilizing capital inflows in excess of what can be absorbed into reserves without pushing money supply growth above 17.5%; and instituting a policy of encouraging capital outflow and discouraging external borrowing for rupee expenditure.

"Instead of arguing for the exclusive use of any of the instruments, there must be a judicious mix of all the three instruments. There are limits to which each instruments can be used by itself," Mr. Rangarajan said. While the rupee should be allowed to appreciate, Mr. Rangarajan cautioned against the possible fallouts. "There are limits up to which this can be done. Beyond a point, it will hurt exports, as also the larger domestic economy. Besides, we need to take into account the behavior of the currencies of other developing countries, most notably China" (PM's panel seeks inflow curbs 17 July 2007).

The report (2007) pegged farm growth at 2.5%; industrial output at 10.6%; and services at 10.4%. It expected inflation to remain close to 4%. Mr. Rangarajan cautioned that unless the farm and power sectors grow, the current rate of economic growth cannot be sustained. "Food security is an extremely important issue. Agriculture should be priority, as 60% people are dependent on it."

Commenting on the power sector, he said if adequate attention was not paid to augment infrastructure, particularly power supply, overheating might persist on account of productivity and supply constraints. The issuance of bonds to oil companies and the Food Corporation of India to meet their subsidy bills and piling up huge dues to the fertilizer industry serve to keep the fiscal deficit looking more pretty than it actually is.

At the state level, losses of public sector undertakings serve the same purpose. While in the current accounting practice these don't show up as part of the fiscal deficit, these items, adding up to 2% of GDP, are part of the public sector borrowing requirement along with the fiscal deficit as conventionally defined. The deficit, as per this wider measure, would still be 8.3% of GDP in 2006-07 and 7.2% in 2007-08.

The Sixth Pay Commission award could widen it further, the report said.

The Indian economy is expected to slow down further in 2007-08 due to surging interest rates, appreciating rupee and poor infrastructure. During the fourth quarter of 2006-07 ending in March 2007 the economy grew at 9.4% compared to 10% in the same quarter of 2005-06. The GDP is now pegged at 9.2%. So even though positive growth is expected for sectors such as agriculture, industry and services, the economy would face a downward pull, CII said in its survey—'State of the Economy'.

Indian Economy: Inflation

If we are going to have strong economic growth, there is a corollary: inflation will always be poised. Managing 9% growth with close to 4% inflation needs close attention and hard work. What is the appropriate level of inflation? We mostly have had a 5% target. Look around Asia, and you will rapidly discover that for many years now India has had the highest inflation rate —two to three percentage points higher than China, Korea, Taiwan, et al., and all our competitors to an extent. Our inflation has, of course, been higher than in the developed world.

Now what happens if we have persistently higher inflation than both the competition and principal export markets? Our competitiveness will suffer—both in world markets and at home. What is the standard policy cure for that? Depreciate the currency, so that the inflation-adjusted relative exchange rate (the real effective exchange rate) is left unchanged. In past years, when we were starved for foreign currency, that was easy to do but now, it is quite different, when foreign capital flows in the country, and when the success of our software and BPO industries create both jobs at home and keeps the current account deficit small. There is pressure on the currency to appreciate.

So what happens when we have both higher relative inflation and an appreciating currency? We are hit with a double whammy. Not just nominal appreciation, but even larger real appreciation. So, how do our enterprises hope to handle it? Productivity is another vital factor. Increase in productivity allows us to gain on the competition, and since the others are also having productivity gains, if we have more, we gain in competitive edge and market share and vice versa. If our currency has had a real appreciation, then some or all of our productivity gains are offset by the appreciation. Thus, the effects of real appreciation is to trade away some of our productivity gains.

This brings us back to the opening issue of the dimension of time and the PM's Economic Advisory Council's (EAC) advice of a "judicious" mix of three instruments to deal with the current situation.

Real appreciation in small doses is possible for business enterprises to absorb by working at greater productivity, where a much larger appreciation would have inundated them. It also helps them stay focused on the adjustment, by keeping it as a living (and moving) component of their business universe. Second, if we want controlled doses, the pace at which adjustment takes place must be controlled through the intervention of the central bank in the foreign exchange market.

That intervention creates exactly the same amount of liquidity in rupees. Some can be absorbed by the liquidity requirements of economic growth. The rest has to be sterilized. Both have to be continuous. It is better to sterilize back-to-back and then re-inject the needed liquidity through open-market operations—the key indicator being the interest rate at the short end, which should correspond approximately to what may be regarded as an interest rate (the indicator of the magnitude of monetary expansion) consistent with the inflation target. It is the way the US Fed gives effect to its monetary policy. If there is active open-market operation in sterilization bonds, the sterilization becomes simultaneous and equivalent to being back-to-back.

Capital outflows must be encouraged, to help our companies become more global, and so also our investors—both individual and institutional. As for limiting some kinds of debt inflows, the

EAC has underscored the importance of these being temporary and very selective. The first and third instruments are limited by time and the response that also builds up over time.

The second must fill the space. But keep working on the other two—to help our economy become more productive and our citizens more comfortable with investing in the world. In the real world, there are no meaningful static choices. The context is dynamic and so must the attributes of the choices.

However, according to Centre for Monitoring Indian Economy (CMIE) the 4% inflation target is possible given the ease in supply-side constraints. The supply-side position in both the primary and manufacturing sectors is improving. While new capacities have been added in the manufacturing sector, the rains have been good for the agricultural sector. While an upward revision of fuel prices is on the cards, the timing of the revision would be crucial, he added. "If oil prices are revised in line with the international prices, it could lead to a further increase in the WPI by 20-30 basis points", EAC's inflation estimates at 4% for the fiscal factors in higher oil prices. Empirical evidence suggests that apart from a small direct impact of fuel price rise on inflation, there is no multiplier effect on the economy. This is because fuel has a small weightage in the WPI basket. WPI consists of three categories: primary articles; fuel, power and lubricants; and manufactured products, with weights of 22.02%, 14.23% and 63.75% respectively.

The objective has to be to curb inflation. To sustain high rates of economic growth we have to keep our productivity gains at home long enough to build a strong and competitive economy. Achieving low inflationary outcomes is thus vitally important to sustained high growth rates over the next 10-15 years (Economic Adviser, ICRA).

The Reserve Bank is more vigilant than ever in checking inflation without choking growth—an uphill task that has been compounded by heightened global financial uncertainties and rising prices of crude oil and farm produce, its Governor Y.V. Reddy said on Thursday. "The policy challenge for Reserve Bank, now, is to manage the current transition to a higher growth path while containing inflationary pressures and focusing on financial stability." But Reddy was pragmatic when he said India cannot remain immune to global inflationary pressures, brought about by global developments—rising oil prices for instance.

Finance Minister's address at the Annual Economic Editor's Conference (12 Nov. 2007) Emphasized that there has been a marked change in the way the Indian economy is viewed, both within the country and in other countries of the world. This is largely due to the sustained, well-directed efforts of the government that have resulted in globally acclaimed rates of economic growth, increased global competitiveness of Indian businesses, strong macro-fundamentals and a highly favourable economic outlook.

The developmental strategies followed by the government in the growth process, the shift in the government's approach to the goal of inclusive growth and restatement of its social and economic objectives.

The 'command and control' economy of India, grew at a rate of 3.5% per annum, during 1950-51 to 1979-80. Growth, which hovered around a little over 5.5% per annum, during the 1980s and 1990s, increased to 5.8% during 1989-99 to 2003-04, and further to 8.6% since 2004-05. Of late, India has been globally acknowledged as a high growth economy. The rate of growth stood at 9.4% during 2006-07. The growth rate, during the first quarter of 2007-08, was an impressive 9.3%, over the corresponding quarter of the previous year.

If we can sustain this rate of growth, per capita income can double in about nine years. This high growth has been facilitated, by an unprecedented increase in the rate of investment from 22.9% in 2001-02 to an estimated 35.1% in 2006-07.

According to Goldman Sachs, over the next 30-50 years, India is likely to grow fastest among the BRIC economies of Brazil, Russia, India and China. McKinsey Global Institute has predicted that India will have the fifth largest consumer market by 2025, with about 583 million people forming its middle class. This implies a huge opportunity for further investment and enterprise.

The rapidly changing sectoral contributions to the GDP are an indication of the significant structural changes taking place in the economy. The share of industry, in GDP, has increased from 25.6% in 2003-04 to 26.6% in 2006-07. There has been a decline, in the share of agriculture and allied sectors, from 21.7% to 18.5% during the same period.

The declining share of agriculture in GDP has been mostly appropriated by the services sector, which increased its share from 52.7% to 54.9%. Industry, of late, has been one of the major drivers of growth of the Indian economy. The last four years have witnessed impressive rates of industrial growth, averaging around 10%. In 2006-07, the industrial growth was a splendid 11.5%, while the rate of growth of manufacturing was even higher at 12.5%.

Though the growth of manufacturing has slightly decreased, to 10.3%, during April-August 2007, the growth in capital goods is at 21.3%, during the period. It is suggestive of a significant addition to industrial capacity. The slackening has been mainly on account of poor performance of the consumer durable sector.

The growing business optimism is manifest in the bank credit to industry and large industrial investments in the pipeline. Outstanding credit, to the industrial sector, by the scheduled commercial banks witnessed a growth of 30% and 28.4% in 2005-06 and 2006-07, respectively.

Year-on-year growth of outstanding credit, as on October 12, 2007 at 23.5%, has exhibited some moderation from the strong pace of the previous three years. However, we should note that industry is able to access funds from other sources as well. Preliminary assessment indicates that in Q1 of 2007-08, access to resources by industry other than from bank credit increased by over 30%, compared to Q1 of 2006-07.

Internal generation of funds continue to provide strong support to the funding.

Economic survey 2008 and current budget 2008-09 furtherhighlights the economic situation in the country:

Economic Survey 2008: The Economic Survey has underlined the adverse impact of slowing down of the manufacturing sector, resulting in overall industrial growth becoming moderate. It has called for removing infrastructural impediments and reviewing labor laws and labor market regulations, apart from proposing phase-out of control on sugar, fertilizers and drugs.

The Survey said that industrial sector recorded a growth of 9.2 per cent in the April-November period of this fiscal as against 10.9 per cent in the same period in 2006-07. For all of last fiscal year, industry grew 11.6 per cent.

The issue of lack of availability of sufficient number of skilled workers affecting the manufacturing sector has been emphasized. This will facilitate research and development and technological innovations, which are urgently called for in important industries like chemicals, automotives and pharmaceuticals. Besides increase in wages, the skill shortage also manifests itself as a problem of retention and attrition in the fast growing knowledge based industries as well as in social sector services like health and hospitality.

Sectoral differentiated initiatives may be required for skill upgradation, supply augmentation of inputs and promotion of research and development. "There is an imperative need to facilitate the growth of labor intensive industries, especially by reviewing labor laws and regulations. This is particularly important in reversing the current, not-so-encouraging manufacturing employment trends," the Survey stated. Despite of setbacks, the Survey said there were sufficient reasons for sounding optimistic as there has been a commendable growth in capital goods sector. "The burgeoning direct investment inflows in the liberalized investment regime supplements the domestic investment to a great extent," it stated.

Budget 2008-09: The Finance Minister has done a commendable job in balancing political, social and economic compulsions in this budget. Riding on the back of a robust growth rate he has focused on inclusive growth with initiatives in sectors like education, rural housing, roads, drinking water, health and agriculture. Recognizing the move towards knowledge based future, the budget provided for the creation of new skills training institutes, IIT's and Indian Institutes of Science. He has shifted focus from outlay to outcome. Monitoring and efficient administration of the various schemes will be critical to effective implementation of these programs.

He has provided growth impetus to several key sectors, especially power, healthcare and pharmaceuticals. The continued focus on infrastructure projects like the national highways and the UMPPs is critical for economic development. By raising the personal income tax exemption limits and rationalizing the tax slabs, Chidambaram has ensured that the common man has a higher disposable income. This will stimulate growth for consumerism.

As one of the few trillion dollar economies in the world, India is firmly on a growth path. The economic growth has been further bolstered by the enhanced collection of tax revenues.

The finance minister has signaled increased investments in the agriculture, infrastructure and education sectors. This balances the expectations of the agricultural sector as well as those of the industry. On the agricultural front, the loan waiver measures announced by the finance minister are welcome. This scheme will benefit the small farmer from the burden of debt besides allowing banks to clean up their balance sheets and thereby increase lending.

Challenges of Globalization: India

Connectivity and transformation are the keywords that pose challenges for India's globalization and these were/are the challenges that nation, society and people faced and are facing. To create equitable development for its diverse population in the face of economic boom through globalization is equally challenging. What extent the population is provided minimum needs of life in reality; and the attitude of people and government to procure it efficiently.

How to balance interests of foreign investors and domestic enterprises? Government is eager to attract foreign investment to fund projects, and to acquire expertise, technology and foreign currency. But how do policymakers ensure that these efforts benefit local enterprises?

India face key challenges to provide solutions to many countries through outsourcing and soon India may face skilled manpower shortages. It is challenging to develop the skilled manpower to keep up with the expanding outsourcing of products and services from many countries. Equally challenging is effectively managing the burgeoning globalization.

Narula (2008b) highlights the developing globalization scenario and its challenges in India. What is the perception of India and its businesses today globally? With increasing globalization, the countries cannot afford to ignore the World's largest Democracy. India is intriguing—a developing economy which has global reach. It is a dual economy. On the one side, India is very sophisticated, on the other side, it has a huge potential to develop. It has elements that you don't find in many places. India's model is a unique one, a story yet to be told. There is a huge shift in perception. But equitable development is still a dream and the challenge for India is to convert this challenge into an opportunity.

India is a very important outsourcing destination for many countries in the world. They are taking note of the quality work being done here and Indians exhibit a very high level of creativity and flexibility. Vendors, too, have evolved both in product offerings and sophistication. That makes working with them much easy. Indian manufacturing centers are quite modern and match up to global standards. In fact, the Indian vendors have scaled up the quality to such heights that they offer many avenues to experiment.

Professional, technical and management support services provide a blend of global reach, local knowledge, innovation and technical excellence in delivering solutions that enhance and sustain the world built, natural and social environments. With a broad range of markets, transportation, facilities and environmental it addresses the key challenges to provide solutions to many countries.

India provides the diversities crucial for testing. With so many segments in terms of income, culture and geographies, acceptance in different scenarios can be tested here. India is among the first markets for launching many products. The dynamics of the Indian market are such that if something works here, then it can work elsewhere.

Soon India may face skilled manpower shortages. Manpower India (2007) points that Industries like financial services, media and information technology require staff to build on knowledge, but they are finding it increasingly difficult to train new workers fast enough. Skill shortages emerged two years back in technology and outsourcing, with attrition rates—the rate of staff turnover—topping 25 per cent, according to industry estimates. With the expansion in services and manufacturing, shortages have now spread to other sectors. A recent survey by Manpower found that finance firms were expecting to hire at the highest rate in 2007, followed by services, public administration and education.

Paucity of talent coupled with high rate of attrition has forced Corporates in India to give more weightage to employees than the customers to ensure their top and bottom lines continue to improve. Finding the right talent has become much harder in today's world and the employers need to create brand value for themselves among the job seekers.

Saul (2006) an economic historian, blames the collapse of globalism on the rise of India and China in a manner that defies the rules as defined by the West. "The economic idea behind globalism and globalization comprised a deterministic belief in the weakening of the state and the ascendancy of the market, which would take economics out of the purview of the State. We see none of this taking place in India or China. They are, in fact, rebuilding the nation State," says Saul.

India's young demographics, says Saul, are more promising than China's, which are already ageing. India has first-rate institutions—judiciary, free press and democracy "however flawed". Saul asserts that although India's rise is impressive, for this growth to last, it has to be more inclusive. At the moment, there are some successful sectors, a small percentage of people growing richer and some expanding cities. But wealth has not spread to the vast majority of the population. And herein lays India's challenge.

"Historically, the rich states of today set off on a path of economic growth only when they began to invest in infrastructure and education for all," he says. Only when wealth is fairly well spread out does the wealth of a nation solidify to form a strong base for further growth. "A healthy, well-educated, well-to-do population is the best wealth-creating tool a country can have," he says.

Does Saul agree with the possibility of an emerging India-China duopoly? "It depends on how unstable the world becomes as India and China grow in importance. Perhaps they will end up as rivals. But, who knows, they may just cannily realize that their interests are best served through cooperation," he says:

Narula (2008a) points that the countries in the interdependency loop not only get involved in economic and social development but one way or the other they also get involved in conflicts, wars and tensions which become global issues through emerging political practices. Globalization should not have escalated political conflicts; rather it should have brought global peace; but the emerging political and religious practices and even business practices such as demand and supply issues of oil worldwide are escalated political and social conflicts. India is also experiencing the negative impacts of globalization through terrorism and which does affect the economy and development of certain states such as Jammu and Kashmir.

Ongoing Process of Globalization

Narula (2006a) discussions have highlighted the Indian economic scenario vis-à-vis economic visions, technology visions and the business visions of its people, its governance and commitment of both to make it reality by facing the ensuing challenges in national as well as globalization contexts. The people and government face these challenges in order to enjoy better quality of life both in national and globalization contexts as they have envisioned. It is not always the bigger issues of globalization or expanding businesses worldwide that will impact its economic growth and prosperity but also to what extent the population is provided minimum needs of life in reality; and the attitude of people and government to procure it efficiently. This is more challenging for Indian economy.

The ideological commitment at the political level is important for shaping the economic policies and choices. The political leaders set salient economic priorities for its people. Narula (1999) points that public opinion and the political system in India symbolize the complex strands of idealism and selfishness, commitment and dismay, planning and bureaucracy, blame and self-justification, and overwhelming discontent that comprise current Indian economic development. The main challenge is to provide economic and social opportunities to people by streamlining economic policies. How they are planned, implemented and delivered through the combined efforts of people, governance and international agencies and institutions is imperative for fulfillment of its economic visions and its economic growth.

Different emerging markets including India have their business strengths and weaknesses according to their specific models of business communication practices. Their markets develop according to models of their predominant business strengths. The competencies of Indian people at all levels, has made India a global player in many businesses and has boosted the business image as well economy of India. India is doing efficiently and cautiously both—opening up businesses for outsourcing, economic liberalization and FDI; and opening the society. These two can develop in parallel. That is how India envisions its problem and development—Emerging and Surging.

Globalizations, technology and economic liberalization and economic reforms, economic policies allowing Foreign Direct Investment (FDI) in Indian enterprises have tremendously changed both business, and business communication practices in India. India is exposed to global business practices through technology and other channels facilitating globalization. The Models of Globalism and Glocalization are operative in this context. In 90s India was getting conscious of the fact that local events such as outsourcing and IT hubs will have global consequences and impact. It did value those business propositions, it did create interest among the business community for its economic potential and developed knowledge-based capabilities in the IT areas. Thus, Globalism has helped India's exposure to global business practices in the context of global offshore outsourcing and accepting them in their business models and in consequences getting global business partners. It modeled these outsourcing business services on Glocalization model by employing the local capabilities and human talents. It further enhanced the capability and appropriate communication skills of the personnel by utilizing local training professional services.

To set up the infrastructure for these services; they did utilize the foreign funding but it was developed and built by Indian professionals. Thus, Glocalization gives Indian businesses chance to cash on their strengths and business cultures. They had strength in IT software applications and development, so they are encashing on that strength and have not so far got into hardware manufacturing of IT that is not its strength as yet. They further strengthen their weakness; such as they needed the foreign funding to set up update infrastructure for outsourcing business.

India's outsourcing model focused on three areas: Customer care through call centers, BPOs for back office professional services and applications, KPOs for knowledge services and products and development of Information Technology services. RIM for remote infrastructure management. India has the advantage of graduate, English speaking huge manpower of youngsters who are ready to join these units after being trained by the local professional trainers. There is huge pool of appropriate professionals such as chartered accountants, medical technicians, radiographers, etc. for BPO services. India has well trained IT professionals for outsourcing services in IT areas. The good point is that India is delivering efficient services in these areas to the global partners and creating potential for getting more outsourcing and in expanded products and services.

Such business practices have created higher employment, higher wages, core competencies and business processes. People have been the main focus and through this process they have gained economically, in competencies, and better lifestyles promoted through more purchasing power and consumerism with high spend. Interestingly, these growing businesses practices are communicating different lifestyles, economic and social values to young growing generation—the iGen. The wealth generated by India's fast-growing information technology and business process outsourcing industries shows that the country has started living up to its economic potential. By contrast, most sectors of India's economy earlier remained shielded from global competition by high tariffs and restrictions on foreign direct investment and were thus woefully uncompetitive. Although some might argue that removing these barriers would threaten social objectives such as the protection of jobs and incomes, a robust economy would be more likely to realize them. If India is to replicate the success of its IT and outsourcing industries elsewhere in its economy, its leaders must lower barriers to trade and encourage foreign investment in many other sectors.

India's $1.5 billion outsourcing business in 2004/05 illustrates how foreign investment and trade have benefited the country. Along with IT and software, business process outsourcing is perhaps the most open sector. In 2006-07 more and more focus is on developing KPO (knowledge process outsourcing) and RIM (remote infrastructure management).

Without early investments by multinational companies, the outsourcing industry probably would never have emerged. The success of these companies demonstrated to the world that the country was a credible offs-shoring destination. Thousands of local workers were trained by multi-nationals and expats also to meet the initial requirements; many of whom transferred their skills to Indian companies that sprang up in response. Although Indian outsourcing firms now control over half of the intensely competitive global IT and back-office outsourcing market, all of the leading ones started as joint ventures or subsidiaries of multi-national companies or were founded by managers who had worked for them.

(based on excerpts from 'Business Communication Practices: Modern Trends' 2006b by author).

Both FDI and consumerism happened in India because the government decided to liberalize economic policies and allowed its people to outsource their skills and talents for products and services in various domains. An important part of India's innovation system is the diffusion of modern and more efficient technologies in all sectors of the economy. Same may be true of China and other emerging markets.

Indian businesses' high cost of labor and low availability of talent specifically for IT is constraint in the coming years. Both domestic markets and global opportunities can be the drivers for growth. Intense competition, increasing innovation from rivals, increasingly sophisticated consumer can be other constraint to growth. Further, they do feel the difficulty of coping with demands of fast developing economy and lack of adequate infrastructure.

How to balance interests of foreign investors and domestic enterprises?

Government is eager to attract foreign investment to fund projects, and to acquire expertise, technology and foreign currency. But how do policymakers ensure that these efforts benefit local enterprises?

Dr. Manmohan Singh—the current Prime Minister led opening up of India's reforms in the early 1990s as its Finance Minister. As a majority party official he was able to drive the process far more forcefully back then than is the case today in 2007, with a delicate left-leaning coalition government. Today's political context is obviously quite different. Mindful of those constraints, the key code word in current coalition governance circles is "inclusive"—emblematic of a development strategy that is being refocused to deal with the income-disadvantaged citizens of rural India. The Prime Minister is very philosophical when it comes to integrating his reform philosophy within the political imperatives of a broader base of Indian economic development. While his government has been stymied by the politics of inclusion on several fronts—namely on infrastructure and privatizations, etc., he does not interpret these developments as fundamental setbacks on the road to Indian reforms. He has the determination to stay the course in the context of major political constraints of Indian infrastructure deficiencies, fiscal constraints, rural employment and income deficiencies, and foreign policies issues such as Nuclear treaties.

The above backdrop of Indian economic scenario and globalization efforts in various domains since 1991 highlights how and why globalization started in India. The process of globalization started and it is an ongoing process. Globalization did create challenges for India from various perspectives and it does face more and more challenges as the process, the structure, the dimensions and face of globalization changes vis-à-vis India. And that is the focus of transformation story of India—the road to growth.

In the next chapters we will be discussing and highlighting the transformation story of India through globalization since 90's within the conceptual framework with its significant concepts of globalization structure, dimensions, and the transformation challenges. The objective has been economic growth through economic boom.

Globalization structure in India is focusing on global business expansions and development of human, intellectual and financial capitals; and the dimensions of globalization focusing on giving connectivity to people and development of infrastructures. Both these have been posing transformation challenges for India to achieve economic growth through globalization.

We will highlight how the key models: Loop model that interconnect people and governance, interdependency model when viewed positively is inter-reliance, inter-collaboration and inter-operability, learned dependency model suggesting self-reliance of people both in national and global contexts and weaning from practices of depending on government and business models for special segments of society; have supported the above conceptual framework in India.

Transformation efforts in India face hurdles such as gaining political consensus for economic growth, policies, plans and targets and most important in implementation of these. The efforts to develop infrastructure and give connectivity to people, the efforts to raise people's income and give them good standard of life and in the process create parity among the majority of people is also an arduous task when it has to be achieved with limited resource and diverse publics of urban and rural, highly educated and low literacy, elite and the down poor. The efforts to maintain the good traditional values when exposed to good and bad social values of multiple countries have been equally challenging.

It has been challenging also to face the collective threats of political, economic, and social turmoil, sanctions and threats externally since India wants to be an important player in the globalization process. The challenge is definitely refutable when India wants to strive for a powerful economy in the coming future through its achievements.

Here is India's Transformation Story—the story of Rising Expectations.

PART II

Transformation Contexts

3. Rising Expectations: India's Transformation
4. Road to Growth: Transformation for Tomorrow
5. Infrastructure for Human Resource Development
6. Capitals Development
7. Connectivity

Transformation Contexts

In the subsequent chapters we present the transformation story of India, its rising expectations and road map of growth. What challenges the Indian nation, business enterprises and social community and the global community encounter in its transformation contexts.

Global Structure: The focus of global structure is on business expansions in key areas of product and services and different geo markets and expansion and development of new business models as applied to expansion and development of new products and services and markets in new geographies. Globalization is further structured through development of human, intellectual and financial capitals. This we present in chapter 3.

Dimension of Global Transformation: Infrastructure Development is essential dimension of global transformation. Development of physical infrastructure and human infrastructure is the focus. Further focus is on connectivity through telecommunication, media channels, various means of transport, travel and tourism; and creating awareness, education, entertainment and consumer consumption and consumerism through these channels. Thus, transformation would depend on economic growth and boom through connectivity, creative educational system, entertainment economy and consumerism. Chapters 4, 5, 6 and 7 discusses these dimensions.

Transformation challenges are posed both by global structure and by the above-mentioned two dimensions of global transformation. Both internal and external factors create Transformation challenges. These are discussed in chapter 8.

The Globalization model with its six significant components: Globalism, Glocalization Globulation, Iconoclasm, Outsourcing and In-forming is focused in discussion about India's transformation from the above three perspectives.

Globalization Models of Global Empowerment and People Empowerment are highlighted in discussing the India transformation story of rising expectations and growth in the above seven chapters. These models are: Loop model, interdependency model, learned dependency model, business models for special segments consumer markets such as rural markets, co-creation business model for poor and bottom of the pyramid model and microfinance practices.

Images of India Model: The six images of Indian business enterprises highlight the struggle, strivings, aspirations and hard work and confidence of businesses as well the people to expand globally and aspire for global power. The first image is of pre-90s when India was a close economy. Second image is when in 90s the economy was opened and economic liberalization and reforms were initiated. Third image is that business economy was progressing not because of growth of enterprises as they were able to import technology; but businesses felt the need to grow not by being compliant, but by being aggressive in being innovative, creative and competitive for developing appropriate and indigenous technologies, ideas, products and markets. Fourth image is when business enterprises and economy became competitive within the domestic markets with indigenous technologies, ideas, products and markets; and this evoked the confidence to expand businesses to different geo areas. Thus, they started to explore global markets for their technologies, ideas and products. Fifth image is of businesses that worked very hard with renewed confidence to be in the global market, reckon with global forces and aspiration to be super power. Sixth image is that role model of the IT companies inspired other businesses to move ahead.

Seven years into the new millennium, India is more globalize than it was in the first 60 years of its independent existence. The power of globalization, both the upside and the downside, has been apparent to investors in India.

It isn't just returning Indians who are willing to embrace a new resurgent India Inc. The image of India has undergone a dramatic transformation. Rajendra Pawar of NITT echoes the same view. "The diffidence of Indian companies in the '80s gave way to reasonable confidence in the '90s. Now there's a lot of positivism as they go global," says Mr. Pawar. "I won't be surprised if companies soon in other countries start saying, 'We wish our company gets acquired by an Indian company.'" In a number of recent deals, Pawar has already been proven right. Pawar says that the world view in the corporate sector globally is changing. "They see India beyond just IT and Indians as good people managers who respect merit and are smart with technology as well." As word goes around, Pawar says there's an acknowledgement of Indian talent. "The condescending attitude is changing to that of an equal level, if not outright respect." And a pack of Indian firms with global aspirations have to take credit for this transformation.

Much like the Japanese wave in the seventies and the Koreans a decade later, India Inc. has launched a wave of attacks on global markets that have made people sit up and take notice. Even though the Chinese may disagree, some like liquor baron Vijay Mallya prefer to call it the Indian decade. "Indian companies have always had opportunities for serious global acquisitions, but government regulations were a handicap. Things have changed now because forex is not a problem, rules and permissions do not come in the way. What you see now is just the beginning, you will see much more. India Inc. can finally do what we want to do", he says.

It's a game that has only just begun. How many Indian companies finally emerge as world-beaters is hard to predict. But that hasn't stopped them from aspiring for global leadership. Consider just a sample: Ranbaxy's CEO Malvinder Singh says he has set his company the target of emerging amongst the top 5 global generic companies in the world and attaining a turnover of $5 billion by the year 2012. "We today have one of the largest product pipelines in the US, the world's biggest pharma market. The company has 17-18 First-to-File (FTF) products that command a market size of over $26 billions. These FTF products are expected to be launched during the period 2007 to 2014. The potential FTF molecules present a huge opportunity and offer a major commercial upside to

Ranbaxy's organic growth plans," says Mr. Singh (Ranbaxy is sold to Daichi in early 2008).

Reform has made the resurgent new India. Yet, it remains a covert operation for the political class, which must learn to celebrate it as politics. India needs a new holistic vision of reform. Reforms are required for higher growth. Financial inclusion is necessary for equitable growth though not sufficient by itself. It's time for the world to stop viewing India as a nation of snake charmers. We are, indeed, charmers and this time our IT, an economy and Indian MNCs will do the trick; India Inc. launches wave of attack on global markets.

We move on the India's Transformation Story—the story of rising expectations of its people.

Rising Expectations: India's Transformation

3

Globalization Structure: Road to Growth

Think Local, Act Global

Think Global, Act Local

It is not just about where your dreams will take you but where you take your dreams.

Global Business Expansion

The India growth story is no longer just the preserve of columns in daily newspapers and speeches of political leaders and civil servants. The number of growing job opportunities in big and small cities, the construction work on the roads, ports and at airports, the healthy balance sheets of companies and the heightened growth in consumerism—all go on to prove that this growth story has begun to change lives of millions across the length and breadth of India.

Statistics only reinforce the all-pervading India growth story. During the past three years, India has grown at an average growth rate of 8.6%, the fastest since Independence. Its global competitiveness ranking has improved from 57 in 2001 to 45 in 2005 and 43 in 2006. According to the latest Global Competitiveness Report, India has the highest rank amongst the BRIC economies, with China at 54, Russia at 62 and Brazil at 66.

India's economy is at the fulcrum of an ever-increasing growth curve. While both the industry and the services sector are growing in double-digits, other indicators—such as the capital markets, foreign exchange reserves, foreign trade and (outward and inward) FDI—too reinforce India's growth story. Today in 2007, India's foreign exchange reserves are at over $200 billion. The Sensex has topped the majestic 20,000 + mark and FDI inflows for 2006-07 are estimated at $19 billion (up from $7 billion during 2005-06). During 2006-07, exports rose 23.9 per cent to $124.63 billion, while imports jumped 29.3 per cent to $181.4 billion.

Gone are the days when the Small and Medium Business (SMB) market was called the emerging market. SMBs have now emerged, and after achieving cogent economic growth in India, have become a fresh target for Information and Communications Technology (ICT) vendors.

India is going through industrial revolutions on one hand and through the velocity of information age; India is being transformed from an ancient agregarian society into modern manufacturing hub and global service provider.

Changing Images of Business Enterprises of India

Six images of India's economic transformation story through business enterprises of India are highlighted.

The first image is of pre-90s when India was a close economy. Enterprises were more creative because they have to work around the technology, tools, funds, money, etc. as whatever was available indigenously. They innovated appropriate technologies to some extent. Bigger businesses were spending funds in research and development and so were able to innovate appropriate technologies though much did not trickle down to smaller enterprises. So as expected contributing of smaller enterprises must be very limited to business and economic growth.

Second image is when in 90s the economy was opened and economic liberalization and reforms were initiated. Enterprises became less creative and innovative because they had access to foreign advance technology as economic liberalization allowed them to import some of them. This is 90s to 2000 period.

Third image is business economy was progressing because of growth of enterprises as they were able to import technology but businesses felt the need to grow not by being compliant, but by being aggressive in being innovative, creative and competitive for developing appropriate and indigenous technologies, ideas, products and markets.

Fourth image is when business enterprises and economy became competitive within the domestic markets with indigenous technologies, ideas, products and markets. Once they gained the competitive edge at home, and the success in outsourcing business not only provided revenues but the confidence to expand businesses to different geo areas. They started to explore global markets for their technologies, ideas and products. This was the period 2000-03.

The businesses worked very hard with renewed confidence in three prongs:

(i) To invite global MNCs to get their business products manufactured from India and also to provide the Indian consumer market as well as to make markets abroad accessible for these products. Thus, it provided manufacturing hub. They worked hard for quality controls to match international standards and invite more and more businesses.

For this not only they were offering low costs but they have to train the manpower for this task.

(ii) A large number of manpower—skilled and unskilled, educated and uneducated was available in India. But these products and tasks needed different kind of skills so they planned to develop matching task force. Lots of efforts by different set of people—academicians, scientists, technologists, policymakers, and trainers contributed in developing this task force and also good work ethics. These were both from national and international levels. Many supporting educational and training institutes have come up. This in turn helped in creating job opportunities for people in different regions of the country.

(iii) The manufacturing hub created for MNCs businesses gave them confidence, inspiration, and motivation to create foreign markets for their own ideas, products and services and also expanding the demand for more trained task force and expanding job opportunities. High level of business acumen of Indian enterprises, trained and educated task force availability, and liberal government economic policies created interest among foreign companies and investors to acquire smaller Indian companies to expand their businesses in India. This gave lift to Indian small and medium capital businesses. Since acquisitions and mergers brought more capital investments, advance technology and new business practices and cultures for these enterprises. The investments by foreign investors also helped these to expand their businesses. This was the period 2000-03 and lots was consolidated.

Fifth image is when India has expanded globally, acquired and merged global companies, got into collaborative and joint ventures of high scale both abroad and in India. And set up world class facilities. The period is 2004 onwards.

Few examples are, Tata acquiring Cores, Land Rover and Jaguar, Reliance acquiring African Oil, Polyster from Malaysia, Laxmi Mittal, for acquiring Arcelor Steel, Jindal Steel and Power in joint venture in steel, Vijay Mallaya acquiring and joint ventures for Liqueur. Aditya Birla Hindalco Group bought Australian Copper Mines, Gujarat NRE acquiring Australian Coal Mines, Ranbaxy in pharma areas and Jet Airlines expanded abroad. There were businesses who have come to India: Porche for steel, Cairn for oil, Holcim for cement, Pfzier for drugs.

Sixth image is that manufacturing businesses gain confidence, inspiration, and motivation to create foreign markets for their own ideas, products and services from IT enterprises. They were the pioneers. They are world class and in global demand, so we can be. If they can bring flow of revenue in the country so can we. That was the start of our global economy.

Entrepreneurs are made in the context of their cultures. The values of a productive culture are the values of entrepreneurship—a belief in progress, wealth creation, disruption change, individual freedom, hard work, skepticism. Whether one acts out of reasoning, by gut feeling, economic calculus, religious mandate, or an irresistible urge just to talk, by any such action every person contributes in some measures to the shaping of culture.

Research studies have shown, it is difficult to measure the political confidence of companies, since there is no direct correlation between a company's financial performance and the political environment of the day. Politics affects business in a subtle manner and it is difficult to quantify it in the immediate term. As such, it is entirely possible that the rise in PCI may have been triggered by an improvement in economic and industrial growth, leading to a 'feel-good' factor among industry executives and proprietors.

The PCI measures respondent companies' confidence in the government across eight parameters—managing overall economic growth, government finance, inflation, unemployment, exchange rate, conducive political climate, external trade negotiations (both bilateral and multilateral) and pushing economic reforms forward. India Inc. has shown greater confidence in government policies across all parameters, except in terms of managing exchange rate and external trade negotiations.

Private limited companies, closely followed by public limited companies, are the most confident of the political environment in the country. In terms of managing overall economic growth, the highest rating of 61.3 has been reported by private limited companies. Proprietary/partnership firms have shown the maximum rise in confidence of 16% over the June '07 quarter. Public sector companies have shown the least percentage increase in confidence over the previous quarter.

Political confidence is highest in the case of mid-sized companies (with turnover of Rs. 100-500 crore). This may be due to good performance of these companies over the last quarter. Very small companies (with turnover of less than Rs. 1 crore) are the least confident, but this segment has shown the highest percentage jump of 27% over the previous quarter.

Globalization structure in India focuses on globalization of enterprises and business expansion of product, global markets and geographies through collaboration, joint ventures, merger and acquisitions. We discuss the planning and policies for globalization of enterprises and business expansion and how these are raising expectations of people and transforming India. There have been three contributory factors for India's economic boom and rising expectations in the years to come.

As changing images of business enterprises have highlighted India's companies are showing strengths in smart management, low costs, and increasing ambition to join the elite ranks of multinationals. India is dreaming bigger and aiming higher. International giants are competing head-on with India's seasoned players. This is testament to the remarkable resilience and endurance of India's conglomerates.

Most of the Indian companies endured decades of socialist rule, which starved them of capital and technology but guaranteed them a captive market. In the early 90s, the economic liberalization opened the door to foreign competition. Companies restructured and were competitive and their success is due to lot of hard work that went to operating in a tough domestic market.

India's global participation started in 90s with business expansion through 'outsourcing' for developed countries. It was a new concept initiated by developed countries to get business services outsourced to developing countries for higher margin of profits because of low cost and cheap labor. The outsourcing could be supported by progress in information technologies. The developed countries believed the profits will trickle down to people in developing countries by more jobs and more earnings.

India experienced more than the trickle effect through outsourcing since India's professionals ventured in developing 'outsourcing' in their own unique way and to their utmost advantage by developing the information technology hubs with software application developments through their strengths of highly educated, English speaking IT professionals. Thus, majority of the IT product services were directed to India. Many BPOs (Back Processing Office) were also set up to avail of back office services for products and services at advantageous prices.

India could also avail of this because of availability of English speaking young educated graduates. Later, outsourcing was expanded to new concepts, new ways of delivering of products and services. We would be discussing about it in later sections.

Initially, India's globalization participation has started with setting up IT 'outsourcing hubs' in India itself. Later they expanded their IT service providers' hubs in different countries for better earnings by being closer to the service providing areas such as setting up in Latin American countries to able to serve USA. They also set up training institutes to train different countries' personnel to work in those hubs and BPO offices. Their motive is of increased earnings through low cost and cheap labor in those countries as well less transportation costs. Those offices are manned by their own personnel as well from host countries. So glocalization principle is operative for better results. More and more Indian professionals are being exposed to foreign countries, their business practices and finding business solutions for them.

Globalized outsourcing was the start of India's transformation story and its sailing through government and private efforts, policies, planning and actions. National efforts, people's efforts and international efforts were significant and essential for ensuing transformation to take place. This was the first significant contributory factor for economic boom.

India is a dominant player in computer software development because it can play on the strengths of its educated, talented and trained manpower in these areas. It is dominant in many areas of BPOs such as radiology, law and accountancy and KPOs in different areas because of its talent pool and expertise in these areas as compared to other countries. Comparatively, China is a dominant player where inexpensive, quality and good design manufacturing is concerned. Manufacturing could be in variety of garments and consumer goods, computer and other technology hardware, and cell phones, etc. It is developing technology hardware both offshoring and indigenous. Its people have inherent expertise and knack for these areas. Whereas, it may not be good in running basic BPOs like call centers as it lacks pool of English speaking personnel. These and other developing countries are selling their ideas, products and services in their expertise areas may be to developed countries like USA, Middle Eastern rich countries and even the emerging countries. Thus, they all seek to collaborate on one another's expertise. Collaboration is the business model for globalization.

Media exposure through national and globalized TV, print, telecommunication computers and Internet has been the second important factor to expose people to foreign lands, their life style services and products, their cultural and business practices. This created a globalized demand for those products, services and practices.

Media impact boosted India's expectations for life and businesses for economic gains and thus economic growth; and it did boost India's transformation story. This was the second significant contributory factor.

Soon it was realized that financial capital must be raised to foray into and expand to global businesses. Financial capital was raised in India by inviting foreign institutions to invest in India directly (FDI) and furthered by foreign investments in collaborative enterprises and venture capitals, etc. Later, this also became two way traffic when India started investing in developed countries as well in developing countries by setting up businesses independently either to serve them or in collaborative ventures.

India has set up guidelines for foreign investments in India through planning and policies and taking cautious actions to safeguard its national interests, interests of its businesses and people and at the same time able to transcend into global enterprises to benefit. FDI directly and through collaborations and joint ventures have expanded to many sectors.

This also highlights the significance of interdependency loop for global participation of India in developing financial capitals through foreign funds and has been the third contributory factor for India's economic boom and rising expectations.

Initially, MNCs started investing in businesses in India through business models of collaboration, mergers and acquiring smaller and supporting businesses and by bringing foreign capital to expand businesses in India. Again principle of glocalization is operative—local talents but foreign fund and expertise both foreign and Indian facilitated these efforts. Liberalization of economic polices, availability of latest technology, and renewed business confidence, new business models and good business and management practices also raised the expectations of businesses as well consumers, and foreign markets to help expand businesses in the domestic markets. Later India, with its gained experience in entrepreneurship started merging and acquiring businesses from domestic markets as well from abroad to expand businesses to become conglomerates. M&A gradually transformed and expanded India's businesses and growth.

Thus, the initial contributory factors were outsourcing and offshoring, media impact, foreign funds investments and capital flow, mergers and acquisitions, expansion of banking and microfinance, and access to business and information communication technologies. Transformation was set in through rising expectations of economic gain through these practices. In the later stages, the transformation is being enhanced by exposure to more and more of emerging best practices in various domains; and India is on its transformation journey by choosing the best practices facilitating its progress in various domains.

The outcome of these initiatives has been increase in job opportunities and demand for specific skills to match these jobs, and increased knowledge, expertise and demand-supply for innovative products and services and innovative business models and functioning styles.

We will be discussing how each of these factors has pushed India for economic growth and gains, and globalization participation and thus contributed towards its ongoing transformation.

Services Globalization Trends

Global services initiatives research report (2007) focuses on services globalization trends. Business transformation will be the key factor this year. Global companies will improve time-to-market, gain new business, and standardize processes and lower costs significantly. Business transformation through services globalization is one of the most important levers that global companies can no longer afford to ignore. A recent research suggests factors contributing to growth in services and has identified several trends. It even analyzed the impact of increasing number of sophisticated buyers with years of global sourcing experience.

On the supplier side, the report adds that competitive forces have led to increased supplier sophistication. Year 2007 will see an increased focus among service providers on developing industry-specific subject matter expertise through acquisitions.

The report further adds that acquisitions will be a continuing trend in 2007. Companies based in the West will take a keen interest in setups in the East to stay competitive as well as explore eastern markets, which are not only cost effective delivery locations, but are rapidly emerging markets by themselves.

Geographically, new locations are emerging, although India will continue to lead the supplier market, with Europe showing strong growth. The research brief says that billing rates will go up amongst the Tier-1 suppliers by 2-3% due to a growing demand for skilled resources, rise in wages, and increased overheads that are incurred in maintaining quality or ensuring tight security.

The report also states that despite the ongoing debate about Tier-1 and Tier-2 cities and concerns of wage inflation, attrition and infrastructure issues, Indian Tier-1 cities (NCR, Bangalore, Chennai, Hyderabad and Mumbai) will grow at a continued pace in attracting offshore delivery work, through 2007. The European market for global services is expected to grow at a faster rate with its companies' offshoring to India, China and the Philippines, and other lower-cost locations, depending on language and culture-dependence of the particular service.

India: Global Business Expansion Focus

India is expanding its businesses with global participation and globalization. It has expanded its business products and a service driven by liberal economic policies, technologies, its unique business strengths in information technology and confidence to achieve and succeed. It has explored new markets at home as well abroad for these products and services thus expanded to different geographies. This unprecedented openness and opportunity for mobility encourages companies, industries and professionals to cover this worldwide market as well as to face the competition from worldwide.

Technology has given promise for the effective progress of businesses. The lower cost, higher performance and advanced features of business technologies have benefited consumers. Therefore, technology not only has to keep pace with changing business requirements but also outstrip them by coming up with the next big revolutionary idea.

The next big growth driver lies in combining technology with business change, i.e. integrated change, as many Indian companies are doing today. However, many businesses fail to achieve integrated change, which involves simultaneous changes in IT, business processes, strategy, organization and culture.

Technology services will continue to play a very important role for enterprises. Even within software services, there are plenty of big ideas considering that the technology integration and harnessing capabilities of companies have yet to see saturation.

Service oriented architecture (SOA)—where products are being integrated with services, seamlessly across all systems, and enabled by the web—will drive the next change in transformation of businesses.

There are early stage venture capital fund Ventureast TeNet Fund II—a seed-stage fund run by the Tenet Group of IIT, Madras and Ventureast Fund Advisors. There is Indian Angel Network, an organization of professionals companies dedicated to supporting entrepreneurship in India.

The Ventureast TeNet II fund invests in technology that enables early stage entrepreneurs to get their businesses off the ground. Emphasis is placed on technologies and solutions focused on small and medium-sized enterprises and bridging the digital divide in India and global markets. The Indian Angel Network (indianangelnetwork.com) brings together entrepreneurs, companies and CEOs from India and around the world to provide money, mentoring and strategic inputs to early stage ventures in multiple sectors.

Google in 2007 announced two partnerships that further its commitment to fostering innovation in India. It has invested in the early stage venture capital fund Ventureast TeNet Fund II and has also joined the Indian Angel Network. Venture capitalists, bankers and angel investors are vying with each other to hunt down the next big idea. The domestic market for goods and services is growing rapidly and so are export opportunities. Internet has simplified the business of business. All this, naturally, must lead to an explosion in the start-up scene across the country.

Diversification of Business

In India, the recent changing business practices by enterprises are widening the scope of their businesses by diversifications. In 2006, the big business houses like Reliance Industries have announced their diversification in retail, agriculture—agro processing, and petroleum and refineries. Reliance capital is foraying into energy and power, entertainment, communications, telecom and Real estate. Bharti Airtel is into telecom mainly but diversifying in Real estate. Zee tele is foraying into entertainment and Real estate. The United Breweries is getting into Airlines beside liqueur business. Many other companies are diversifying and thus expanding with domestic or global partners and also finding business scope in other countries as the government policies change.

Such as in 2006, the foreign investment is opened in Retail and Real estate, in 2004-05, foreign funding and equity for airlines was opened. This has been possible because of changed practices about economic reforms, liberalization and opening of certain areas for foreign funding and equity as communicated by government policies and the businesses accepting the globalization challenges. Because of these diversifications of businesses, Indian companies have expanded domestically by either merging their subsidiaries—thus integrating or merging other businesses by acquisitions in diverse businesses. Since late 90s the trend has been that global companies were acquiring Indian companies, merging in their business expansion plans because of their changed attitudes towards Indian companies adding value to their companies. But this business model has been changing later on.

The business model being followed by India is: open economy, liberalized economic policies, collaboration and interdependency, export-oriented economic growth through export of products and services specifically produced for exports to developed countries; and import and transfer of technology, innovations and innovative business ideas from developed markets, expertise through foreign experts and expats. These kinds of exports and imports will create economic growth and steady the economy by producing more employment, circulation of money through foreign funding, more infrastructure and consumerism.

The products produced in emerging markets for export to developed countries, as fallout may create consumerism in the domestic markets and consumerism may be further promoted by higher disposable income of the younger generation. The higher disposable income is also the result of higher employment due to changing businesses and practices due to globulation, glocalization and globalism. The emerging markets of India, China, Brazil and Russia and many other developing countries are participating in globulation by opening their economy, liberalizing economic policies, by allowing circulation of money by investing in foreign markets as well as allowing foreign investments in their countries. Thus, businesses get expanded. Businesses get further expanded by acquisitions and mergers and by collaborating with foreign businesses to gain technology edge and markets and to expand in scale.

Secondly, foreign funding is invested in emerging markets in businesses in general, manufacturing of products and investments in stocks and bonds. Foreign investments create different kind of, and mutually facilitative opportunities for emerging markets, developing countries and developed countries. Thirdly, technology changes the business practices these days. It is a great facilitator in many ways. (i) There are quick travel modes, innovative telecommunication modes such as computers, cell phones, Internet functionalities, digitalization, data banks and data storage, and telephone, audio, video conferences, etc. (ii) Innovative business technologies shared by transfer and buying technologies, hiring expertise, business collaborations and creating innovations.

Business Competition: The impact of competition and business innovations is global as well as globally shared. Competition drives businesses to adopt new practices; as well competition pushes businesses to look for new and best practices to produce the products and services as well to deliver them to the consumers. Market openness with globalization has increased the speed, frequency and magnitude of access to worldwide markets, including all tangible and intangible aspects of commerce, by a new and more diverse set of competitors.

The knowledge management competencies focus on knowledge development of global customer, competitor and supplier; and inter-functional coordination and value chain coordination.

India by their business strategies, talent pool and getting into update technologies; forayed into competition both at home and in global markets for enhanced range of products and services, new business practices, advance management techniques, innovation management and expanding consumer profiles and markets for themselves as well foreign enterprises to foray into businesses in Indian markets. These skills have equipped them well for operating in different geographies. These have created strong sense of competition and have been the changing the business scenario fast at home and in global markets.

The snapshots of Indian enterprises given in other section highlight these competitions and how such competitive spirit have enabled them to create strong niches for themselves in different geographies and markets of both developed and developing countries in various domains and change of attitude towards Indian enterprises as the dominant power player, and stable political environment and secure business environment and respected business leaders to invest and do business (Narula, 2008a).

Business Innovations and Opportunities

Innovation consists in the design, development and diffusion of technology (or a practice) that is new for the society concerned. In order to take shape innovation requires: (i) climate favorable to entrepreneurs without the hassles of bureaucratic, regulatory and other obstacles, and (ii) appropriate interactions between the local business world and different sources of knowledge. Those knowledge sources include 'classical' establishments such as universities, public labs and research centers, users and indigenous communities.

Innovation systems are made of interactions among those actors. They are complex and sophisticated depending on the level of development. The role played by domestic research capabilities increases as an economy develops. In low-income countries, innovation is much dependant on foreign technology and its adaptation to local contexts.

In developing countries, the role played by domestic research capabilities increases as an economy develops innovation systems do not take shape easily because the groups and organizations are more concerned with the day-to-day survival issues, or the defense of vested interests, or because they are lacking the necessary technical culture. This affects communications and exchanges of information. Therefore, innovation policies in developing countries primarily deal with the building of an appropriate technical culture and with the establishment of incentives to stimulate cooperation and entrepreneurship.

Derek H. Chen and Carl J. Dahlman (2003) research highlights that stock of human capital, the level of domestic innovation and technological adaptation and the level of ICTs infrastructure exert significant effects on long-term economic growth. Developing countries do learn from other developing countries as well as from developed countries. They learn the lessons both from success and failures. Lessons learnt must be contextualized to local contexts. They can leapfrog their performance by using knowledge and experiences of others coupled with their own knowledge of local circumstances.

Most entrepreneurs start their business with some innovative ideas. The problem occurs when they stop innovating without realizing that in a rapidly changing global market innovation holds the key to business success. Innovation is significant in the perspective of the changed market scenario in the country—from a closed economy to an open economy. The change demanded big strides in progress as against a gradual incremental development. "And innovation alone gives you quantum jumps. As we have observed Indian companies need to be promoting continuous innovation in order to maintain sustained competitive advantage over the competition. Hence, the emphasis on continuous innovation by companies and promotion of sustained innovation culture in companies. We observe, the companies strive for, and gain global market competitive advantage through alliances of strategic partnerships, through business innovations in technology and management; creating diverse skilled as well global culturally adaptable work force, and by creating values for their businesses."

'5th Global SMEs Conference' on "Innovation and Competitiveness for World Market" in November 2007 in Mumbai highlighted the importance of innovation for SMEs and entrepreneurs in the highly competitive global market. SME Chamber of India remarked that the SMEs had emerged as a vibrant segment in India and were at the forefront of the country's economic development. "SMEs are facing a challenge of a fast changing world and innovation will be an important tool in taking up this challenge." It was further stated that small scale of operations and limited resources were the main concerns for all SMEs and therefore it was necessary for them to focus on innovation for enhancing productivity and increasing competitiveness. Three key areas are where SMEs need to focus for innovation. "SMEs need to look at innovation on managerial, financial and technological fronts."

Many MNC make better use of Indian engineers, factories, and supply chain based in these countries. They thus neutralize an emerging challenger's low-cost advantage. Realization is fast dawning, as foreign companies, attitudes have changed that leading companies in India can be great partners; these are great to hold equity into and add values to their businesses. The smaller companies and startups can be acquired to add value to their businesses that these MNCs plan to set up in India. These companies know the changing business environments and practices, terrain, and real market needs at home and in other key emerging growth markets with which they are dealing. MNCs businesses can cash on these added values also.

Creativity and innovation both define how we compete and re-define who will own and control the greatest market opportunities in the world. This is true for both online and offline. Those businesses that can re-invent themselves, change the rules of an industry by accepting change itself, define new markets; and offer entirely new ways of doing business will not only compete but break away from competition itself. That is what Indian enterprises are doing constantly and continuously, and foray into best and next business practices.

The corporate structure, board structure, accounting methods, reporting processes are all getting re-invented to fit in the global practices of standardizing. The essence of re-invention is innovation, invention and risk-taking in order to take the businesses to the next level of success. Reinvention of businesses at home will have the impact across global businesses. We need to rebuild a business culture with new global point of views.

What is significant is how these business practices are communicated to consumers and businesses worldwide due to changing modes of communication and also due to impact of practices changing in other domains. The significance lies in thinking globally and coping with global trends by capacity building and improved management techniques and facing challenges of changing business practices and redefining and re-inventing businesses. India is focusing on these dimensions to do business in global markets and as well make it attractive, challenging and profitable for global businesses to do business and investments in India.

Innovation has changed, in 90s it involved dealing with vast technological shifts that disrupted and threatened companies. Today, it means building the process that promotes an idea generating culture. Increasingly, large companies are also globalizing innovation as well (Narula, 2008a).

Mergers and Acquisitions (M&A): The external growth through partnerships, through M&A, strategic alliances, and creative deal-making is now an essential ingredient for continuously reinventing any business. M&A also creates diversifications in businesses both globally and at home and that widens the scope. Heightened economic activity usually leads to a spurt in M&A transactions, as companies with motives as varying as buying growth to staying afloat decide to merge.

M&A of companies from BRIC nations (Brazil, Russia, India and China) are fast closing the gap on their counterparts in developed nations in terms of cross-border acquisitions. Though the number of deals involving a developed economy buying into an emerging economy is still much larger than that of emerging-into-developed, the divide is narrowing fast. According to KPMG's 'Emerging Markets International Acquisitions Tracker' research study, Indian companies also see acquisitions and mergers as new strategy and practice. For decades, the corporate India has been sticking close to home and protecting its markets from foreign incursions. Now, Indian companies are scouting for international acquisitions and mergers for wider growth. The trend is changed by economic liberalization policies, cheaper capital, low Indian interest rates and low (though it is changing with changed economic scenarios) global interest rates. At the same time Indian government has liberalized restrictions in tapping international debt markets and the boom in Indian stock market is also providing an easy source of funds. Over and above, the new breed of Indian executive is leading this practice. They are educated at western management schools, and elite Indian management schools, trained in multinationals and global in outlook. Their approach marks a radical departure from conventional approach to oppose any market opening moves and market economy. Now some of the same companies, with younger generations with global outlook at the helm, support proposals that would open Indian economy wider and wider.

Indian companies are getting strong, cost-efficient and with greater opportunities, are acquiring companies to build their own competence and scalability. In India, M&A market is heating up with local companies aspiring to become global, capital becoming much more easily accessible and the regulators adopting a positive stance.

Business Model of M&A: Most of the acquisitions have been so far for small companies. But as Indian companies achieve global scale; their acquisition sizes will also grow. Indian companies are getting confident of their ability to manage global enterprises. By pushing overseas, many Indian companies hope to gain expertise, build brands, and add scale to set themselves up in business abroad and competition at home.

Over the years the M&A business model has changed. New dimensions were focused. In dimension one, initially, in the domestic markets; (i) Indian companies were merging their subsidiaries to consolidate businesses. (ii) When they started diversifying businesses, they started acquiring small companies and start-ups either to expand their businesses, or bail out companies with good ideas and products and talented expertise of workforce but not able to go ahead because of money liquidity. (iii) They were merging some of the subsidiaries set up by global companies in India to focus on Indian domestic market or make India as hub for exporting to other nearby countries, as well as back home.

In second dimension, as India's economy grows faster; its newly confident companies are showing their global ambitions. They are investing abroad and adding substantially to their revenues as well as investing their expertise for the benefit of other countries. Indian companies are expanding their businesses and are acquiring bigger companies abroad as well acquiring stake in those companies; and have been successful in bidding for them along with other big bidders.

In March '07 Tata Steel finalized $11.3 billion purchase of Dutch steel maker Corus. In June 2007 wind turbine maker Suzlon Energy paid $530 million for controlling interest in German rival REpower systems. Suzlon founded in 1995 is now one of the world's fifth biggest producers of wind turbines. Aditya Birla Group acquired copper mines in Australia in, Novalis a aluminum company from, paper pulp companies in Canada, Reliance has acquired Polyester Company from Malaysia, oil company in South Africa. Appolo Health acquisition of US-based BPO Zavata. Other biddings in progress in 2007 are: Sun Pharmaceutical is bidding for Taro Pharmaceutical Industries, an Israeli generics maker. Tata motors bid for Jaguar and Land Rover. And India's drug makers are plowing more of their profits into research and development in the hope of devising cures for diseases such as HIV/AIDS, diabetes, malaria, cancer. Indian pharma is at the cusp of dramatic change where the IT sector was a decade ago. This diversity is reversal from just a few years ago when the entire world knew about corporate India was its software companies.

2004 was hot on M&A front and 2005 saw a large increase in the number of mergers, a large number of which took place in group companies. Mergers in group companies were the highest in 2007 as companies realized that multiple operating entities are not efficient either from a business or overheads perspective. Among sectors, the financial services sector had the largest number of mergers followed by other services, chemicals, textiles and trading sectors. While acquisition activity has slowed down in terms of the number of deals, the value of deals has gone up significantly when compared.

KPMG study indicates that financial sense is not enough to make a success of global mergers and acquisitions. Several M&As fail when diverse business cultures, work ethics and country cultures fail to integrate. Communication is the key for

M&A success. Language plays an important role, and communication skills are important to understand these diverse cultures for the employees get the right cues.

India and China's hunger for foreign assets and a frenzy of activity in the booming commodities sector triggered record merger and acquisition volumes in Asia outside Japan in 2007, with outbound acquisitions on track to triple last year's total. That momentum is poised to continue as Asian buyers using swelling foreign exchange reserves look for natural resources, brands, distribution and know-how.

"M&A volumes will be higher in 2008 than in 2007, and will be more China-driven than India-driven," "The reason why you've seen increased acquisitions taking place in the financial services industry is partly because people don't want to hold US dollars in the form of treasuries," said Colin Banfield, head of Asia ex-Japan M&A at Lehman Brothers. "If you're going to hold US dollars you might as well as invest in an actual operating entity given what's happened to relative valuations on assets and the weakness of the US dollar," he said. The dollar has fallen almost 10% this year against a basket of currencies, while the yield paid on benchmark 10-year treasuries has declined to around 4.15% from a peak above 5.30% in June 2007. China's Sinosteel offered $1 billion for Australian iron ore miner Midwest. On the same day, China Minmetals Nonferrous Metals and Jiangxi Copper launched an agreed $450 million offer for Canada's Northern Peru Copper.

Collaborative Business Model focus on joint ventures in domestic market, with other global corporates in multi-geographies. It could be bilateral or multicountry; with one company or with multicompanies. Joint ventures are sought to get expertise of the other company, to get markets and geographies of other country, leverage the talent pool and to get capital from other company. Many MNCs in India get into joint venture with Indian companies to cut development time and cost such as:

US defense contractor Lockheed Martin Corporation is looking at the possibility of making some new commercial products in India for the global market to cut development time and cost, a company official said in September 2007. The $39.6 billion company was looking to make products in India that would be cheaper and better to compete in the global marketplace. "Increasingly in the global economy where we live, you don't have the luxury of taking 20 years to bring a product to marketplace", he said adding the products needed to be made at a cheaper cost. "We are approaching India on a very broad front but excluding defense sector. We are looking at business opportunity. What's the thing we can do in India. The company would explore possibilities of setting up an R&D centre in India to leverage the engineering talent pool."

Indian companies can also collaborate with Indian an Indian company. ONGC and Laxmi Mittal collaborated into bid oil sector through their joint expertise. Indian companies can collaborate with foreign companies to get their expertise just as Reliance is seeking to collaborate with Petrobra for their expertise in drilling in deep waters for his Krishna basin oil fields.

India uses Collaborative Business Model for collaboration and joint ventures with other global corporates in multi-geographies. Global technologies, global participation has been the major drive for such business expansion.

India is ahead of China on many counts. In its report, doing business 2008, the World Bank has ranked China at 83rd whereas India occupied the 120th place. However, India's score is better than China in terms of starting a business, dealing with licenses, getting credit, employing workers protecting investors and paying taxes. India is below China in registering property, enforcing contracts, closing business and trading across borders. The report, said four hurdles such as delays in litigation, inadequate bankruptcy laws and taxation system, besides dealing with licenses led to India's low ranking among 178 economies.

The report brings out a wide disparity between efficiencies of different cities within India. "If the top score among Indian cities in each of the indicators were used for the country as a whole, India would be up to 55 places in the aggregate country rankings". The Indian government is using this information to plan further reform.

"China has liberalized trade far more than India. India is still reluctant to open up significantly", the Yale University Professor said while delivering a lecture on economic reforms in India and China at the India Policy Forum in July 2007. He said India could leverage its democracy as the safety valve to rope in more investment and compete with China as the latter's "authoritarian system still depends on repression."

Other speakers pointed out that the biggest challenge before India is to address infrastructure issues particularly power and financial sector reforms. The country's agriculture sector also needs to be re-formed with a view to shifting excess labor from the farm sector to the industry. The hot topic is inclusive growth.

Maharashtra's industry department in India has approved a proposal to develop an 'International Standard Trade Point' at the World Trade Centre building that would provide the domestic industry, in particular the Small and Medium Enterprises (SMEs), a window to global trade and a platform to take part in global e-commerce economy.

Mumbai becomes only the second city in India after Delhi to boast of a Trade Point which is part of a United Nations Conference on Trade and Development (UNCTAD) program to increase international trade participation of SMEs from developing countries, sources said. Since November 2002, the program is being implemented by World Trade Point Federation (WTPF). "The establishment of a Trade Point would put Mumbai in the league of 70 nations which are already on the information highway on global trade. The World Trade Centre in Mumbai gives inputs on global trade and requirements to the domestic industry."

The Trade Point would go further and provide SMEs access to international market and trade scenario in all affiliated countries. A trade point is a locally based trade support office with global reach through WTPF. It helps its affiliated companies navigate easily through the complexity of international trade procedures and provides them with relevant data that help them take informed market decisions, sources said. A trade point is a one-stop-shop providing trade information, trade facilities, and trade transaction services. The trade point will be a source of trade-related information for current and potential traders. The information could range from data about business opportunities, potential clients, suppliers, trade regulations, etc. It also serves as a trade facilitation centre for participants in foreign trade transactions like customs, banks, chambers of commerce, freight forwarders, transport and insurance companies. It is a gateway to global electronic networks as all trade points are inter-connected to facilitate the SMEs sector's participation in the e-commerce economy.

Industry department officials reckon that by becoming a member of the trade point network, the World Trade Centre in Mumbai would gain not only from its association with its counterparts worldwide but also share the existing strength of WTC with other trade point centers so that more business and competitiveness could be provided for the SMEs sector. Some of the direct benefits of the trade point to Mumbai WTC would be a direct access to reliable counterparts and their governments, an opportunity to become a preferred supplier for SMEs, and attracting trade point customers from over 43,000 companies based in 61 countries which are on the global company database of WTPF as of 2007.

Snapshot of Indian Enterprises

Snapshot of randomly selected Indian companies highlight their foray into expanding products and services, new technologies and multiple geographies. We have illustrated a few big companies, medium to small, upcoming companies in various domains to give glimpse of the entrepreneurship, progress, global participation and acceptance, collaboration and joint venture and highlighted their 2007 current business product focus, collaboration and joint ventures with other global corporates in multi geographies. Global technologies, global participation has been the major drive for these.

Current Scenario 2007-08: The everyday news in the media point the Indian companies are moving on in various domains to different geographies abroad and at home focusing on varied products. They highlight their product range, operation areas development, geographies and expertise. These tell the story of progress, transformation made by these companies, and getting into diversified businesses that was not the earlier norm before 90s, their developing and growing into MNCs, and Conglomerates; and thus giving way to rising expectations among people, experts, businesses, policymakers, and among national and international economic and political leaders.

Sample Corporate Announcements through media news highlight the entrepreneurial activities and acquisitions of Indian companies on October 23, 2007:

- Reliance Industries, which is set to begin production from the country's largest gas block, is in talks with Peru for picking up-stake in two oil blocks.
- ONGC Mittal Energy has acquired a 30% stake in an offshore exploration block in the Caspian Sea, Turkmenistan.
- Wipro Consumer Care and Lighting is setting up a plant to manufacture modular switches to strengthen its switches and lighting business.
- Tata Chemicals expects its bio-fuels manufacturing unit at Nanded, Maharashtra to be operational within the next 18 months.
- BSEL Infrastructure Realty Ltd. has set aside an investment of Rs. 1,000 millions for the state to tap the growing hospitality sector in Gujarat.

Sample Corporate Announcements through media news highlight the entrepreneurial activities and acquisitions of Indian companies on 24 October 2007:

- Siemens has bagged an order worth Rs. 3.3 billions for power distribution network solutions from Tata Steel for its green field steel plant at Kalinganagar, Orissa.

- Satyam acquired UK-based Nitor Global Solutions which provides infrastructure management services for $5.5 millions in an all-cash deal.
- Reliance Communications is likely to list its tower arm—Reliance Telecom Infrastructure Ltd. (RTIL)—by March 2008. The Company plans to sell an additional 10% in RTIL through an IPO.
- Apollo Health Street is planning to float an IPO to repay its debt for its recent acquisition of US-based BPO Zavata for $170 millions as well as fund future expansion plans.
- Sun Pharmaceutical Industries has received USFDA's approval for the abbreviated new drug application to market its generic version of Novartis's Exelon.
- BEML opened a global warehouse in Malaysia for sourcing and supplying of mining and construction equipment and spares to over 43 countries.

Big, medium and small Indian enterprises are operating in multiple global geographies through variety of products and services and which are on the anvil of ever expansion.

Sample products and services in multiple global geographies in 2006-07:

Telecom transformation operations—Asia-pacific region, Israel, Africa.

BPO—North America, Latin America, Brazil, Africa.

Prescription generic drugs—Nigeria, Brazil, USA, Africa, UK, Ireland.

AIDS and Malaria drugs—Africa.

IT—US, China, Latin America, Lanka, UK.

Construction and engineering—South Arabia.

Switch gears, MV, LV low voltage switch gears—Malaysia, Middle East.

Turnkey solutions—Middle East.

Iron ore—Brazil, China.

Refinery in Turkey, refinery-cum-petrochemical in Paradip.

Oil exploration at East Timor oil blocks, Peru, South Africa.

Areas of geothermal, hydrogen and fuel cells and wind energy—Iceland and India.

Transformers and rectifiers—Germany.

Copper Mines—Australia.

Business of mining and processing of Calcium Carbonate, Gypsum, Kaolin and other Industrial Minerals—UAE, Oman.

E-learning Solutions—Singapore, China.

List of some other products:

- Technologies in the crystalline silicon, concentrator and thin film domain in the photovoltaic industry.
- Setting up high technology methyl amines and dimethyl formamide plants, bio-diesel, coal bed methane.
- Iron ore and steel business.
- Telco transformation domain, cable and direct broadcast satellite market, OSS/BSS solutions, CRM domain, BPO space.
- Prescription generic drugs, pharmaceuticals products.
- Nuclear power plant equipment.
- Refinery and pipeline capacity.
- BPO services providers.
- E-learning solutions, IT sector, heavy industries and power equipment.
- Biometric segment.

Business Expansion Geo Areas

Middle East: India has launched a major drive to step up exports of agricultural and processed food products to the Gulf countries and attract investment in the sector. The six Gulf Cooperation Council (GCC) countries offer huge potential for Indian food since the region has historically been reliant on imported food, officials said. Driven by the buoyant economy and growing population, the market in recent years has reached an all-time high in terms of volume of imports, they said.

India's exports to the Gulf had been steadily increasing over the years, but there was still considerable potential to expand shipments of processed agricultural and food products, Chairman of the Agricultural and Processed Food Products Export Development Authority (APEDA), who recently led a high-level delegation in 2007 to the visit to Gulf region, said.

The Gulf region offered tremendous opportunity for Indian food exports, he said, adding the value of trade in agriculture and processed food between India and the Gulf had "grown from $5.5 billion in 2001 to $48.6 billion at the end of 2006".

Food exports to the GCC region is worth an estimated $3 billion a year with agricultural and processed food exports from India to the UAE alone accounting for more than $273 million in 2004-05. Total annual trade between India and the GCC currently exceeds $15 billion, 15 per cent of India's total foreign trade. Dubai plays a key role in the distribution of food in the region, with over 70 per cent of the total UAE food imports re-exported to more than 160 countries including the Gulf, North and East Africa, and, increasingly, the Central Asian Republics.

A snapshot of diversified activities of companies reflects their growth in different segments and in different geographies with varied business partners through varied modes of collaboration and acquisition.

The randomly selected companies highlight their growth through an going business orders in power and heavy industry, pharmaceuticals, telecom transformation, information technology, oil, energy and petrol, mining sector, thermal imaging, and avionics, etc. textiles, biometrics, real estates and BPO services. The snapshot with Outlook and Key Events 2007 and Prospects is given in Appendix 3.

Outsourcing Growth

The expansion of business content focus is through new products and services in globalization contexts such as widening the scope of outsourcing through KPOs focuses on analytics and research in various disciplines such as medical, law, accounts, etc. in addition to BPOs for many sectors; the scope of RIM (remote infrastructure management) is widened. Outsourcing is further focused on insurance, health, pension funds, foods, etc. New business models are developed and applied for new products and services and new geo areas and markets are entered and developed.

Offshoring has also expanded the outsourcing and BPOs. The MNCs started setting their businesses—hardware or software development in India itself such as IBM, Nokia, Motorola, Oracle, Microsoft. Offshoring brought foreign investments, knowledge, expertise and jobs for the country.

India, already known as the back office of the world, will account for two-third of the global Knowledge Process Offshoring (KPO) segment that could create up to 1.8 lakh new jobs here by 2011. The worldwide KPO market is expected to grow to 16.7 billion dollar in revenues by 2010-11 at an annual growth rate of 39 per cent. Of this, India would account for 11.2 billion dollars, according to the study by business research and analytics firm Evalueserve. The industry would employ about 3.5 lakh professionals by March 2011 globally. This includes nearly 2.55 lakh in India, where only about 75,400 people are currently employed. According to Evalueserve, the KPO industry in India had only 9,000 billable professionals in India, generating revenue of 260 million dollars during 2000-01. This number has grown to 75,400 by 2006-07 with 3.05 billion dollars in revenue at an annual growth rate of 51 per cent.

The anticipated success in KPO comes after the success of BPO in the country, which accounts for revenues of 15.8 billion dollar in 2006-07, a jump from just 7.7 billion dollar in 2003-04.

These numbers will doubtless grow as the Indian economy expands. Software and BPO exports, for instance, are expected to double from the current $30 billion to $60 billion by 2010, according to Nasscom. India already has 50% share of the world outsourcing market, though the total addressable market is estimated to be $1.5 trillion in 2010, according to Nasscom. Exports of skill-intensive manufacturing alone could reach $300 billion in 2015, according to McKinsey. Yet these figures pale besides China's current figures $1 trillion of exports and FDI of over $100 billion per year. China's trade surplus exceeds India's total trade.

IT export turnover is expected to touch the $80 billion mark by end of 2011. The Commerce Minister expressed confidence on the export boom irrespective of the perceived odds against outsourcing, and increasing competition. He assumed an average growth rate of 30% per annum. Currently, IT exports are at about $37 billion. Software services currently dominate the export basket and he noted that the electronic hardware would be an equally significant export driver in future. The government is closely looking at a strategy to build capacities in the hardware sector.

The huge growth in the global KPO space would be driven by the vast pool of educated and experienced professionals in countries like India, China, Russia, Poland, the Philippines, Hungary and many republics from the erstwhile Soviet Union. It is quite likely that companies—both with their own captives and those using third-party vendors—may use a "hub and spoke" model in which a provider in India may constitute the "centre" whereas other units in the world may provide appropriate "spokes".

With the slowdown in the US economy, a strong rupee and questions over extension of the Software Technology Parks (STP) scheme looming large, 2008 will be a crucial year for the Indian BPO industry. While players and analysts agree the troubled American economy is unlikely to have a significant impact on the industry, the decision on STP-extension closer home is seen as a clincher.

Analysts also see greater investor interest, due to more realistic valuations. "One can expect greater interest among private equity (PE) firms to invest in BPO/KPO firms. After an upbeat 2007, where valuations were a bit on the higher side, 2008 will bring more realistic valuations, giving a boost to consolidation," says offshoring advisory firm Tholons president.

However, players think the impact would be insignificant. "Considering the recession in US, offshoring is an imperative and hence, anti-outsourcing rhetoric won't have much impact. BPOs in India are going to benefit from the global credit crunch as companies will resort to more offshoring to minimize impact on falling margins," said HCL BPO chief executive. "It's expected that banks and other financial institutions will downsize staff in the first half of 2008. After the restructuring, these institutions will start outsourcing their back-office work to cut costs."

Allied Digital Services has announced the launch of its remote management services consisting of network operation centre (NOC) and information security operation centre (SOC) at Millennium Business Park, Mahape, STPI. These remote management services are supported by Intel Inc., E-Cop Singapore and HP. Appendix 1 gives the historical perspective of outsourcing in India.

BPO and knowledge process outsourcing (KPO) are set to be joined by business transformation outsourcing (BTO). BTO, the study says, involves the outsourced service company sharing the client's risk that thinks not as a supplier but as some kind of a strategic partner, who innovates on processes. BTO combines elements of BPO and information technology outsourcing. BTO changes how the business operates. It acts on the processes to create new capabilities.

The percentage of BTO services in the outsourcing spectrum is expected to rise to 31 per cent in 2009 from 19 per cent in 2004. BTO work is being offered currently out of India by companies such as IBM, Accenture, Wipro BPO and Nipuna, a subsidiary of Satyam Computer Services.

Business Initiatives Abroad: India to help build second Silicon Valley in US. This could very well turn out to be the making of a second Silicon Valley in the US. Over 40 Indian IT software companies who have been jostling for space and market share in the Silicon Valley are now moving on to set up Silicon Valley II at New Jersey and Chicago backed by the India commerce ministry. The government and industry would set up incubation centers in New Jersey and Chicago for providing easy operational facilities to the start-ups. The incubation centers would be set up on 50:50 financial supports.

"The commerce ministry has agreed to provide support for setting up the incubation centers. The industry and government would put equal money to start the centers from where any new company can start operating without actually putting up their independent facilities", Electronics and Computer Software Export Promotion Council (ESC) India executive director said. "It is for the first time ever that the government is setting up an incubation centre outside the country".

Apart from providing support for setting up the centers, the government would also bear the operational cost of the facilities for a period of three years, after which the scheme would be reviewed.

"Silicon valley is saturated. New software companies were finding it difficult to get orders and so they were in search of newer markets. Places like New Jersey and Chicago provide them an alternative. Plans for setting up the first such center in New Jersey is in its final stage and the facility would be operational by January 2008. We are looking at markets where we can sell our software. Already big software producers are at Silicon Valley, cities like New Jersey provide new marketing opportunities" (Sept. '07).

India Business Center is set up in USA to provide business intelligence to American countries which is critical to do business with India. USA is also encouraging foreign investment and long-term investment by Indian companies is being encouraged. The government could create conducive environments for trade and investments; but the onus of optimizing these sectors lay with private sectors, particularly companies that are global leaders in their respective fields. There is two-way trade, investments and job-creation between India and USA, and UK and also between India and many developing countries like Latin America, South America, Brazil, China, Africa, etc. but there is still one way trade, investments and job-creation between these countries and India.

As part of world's second fastest growing economy, Indian businesses are investing in creating best global practices and standards that establishes a relationship of mutual trust with their customers.

FICCI India collaborates with 80 business bodies in the world and now in June 2008 it is collaborating with US council of Better Business Bureaus (BBB) to promote standards and responsible business practices in Indian and American markets based on voluntary self-regulation. It is the role of FICCI and BBB to ensure that best business practices and standards for the market place are also being exchanged.

Their collaborative efforts focus on:

- Information exchange where a knowledge bank will be shared on global best practices in the areas of market place trust and consumer care.
- Collaborative research in the areas of market place trust and consumer affairs.
- Organizing together international events to promote global best practices to strengthen market place trust between consumers and businesses.
- To develop and organize training and capacity building programs for businesses in India—including US businesses operating in or marketing to India and Indian companies operating in or marketing to US.
- On as 'as needed basis' consultancy services to facilitate development of codes of conduct, standards and mechanisms of voluntary self-regulations based on successful models implemented in North America by BBB.
- To extend consumer mediation and arbitration services to industries including US businesses operating in India—based on systems to be jointly agreed to and developed.

(FICCI and US council of Better Business Bureaus (BBB) enter MoU on best practices in June 2008).

Special Economic Zones (SEZ) Development

Kamal Nath, India's Commerce Minister said that his ministry would pursue with RBI to ensure that SEZs were treated as infrastructure projects. He underscored the need for coordinated efforts by all the stakeholders so that the SEZ scheme could fulfil the objectives and could be implemented efficiently by the State governments by providing single window clearances and other promised benefits.

He commented that SEZ, specifically the new ones, which had come in the last 18 months, had performed exceedingly well on the export front, employment and new infrastructure. Once all the 366 formally approved SEZs become operational, four million additional jobs would be created and the country's manufacturing sector would get a shot in the arm. He called for a coordinated effort by all stakeholders so that the SEZ scheme could fulfil its objectives [interactive session with SEZ units and developers as also export-oriented units (EOUs) organized by the Export Promotion Council for EOUs and SEZ units on July 2007].

Dani Rodrik (2007) argues that it is important to differentiate between igniting growth and sustaining it. India is now exposed to the full weight of global competition. For the country this means that it has to act rapidly and effectively to address production failures and bottlenecks. Future successes will rely upon a continuing commitment to the improvement in our competitiveness. SEZ is a long-awaited initiative taken by the government in that direction.

Finally, the impact of SEZs may be small on the overall economic activity level, but the deep sense of purpose and commitment to the promotion of industrialization that it has generated in the government and bureaucratic machinery is likely to make an enormous impact. State governments in their pursuit to attract SEZ investment have engaged in compelling ways to promote an industrial climate. It also has a signaling effect, signaling to the investors, domestic and foreign, that the government is receptive.

SEZs in Insurgency-prone Areas

Government plans to invite private companies to develop SEZs, or industrial clusters, in some insurgency-prone areas of the country. The pilot project is proposed to be initiated in the north-eastern region, in the Bodo-affected areas of Assam. Later, similar projects will be initiated in areas like Chambal Valley and MCC-prone belts in Jharkhand and Telangana (Andhra Pradesh).

The ideology behind the move is clear; it is an attempt to solve the problem of insurgency and youth restlessness in sensitive areas by creating economic activity and generating employment opportunities. Tribal affairs minister who himself hails from an insurgency-prone area on the Assam-Meghalaya border, is taking a keen interest in the matter and has met developers of some SEZ projects.

"Only barren land tracts will be earmarked for the projects where there is no agricultural yield, wildlife or greenery", an official in the tribal affairs ministry said.

In recent times, the government has given tax concessions to corporates setting up units in the north-east. However, only a few companies, such as Delhi-based DS group, have set up industrial base in the region. "The development of dedicated industrial zones, added to the existing industrial policy in the region, may attract more companies and foreign investment in the area," the official said.

Developers are, however, not too sure how the plan would shape up. "There are many issues involved. Certain exclusive incentives will have to be extended to motivate companies to invest in the disturbed areas. Security is also a major concern," an official of a well-known corporate developing an SEZ in the NCR said.

The plan will come up for discussion at the parliamentary committee meeting of the ministry of tribal affairs early in August. Subsequently, proposals will be sent to home, finance and commerce ministries (July 2007).

Other SEZs

Outlook and Key development 2007 and prospects:

- The 70-acre IT Park, named HDIL Cybercity, will be built at a cost of Rs. 20 billion in Kochi.
- Videocon Industries on 9th September 2007 announced its decision to set up a multi-product special economic zone spread over an area of 1000 hectares in Punjab with an investment of Rs. 100-500 crore. "We will be developing a 1000 hectares SEZ in the field of agriculture as well as electronics and hardware sectors in Punjab which will involve an investment of over Rs. 100 to Rs. 500 crore," Videocon Industries Chairman and Managing Director, VN Dhoot told reporters. The company will acquire land for this purpose on its own rather than asking the state government, he said.
- Videocon Group is also looking for a suitable location to set up a semi-conductor unit in the country. "We are scouting for the land for setting up a semi-conductor unit but the location has not been finalized yet," he said. The company, which proposes to invest over Rs. 1000 crore on semi-conductor unit, is also looking for some incentive from government for this unit. "We will be setting up this unit in that state which will offer us land and power at reasonable rates. In addition to it, the government should also provide us enough water for our semi-conductor unit," he said.
- L&T also plans to develop two SEZs close to its manufacturing facilities. While one IT zone SEZ will be located near Vadodara for engineering services, the other will be built after its shipbuilding plant gets finalized, say sources.
- Man industries is mulling to put up an engineering SEZ at Anjar in Kutch.
- Ahmedabad-based Chiripal group too has filed an application with the state government to set up an IT zone at Koba in Gandhinagar.

- The government has received three more applications, one each by Rajkot Engineering Association (REA), Kandla Port Trust for port-based multi-product SEZ, which has already got the necessary clearances from the Centre.
- PR SEZ is setting up a pharma SEZ near Valsad. The pharma project envisages an investment of Rs. 11,650 crore.
- Rajkot Engineering Association plans to set up a SEZ in Devgam near Rajkot. Sources say that the SEZ will attract investments worth Rs. 800 crore.
- REA had already signed an MoU during the Vibrant Gujarat Global Investors' Summit, which saw pledged investments to the tune of Rs. 1,70,889 crore in 28 SEZ projects.
- Gujarat has 51 approved SEZs in the state. Some of the country's top corporates including Tata, Reliance, Essar, Adani, Welspun, Satyam have lined up huge investments in the state.
- Haryana state governmentt has forwarded 87 proposals to the Centre for setting up SEZ in the state.
- Japanese ink-maker Danippon Ink and Chemicals (DIC) and Pidilite industries, makers of Fevicol brand, will invest Rs. 300 crore and Rs. 400 crore each at the Dahej SEZ.
- Rewa SEZ by Reliance for shipyard building and Dredgers building and repairs in Kakinada. Rewas port is in the vicinity developed by Reliance Industries.

SEZ Land Compensation

Farmers are not thinking in the terms of the land that belonged to his family for generations, and now it will go away forever." The reality is that in many cases farmers do not even own the land. Land is mortgaged with moneylenders. Is it then any wonder that most farmers see SEZs as an opportunity to get out of agriculture and abject poverty, educate their kids and get them well paying jobs to improve their living standards. They do need good and adequate compensation plan and not to be duped by SEZ stakeholders.

Commenting on SEZ land compensation CII was working in closely with the government to work out a formula to appropriately compensate the landowners.

We do not want the government to subsidize land cost but only facilitate its availability. At the same time the stakeholders should be looked after so that the balance is maintained. So far different SEZ groups are working on their own compensation formula. Some are accepted, some are agitated as felt being exploited. This can at times jeopardize setting up SEZ plans.

Navi Mumbai SEZ by Reliance Industries outlined the extensive rehabilitation plan the company was offering for the land. "We pay Rs. 10 lakh per acre for the land, we give them 12.5% of developed plots, so they can be partners of our development. In case they don't want the 12.5%, we will give them additional Rs. 5 lakh per acre. Assured employment and training is given to one person per family, or Rs. 3 lakh per acre extra. Landless laborers will have 3 yrs salary and will be trained for work. No villager will be dislocating."

RETAIL INFRASTRUCTURE

India has the market, the consumers and infrastructure. We should have organized retail sector. Wherever consumers go, retailers will follow, from cities to smaller towns to even rural areas. It will create organized consumerism as well jobs in various divisions from sales, marketing to procuring. Large retail outlets mean more jobs in storage and logistics departments. Retail sector will create millions of jobs.

Organized retail besides benefiting the consumers by way of competitive product pricing and quality service, is introducing the Indian consumer to a shopping experience like never before. The modern shopping complexes are becoming the destination point for shoppers as well as 'window-shoppers'. There is everything for everyone—shopping, entertainment, and food, all of it under one roof. Further, being largely labor-intensive, organized retail is likely to unleash huge job opportunities.

Further, to the surprise of many, retail also requires application of global best practices in terms of processes, systems, quicker assimilation and implementation of new technologies. If organized retail in India has to grow as forecasted and estimated, it requires significant capital, technology and application of latest global best practices. The food supply chain in India remains fragmented and unorganized. From farm to fridge, distribution of most food items involves multiple intermediaries and wastage during transportation and storage. Organized retail is expected to result in significant investments in upgrading the technology and practices in the entire value chain, and the removal of intermediaries. This will reduce wastage and duplication of efforts resulting in farmers realizing both higher productivity and better price.

Defending the entry of major companies in the retail farm products market, it is pointed out that organized retail would be the way out of stagnation in agricultural growth, as farmers would start getting attractive returns for their produce. Organized retail in food and groceries is emerging as a sector which will create a huge market leading to demand-driven farming. "The day the demand-driven agriculture picks up, farmers' bargaining power will increase and their economic conditions will improve." It will eliminate the wastage of agricultural produce, which is to the tune of Rs. 40,000 crore per year, which can contribute one per cent to the GDP by value-addition. It will also improve farming infrastructure. Contract farming can have both positive and negative connotations. On the positive side, farmers' bargaining power improves, secondly they have the advantage of getting assured returns, thirdly the MNCs negotiating for contract farming provide good seeds, improved techniques for the crops and monitor it also; that is also learning experience for farmers. State government also enter into contract farming.

The Punjab Government has decided to enter into contract farming as part of its efforts towards diversification of crops from wheat-paddy cycle. It promised to offer competitive global rates to farmers by exploring domestic as well as international markets. Minister added that as a pilot project of contract farming, agreements have already been signed for cultivation of basmati and potato. He revealed that as part of its move for diversification, Markfed the state enterprise has indulged into contract farming of potatoes with farmers of Jalandhar and initially as many as 50 farmers were enrolled for certification of their crop with European standards.

He criticized the private efforts for contract farming in Punjab state. "It has been witnessed that private companies enter into contract farming for any specific crop but later they backtrack if they don't see any profit. As such companies have a sole motive of earning profit, state government has decided to enter into the field of contract farming". Earlier, a big-time private company had entered into contract farming of tomatoes in Hoshiarpur district but later breached the agreement by disappearing. Again another big industrial backtracked from buying crop of baby corn, for which they struck a contract with the farmers of Jalandhar district, the minister alleged.

The Field Fresh Agri Centre of Excellence is set up in India for collaborative farming by Field Fresh Foods Pvt. Ltd. under cultivation in Punjab and growing partnerships in Rajasthan, Uttarakhand and Maharashtra. The Centre will showcase advanced technologies and agricultural best practices and serve as the hub to impart knowledge and training to the grower partners of Field Fresh. The focus will be on early adoption of best practices across the fields to enhance agricultural productivity in an environmentally sustainable manner. 'Link Indian farms to the world' by creating the country's first global outsourcing opportunity in fresh produce.

In addition to this, the Company is working in close partnership with Punjab Agriculture University on several R&D projects for development of world class produce for international markets. 'R&D will be one of the strategic drivers for ensuring delivery of superior, innovative products to our global customers.'

Retail Food Superstores are being set up in many of the emerging markets and developing countries on Western models. These are the new practices. Many big retail and food chains from USA, UK and other European countries such as Wal-Mart, Carrfour, Tesco, etc. are ushering into this area. The practice in

India has been to tie up with big Indian MNCs like Bharti, etc. Many big companies on their own are developing the retail superstore model such as Reliance. In India, most hyper or super markets are essentially westernizing the Indian model. They want to connect with the local vendors to know each area and understand people consumption habits better. The food sector in India is huge, but it has been faced with a lot of internal challenges. If we are good locally, one challenge is conquered. Our aim is to replace 'Kirana (grocery Pop and Mom) Stores'. The market is big enough to accommodate many players.

"While it is true that there is space for mid-level retailers, the bigger players might just come and tie-up with these mid-sized retailers. A lot of them might get taken over by the big chains, since for such operations scale is required. Many of them could be converted into franchisees." The deal values that bigger chains can provide by way of wholesale will definitely be much better than the mid-size retailer. Indian retail model has space for 6-8 big retail players since right now only 3 per cent of retail market is organized and even in the next 6 years only 10 per cent will be organized. Players like SPAR International have already attempted to bring together small, independent retailers together and thereby compete more effectively with the giant retail chains.

The key issue in India is to manage a smooth supply chain right from the farmer level right up to the retail level, say experts. While chains like Wal-Mart are known to be experts at the retail model, Reliance too aims to build a 21st century retail supply chain from growers to grocery-store shelves, i.e. from 'farm to fork'.

Experts suggest that organized retail should address the 30-35 per cent crop and food wastage in India and hope to reduce it drastically, the immediate concern is whether independent retailers choose to come under a common brand or retain their brand and hope to withstand the pressure from the big chains.

Agribusinesses aligned to organized retailing will drive the next big change in agriculture, unlike the green revolution which was a government initiative and a wheat and rice affair. Together with logistics firms and cold chains, they will cut the slack in moving produce from farm to fork, eliminate wastage, enhance productivity, increase farm incomes and make farmers respond to market whim. But with the average size of farms at under 4 acres and average annual farm incomes around 25,000 per acre, most farmers cannot make the capital investments necessary to scale up productivity to global levels. Companies like Bharti Enterprises are prepared to make capital investments in leased land provided the leases are of a longer tenure. For that farmers will have to shed the fear of losing ownership. But that would require changes in law. "If I got a lease of 5 to 10 years, I will put money tomorrow on that land," Drip irrigation is a case in point. The government's 50% subsidy is unutilized because farmers cannot fork out the balance. For agribusinesses to power the rural economy, government will have to realize that it cannot be business as before.

The overall retail business in India is expected to grow to 500 billion dollars out of which the organized retail will get 300 billion dollars. The balance will go to the small sector and create a situation where the two can co-exist.

Besides allowing FDI in retail, to unleash the growth potential of retail sector, government will also have to give infrastructure development its due attention, so that it keeps pace with the current retail transformation. Further legislative reforms, and rationalization of fiscal laws, is also required to keep the momentum going.

The rising demand for cornering prime locations has hiked the property lease rentals across the country. The recent levy of service tax on such rentals has further aggravated matters. Further, a typical retailer is subjected to service tax levy also on security, storage and warehousing, commission and collection agents' services, and transport services. This becomes a significant additional cost, given the wafer thin margins in this industry. In most cases, the retailers are not able to utilize the credit of service tax paid on the input services consumed by them.

Similarly, the credit regime is also not very friendly in respect of central sales tax and entry taxes.

Retail sector needs a much better set of regime, till an integrated goods and service tax (GST) is introduced. Given the huge benefits of organized retail, and the likely spiraling effect of the sector's growth on the growth of Indian economy, including the rural economy, it is high time that this sector receives its due attention, and measures are introduced liberalizing and rationalizing regulatory and tax environment.

Retailing Next Practices from India

Globally, retail is a localized business. Retailing demands a thorough understanding of local customs, consumer tastes and culture. That probably explains why unlike other sectors like energy, FMCG or automobiles where multinationals are often present in more than 100 geographies, there very few multinational retailers with a large footprint. Of the 250 largest retailers, 104 retailers do not have any international operations. Of these the largest international operations is that of French retailer Carrefour and it is present in only 29 countries.

This need for customization takes a whole new meaning in India wherein a retailer has to adapt, change and modify its customer interface for every city that it sets shop in and every community that it caters to. The language we speak, the religious customs we follow, the food we consume, the fabric we wear and the festivals we celebrate changes every few hundred kilometers in India. Logic and emotion, individual and social, poverty and affluence, capitalism and socialism, life and lifestyle, value and indulgence, and the past and the future simultaneously co-exist in India. All these paradoxes converge to make India what it is.

The economic, social and cultural diversity of Indian consumers force marketers and retailers to view this mass of consumers not as one single market but as a 'mass of niches'. Retailers are therefore forced to develop multiple formats that cater to different customer segments and even within these formats they have to customize it significantly for every city they operate in. Retailing in India isn't about catering to one single market, but catering hundreds of communities and sub-communities.

Therefore, even the foreign investors are looking for Indian partners in setting up retails. Wal-Mart has partnered with Bharati and others are seeking the same.

This characteristic differentiates itself from the standard development of modern retail anywhere in the world. Conventionally, retailers focus on homogeneity and continuity in order to derive benefits of scale and efficiency in their system. Globally, retailers develop two or three major formats which are largely standardized.

This however, may not work in India. As a significantly large, truly pan-Indian, multi-format modern retailing model develops in India, and that is still quite a few years away, the Indian market will develop a model for globalizing retailing. And that will be the biggest contribution of Indian retailers to the world.

Another significant area where Indian retailers can establish leadership is in the field of technology. Unlike in developed countries, Indian retailers do not have legacy systems on which they have to build their technology platform. As we grow and develop fresh technology-led solutions, we will take a leap and the next generation retail technology solutions may well come out of India. While most technology solutions are data-intensive, we see a significant scope for developing visual-based retail technology that benefits from recent developments in network management, business intelligence and information gathering. Usage of RFID and the next practices in technology-based retail solutions may well emerge from Indian retailing.

Latin American retailers like Grupo Elektra and Casas Bahia have developed admirable retailing models that cater to lower income groups by developing innovative consumer credit models. Most retailers in Latin America have formidable consumer finance arms that drive consumption growth.

Indian retailers can learn a lot from these models and at the same time set new benchmarks in building innovative consumer credit solutions that catalyze consumption and bring in low-income groups into the fold of modern retailing. In a few years from now, one can expect Indian retailers to show the world how to capture consumption among the lowest income groups. Indian retailers would develop their own systems and benchmarks; and that will form the genesis for the next-practices in retailing the world over.

Experian Inc., a global information solutions company announced the launch of its enhanced retail marketing database offering, Totalvue Retail helps marketers make sound investments across their different channels by providing analysis of all marketing efforts within the database along with increased ROI measurement and reporting. It is critical that each investment, decision marketers make be the most effective one possible. Totalvue Retail helps marketers better understand where and how customers prefer to shop by compiling and tracking their purchase behavior across the entire business. It integrates this single customer view with an advanced business reporting suite that mines the database to help marketers better understand the performance of campaigns, products and channels in order to improve and increase marketing ROI. It takes the complexity out of campaign management and measurement by providing seamless interaction between the marketing database and online marketing efforts, while identifying and reporting on customer responses across various Internet promotions, catalogs, direct mail, call centers and stores (Kishore Biyani Group CEO, Future Group 2007).

The latest retail practice that Indian retailers are taking up is not to disturb the neighborhood kirana stores but integrate with them by co-opting with them and training them for organizing good supply chains.

Retail Enterprises

Upcoming retail enterprises are, Reliance Retail, Aditya Birla, Wal-Mart, Spencers, Hypercity Retail (India), Aditya Birla Group, launched its retail operations in May 2007 under the brand name 'More', plans to set-up 1,000 super-markets across the country in the next three years.

UK-based Diageo had recently tied-up with retail giants Reliance Fresh and Shoprite Hyper to distribute its wines portfolio in cities like Mumbai and Pune; and also with Aditya Birla-promoted retail venture 'More' to sell its wines across the country. Through the tie-ups, the British firm plans to expand presence to other centers like Delhi, Bangalore and Gurgaon and to expand its market share in India.

The consumer electronics retailing arm of Videocon Industries 'Next' retail has acquired Planet M, the music and entertainment retail chain, reportedly for Rs. 200 crore with an aim to leverage the brand to tap the young generation.

Rural retail enterprises are: Tata Kissan Sansar, Bharti-Wal-Mart, Haryali Kissan Bazar, DCM Shriram Indian Oil Corporation's outlets for fuel and non-fuel retails.

Wal-Mart gears up to open stores in India, it's ramping up procurement from India for global operations. The world's biggest retailer is betting bigger on India. After sourcing products worth USD 600 million in 2006, comprising largely of apparel, jewelry and textiles, Wal-Mart is scaling up. This year 2007, it is adding electronics, leather accessories and footwear to its portfolio of products being sourced from India to be sold through its 7,000 stores globally. General Manager, Wal-Mart Global Outsourcing India said, "Some of the new initiatives we are taking are more and more penetration in footwear and electronics. We see that as a growing opportunity from India and we are exploring our opportunities there. So if there were merit, and it is established that electronics is an opportunity, at least five or six vendors add up in the category."

Wal-Mart is expanding its presence as well with two new offices planned in Mumbai and Delhi. This is aimed at penetrating deeper into smaller towns and cities for procurement. "We have been going to smaller towns in India aggressively for sourcing, so we are setting up offices closer to the bases, in Delhi and Mumbai. We see a huge growth opportunities in small towns and the idea to go to a small town is inclusive growth." In the six years since it began sourcing from India, Wal-Mart has focused largely on SMEs and at times even cottage industries. In some cases, exports to Wal-Mart account for over 50% of the Indian company's turnover.

Reliance Retail notwithstanding the unabated protests against its stores in some parts of the country, it is planning to increase its workforce to one million within the next four years. What took Wal-Mart to achieve in 30 years, Mukesh Ambani plans to do that in four years.

As part of a big restructuring process, Reliance Retail is likely to be split into 34 separate companies which will be independent profit and loss centers for the group. The plan, said a source, will be executed by the company in a phased manner over a period of time. Some of the important verticals that the company is looking at hiving off into separate profit and loss centers in the initial phase include the hypermarket Reliance Mart, health and wellness chain Reliance Wellness, consumer durable format Reliance Digital, lifestyle chain Reliance Trends and the proposed footwear chain Reliance Footwear. The company's food and grocery chain Reliance Fresh has already been hived off into a separate company, Ranger Farm.

Reliance is set to take giant steps in the footwear segment. It has launched a footwear store in Bangalore and has set its sights on big revenues. Reliance is also said to be in talks with foreign entities to license and sell mid-segment branded footwear and accessories outside its footwear stores. Reliance is looking at five players initially. But the investment will depend on the number of brands it can bring into its fold.

All these companies will have their own infrastructure for procurement, supply chain, logistics and marketing. At present, Reliance Retail has a centralized pool of resources which caters to all formats. "At a later point of time, as and when each of these individual businesses attains the necessary critical mass, the promoters would also look at the option of listing these companies. But that's just a thought right now," a source close to the development told. Though the move is primarily part of a major restructuring exercise at Reliance, a source also indicated that it could be aimed to check political controversies surrounding the retail business.

"All political objections are mainly targeted at food and grocery retail. By hiving each one of the verticals into separate company, Reliance would be able to protect its other formats on one hand, and on the other hand tackle political controversies around Reliance Fresh in a dedicated manner," a source said.

Also, the operating margins vary significantly in various retail formats and with independent profit and loss centers; it would be in a position to make a better financial leverage. "For instance, at present, while Reliance Retail has a fairly high operating margin in its health and wellness format, it has to take a hit in food and grocery," the source said.

In addition to accountability and focus, the formation of new companies will make it easier for the various Reliance offshoots to enter into joint ventures and alliances with global and domestic companies. RIL chairman Mukesh Ambani, in his recent AGM speech, had said that joint ventures and partnerships are key growth drivers for the group in the years to come. He said Reliance Retail is building global partnerships with global leaders in all aspects of retail including fast moving consumer goods, health and wellness, apparels, electronic goods, lifestyle products and services, home and furniture, luxury goods and financial and advisory services.

In 2007 Reliance Retail, has decided to shut its agricultural collection centers in Punjab, Rajasthan, Madhya Pradesh and Haryana. In the last one year or so, the company had set up more than 2,000 collection centers in these states for procurement of agricultural produce. The idea was that direct procurement from farmers will help the company save on costs and make products cheaper for retail consumers.

Sources said the company's decision to close down the collection centers is in sync with its earlier decision of going slow in the food and grocery part of the retail business. Besides, the move comes close on the heels of its decision to completely withdraw from the retail business in Uttar Pradesh. The sources linked the company's decision to go slow on the food and grocery part to the political opposition that these formats are evoking.

They said Reliance Retail could shift its focus to other formats such as apparel lifestyle retailing, consumer durables and hypermarkets. "The company will continue to operate state-level collection centers, but will close down the ones at the level of mandis," said a source. In effect, it means that the company will put contract farming on hold, as only the mandi level centers were involved in direct procurement from farmers. The decision to exit contract farming, at least for now, is in line with company's view that its businesses do not end up becoming part of the election agenda. "It will stay away from contentious issues like contract farming till there is more political clarity on the subject," said an official (2007).

Although it is argued that contract farming is in the interest of farmers, yet it has been mired in political controversies. Some farmer associations have been pressurizing farmers to stay away from the "trap of corporates". Farmer leader Mahendra Singh Tikait had recently told ET: "Organized retail is a vicious circle and if farmers get into it, in the long run they will become dependent on the companies' whims and fancies."

Reliance Retail has clinched an exclusive marketing and distribution deal with the $19.3 billion iconic maker of iPods and Mac computers, Apple, for standalone iStores. This is Reliance Retail's first exclusive alliance with an international brand. Store will come up by October-end 2007 in Bangalore. Globally, Apple stores are not mere retail stores, they feature a theatre for presentations and workshops, a studio for training with Apple products, and a Genius Bar for technical support and repairs, and also offer free workshops to the public.

This is the first time Apple is tying up with a big corporate house for distribution anywhere in the world. The iStores would be standalone stores selling Apple products ranging from Macintosh computers to iPods and Apple introduced its all new ranges of iPods with enhanced user interface and new designs in the country. This new range from Apple comprises of the iPod Touch with a multi-touch user interface; the all new iPod Nano with video playback; later, once it's launched in India, the latest cult offering from Apple, the iPhone. Reliance Retail is likely to open ten stores by the end of the calendar year 2007. Apple would invest in market development.

Reliance Communications is readying itself for Rs. 20,000 crore GSM handset retailing in May 2008. It will enter into the new avenue in a month by selling GSM handsets in the existing eight circles of Reliance Telecom, a part of R.Com by the end of next month. It has signed agreements with major handset vendors, including LG, Samsung, Motorola, Sony Ericsson, Spice, Fly Mobile and HTC. It is expected to sign a similar agreement with Nokia shortly. The move is expected to create ripples in the organized handset retail market, as the company would achieve significant discounts based on the huge order size, analysts say. It has been distributing its own cutting-edge and affordable CDMA handsets at the entry price of Rs. 777, the cheapest handset in the world, and has also launched color handsets at Rs. 999. The company plans to sell GSM handset in all of its 2,500 retail outlets. The target is to sell 15-20 million handsets in the first year of operations. The handset market is expected to cross 100 million this year against the last year's estimated size of 70-75 million units.

"The Company has built significant capabilities in CDMA handset retail business, which can be readily utilized to channelize a diverse suite of consumer electronic gadgets. We have always believed in giving better than the best quality and prices to the many million Indian consumers, and the same philosophy is the guiding force whenever the company plans to evaluate opportunities for portfolio expansion." R.COM is the second largest handset distributor. It sold over 15-16 million CDMA handsets last year.

Retail Needs FDI to Reach its Potential

In 2003, India's economy was projected to overtake the US to become number two soon after 2060. However, given the revised estimates, the chances are that the 'overtake' may actually happen even earlier! With such growth prospects, rising incomes with increased per capita spending, changing consumer tastes and high proportion of young working population—no doubt India tops the list of emerging markets for global retailers!

These are clear signs that multinational corporations are also betting on the Indian consumer. As long as the government doesn't get in the way, I suspect that the momentum of market-based reforms will continue to outweigh the political constraints.

However, the retail sector is presently grappling with certain policy, regulatory and tax issues, which if not quickly addressed, may impact not only on the prospects of retail sector but also on the long-term India story to some extent.

The political issues involved in retail are which foreign retail chains of a particular country will allow to enter in domestic business, how much foreign equity will be allowed in this as partnership. The governance of a country has to protect the interest of the small retail businesses as well the consumers served by them. The government has to protect the farmers' interests when MNCs enter into contract farming or their land is acquired.

At the regulatory front, presently, FDI is completely prohibited in multi-brand retail. Further even in case of single-brand retail, only 51% FDI is allowed with prior government approval. However, if organized retail in India has to grow as forecasted and estimated, it requires significant capital, technology and application of latest global best practices. In such case, restricted FDI regime may be an impediment. Growth of organized retail is likely to have a positive impact not only on the end consumers, but also on the employment generation, supply chain efficiency, agricultural practices, sourcing from India, etc.

Opening up the sector to global retailers will only result in further investments to help farmers scale up and modernize farm practices. Direct inclusion of farmers into this process on fair terms would give them the first real opportunity they have had in centuries. The extent of sourcing from India will also grow manifold when global retailers are allowed to operate in the Indian market. Global retailers have invested significantly in the local economies presently. In the process, they have improved living standards of consumers, suppliers, farmers and employees and generated greater quantity and quality of employment.

All of the above strongly advocate a case for allowing FDI in retail sector. A gradual approach, similar to telecom sector, may also be explored, such as, opening up the sector for 51% FDI now, with a clear road map for further liberalization. In a scenario where large Indian business houses and conglomerates like Tatas, Reliance, Birlas and Bhartis have already entered the field with huge investment plans, there does not seem to be any logic in arguing against FDI on the ground of impact on mom-and-pop stores.

Rural Retailing

Rural business model focuses on five characteristics of rural markets and consumers: (i) purchasing capability, (ii) durable and non-durable consumer needs according to rural life styles, e.g. they would need a different kind of food, different kind of soaps and detergents. Quite likely, there may not be any market for toilet tissue and paper napkins, (iii) sachet economy will be the priority for durable consumer goods, (iv) businesses need to tap the market for farm implements, accessories and farm goods and provide doorstep delivery system, (v) delivery system is the most crucial part of the marketing strategies since villagers have low mobility, less knowledge and familiarity with the urban markets for purchasing negotiations.

In the second phase of their marketing strategies the focus should be on, (vi) to enhance villagers purchasing power by providing micro-credit, (vii) through micro-credit, businesses also capture some share of market for regular products and services in course of time thus increasing their total market share.

Another peculiarity of the rural market will be the fast changing consumer scenarios due to their exposure to media channels of TV where they are exposed to life styles of various Indian regions and the world around (Narula, 2006).

Organized retailing may have not set its foot firm in metros and other major cities yet, but Corporate India is already firming up concrete plans to tap the 100 billion dollar rural retail market with innovative schemes and human resource policies.

What have prompted India Inc. to turn its energies to rural retailing are a slew of facts that rural markets are growing at double the rate of urban markets, more than 60 per cent of the country's 1.12 billion population live in rural areas and 87 per cent of rural markets do not have access to any sort of organized marketing and distribution.

Meanwhile, India's $200 billion rural economy is also poised for sharp growth due to greater efficiencies in a notoriously wasteful food supply chain driven by the growth of an organized retail sector.

While a number of products on the rural retail shelf are agro-based companies are eager to make available products varying from cricket bat to customized credits in association with banks in rural areas, following the expansion and entry of new players into this emerging sector.

A report released by CII and Yes Bank on 27 September 2007 has estimated India's rural retail market to grow 29% to Rs. 1.8 trillion by 2010 driven by rising rural incomes and changing consumption patterns. Rural retail includes fast moving consumer goods, durables, agricultural inputs and autos like tractors. Rural per capita income is estimated to double to Rs. 14000 by 2012 as more rural families would switch over to commercial from subsistence farming. Village households are expected to rise to 153 million in 2009-10 from 135 million in 2001-02, probably making rural India the market with the largest potential in the world.

According to the report's findings, poor infrastructure, supply chain inefficiency, unorganized marketing and product pricing can be the major bottlenecks for the growth of rural retail. There exists no organized marketing and distribution in 87% of India's villages, wherein 50% of the rural population resides.

Corporates are touting rural markets as drivers of future growth. Such firms need to view rural retail development as a long-term commitment, and must be continuously innovative as rural consumers are often more price than quality conscious, observed the report. The development of organized rural retail in rural India will create jobs, check rural migration, raise tax generation and improve agricultural efficiencies.

Bharti-Wal-Mart joint venture, for example, plans to invest substantially in the next 3-4 years for establishing supply chain network in rural India. Reliance Retail's Rural Hubs (procuring-cum-processing hub and one-stop farmer shop) has plans for Punjab, Maharashtra, West Bengal, Andhra Pradesh and Gujarat. Pantaloons also plans a similar procuring-cum-processing hub for setting up farm input malls in rural areas.

A few others are already set up; DCM Shriram launched its Hariyali Kisan Bazar in 2002 in Punjab, Haryana, Rajasthan, Madhya Pradesh, Uttar Pradesh and Uttarakhand. It has more than 70 stores with an average store area of 9000-10000 sq. ft. and a catchment's radius of 25 km. "Our focused expansion is into Northern and Central India and eventually into Southern states. We plan to add another 200-50 stores in the next 12-15 months," said DCM Shriram Consolidated President.

"Our stores are one-stop shop for farmers with agricultural consultancy as an add-on service by sales executives who are agronomists and not smart executives as in urban retail. We also have produce buyback arrangements," he added.

Even public sector companies entered the fray. Indian Oil Corporation's (IOC) rural retail initiative was launched in 2006 in Uttar Pradesh, Madhya Pradesh, Punjab, Tamil Nadu, Karnataka and Bihar with more than 1,400 stores and an average store area of 4,400 sq. ft. covers a radius of 10-15 km. "Ours is a low-cost and de-risk model and leverages on IOC network for fuel and non-fuel retail. Our thrust is mainly agricultural inputs and FMCG products. We have plans to add 3,000 stores in the next 4-5 years," said IOC General Manager, Retail Sales.

Tata Chemicals (TCL) too launched its Tata Kisan Sansar (TKS) three years ago in Punjab, Haryana, Uttar Pradesh, Bihar, West Bengal and has already more than 800 TKS franchisees with an average store area of 300 sq. ft. and cover 10 km.

"The thrust of TKS is a link to states where TCL has a majority market share in fertilizer business. Our success is due to factors like strong relationships and brand awareness among farming community. Focused approach on agricultural inputs and consultancy, produce buyback and farmer credit arrangements," said Tata Chemicals COO (Agro-business).

The corporates are taking special efforts to ensure the quality of products and services offered to rural customers. The 'trust' factor has been highlighted to their employees in rural retail.

Unlike urban retail customers, in rural retail there are fix set customers. The area that would be addressed is within 25-30 km range. And again unlike urban retailing, customers come from far-flung areas and are visitors from other states.

"The relationship factor is stronger in rural and smaller towns. They just keep coming to you or stop if they are not convinced about the quality, price or service."

'Rural Retail: The Next Phase in Retailing', a report prepared by CII-Yes Bank (Sept. 2007) has pointed out that once the rural retail grows there would be a slew of positive implications like boost in employment, infrastructure, increased revenue and tax generation and check rural migration. However, poor infrastructure, seasonality of demand, heterogeneous population, complex buying behavior and price sensitivity are the main challenges that need to be overcome by the companies planning to enter the rural retails, said the report.

Another changing practice in India for rural markets retailing: "With the high-level involvement of CII and different wings of governments and panchayats, we may be able to transform the image of rural India. The government has identified 846 products for which the business community could have a partnership with panchayats for establishing rural business hubs based on Chinese model. The rural business hubs scheme, launched in 2004, to be set up in partnership with CII would upgrade and up value the skills and the products made by the villagers. This is a new experiment based on P4 model (public-private-panchayat-partnership) and so far 72 companies have shown interest in setting up such business hubs."

A total of 31 MoU have been signed towards the rural business hubs (RBH) project involving Reliance, Tatas, Coco-Cola, ITC, Mahindra and Mahindra and Microsoft among others. RBH is a P4 model initiative wherein the industry will be involved with rural resources and skills to develop products of internationally accepted quality. "Ministry is ensuring the convergence of the Central Government and the State Government scheme relevant to various RBHs and there will be 55 of them very soon" (News item, 2006).

Retail and Financial Services

Indian retailer is getting into money lending business. Bank may be closing the door on some loans, but retailers are opening up a window. Most large retailers are gearing-up for the loan business, reports CNBC-TV18. Consumers are taking a loan to buy their new TV. But instead of a bank, they are being financed by the shop itself. Future Money, from the Big Bazaar and Pantaloon stable, is the first attempt by an Indian retailer to get into the money lending business. In three years, it is expected to be a Rs. 10,000 crore business for the Future Group. Newer entrants into retail, like Reliance and Hypercity, have tied up with banks for financing. They say it drives up volumes. Future Money plans to issue credit cards, sell personal loans, travel loans, mortgages, insurance products, mutual funds and do money transfers, or basically become a non-banking financial company, within the next three years. The company estimates that its cost of acquiring a customer is about 40 paise versus about Rs. 2.60 for other financial services companies. "We are acquiring customers in our retail business. So, we have already acquired that customer. Now, the idea is to sell him more," said Kishore Biyani, Group CEO, Future Group.

Sources said that many Indian retailers want to get into the business of lending money like their contemporaries abroad. But with most of them, still in the process of establishing a national footprint, it is expected to take at least a couple of years before they get into the lucrative financial services space.

Retail and Food Processing

Retail players are all set to get a boost with a possible Rs. 10 crore grant from the government to revamp the cold chain facilities reports CNBC-TV18. There are 1300 cold storage facilities in India but they are completely unused for most of the year even as 40 per cent of India's fruit and vegetables get wasted due to the lack of a cold chain. But Reliance and Bharati entering into the agricultural space and demanding better infrastructure, things might be set for a change. "Give industry status and tax benefits to companies wanting to set up cold chain infra." The government in its 11th Plan is launching a revamped comprehensive cold chain infrastructure scheme to set-up cold chains at different levels.

The government is looking for private investment in the agricultural sector to remove infrastructural hurdles by developing cold chains, warehousing and transport facilities to see to it that wastage is minimized and the agricultural produce is of high quality. The private sector should supplement the public investment in agro-exports sector.

The government has also conducted a feasibility study for mega food parks in the country, which will function as sourcing hubs for the retail outlets. Thirty mega food parks are in the pipeline. These food parks will have cold warehousing, grading centers and research laboratories, all with the aim to promote the untapped food-processing sector.

The agricultural and processed food products exports developments authority (APEDA) plans to set up 12 centers across the country at a total cost of Rs. 25 billion for handling agro-perishable exports. In the same line, regional quality control laboratories would be set up by the spices board at Guntur, Mumbai, Chennai and Delhi. Government is likely to give a major thrust to the export of organic agro-products and will take up the issue of greater market access for agricultural products with other countries.

As per data collected by the department of industrial policy and promotion (Dipp) there are just 1,500 refrigerated trucks in the country while there is a requirement for 15 lakh. Although the country is the largest producer of milk and produces huge quantities of fruit and vegetables, much of it gets spoilt in transit due to lack of adequate infrastructure.

Retail and Trained Personnel

Retail needs trained personnel in its thousand skills to make it really remunerative. As we have discussed India had to adopt multi-format retail model, so it would need diversification of personnel skills on account of this factor also. For rural retailing format they would need different handling skills.

CII vice-president K.V. Kamath expressed concern about the lacunae in teaching skills for retail industries. There is no structured coaching for nearly a thousand skills in these divisions of the economy.

Since big Indian business conglomerates are entering into retail business various formats, they do want to focus on drawing personnel from already skilled areas as sales, procurement and supply chains. Still workforce may not be sufficient for the million jobs that it intends creating both from metro to small towns and rural hubs. These need to focus on offering Retail Training Modules for selected candidates, both in the set areas of retailing like sales, procurement and in new areas of logistics and storage. Even the already skilled personnel from specific areas would need on job training to fit the needs of ever changing retail industry in the new set up of economic boom in India. Trained workforce will make the retailing a success.

Moreover, the private institutes and agencies have to come with the different skill training programs in different segments of organized retailing. Even the institutes of management and other higher learning institutes can introduce skill training programs in organized retailing. The manpower forecast is there, we have to match the needs fast. In fact whether it is IT, or financial investments or retailing, we need trained workforce speedily. Then we cannot complain about unemployment.

Metro AG, a German retailer company, plans to empower Kirana (grocery Pop and Mom) Stores with latest business practices to tackle emerging competition from organized retail chains. They will train owners of these stores in latest practices in accounting, merchandising and other areas. German retailer already runs such academies in Turkey and has set up outlets in Hyderabad, Bangalore, Mumbai and Kolkata in India. This initiative comes at a time when there is controversy of modern retail encroaching into the business and existence of small Kirana stores. Even Bharati Resources has tied up with GRS (global retail school) a unit of Cosmos training school to train people for front-end jobs in retail. This alliance will offer courses in retail management, sales and marketing, buying and merchandise management and supply chain management.

Hurdles

Politicians need to support the retail sector. Political controversies are surrounding the retail especially of food and groceries. Uttar Pradesh government has been forcing Reliance Retail and Spencers to close their retail stores in the state. Kerala is also mulling a law to ban big organized retail chains in the state. States should not take decisions in panic and should not be influenced by "political slogans", interest of both farmers and consumers would be hurt by making retail as a political slogan.

Moreover, the political activists and the government must consider that the big retailers would not waste their time and money in fruitless controversies. They would divert their funds elsewhere in productive avenues.

The political activists are concerned about the small grocers in the markets close to residential areas; they feel their business and profits will be absorbed by the big retailers. This is not likely to happen in Indian situations. As big retailers will not open shops in each and every nook of the city, people will buy from business close to residences since 90% of consumers will not and cannot rely on their private transport to buy each and everything of daily use from the big retailer store in far flung area. That will add to the price. Big retailers should include small shopkeepers and intermediaries like Mandi commission agents in their large supply chains for effective retailing. Moreover, the good point is that organized big retailing will also keep check on high prices of small businesses for various goods and services. Small businesses will do business but consumers will not tolerate their arbitrary practices and prices.

"All political objections are mainly targeted at food and grocery retail. Sources said the Reliance decision to close down the agriculture collection centers is in sync with its earlier decision of going slow in the food and grocery part of the retail business. Besides, the move comes close on the heels of its decision to completely withdraw from the retail business in Uttar Pradesh. The sources linked the company's decision to go slow on the food and grocery part to the political opposition that these formats are evoking. Reliance will stay away from contentious issues like contract farming till there is more political clarity on the subject," said an official (2007).

However, the retail sector is presently grappling with political controversies, certain policy, regulatory and tax issues, and lack of trained personnel which if not quickly addressed, may impact the prospects of retail sector.

The retail revolution, apart from bringing in sweeping, positive changes in the quality of life in the metros and bigger towns, is also bringing in gradual changes in lifestyle in the smaller towns of India. The retailers are not only bringing in more merchandise to their stores, but are also continuously working on enhancing the shopping experience.

REAL ESTATE SECTOR

Demands on Real Estate

The business expansion in different domains of diverse products and services needed space to set up offices, commercial complexes, factories and residential for the workforce. Before the 90s decade real estate was a small time activity spread over a time period to develop and build office areas or residential complexes, factories whenever a new one was set up or expanded. But there was never that frenzy to build to expand the real estate. With expansion it gradually turned to be an organized business associated with the expansion of many diversified businesses—a part of domestic and global business boom and economic boom for India.

In 90s there was the setting of outsourcing business which Indian IT companies set up in metro towns of Bangalore and Hyderabad in India. They had plenty of land to set up both commercial and residential complexes and even for the foreign offices to which their business was catering; as well as the associated lifestyle changing demands, the hotels, restaurants, shopping and entertainment complexes, and even training institutes and job placement agencies were set up and there was tremendous increased of vehicular traffic on roads and pressure on other civic amenities of metro towns. Everything needed land. The outsourcing business was growing fast and with it the demand for land and the real estate spread over to other nearby satellite towns of Whitefield near Bangalore, Pune and Mysore towns. IT companies, with leading firms such as Tata Consultancy, Wipro, Infosys, Satyam and HCL were spreading to Delhi NCR and Chennai.

The second demand for real estate happened when manufacturing industries and associated business enterprises moved fast since the economic reforms of 90s, letting the businesses expand, diversify and let the FDI flow. The third demand occur in 2000 decades when the global industries started setting up their commercial and manufacturing hubs in India and its eventual lifestyle demand changes. In the south and west the metro like Bombay, Ahmedabad, Chennai and its satellite towns were full to the seams.

Already IT companies, and other leading companies such as Tata, Wipro, Infosys, Satyam, HCL, Reliance and other medium and smaller enterprises were lining up for land in Tamil Nadu, West Bengal, Punjab and Rajasthan states. There were two reasons to move all over, the paucity of land, the high prices of land and with it the cost of land settling the migrating workforce away from home cities. With this the real estate became an organize business enterprise. Many big companies diversified into real estate business, thus giving it more credibility for FDI flow. Thus, from Mom and Pop companies real estate developed into an organized business handled by professionals.

We are seeing a very active dispersal of the industry from the bigger to the small towns and small to even smaller, because of high land prices. It will result in a more even dispersal of employment and economic development across the country.

Even state governments are luring firms to the hinterland by promising quick land allotments, a vast pool of engineers, uninterrupted electricity and telecoms, good roads and air links.

Region Shifting: Factors like rising manpower and real estate costs are causing IT-ITES companies to move to newer Tier-II and Tier-III destinations which have lower real estate and manpower costs.

Tier-I Cities: One of the key developments in the office sector in recent times is the move, especially by IT-ITES companies (which account for two-third of the total demand for office space in the country), to Tier-II and Tier-III cities. According to a Jones Lang LaSalle Meghraj study, this was driven mostly by rising manpower and real estate costs in Tier-I cities. At the same time, the new centers have positioned themselves to take advantage of the emerging opportunities by developing IT Park facilities. State governments have adopted proactive policies and are offering incentives in order to attract IT-ITES companies. These newly emerging centers include Kochi, Bhubaneshwar, Thiruvananthapuram, Coimbatore, Indore, Ahmedabad, Jaipur, Nagpur and Nasik and so on.

As per the Nasscom-McKinsey estimates, the IT-ITES industry will require nearly 100 million sq.ft. of additional office space by 2010. At the same time, competition from newer locations in other countries is set to intensify. Hence, in an effort to lower their costs, more and more companies are expected to move to Tier-II and Tier-III cities.

These include established IT-ITES hubs like NCR, Mumbai, Bangalore, Chennai and Hyderabad. These are established destinations. They enjoy an established brand image, and will continue to be the centers where new companies, which have just entered India, will establish their first offices. On the positive side, Tier-I cities also have much larger pools of human capital which can be tapped by IT-ITES companies. However, now IT-ITES players have to contend with rising salaries, rising cost of real estate, and a very high rate of employee turnover in these centers.

Tier-II and Tier-III: These include state capitals and other important cities. Though they have a much smaller population compared to the metros, they are now emerging as the new destinations for IT-ITES companies. Let us now examine in detail what factors are compelling IT-ITES companies to shift to Tier-II and Tier-III cities.

Rising turnover of employees in metro is one factor. The competition for the best talent among existing companies, and the constant influx of new companies into India has led to very high employee attrition rate in the IT-ITES industries in Tier-I cities. The second factor is rising salary cost. Growing competition among companies to attract and retain the best talent has resulted in double-digit salary raises in the Indian IT-ITES industry. According to estimates, the salary differential between a Tier-I location and a Tier-II location at the entry level is 19-22%. The salary differential between a Tier-I and a Tier-III location could be as high as 42-57%. This steep difference is one of the major reasons why many IT-ITES companies are seriously examining the option of moving to Tier-II and Tier-III locations.

Large IT-ITES companies need to maintain business continuity. In this age of global terrorism, one of the ways they can mitigate risk is by dispersing themselves geographically across the country, and by locating themselves in multiple cities. This third factor too has resulted in IT-ITES majors setting up new centers in Tier-II and Tier-III locations.

In the '90s, when the central business districts got congested, companies moved to the suburbs. But now, the infrastructure of the suburbs is under great strain. Traffic jams, power shortages have become the order of the day. While the situation might be slightly better in Tier-II cities such as Hyderabad, Pune and Kolkata today, the huge influx of new companies and their employees means that very soon these centers will also struggle to cope with the demand based upon their infrastructure; hence the move to newer locations.

In the suburbs and NCR regions of Delhi metros, say Gurgaon, the rental rate for IT-ITES space has risen and even buying real estate cost is rising. Since demand is strong, and supply cannot come up; rental rates and real estate cost tend to firm up in Tier-I locations. Hence, companies are looking at newer locations.

While Tier-III cities offer several advantages such as lower real estate and manpower cost, and also lower attrition rate, companies need to take a close look before deciding to move to these cities. But the flip side for these is: the quality of office space available in these cities; and quality of life these smaller cities offer for its employees.

Real Estate Investments

A new report commissioned by Cityscape Market Intelligence Service and published by the Oxford Business Group (2007) said, India is a top place for investment opportunities in residential, commercial, hospitality and retail development. This kind of foreign investment in real estate increased once India Government opened this area for 100% FDI in 2005. With India Inc. emerging as a serious investor around the globe, various cities, businesses and governments, are now courting Indian companies, seeking their investments and joint ventures and setting up their global or regional offices and manufacturing or services units in India.

After the launch of a USD 750 million, real estate fund, Tata Reality and infrastructure has signed a 50:50 joint venture with Dubai's Jafza International, the parent company of Jebel Ali Free Zone. The JV will develop and operate 27 business and logistics parks across India with investment of Rs. 10,000 crore. Tata Reality has already identified 100 to 500 acres of land outside Mumbai, Hyderabad and Chennai for these projects. The first phase of 7 such parks will be launched in 2008 with an investment of Rs. 2,400 crore.

UAE-based property developer ETA Star plans to foray into the Indian property market with the launch of new projects in Bangalore in 2008. The company will use a land bank of 300 acres on the outskirts of Bangalore for the planned mixed-use developments. Apart from that, ETA is also developing commercial and residential property. ETA Star is also working on a Dh11-billion project that includes residential buildings and industrial zones in Tamil Nadu.

Global Best Practices

Real Estate Investment Trust (REIT) is today considered a global best practice in real estate as it benefits both real estate companies as well as their investors. It is a label attributed to a corporation that does away with or reduces corporate income taxes. Thus, REITs have a two-pronged effect—they allow investors to diversify through investing in a portfolio of properties rather than a single building and management by experienced real estate professionals. Initiated in Australia, US and Japan, REITs are now gaining ground in other Asian economies with liberal tax environments like Singapore.

Sustainable architecture establishes a number of compatible and simplified construction methods underlined by a cooperative and participatory process, e.g. the rehabilitation of the Thao community post the 1999 Taiwan earthquake received international attention as several houses were rebuilt by 10,000 volunteers from marginalized communities. The Khuda ki Basti project in Pakistan is another good example of this architecture being used to address socio-economic problems of the poor. The Incremental Development Scheme in this project has ensured that the homeless create communities for themselves.

Transparency seeking reliable performance benchmarks, accurate financial information, enforceable contracts and property rights, the Real Estate Transparency Index effectively ensures clarity in taxation and regulation, fair treatment in the transaction process and sets ethical standards in this industry. As of now, Australia, USA and New Zealand top the Transparency Index. Further, the opening up of many Asian markets to international competition has pushed emerging economies like India from low transparency to the semi-transparency segment.

Greening real estate helps in reducing adverse effects to the environment by adopting eco-friendly methods and material to aid the expanding real estate industry. A good example is the Energy Star program undertaken by the USA Environmental Protection Agency which reduces energy use by 40%, produces an annual savings of $0.90 per square foot, and is paid back in 2.5 years. Also the British Land of London, Windmill Developments of Ottawa, Ontario and certain initiatives in Australia are some more examples paving the path for a greener and cleaner tomorrow.

Urban Affordable Housing

India has a shortfall of 24.7 million housing units. "Affordability has gone up and the tendency to have a second-home among the youth is contributing to the spurt in demand. The real estate sector would require a mammoth USD 40 billion dollar investment to bridge the gap and another USD 65 billion to create the supporting infrastructure. Lot of equity money is coming into Indian real estate sector sensing huge demand.

Real estate consultancy firm Knight Frank's chairman said the real estate sector was growing at such a rapid pace that it might lead to shortage of workers at the ground level. He said the growth of the industry would be more widespread and volumes would remain buoyant. With the growth of the knowledge sector, the office sector will grow. The housing sector will continue to witness growth as long as mortgage finance rates remain stable.

There will be demand for over 24.3 million new dwellings for self-living in urban India, and over half of this will come from outside top 100 cities, according to 'Housing Skyline of India 2007-08', a study by research firm, Indicus Analytics suggests that Delhi will be the biggest generator of demand for residential housing in the country, followed by Mumbai and Thane. Easier credit availability is likely to drive greater ownership in future, changing family structure in urban India will be fundamental driver for housing growth.

Investments in real estate have a multiplier effect on income and employment. HUDCO-IIM Ahmedabad study estimates that every rupee invested in this sector adds 78 paisa to the state's GDE. The study estimates that for every direct job created in the industry, eight jobs are created indirectly. Indian real estate sector is on a high growth trajectory.

And according to global consultancy firm, Merrill Lynch, the sector will grow from $12 billion in 2005 to $90 billion by 2015. Much of the growth will come from the housing market. Despite the good news that the average age of house ownership has come down from 45 years in the 1980s to 32 years now, India's realty sector is still dominated by the unorganized and fly-by-night players. Very few corporates and large players have a national presence.

It is well-known that rising middle class salaries, easy access to finance and affordable housing have given a boost to the industry but restrictive legislations and non-transparent transactions have nullified some of these gains. India is governed by over 100 and mostly archaic laws, some even dating back to the 19th century. These barriers extract an exorbitant cost. McKinsey study calculates that removing land market barriers can contribute an additional 1 per cent to India's GDP growth rate. Confirming the trend, a World study estimates that an average housing project in India takes anything up to six years to complete as against 15-18 months in China.

India also charges one of the highest levels of stamp duty in the world. In most states it ranges from 10 to 15 per cent, though Delhi has brought it down to a low 6 per cent recently for certain categories of home buyers. High stamp duties have lead to unregistered—and all property transactions and transfers through the Power of Attorney, entailing considerable financial loss to the exchequer and giving low transparency. The National Housing and Habitat Policy of 1998 recommended a stamp duty rate of 2-3 per cent across the country.

The Urban Land (Ceiling and Regulation) Act 1976 hinders availability of land for housing projects. The Center in 1999 repealed the Act, but it still remains in force in states like Andhra Pradesh, Assam, Bihar, Maharashtra, Jharkhand and West Bengal. Similarly, a creaky land title monitoring system often results in ordinary people being duped. The revenue records are not documents of titles, and ownership is established only by the sequence of earlier transfers. This has led to enormous litigations. All India Bar Association estimates that about 40 per cent of all litigations filed in lower courts and state high courts put together are related to land ownership or property related disputes.

Under the Rent Control Act, many tenants still pay the same rent that they used to pay decades ago. This has not only discouraged fresh investments in housing for rental purpose, but has also led to deterioration in the physical condition of many houses, with landlords reluctant to invest in repairs. Municipal property tax collection is stagnating as it is based on the rent. The number of litigations between landlords and tenants has been piling in various courts across the country.

Comprehensive legal reforms will be taken up by the proposed National Housing and Urban Habitat Policy 2006. It envisages that by 2021 every homeless Indian would have a house of his own. Many analysts feel that along with legal reforms, the sector also needs to get the status of an infrastructural industry, which attracts lower taxes and gets low cost funds. All this would help the Indian real estate sector realize its real potential even though it will be overoptimistic to assume that universal housing is within our reach.

There will be a shortage of 24.71 million houses by the end of 2007. In the next 10 to 15 years, 80 to 90 million houses will have to be constructed in India. Office space requirement is slated to triple to at least 60 to 80 million square feet by 2010. Six hundred new shopping malls are expected to be in place by 2010, as compared to 1999 when India's first mall opened. The Indian realty sector is expected to expand from $12 billion in 2005 to $90 billion by 2015. In 2005 the government permitted 100% FDI in housing and town ships. Around $7 to $10 billion FDI in real estate sector is expected in the next three years. (Sources: Planning Commission, Merrill Lynch, Ficci, Jones Lang Lasaile.)

Challenge of Indian Consumerism

The expansion of diversified business enterprises have created more jobs for people earning good salary, many of the foreign brands are available through retail revolution in India which attract the youth with disposable incomes.

The resulting economic boom and combined with young demographics and exposure to global lifestyles and availability of consumer products and services has created consumerism. The increase in disposable income for the younger generation may develop certain changing societal values that may not commensurate with traditional values and lifestyle of people. The society will undergo change through push and pull process. The transformation of India into consumer society is changing the core social values and challenging old identities.

Changing Lifestyles

Access to cheaper credit and high disposal incomes to fulfil aspirations for private homes, cars, and a plethora of other consumer durables was a distant dream for Indians. However, this has changed dramatically over the past decade. The Indian economy has evidenced an unprecedented resurgence, with strong GDP growth placing India amongst the fastest growing economies in the world. It is not merely the market size, but the manner in which consumer tastes and preferences are evolving that creates interest in the sector; and also the availability of products.

Indian consumption story is, first and foremost, one of accelerating growth off a low base. The potential comes from the structure of the Indian economy: India's transition to 8.5% to 9% growth in recent years is very much an outgrowth of the emerging consumerism of one of the world's youngest populations. The increased vigor of private consumption provides a powerful leverage to the Indian growth dynamic that is rarely found in the externally-dependent developing world.

The 55th round of the National Sample Survey (2006), states that the Indian middle class (about 23 per cent of total population) accounts for about 42 per cent of the total consumption expenditure of the country. However, domestic demand for such branded products remains the key driver. This provides a boost to premium and luxury brand retailers, servicing select clientele.

In India the new consumerism is changing lifestyles. The retail revolution, apart from bringing in sweeping, positive changes in the quality of life in the metros and bigger towns, is also bringing in gradual changes in lifestyle in the smaller towns of India. The retailers are not only bringing in more merchandise to their stores, but are also continuously working on enhancing the shopping experience. The stores are spacious and visual merchandise is being re-worked with focus on customer interaction.

The increase in the number of young consumers and rising income levels is witnessing a rise in aspiration levels. Within overall transformation in spending pattern, there is a high propensity to spend more on lifestyle products. Growth opportunity is widespread. Demographic trends are charting a new growth path for lifestyle goods that have emerged over the last few years due to strong growth in the Indian economy post-liberalization.

Despite the rising consumption and changing spending habits it is the lack of priority given to quality of life that is the main stumbling block. There's a growing need among Indians, especially of the younger ages, to enjoy life and find a balance between work and play, which was not the case earlier.

Rural Consumer: The "inclusive economy" is viewed as one that is biased toward consumption-led growth—reinforcing on the coming shift to Indian consumerism to the extent that rural development will result in Indian productivity enhancement. Real incomes and consumer purchasing power should rise in rural areas. The bulk of the early dividends from rural reform are widely expected to come from small and medium-size businesses. Successful agricultural reform would further help it. Given the already large consumption share of the Indian economy, rural development could actually end up being a levered play on the Indian consumer. It must come up with new sources of growth such as those that are evident in India's consumption-led model.

IT Infrastructure Management Services

IT major IBM is investing $1.5 billion globally to strengthen its security offerings that complement its range of technology services, including IT infrastructure management. These services would encompass hardware, software and cover new areas such as intrusion detection and prevention, all aimed at providing holistic enterprise-wide infrastructure risk management services. "IBM has made a string of acquisitions in the security related space, including Internet Security."

Systems Inc. and these, along with the services capabilities, would now complement one another and enable us to offer end-to-end IT risk management. "As part of the recent announcement of $1.5 billion into security products and services, we see part of investments in India too, which would cover security services and customization and localization required for specific markets," IBM has taken a leadership role in providing IT infrastructure management services and continues to expand the offerings. During the year, some of the larger IBM deals include that of the Central Board of Direct Taxes (CBDT), Delhi International Airport Ltd., DLF Ltd. and Idea Cellular and FINO (Financial Information Network and Operations Ltd.).

The company is also engaged with Apollo Hospital Group to create a health data network. Significantly, infrastructure management deals are going beyond the larger sized ones with a host of small and medium-sized enterprises looking to take these offerings. This is because most of these enterprises are going global and have taken IT infrastructure and security management proactively.

Traditionally, financial services, telecom and manufacturing are those which opted for integrated IT infrastructure management services. But lately, retail, real estate and infrastructure are taking to security pro-actively, be it through digital video surveillance or access management.

Quoting IDC data, about 70 per cent of chief information officers (CIOs) hinted at increased spending on risk mitigation and that too to ensure that their technology infrastructure is up and running all the time. Therefore, security is not a one time mantra but an ongoing engagement which changes as business keeps transforming. This is both in the virtual world and real time requirements in large distributed infrastructure companies; for instance, when a large enterprise opens up its SAP applications to its external agents and suppliers, the nature and scope of the engagement changes. Even if the entire system is secure, look at the power of a pen drive that can potentially carry the most important enterprise data. It is here that the role of identity management has become central for corporations. Apart from these sectors, IBM is engaged with IT and BPO services providers, managing their ever-growing data centers, all of which require integrated risk management solutions.

Managing Global Business

In India, the businesses are expanding in diversified products and services in different domains. They are expanding into far flung geographies which necessitate dealing with three forces: diverse business cultures and political cultures, and equally important is to deal with people's culture—as their characteristics, work ethics, motivations and expectations, languages with their subtle nuances, and lifestyles of people in every country differ and that is why it is very important to be well-versed in these to be effective in business dealings. These three forces have to be managed well for the success of the enterprises big or small; when people are interdependent and collaborative in globalization contexts. The exposure through various media and travel modes facilitate an understanding and ambiance to act and mange well different actions.

As discussions in the earlier sections highlight that globalization structure in India focuses on globalization of enterprises and business expansion of products and services, global markets and geographies through collaboration, joint ventures, merger and acquisitions. India could generate funds internally and expand businesses internally because of economic reforms at home and consistent economic polices, as well as allowing diversifying business portfolios. These are raising expectations of people; and aims at transforming India. Innovative business and management practices as well as managing peoples' expectations in both national and global contexts are important for successful and effective transformation.

The Seven Factors

There are seven factors which facilitate in managing global businesses. First, the businesses workforce have to manage people with their cultural practices, ways of doing business, the market forces, the ever increasing range of products and services and expanding markets and innovation practices and above all technology with its newer and newer breakthroughs.

Secondly, India needs to leverage its soft power. Expansion of business needs to generate funds both internally and externally. As our discussions in subsequent chapters would show India could attract foreign investment funds because it offers stable political environments, stable and consistent economic policies, business and management expertise of its business leaders and a talented work pool. Lower level inexpensive manpower also attracts foreign businesses to set up their offshore manufacturing, software, administrative and export units here. All told India could offer soft power.

The third essential factor for managing businesses successfully and its growth is a vast pool of skilled workforce at all levels. India is making efforts, pooling its private and public resources to educate the people and impart vocational skills both hard and soft skills. These skills need constant updating. Thus, with this ever increasing demand, the supporting businesses expand more and more.

The fourth factor is updating technological needs of businesses. India is able to meet its technology needs both by innovating indigenous technology by research development; and importing advance technologies as now government has open policies for import of such technologies. Secondly, when foreign MNC are opening their units in India, they are bringing with them latest advance technologies, or setting up research and development units for advancement in technologies and the best part is, they train manpower to operate these technologies. Thirdly, when Indian MNCs acquire and merge foreign companies, they acquire their operating technologies also. Also, the expats returning home bring their expertise and knowledge in advance technologies. Even the Indian workforce that work in Indian business units set up in different countries when return home or get transfer to one of their other units in different country bring differing expertise and business practices.

The fifth factor is trained and skilled workforce. The training and skills have to be updated with changing technologies, changing business focus and practices. In India, there is continuous effort to create a trained and skilled workforce but much is needed to take advantage of the young demographics of vast ever increasing manpower. Returning expats and Indian workforce do contribute to this need. As employees become scattered around the globe, virtual teamwork has become crucial.

Sixth factor is the business practices which need to be the best, assimilating to the business, political, administrative and social cultures of the host countries. Many such cultural practices intermingle as businesses get multilateral with close personal interactions.

Seventh factor is the business models. India experienced that business success depends on its business models. India did move ahead from its traditional business models to innovative and newer and newer models as it fitted its expansion programs. It reiterated its low end markets and rural markets, and microfinance models and give new lease to these models to boost more economic growth for the low end population but in return boost more business volume for Indian businesses.

India is experiencing economic growth as businesses are expanding both nationally and globally. The business expansions must be managed well so that economic growth and even economic boom is continuous and remains stable. We find the three essential concepts of globulation, glocalization and globalism conducive to expanding and managing businesses well.

Concerns and Challenges

Global businesses can be managed well if enterprises and workforce have competitive spirit and global skills and manages information security and disasters challenges from within and outside with business continuity plans.

Competitive business environment and disruptions that could be man-made or otherwise in a world where 24/7 is the norm, organizations need to not just survive but thrive. The ability to recover and get the business back on track in the minimum possible time is a must in an increasingly globalized environment.

Globalization brings with it complexities that require companies with global growth strategies to prepare for 24/7 operations. In order to help organizations cope with the changing business needs, both enterprises and people have to have competitive spirit and global skills.

Information security, business continuity and regulatory compliance are other enterprise-wide concerns and challenges. The Economic Times Panel discussion in Sept. 2007 on 'Business 2.0: Managing a Global Enterprise and Preparing for the Future' proposed the need for a 'Business Continuity Plan' when businesses are threatened by disasters such as bomb threats, rioting.

The discussion addressed the above-mentioned enterprise-wide concerns and these are significant challenges for CIOs who are largely responsible for managing these risks. CIOs must contend with ongoing threats from within and outside including corporate espionage, disaster recovery and business continuity scenario planning.

"Business continuity processes (BCP) are constantly evolving and organizations should adopt best technology and practices to ensure business continuity," organizations are increasingly dependent on Information Technology (IT) infrastructure for disaster management and business continuity. The cost of disaster depends on the nature of the industry. Some are more susceptible to disasters and need to provide in full measure. "The security industry, including stock exchanges, clearing houses, depositories need to be prepared to fullest extent." In such cases, the disaster recovery (DR) sites need to be exactly identical and needs to ensure that data is protected at rest and also in transit. The cost of setting up DR sites is a major issue for most companies. We should mirror what we can afford. For that which cannot be mirrored, we should tie-up with vendors to set up DR sites.

An important point was raised, there was a tendency to mix together the resilience, disaster and continuity aspects and then start working on a business continuity plan. "There is a need to desegregate the resilience aspect from the disaster and continuity aspects."

The panelists also felt that a BCP should be tailored to meet all kinds of events, not just disasters. "BCP is not related to disasters alone. It is related to business. For instance, if a particular business sees unprecedented growth, then it may not be a disaster but it would lead to a degradation of the response time. In such scenarios too, the BCP should kick in. BCP needs are changing constantly, for management, the challenge is how to manage their time or bandwidth and come up with business continuity scenarios when they could be dealing with demands of new businesses. There is also the issue of educating the consumer about BCP.

Business resiliency should be an organization wide initiative. It should be the concern of every department so that everyone rises to the occasion when required. In order to enable that everyone participates, it is necessary that the business continuity process is understood by everyone. The definition of failure needs to be specified and understood by all—technical or non-technical.

We say again that business expansion knows no bounds in India and there is rising aspirations and growth; we reiterate.

It is not just about where your dreams will take you but where you take your dreams.

Road to Growth: Transformation for Tomorrow

4

For any nation to maintain its Competitive value, proposition and Improve, it will need to go through Constant reforms.

Dimensions of Global Transformation

Global structure sets the stage for transformation and it becomes an ongoing process seeking support from globalization dimensions of connectivity and infrastructure to give it more stability.

Rising expectations and stability is necessary for transformation success of India and expanding its global participation to an extent that it is being reckoned as powerful country with its booming economy. To be a global power, it has to focus on developing more of connectivity through telecommunication development and transport development for its people, country and businesses to participate in globalization effectively. Physical and human infrastructure development is equally important for effective globalization participation. These two would upgrade both urban and rural communities to facilitate global participation.

We discuss Physical Infrastructure development in chapter 4 and Human Infrastructure development in chapter 5. Chapter 7 focuses on connectivity.

Physical Infrastructure Development

People around the world are realizing that good infrastructure leads to economic development; therefore infrastructure development is the buzz word in booming economies. World's fastest growing economies pour money into new ports, power plants, highways and expressways, good roads and rails to telephone and water, etc. Infrastructure spending can be difficult to quantify since it encompasses both private and public spending. Much of the Infrastructure growth will come from the developing countries particularly in Asia. China and India are moving ahead aggressively in this direction.

Good infrastructure development is necessary both for global and domestic development and gives connectivity to people. Connectivity and transformation are the keywords. Connectivity through better means of transporting people and goods, roads, highways, expressways, railways, airlines, airports etc. Connecting people through better telecommunication systems. Such connectivity transforms nations and people's lifestyles. But to facilitate such transformation the other infrastructure development necessary is power generation—so power plants are needed, fuel—oil, gas, coal or other kind of fuel; these are to be developed in country or bought from other countries; and water resources both for human, industrial, and agriculture consumption need to be developed. The focus has to be on products and services in agriculture, industrial and service sectors.

Globalization demands as well facilitate infrastructure development through joint ventures, collaboration and cooperation in businesses, technical expertise, financial and capital flows and investments and above all manpower use. Interdependency loop is operative in all these areas. We agree road to growth is through optimum infrastructure development.

Our discussion about infrastructure development in India will focus on development of physical and geographical areas, technologies for development of physical and geographical areas, and manpower skill development and training in expertise areas for planning, appropriate technology development and applications. Over and above such world class infrastructure development (which is need of the day) on vast scale would need a fair amount of capital and money resources and that would need global financial resources and capital investments. Global funds as well global expertise are needed. Developing countries are aggressive and assertive enough to negotiate such resources from other countries worldwide by offering some of their strength areas such as India may offer IT expertise and low cost skilled workforce and a vast consumer market; China may offer low cost labor and manufacturing strengths and a vast consumer market. Therefore, globalization market forces and interdependency loop are important in this context.

A top government policy advisor Montek Singh Ahluwalia said, "Billions of dollars must be spent to improve India's creaking infrastructure to achieve the economic growth needed to lift millions out of poverty, India's dilapidated ports, roads, power supplies and other infrastructure are a 'critical constraint' to stronger growth. Investment in infrastructure in 2006-07 was five per cent of gross domestic product and was inadequate. We need to increase it to about nine per cent by the financial year 2011-12 to around five billion dollars. India's goal of attaining 10 per cent growth by the 2011-12 financial year would be unachievable unless infrastructure spending moves into much higher gear. The Indian Government will pick up the tab for 70 per cent of the infrastructure spending but the rest—around 150 billion dollars—must come from private sources. (India Economic Summit on Dec. 4, 2007).

India also realizes the equal importance of development of human infrastructure in key sectors of Health, Education, Energy, Banking, Retail, Real Estate and IT; and also training the workforce to develop physical infrastructure.

Decision-making for infrastructure in India has involved two important decisions: (a) decision to go global. In this context does it have adequate physical, financial and human resources, (i) to liberalize economic policies, (ii) to invite global players and also let its people participate in globalization process with those global players? (b) If not, how it intends to develop physical resources such as oil and gas power, setting steel plants, or even at the lowest rung—setting BPOs and telecommunication centers, etc. and develop roads, highways, bridges, road transportation, railway, airport, ports, airlines etc. water and land; and to set up these facilities as world class facilities to encourage global players to do business in India;

and also to handle the growing demand for infrastructure due to expansion of economic activities at home. To illustrate, when there is economic boom and people are earning more, let them enjoy quality of life with increased availability and better standard of infrastructure; such as they may travel by air calling for more and better airport facilities. They may use self/own cars rather than public transportation. With industrial production more cargo may be transported through roads, ports and airports. More transportation of goods means better roads. With increased population and to ease the vehicular traffic jam, metros and subways may be needed.

What are the modes of development of infrastructure? Finances and investments are needed to develop these. India has invited foreign entrepreneurs to invest their financial and other physical resources, as well as their expertise to set up such industries. This may be facilitated by collaborative or cooperative business models. These may be built through foreign funding as joint venture or by total foreign investments on BOT (buy-operate-transfer) basis depending on again country's openness of economic policies about the foreign capital flow in without reservations and restrictions or it may levy certain conditions. The other modes could be public-private investments, collaborative investments of domestic private enterprises and foreign business enterprises as approved by the government. It has been encouraging the domestic industrialists by allowing them to import relevant technology, finances and expertise—all of them or either of them. Liberal economic policies with certain world-class economic reforms, opening up of markets will be necessary for such an endeavor.

Who are the decision-makers for development of infrastructure? It could be country 'A' that invites other countries to do business with it. Other countries may be willing to do business with 'A' if there is appropriate world-class infrastructure as that would facilitate progress of their businesses; otherwise they may look for country 'C' who has or is willing to provide such infrastructural facilities. Therefore, government and enterprises of country 'A' would make-decisions about development of infrastructure to meet the needs of countries doing business with them. Chapter 3 highlights the business expansions in multi-geographies and expanding in volumes and domains which demands more and more of these infrastructures of world class to develop fast, reliable and updated to have easy access to do business. If roads and road transport is outdated, if airlines and airports are not modernized, and if ports are not conveniently accessible and modernized for cargo containers, the developed countries doing business with India may start looking elsewhere and the strongest competitor is China, which has moved much ahead in infrastructure development and is also a preferred destination for businesses.

The second scenario is when country 'B' does want to do business with India because of low cost factor and other expertise and talent workforce and it decides to develop some of the infrastructure—physical or human for business profitability. Country 'B' takes this decision in coordination with India. Human resource development is important component of doing business and investment in it both by India and other countries is essentially treated as part of business recurring expenses and investments for good return of investment (ROI).

Keys for World Class Infrastructure Development

There are six essential keys for world class infrastructure development. It involves high quality of construction activities involving construction material and equipment, skilled and unskilled manpower and engineering, designing and management expertise, oil, gas and power to operate it, real estate availability, transport modes, consumers and funds.

India's economic boom has resulted in an exponential growth in demand for construction equipment and services. The construction industry is expected to play a critical role in the building of modern India.

According to consulting firm McKinsey study (2007). Indian earthmoving and construction equipment sector (ECE) can grow to $12-13 billion by 2015 provided it gets support from the government and the industry; the current growth levels would create a market of eight billion dollars by 2015. A concerted push given by the industry and the government would promote exports and generate additional 4-5 billion dollars in revenue, it said. The industry has recorded a year-on-year growth of 40 per cent in revenue since 2004 to reach 2.3 billion dollars.

Growth opportunities for the industry include investment of 750 billion dollars in infrastructure development, increased involvement of global equipment manufacturers in the country and rise in exports. Low cost imports from countries such as China could pose a challenge, but at present it is low at only five per cent of the total ECE consumption.

India can become the major global construction outsourcing hub for construction equipment, components and construction related knowledge based activities. Already it does vast turnkey projects for outside countries (using indigenous resources of material and equipment, and skilled and unskilled manpower).

The second key is to have power, oil and gas to operate the infrastructure. All these are in inadequate supply in India. But our Chapter 3 on business expansion oil and energy shows that Indian companies both private and public are forging ahead in big way, investing billion dollars and collaborating with other foreign big companies in this sector to explore oil, to refine and produce gas. Ultra mega power projects are being set up in different states with funding from private, government and international conglomerates.

We need power equipment to match the mega investments in power generation; we need power producers, and power distributors. Indian companies are booming in these sectors. There are power producers like NTPC, Neville Lignite, power equipment and the transmission companies like Power Grid, KEC Infrastructure, Jyoti Structures, Kalpataru, and power distributors like Reliance Energy.

The third key is the Real Estate availability for making roads, highways, ports, airports, expansion of rail lines and rail stations, SEZ and retail super stores, etc. setting up power and steel plants, industries, etc.

The fourth key is the transport modes such as both passenger and commercial vehicular modes and airplanes and airlines for using airports for air travel, businesses and consumers utilizing these infrastructures.

Fifth key is manpower—the skilled manpower and engineering, designing and management expertise to equip and operate these infrastructures. It also needs unskilled manpower for supportive and basic services. Sixth key is the infrastructure funds for the infrastructure development.

Infrastructure Fund Needs

Finance for Infrastructure in India: The rules for government-owned infrastructure companies for raising funds through initial share offerings are made flexible by the Securities and Exchange Board of India, which naturally will increase the flow of investment in the infrastructure of India. To bridge the wide gap between the potential demand for infrastructure for high growth and the available supply, there is urgent need for a close partnership between the public and private sectors, and for foreign capital. In India infrastructure sector itself is becoming an attractive investment area for FDIs. To encourage foreign funds flow into the infrastructure in India, the Indian Finance Ministry has allowed Foreign Institutional Investors (FIIs) also to invest in unlisted companies. FIIs now can invest 100 per cent of their funds in the infrastructure in India. In order to make the core sector more attractive for FDI, the Cabinet Committee on Foreign Investment (CCFI) has modified the 49 per cent cap on foreign equity in the infrastructure sector to make fund mobilization easier. This major policy decision will indirectly raise the foreign equity investment in infrastructure sector to well over 51 per cent.

Besides, even if allocation in the infrastructure in India is raised with a greater inflow of FDI and a large participation of private sector, the immediate problem will still remain, since, infrastructure is subjected to long gestation period. Consequently, the inadequacy of infrastructure in India will continue for quite some time, unless technology upgradation can be done in the infrastructure production, including construction activities, for reducing the gestation lags and simultaneously improving the quality of products. With this infrastructure limitation any indiscriminate growth may lead the economy of the country to a situation of over-heating and a further rise in inflation.

In India, the most essential field is urban infrastructure development. Except for a few large projects in a handful of cities, paucity of urban infrastructure projects is a standing problem. Although city mass transport systems and airports have found place in developmental plans, essential services such as roads, drinking water, sewerage management, drainage, and primary health are still greatly under developed. However, with the economy growing at more than at the rate of 8 per cent in 2007, the government is aiming at an economic growth rate of 8 per cent during the Eleventh Plan (2007-12), for which the government is taking necessary steps to develop the infrastructure in India.

Infrastructure development in India is challenging and it needs tremendous amount of financial funds and human resources to meet the needs. India's robust growth in GDP has exposed the grave inadequacies in the country's infrastructure sectors. "It is now widely acknowledged that the state of the infrastructure is a drag on the economy, perhaps by as much as 1-2 per cent a year", India's Finance Minister Chidambaram said. He highlighted that the Committee on Infrastructure Financing, which submitted its report in May 2007, has advised that the target for infrastructure investment should be revised from \$320 billion to \$384 billion at 2005-06 prices, which is equivalent to \$475 billion at current prices. It had been earlier estimated that during the Eleventh Plan period (2007 to 2012), the country would need to invest over \$320 billion in infrastructure alone.

India's Finance Minister asserted further, "I can say with confidence that no country than India needs and no country than India can absorb so much funds for the infrastructure sector", stating that the real challenge lies beyond the resources. He underscored the need to look for innovative mechanisms and instruments to channelize the funds into the infrastructure projects. Outlining some of the innovative measures of the government like viability-gap funding and establishment of India Infrastructure Finance Company Ltd. (IIFCL), he said that the government has also persuaded the Reserve Bank of India to lend $5 billion from the foreign exchange reserves to the IIFCL to enable the company to on-lend to infrastructure projects for their capital expenditure. IIFCL would finance the infrastructure projects of Indian companies, especially for capital imports, finance ministry sources said the proposed borrowing from the RBI would not be spent in the domestic market to avoid increase in money supply and inflation. The Reserve Bank has given an in-principle nod to invest $5 billion of foreign exchange reserves annually in infrastructure projects.

The state governments' apathy toward infrastructure was noticeable. Although finances were available, there were not enough infrastructure projects on the shelf in states development. It prompted the Centre to announce Rs. 100 crore corpus to help them in preparatory work of projects coming up with public-private participation. Highlighting the logistics of 'India Infrastructure Project Development Fund', India's Finance Minister Chidambaram commented. "It would be a revolving fund that will get replenished from successfully bid projects. In case it needs to be topped up, it would be topped up through budgetary support. States would bear up to 75 per cent of development costs of projects till the bidding stage", he said. If the bidding is successful, the amount given to states would be treated as interest free loans and in case the exercise fails, the assistance would be converted into grant. In case of successful bidding, the money would be recovered from those who get the contract (Finance Minister P. Chidambaram addressed at conference of chief secretaries on public-private partnership—PPP Oct. 2007).

Finance ministry sources said the fund would be sent to the Cabinet committee of economic affairs after approval of the Finance Minister, who had proposed it in the budget for 2007-08.

In 2007, it is estimated that infrastructure investment would rise to 9% of gross domestic product by 2011 and 2012 from about 5% GDP today. India's infrastructure investment would come to $50 billion a year at about 5% of India's $1 trillion economy.

People will be using more steel, oil, copper for infrastructure development.

With an estimated investment of about $500 billion in infrastructure during the 11th Five-Year Plan, the private sector is expected to pump in up to $125 billion during the period. "The private sector expects to invest up to 25 per cent of the total investments needed in infrastructure sector in the next five years which is more than the international average of about 20 per cent participation in infrastructure investment by the corporate." On attractiveness of the sub-sectors, majority of CEOs considered power sector as the most attractive sector for private sector investment (snap poll of CEOs, CFOs 30 Sep. 2007).

"The government will not be able to meet the growing funding need on its own for infrastructure. The country will need massive private investment," Chidambaram told a conference on infrastructure here. Private investment need is around $18-20 billion a year. Chidambaram commented that large private funds are looking at India with interest. After launch of two funds for infrastructure projects, including the $5 billion fund by Citigroup, Blackstone, IDFC and IFCL combined; other similar initiatives are waiting to be launched in India, he said.

The pace of infrastructure projects had gathered momentum in 2006-07. As many as 12 states have agreed to sign MoUs with Asian Development Bank for providing technical assistance to PPP projects. Two such MoUs have already been signed.

Thirty-First proposals under PPP were received during 2006-07, out of which 21 involving a project cost of Rs. 9,325 crore were given in principle for final approval. Similarly, 25 proposals under viability gap funding were received from state governments in last fiscal year, of which 18 were given in-principle approval.

The Asian Development Bank on 11 Dec. 2007 has allocated 9.2 billion dollars for funding infrastructure and development projects, mainly in India's less developed states, viz. Bihar and Jharkhand and those in the North-East, in the next three years.

"ADB has 31 projects under preparation for states like Bihar, Jharkhand, Orissa and North-East and other states," Shigehiko Muramoto, Project Head of the Manila-based multilateral bank said. Energy, transport, urban development, finance and agriculture would be the focus areas of the ADB funding.

For 2008, the multilateral funding agency has approved a loan of about 2.9 billion dollars for different projects which include agri-business and infrastructure development plans in Bihar and Maharashtra. They also include Integrated Irrigated Agriculture and Water Management in Orissa. About 3.1 billion dollars would be disbursed in 2009 for projects like Integrated Flood Control and River Erosion Mitigation, Assam Energy Efficiency Enhancement, Mizoram Public Resource Management and Development Program, Bihar Urban Infrastructure Development Sector.

For 2010, the ADB has approved about 3.2 billion dollars for funding projects which include Clean Power Scheme in Jammu and Kashmir and North-East Region Urban Development investment program. The money would also be used for improving roads in Bihar and Jammu and Kashmir.

India hopes China will boost investment in the south Asian nations' under funded infrastructure sector, but Chinese firms are wary about opening their wallets for Asia's third-largest economy due to worries about returns.

At a seminar in Shanghai on 11 Dec. 2007, Indian Government and company officials called on Chinese firms to pour funds into India's road, port, telecoms, power and property projects, which need $500 billion over the next five years. They said China's experience and expertise developed through a more than two-decade infrastructure construction boom at home would help India achieve its goal, and the Indian Government is offering tax and other incentives to woo private investment.

"India can certainly learn from China in terms of infrastructure investment," Prakash Gupta, consul and head of chancery of India's Consulate General in Shanghai, told the seminar about infrastructure investment in India. The rapid expansion in bilateral trade between the two giant Asian economies means there is much room for China to boost its direct investment in India from around $6 billion, Gupta said. Bilateral trade soared to $30 billion in January-October from just $3 billion in 2000, he said.

Chinese firms investing in India include Shanghai Urban Construction Group and firms based in eastern China, such as Ningbo Bird Co. Ltd. and Haier Group, and a company from eastern China's Jiangsu province is to build an industrial park in India. JJ Shrikhande, China head of Indian construction and engineering firm Larsen & Toubro Ltd., said his company is working with Chinese firms on infrastructure projects in India.

Nitin Sen, Beijing representative of Indian law firm Remfry & Sagar, said Chinese capital and technology are well suited to a developing country such as India. "The Chinese service is okay and their prices are also good," said Sen. "Only Chinese can help India."

But some Chinese company officials said they currently had no plans to make any significant investment in India's infrastructure sector because of risk concerns. "We are interested but we are not familiar with the risks in India. For example, if they get a new government, can we still recover our investment as planned?" said an official of a Chinese construction firm. Investment in India's infrastructure sector has lagged an economy growing at 9 per cent a year, partly because of regulatory issues. China is moving much faster in infrastructure development, particularly in the power industry.

China added 2,83,000 megawatt (MW) capacity in five years, dwarfing the 21,100 MWs built by India in the same period, said M.V. Rabade, chief representative of India's Adani Group in China. He said India's steel and cement capacity could not meet the power sector's requirements, and imports are increasingly essential (11 Dec. 2007).

The Urban Development Ministry has sought a massive Rs. 2,89,615 crore in the 11th Five-Year Plan to develop infrastructural facilities in urban areas. "So far five-year plans failed to focus on urban transport system in a big way. This time we have earmarked Rs. 1,32,590 crores specifically for developing transportation system in urban areas. Beside transport, we have set a target to make available for the entire population in urban areas with water supply and sewerage system by the end of the 11th Five-Year Plan."

"Urbanization is a key indicator of economic development and should be seen as a positive factor for overall development. Also as an economy grows, its towns and cities expand in size and volume and the contribution of urban sector to the national economy also increases."

Low income of municipalities is one of the reasons coming in the way of development of cities. Government launched the Jawaharlal Nehru National Urban Renewal Mission on December 2005 to give focused attention to integrated development of urban infrastructure and services in select 63 cities.

Delhi-Mumbai Industrial Corridor (DMIC): India has decided to ask Japan to contribute half of the proposed $250 million project development assistance fund for the Delhi-Mumbai Industrial Corridor (DMIC). The DMIC task force met in Tokyo on July 23-24, 2007 where senior officials from both sides discussed Japan's contribution to the project and the possible inflow of Japanese investments into the project.

For attracting investments from Japan into the 250-odd projects—like roads, ports and SEZs—that would be part of the corridor, Indian officials will hold meetings with Tokyo Stock Exchange representatives and financial institutes to explore the extent to which India could bank on Japanese investment.

Speaking to the media on the project development assistance fund, industry secretary said, "While the Japanese government would provide $125 million, the rest would come from Indian entities including the Centre and State governments" (July 2007).

Germany has sought to enhance its economic ties with India by investing in the infrastructure field with its cross-sector expertise and modern technologies. The interests of German companies range from construction of express roads and power plants to the construction or reconstruction of ports and airports to setting up of a telecommunication network linking the entire subcontinent, he said (Sept. 2007).

Physical Infrastructure Development

Infrastructure in India include transportation, agriculture, water management, telecommunications, industrial and commercial development, power, petroleum and natural gas, housing and other segments such as mining, disaster management services, technology-related infrastructure. Within the infrastructure of India, the transportation sector is the most important, including the aviation, ports, roads, rail system and logistics. The agriculture sector comprises infrastructure-related storage facilities, construction relating to agro-processing projects and reservation and storage of perishable goods. Among others essential sectors, real-estate development, including industrial parks, special economic zones, tourism and entertainment centers, educational institutions and hospitals and solid waste management systems, also play significant role in Indian economy.

Transport Development would need development of roads, highways, airports, metros, railways, ports, dams and bridges.

Good public transport infrastructure is drastically needed in India to decongest the roads with more private vehicles and also to give affordable transport to people. These modes could be public buses, taxis, metros for passenger transport and trucks, vans, tempos for commercial transport. The government has recently come out with a National Urban Transport Policy in 2007.

We need efficient transport system. This is possible but many things will have to change before this becomes a reality. India is a vast country with long distances and therefore quick, reliable and safe transportation systems are most essential for its economic growth. Planners have not realized that investments in the transport sector come back to the nation manifold, fueling growth in many other sectors. More than 70% of the country's goods and population move by roads. A lot of needs to be done to lay new roads and improve existing ones, and national highways and expressways. Development of such a system also needs resources and finances. The planners are realizing the needs as well as the need for resources. They are also aware that this could be made possible by private-public joint imitative, as well domestic and global joint ventures and collaboration both for finances and expertise. The golden quadrilateral project is a beginning, such projects will gather momentum.

Roads connect cities, villages and gives connectivity to people and to diverse facilities like work place, market places, farms, educational institutes, hospitals, banks, and entertainment centers etc. In this way, they connect people to products and services and thus enterprises. Well connected and well maintained roads and in good condition add efficiency to businesses and life.

India needs to spend more on providing roads to connect villages to farm facilities and other facilities, interconnect villages, and connect them with cities. A road grid around villages and cities is important to upgrade both villages and urban communities' vis-à-vis economic growth and quality of life. Presently, at many places only dirt roads exists, which even make transport reach inaccessible.

Within metros and bigger cities we need highways both to regulate the traffic and efficient movement of traffic. We need expressways to interconnect metros with outlying cities and villages.

Environment: The government may make it mandatory for all arterial roads to have a minimum 2.5 metre pedestrian path and proper street furniture and 2.5 metre bicycle path preferably in each direction. "This would help reduce fuel consumed per passenger traveled through the modal shift," the official said. The safety of walking and bicycling is a prerequisite for controlling global warming. The government is of the view that these measures would also help attract large players to invest in the industry.

According to government officials, greenhouse emissions can be reduced by linking urban development with transportation planning to improve access to goods and services while minimizing the need to travel by charging the cost of externalities, such as congestion, pollution, climate change, public infrastructure, and reducing subsidies for private vehicles.

Transport Authorities will soon set-up in mega cities with a population of more than a million for implementing urban transport programs and projects for sustainable urban transport. The present land use and transport policies in India have led to the excessive use of the personalized modes of transportation that causes congestion, air pollution and noise. Urban transport is 'bloodstream' of the cities, there is need of including private parties in the sustainable development of urban transport. Increased traffic jams, increased road accidents, and air pollution level are the few challenging problems in the urban cities. The conference discussed various aspects and options to identify sustainable urban transport.

Automotive Development: India is among the world's fastest growing automobile markets, due to a booming economy that has enhanced middle class disposable incomes and encouraged demand for cars. To tap the market, auto firms are beginning to respond to the common man's desire for small and affordable cars. As a result, car companies are reinventing the wheel to make cars more affordable to meet inflated consumer aspirations.

With approximately 56% of the population comprising youth and a rapidly expanding middle class, India could overtake China within a couple of years as the fastest-growing car market, according to analysts. Car companies are targeting India's approximately 65 million two-wheeler owners to market the small car. The reason why global majors are flocking to India is not hard to find. There are three reasons. Firstly raw material is cheaply available in India, secondly the cost of production is less and thirdly firms would be able to source components from various two-wheeler component producers across the country. The small car would be fuel efficient and would be a huge success in India because the segment constitutes 70% of car sales annually.

And who exactly are the small car dream merchants? Tata's dream car, in India, Tata Motors pioneered the concept that is about to change the rules of the automobile market. By mid-2009, India's third largest automaker is scheduled to introduce its long-awaited Tata's dream project—the People's Car. Many more are joining the race.

Airports and Airlines Development

Boosted by robust economic growth in India, the business expansions in multi-geographies around the world, both domestic and global demand for air travel has risen considerably in the recent past, reaching an all-time high. Newer airlines with new air routes have come in the market. Air traffic growth has increased even creating air traffic jams which need to be addressed by creating more runways, modernizing airports, and setting up new facilities at airports. Both passenger and freight demand has increased.

Air travel is much in demand both within the country and worldwide both by Indians and foreigners because of business expansions and also invoking tourist interests and due to special events like Commonwealth Games scheduled for 2010. The country needs modern airports and at least three to four times more than the number available today. Airports at the metros of Delhi, Mumbai, Bangalore, Kolkata and Hyderabad are being upgraded and even a second airport is also being constructed to meet the increasing air traffic such as in Bangalore which is the hub of IT businesses. Greenfield airports are coming up at Devanahalli near Bangalore and Shamshabad near Hyderabad, but many more such projects, especially in remote areas, are required.

Air connectivity to all corners of the country should be a reality in the future. More new domestic airlines such as Jet Airways, Kingfisher, Go Air, Deccan Airways are licensed on different routes; both metro routes and feeder routes to smaller cities. Earlier, there was only one airline—Indian airlines operated by government. Now that is also revamped and has become efficient due to private competition. This has created competition and also reduction in airfares and thus more air travel but also air traffic to congest the airports.

Impressed by the unprecedented 40% growth in the domestic air traffic during the first nine months of 2007, Civil Aviation Minister Praful Patel said 20 more civilian airports would go operational next year. Nearly 100 airports in the country would be operational in 2008 as compared against 80 now. Policy on Greenfield aspect for airport development would be in place by early next year.

There is huge demand on power with the airport development and companies have to harness it. Ministry of Civil Aviation is considering a proposal to allow more than one airport in a particular region. Currently, the government policy does not allow an international airport to come up within 150 km. of an existing airport. The ministry is reconsidering this as the policy may hamper the growth of the industry, officials said.

There is optimism over growth of cargo traffic. Logistics infrastructure is being developed across the country, both public and private airlines will have to expand more cargo planes. Public sector Air India has already started a subsidiary dedicated to cargo, Jet Airways is planning to launch a separate airline for cargo operation.

The country would need 1,000 aircraft by the end of next decade. "Just three years back, India had only 125 aircraft. In the last three years, the number of aircraft in the country has neared the 400 mark. Aviation activities which were limited to a few metros serving only elite classes have now percolated to smaller cities and the lower-middle class. Ministry of Civil Aviation is now scrutinizing business plans and financial health of the promoters before giving approvals to allow more airlines to start."

Air connectivity growth would need urgent focus on upgrading airports and ensuing facilities with modernized and advance technologies, fuel and power growth, modernized airport equipments and trained pilots and supporting airport ground and air crew staff. An academy is set up to meet this manpower need.

Companies like GMR infrastructure and other infrastructure companies are putting their expertise and funding. These are being developed as joint ventures with foreign Corporate with their foreign expertise and funding; and are also time-bound.

Delhi International Airport Ltd. (DIAL) is a public-private partnership initiative that has been awarded the mandate for modernization and restructuring of the Indira Gandhi International Airport in New Delhi. DIAL comprises the GMR Group, Airports Authority of India, Fraport AG, Eraman Malaysia and India Development Fund. GMR Infrastructure generates, transmits and distributes electrical power. It also develops, maintains and operates airports and roads. On 17 September 2007, DIAL commissioned a new Internet Protocol (IP) based digital EPABX system with advanced multimedia applications and services to improve passenger facilitation at Delhi International Airport.

A strategic alliance may be in the works between the Reliance Group and the GVK Group for the proposed Navi Mumbai Airport. Various options, including Reliance Group picking up a possible stake in MIAL—the Mumbai airport operator—or the GVK Group first increasing its stake in MIAL and then diluting in favor of Reliance Group, or associate company or fund are being considered.

Sources said exploratory talks are on, though at informal levels—with the preliminary understanding that Reliance Group will support the GVK-led consortium's bid for the second airport in the city. The Greenfield airport—expected to be ready by 2012—will be the gateway for two SEZs at Navi Mumbai and Maha Mumbai promoted by Reliance Industries chairman Mukesh Ambani and his close associate Anand Jain.

MIAL airport is a joint venture owned by the GVK Group (37%), Airports Company South Africa (10%), Bidvest Group (27%) and Airports Authority of India (26%). MIAL operates the existing Mumbai airport at Santacruz, India's largest in terms of the volume of traffic. Sources said that South Africa-based investment holding company, Bidvest Group, may sell some equity to the GVK Group, giving the lead partner a majority control in the JV. Subsequently, the GVK Group may give a strategic stake to a Reliance Group company or a fund backed by the group.

Airport Infrastructure

The real makeover in airport infrastructure is taking off in the hinterlands with 200 small airports to mushroom according to different models. Non-metro airports cannot generate profits from passenger traffics. Their leverage will be other activities which will generate passenger and or cargo traffic and feed city-side revenues. The emerging five non-metro feeder models of airports are:

- **Cargo Model:** Dedicated hubs that can handle logistics. Planned airports Nagpur, Kochi and Hassan.
- **Tourism Model:** Bellary has converted the seven hour Bangalore-hampi-cross country into one hour 45 minutes journey. Planned airports Ballery (hampi) Shirdi, Puttapurti.
- **Sez Model:** Reliance industry 5000 Acres SEZ in Jhajjar Haryana. Planned airports Jhajjar, Shimoga and Hassan.
- **Industry Model:** Good and populated industrial belts will breed an ecosystem that will demand movement. Planned airports, Navi Mumbai, Sholapur and Rajmundry.
- **Aerotropolis Model:** Develop an entire sub city, houses, offices, factories, hotels, leisure. It will serve the airport and airport will serve it. Planned airports, Durgapur, Kochi and Hassan.

There will be 300 small and regional airport projects through PPP route over the next 20 years. India's thrust on small and regional airports will demand for at least hundred, 70-120 seater planes in the next 10 years. Aircraft orders is one of the many economic pockets that will get fillip. There will be trickle down impact on local services like catering, taxi, F&B and courier services. Locals from nearby villages will get jobs in the day-to-day maintenance and development of airport areas both on full time and part time basis.

Non-metro airports will help in decongesting the metro airports also. Eventually, every state will have one international airport fed by a mix of regional and metro airports. The hub-and-spoke model where non-metro airports will feed metro airports, which will feed international one, will evolve overtime. We will also need regional airlines; the current policy to restrict the regional airlines to fly in one region only is not encouraging many. Some regional airports are exploring strategic relationship with regional and budget airlines. For a smaller airport to work, it should be sponsored by airline. Each airport should be viable by itself. Many investors feel, the return on small airports will depend on the amount of land available for commercial use.

Non-metro Airport Modernization: The ministry of civil aviation has clarified that the air cargo management at these airports will be vested with private players as envisaged in the original bidding document. The ministry had decided to give the mandate to the winning bidder for commercial operations, maintenance of terminal buildings, cargo management and city-side development.

The target date for completion of modernization process of the 35 non-metro airports by the Airports Authority of India (AAI), is March 2010. New terminal buildings expandable on modular basis are being constructed at Ahmedabad, Amritsar, Aurangabad, Agatti, Bhopal, Bhubaneshwar, Chandigarh, Dehradun, Goa, Jaipur, Lucknow, Indore, Khajuraho, Madurai, Mangalore, Port Blair, Ranchi, Raipur, Rajkot, Trivendrum, Trichy, Udaipur, Varanasi and Vishakhapatnam airports.

Modification and expansion of existing terminal buildings are being undertaken at airports in Agra, Agartala, Coimbatore, Dimapur, Guwahati, Imphal, Jammu, Nagpur, Patna, Pune and Vadodara.

Companies including Reliance Energy, Fraport AG of Frankfurt, Tata Power, Lanco Infratech, Larsen & Toubro, Maytas Infra and GMR Infrastructure are among the companies vying for business opportunities in modernization of the non-metro airports.

Meanwhile, the government is also developing a world-class multi-modal international passenger and cargo hub in Nagpur.

Infrastructure bottlenecks make the infrastructure inefficient. One has to address these bottlenecks, for instance, infrastructural bottlenecks in airports force aircraft to hover in the skies for far too long, resulting in a loss of around $80 million to the airlines every year, a top aviation industry official said. Jet Airways alone incurs a loss of about $25 million per annum, he added. To avoid such bottlenecks, airline traffic planning is of utmost importance to save cost as well commuters' time and energy and environmental hazards.

Aviation Industry Faces Challenges: There is the shortage of trained personnel, non-availability of secondary airports and the competitive pressure on full service carriers to reduce fares on a par with low-cost carriers. It is observed that the aviation turbine fuel (ATF) charges comprise 35-40 per cent of the operating cost for airlines and is higher compared to those in other countries.

Boeing Investment to Support Indian Aviation: India has a tremendous need for aviation infrastructure as its aviation market keeps pace with a soaring economy. Boeing is investing in India to support India's development of a strengthened air transportation infrastructure. It benefits Boeing both directly and indirectly to participate in developing a system to accommodate many new Boeing products and services.

Boeing Commercial Aviation Services (CAS) plans to invest up to $75 million in India for training facilities, most of which will go to pilot training. A unit of Boeing Commercial Airplanes, CAS provides products and services to support its customers and help them improve fleet utilization, reduce costs and ensure passenger well-being. CAS will invest up to $100 million in maintenance, repair and overhaul (MRO) facility for Boeing airplanes in Nagpur city. Boeing anticipates joining with an in-country partner to work with Boeing on the MRO facility. The keen level of interest within India among outstanding companies that would like to work with Boeing on this has been gratifying.

The order for twenty-seven 787-8s, fifteen 777-300ERs, eight 777-200LRs and eighteen 737-800s will allow the airlines to upgrade their fleet and expand operations in many market segments—the Gulf, Europe, Asia-Pacific and the U.S. Deliveries of the jets are scheduled to begin in November 2006. Air India's fleet will have the most modern, most efficient airplanes—including Boeing's new, state-of-the-art 787 Dreamliner. With its new airplanes, Air India plans to start a range of new services including nonstop India-U.S. and India-Australia flights. Other Boeing Commercial Airplanes' customers in India include SpiceJet, Jet Airways, Air India Express, Alliance Air and Blue Dart Aviation.

Boeing's 2006 annual "Current Market Outlook" projected that India would need 856 new commercial jet airplanes worth $72 billions from 2006 to 2026.

Rail Road/Metros

Indian Railways need an aggressive policy for modernization and improving the safety record. The focus of the Railways should change from dedicated freight corridors to dedicated high-speed passenger corridors, to which all mail and express trains should be diverted. Capacity thus released will be more than what is needed for freight movement.

While our cities are growing very fast, the urban transport infrastructure is lagging behind. Modern public transport systems like the Delhi Metro are essential to sustain economic activities in our cities. Measures to reduce private ownership of cars and encourage use of public transport are urgently required. After the success of the Delhi Metro, several Indian cities such as Mumbai, Bangalore, Hyderabad, Ahmedabad and Chennai are now taking up Metro projects.

The government should also set up a separate ministry to oversee and expedite Metro constructions in all cities with populations over three million. Only such measures will solve the transportation problems of medium and large cities. India also needs an administrative environment where decision-making is very fast. Procedural shackles slow down such projects. Delhi Metro Rail Corporation has been quite successful in this respect and there is no reason why government departments and public sector undertakings cannot follow the Delhi Metro example. Undoubtedly, public transport is one area where vast improvements will have to be made to build a dream India. Ultimately, the benefits of the country's progress should reach the poor and the villages.

The Indian Railways is considering running suburban railways on the public-private-partnership (PPP) model by forging partnerships with state governments. The Railways have been incurring a loss of Rs. 900 crore every year running the suburban railways.

According to the proposal, the railways would own the land and state government and private players would operate the system and arrange required rolling stock for maintaining train frequency. Several states including West Bengal, Maharashtra and Gujarat have decided to insulate the Railways against losses in suburban railways.

Streamlining railways operation is very critical for people to feel attracted to travel. Safe and clean travel is important. Recently, the railways authorities are on cleaning drive, the bathrooms in rail compartment were so far not fit for human use. So the drive is to get them cleaned even frequently where trains may stop and water available in the taps in running trains. Compartments seats will be cushioned and would be cleaned regularly. The rail platforms have also come under cleaning scrutiny to take away the stink. Clean food stalls will be on the stations and safe drinking water kiosks are being put up; the food will be clean, safe and of good quality if being served in certain trains. Even there is proposal to have cinemas closer to metro stations where people can utilize their waiting time. Majority of people and all from low incomes would like to travel on railways as the fares are affordable.

Delhi Metro Rail Corporation (DMRC) in India is seriously considering creation of a consultancy wing to cater to global clients. After Sri Lanka, Syria, Pakistan, Bangladesh, Indonesia and Ireland, Vietnam has shown interest in Delhi Metro's success story. Although talks are at initial stages, DMRC may be roped in for preparing the blueprint for a 12.5 km. long metro line in the capital city of Hanoi, sources said.

"If more countries want to use DMRC's expertise, we have to play a larger role at the global level." In fact, DMRC undertook preliminary studies both in Sri Lanka and Syria to build metro systems in Colombo and Damascus, respectively.

The Colombo project, however, got shelved because of political reasons. Many Asian countries are turning to DMRC because of its expertise on low cost metro system. "Ours is the latest technology, yet, it's the cheapest. Many countries want to involve DMRC mainly because of its cost-effective techniques. We are familiar with the environment here, and also, good at working in high density areas where problems like acquisition of land etc. often crop up" (2006).

Highway and Expressways Development

Highways are being developed in India with high technology support and features to efficiently handle high-flow traffic as well commuters' time and wherever surveillance is needed for security.

A completely new experience is being promised for commuters on the Delhi-Gurgaon Highway in the 32 lanes toll plaza. Slated to be the largest of its kind in India, the hi-tech plaza would assure speed, transparency and efficiency. Spokesman of D.S. Constructions, said, "The automated tolling system at the plaza would also have lanes for commuters where they would not have to stop and pay the toll if they already have toll tags on their vehicles.

As it is expected that in the next few months the 27.8 kilometer stretch will witness a huge traffic flow, the plaza has been designed to be flexible enough to be able to change at short notices. Besides 16 lanes per direction, another three special lanes have been planned on both sides to accommodate the slow moving vehicles. However, slow moving traffic will not be allowed in the toll lanes."

Significantly, out of the 32 lanes, four lanes in the centre would be 'reversible lanes'. This means, according to the requirements of the volume of traffic flow, lanes on either side could be changed to the configuration of 18 lanes and 14 lanes per direction.

There will be three different color schemes for three different kinds of tolling systems. The lanes with orange signage would be for those vehicles which would have a smart tag attached on the inside of the windshield and expressway. These lanes will be unmanned and will be in the middle of the toll plaza. The lane with blue signage would be for commuters using a prepaid card called the Contactless Smart Card (CSC) with a transaction time of under 3.5 seconds. With touch and go technology, the commuter has to stop and manually swipe the card without worrying about carrying cash for paying toll. The lane with green signage would be the cash lane and the commuter would have to stop and pay cash at the counter.

Another feature, "the cameras installed would generate photographs of all vehicles at the toll plaza. This would not only ensure 100% revenue collection, even local police can get the details of stolen vehicles which pass through this stretch," said an NHAI official.

Besides toll, SOS phones installed at every 2 km. on the highway would help the users to contact control room in case of any emergency. While on an average the light system would be of 40 lux throughout the stretch, the lighting at the toll plaza would be 100 lux.

In order to give the expressway a unique character, the entire expressway has been divided into three zones. The stretch from RTR Palam to Delhi-Gurgaon border would be the VIP segment and white light bulbs will be used with 12 metre inclined poles. The developer would install CCTV cameras till IGI Airport for surveillance of these areas.

The urban segment, which stretches from Delhi-Gurgaon border to Rajiv Chowk, will be using green light fixtures and the third phase from Rajiv Chowk to the place where toll road ends would be known as the trucker's paradise. The color scheme for this stretch will be orange.

The highway is operational since Feb. 2008 and people are having their toll woes and creating traffic jams; more due to people's lack of patience to use it properly. It is necessary traffic thus planned should be strictly enforced.

Many such highways are being developed connecting metros within and connecting to passenger and business hubs. In North, from Delhi to Chandigarh and further excellent Highway is developed connecting Panipat a petrol refinery and textile hub, Kurukshetra an old historic town as a developed tourist and religious pilgrim town and connecting business hubs in Ludhiana, Amritsar and Chandigarh and building good ancillaries roads to Punjab villages and giving flip to rural community. In west Bombay-Pune new highway has expanded the business along; as many manufacturing industries and IT industries are around the areas. This highway is used extensively by commuters and goods carriers. Bangalore to Mysore is another one recently developed to meet the demands of expanding IT and industrial infrastructure around it. Many more are coming up to meet the ever increasing traffic snarls. But important point is people should use it properly for traffic management.

To manage traffic snarls recently, NASSCOM has floated local BPO forums in metro cities, including Gurgaon with high concentration of call centers and BPOs to render support to the local administration in solving infrastructure-related problems. The move aimed at sharing best practices between the administration and the BPO industry in key areas such as safety and security of working women, traffic management and others, the NASSCOM chief said. The cities where these forums have come up include Noida, Bangalore, Chennai, Mumbai, Pune, Hyderabad and others. Since the local administration and police lacked infrastructure in some of the metros, the local BPO forums would assist in certain areas such as road traffic management. "In Bangalore, the Local BPO Forum has offered to assist the traffic police department in managing the traffic of the city in more efficient manner. In some of the metros, the police departments lack the required infrastructure and this is where we can offer to assist them on man power front. The BPO forums also can come forward to share ideas on improving the infrastructure."

RFID is another advance technology being considered to make highways traffic movements a success. The ministry of heavy industries is considering a proposal to make it mandatory for cars manufactured in India to have RFID-enabled tags. It will be the responsibility of car manufacturers to ensure that all new cars have these radio-frequency identification (RFID) tags.

It is believed that RFID tags would help in traffic management as traffic violations by motorists could be tracked and identified. Also, motorists would get charged automatically as soon as they enter a toll area.

In Singapore, public transport buses and trains use passive RFID cards known as EZ-Link cards. Traffic into crowded downtown areas is regulated by variable tolls imposed using an active tagging system combined with the use of stored-value cards (known as cash cards). RFID is also used in Malaysia Expressways payment system, known as 'Touch n Go'. Due to the name and design, the card needs to be touched for usage.

The ministry of urban development has already discussed a similar agenda with many states. The ministry has proposed a 'core area charge' for different cities to reduce traffic congestion in the city's nerve centre. Such as people could end up paying a special levy to drive into Connaught Circus, the heart of the capital city of Delhi.

There are other showcase highways being developed in other metros of Bangalore, Chennai, Mumbai, Hyderabad, Pune, etc. to boost the businesses, commercial and passenger traffic efficiently.

Another technology for intelligent transport system (ITS) is in the offing. You may not have to stop at every toll junction to pay charges. You could be able to pay toll even while driving at 100 km. an hour. The government is planning to frame a policy for intelligent transport system (ITS) that will allow cars to be fitted with onboard unit for deduction of toll charges and various other taxes through credit card.

Another systems being considered under ITS are providing real time data on traffic and routes to the drivers. Travelers will also be able to save time or switch transport modes as per their convenience. They would also be able to pay for parking without cash.

Top officials from ministry of information technology and telecom, urban development ministry, ministry of science, health, ministry of heavy industries, finance ministry and home ministry had a meeting on 12 October 2007 to prepare the guidelines for the proposed ITS policy.

The core group comprising senior officials from all the ministries would frame a model ITS policy and circulate it among all the states for its implementation. If implemented in a time-bound manner, the policy can bring a sea change in traffic management on Indian roads. Increase in the average speed of vehicles and maintaining all safety disciplines simultaneously would be the greatest advantage of the policy.

According to sources, the ITS can also be used in emission based speed enforcement which is based on automated speed enforcement technologies. The goal is not to avoid speeding as such, but to reduce emissions by improving the flow of traffic, avoiding the stop-and-go dynamics that can raise large variations in vehicle speeds and maintaining traffic speeds within a range at which emissions on a gram per km. basis are lowest.

The officials have had several rounds of talks with policymakers of countries like Japan, South Korea, Singapore, China and the US.

Hong Kong has arguably some of the most diverse public transport options on offer. For example, a densely populated, bustling region in Hong Kong is extremely well connected through metro lines, buses, ferries, tram. To assist people make choices based on individual priorities of speed, modes and cost, the Hong Kong Government has developed a Web-based multi-modal public transport query system called Easy Go. It is a bilingual system and helps travelers find optimal traveling routes for users in terms of fewer transfer modes, shortest traveling time and lowest fare (Nov. 14, 2007).

The ministries are together working on single emergency management services where police, fire service, ambulance and accident services can be reached at a single telephone number in case of road accidents on Highways or otherwise (Nov. 14, 2007).

Shipbuilding and Dredging Infrastructure

Shipbuilding, scarcity of bulk carriers and offshore supply vessel in the global market has forced several Indian companies to look at setting up large shipbuilding yards in the country at a total investment of Rs. 10,000 crore. The shipbuilding yards would make specialized offshore vessels, jack-up rigs and chemical tankers, up to 75,000 dead weight tons.

Mukesh Ambani-owned Reliance Group is set to make a splash in shipbuilding and dredging with two separate companies. Sources said Reliance is expected to invest around $1 billion each in two companies and has begun talks with international majors for a strategic tie-up for the dredging business. This $2 billion investment is over and above the $1.3 billion investment committed for the Rewas Port, off Navi Mumbai.

The shipyard will come up at Rewas, where Reliance is setting up a mega port and a special economic zone (SEZ). The company is also looking at a ship repair yard at Kakinada for servicing offshore/platform vessels and rigs. This facility is expected to be the hub for all its offshore activities in the KG basin, where Reliance Industries (RIL) has struck oil and gas in abundance.

The group will spend around $1 billion to build dredgers at its own shipyard and other yards. Plans are to set up a mega dredging company, which will compete with international giants such as Van Oord and Dredging International. Sources said Reliance wants to cash on the two booming sectors of shipbuilding and dredging. As a majority of existing foreign shipyards are full with orders, shipbuilding prices are expected to remain firm for another couple of years. On the dredging side, almost all Indian ports are trying to deepen their berths and approach channels in order to accommodate larger ships. This has increased the demand for dredgers, pushing up charter rates to new highs, while the supply remains sluggish (Sept. 2007). ABN offshore is one of the big shipbuilding company, and Jindal Dredging is big in dredging business.

In Dec. 2007, H.K. Mittal family, promoter of domestic shipping company Mercator said it is setting up two shipbuilding yards, one each in Gujarat and Maharashtra with an investment of Rs. 1,500 crore. Besides the Mittal family, Larsen & Toubro, Reliance Industries, Shipping Corporation of India, SKIL Infrastructure, Good Earth Maritime, Apeejay Shipping have announced plans to enter shipbuilding. Even Tata Group is mulling over to enter shipbuilding because of the huge opportunities that the industry promises.

Existing players such as ABG Shipyard, Bharati Shipyard, Cochin, Hindustan, Mazagon Dock and Goa Shipyard have announced plans to expand their existing facilities. The Central Government has announced that it wants to set up two big shipbuilding yards, one in east coast and another in west coast, each attracting an investment of Rs. 2,000 crore each.

Telecommunication Infrastructure

Telecommunications infrastructure costs form a very high proportion of global investment. With the Internet economy, digital media and other telecommunications activities becoming more established; the need for modern and efficient infrastructure is becoming more critical. The growing demand for broadband services has made this even more so. Some countries like Japan and Korea are leading in this area, but most countries are failing to keep pace with demand.

Telecommunications infrastructure services include setup, maintenance and consulting for all data and voice communications technologies. These products and services include both hard and soft infrastructure both for landline and cell phones and other wireless devices. Hard and soft telecommunications infrastructure focus on hardware products and services.

Hard Telecommunications Infrastructure

- Cable laying services install fiber optic cable or copper cable in buildings and office complexes, or over large distances. LAN and WAN network design services design large-scale networks for communication provider or large enterprise businesses.
- Erect communication towers, set up satellite dishes and install related communications equipment.
- Specialty communications and wireless chips are specialty or proprietary products and accessories related to communications, wireless and telecommunications chip products.

- Network and communication chips are semiconductor integrated circuits (IC) used in telecommunication devices and systems.
- Telephone Software products are also being developed by many Indian companies, in collaboration with foreign companies and outsourcing for foreign telephone companies to be used in telecommunication devices and systems.
- Manufacturing telephone handsets both for landlines and cell phones, and routers.
- Instrument calibration, test equipment and calibrate them to various standards.
- Calibration and repair for vibration, acoustic, electrical/electronic test, environmental, dimensional, NDT, analytical, process and other specialty instruments, sensors and related equipment.
- Communication Link Sub-System: Satellite Communication Link and Terrestrial Communication Links.

Soft Telecommunication Infrastructure

- Specialty communication services are specialty or proprietary services related to voice and data communications.
- Telecommunications infrastructure providers implement technologies such as Voice-over-Internet Protocol (VoIP), broadband exchange, and integrated services digital networks (ISDNs) to facilitate real-time voice, data, and video communications over great distances. These specialty communications infrastructure services may also provide streaming video, network or Internet platform meeting applications, and software demonstration packages. Web-based plug-in technologies include Macromedia Flash, Shockwave, and multimedia players.
- Wireless communications services provide cellular phone service, SMS, WAP and GPRS services to mobile phones.

- Communication services providers include phone companies, satellite companies, and internet service providers (ISP).
- Telephone service providers furnish telephone both landline and cell services to customers.
- Communication site maintenance, services maintain remote communication sites and client-owned (CO) infrastructure and equipment.
- Communications can also be implemented through a wireless infrastructure that permits e-mail, voice, and data communications. For example, users in different areas of a building or worksite can access broadband wireless services to speak with one another via portable, handheld devices that use radio frequency (RF) or satellite communication technologies.
- Specialty communications infrastructure services may also offer hosting services, which provide servers, server-side applications, and scripting to deliver a variety of communications infrastructure technologies.

The globalization has impacted the rapid progress of telecommunication in India. Since 90s, the pace has been very rapid in both landline/fixed lines and cell phones. The cell phones use was revolutionary, increasing the subscribers rapidly and with the increase of new features in cell technology and in cell handsets. It has also expanded from urban telephony to including rural telephony and from luxury and status symbol to necessity and it is ubiquitous in all strata of society. It gives personal as well business connectivity to people and has brought tremendous social change.

This tremendous progress since 90s to date has created the demand for developing telecommunication hard and soft infrastructure, telecommunications infrastructure is being developed to provide landline and mobile telecommunication, VSAT, Internet and broadband services in India. These are being developed by many Indian companies, in collaboration with foreign companies and outsourcing for foreign telephone companies to be used in telecommunication devices and systems.

The snapshots of Indian communication companies in Chapter 3 and Appendix 3 substantiate that.

Defense Infrastructure

The domestic capability of the Indian defense industry is largely concentrated around the production of the PSUs (Public Sector Undertakings) and ordinance factories. This trend is expected to change with the recent selective liberalization of investment in the defense industry both by domestic and international companies; and a sound offset policy. These are expected to create greater private sector participation and facilitate bigger FDI inflows into the Indian defense industry.

Private Investments are on the rise in the Indian Defense Industry. The defense industry in the past has been dominated by the government-run PSUs. This scenario has changed significantly with the Ministry of Defense providing license to private companies to manufacture select aerospace and defense products.

In 2001, the country opened for 100 per cent Indian private sector investments in the defense industry and even allowed foreign direct investment (FDI) of up to 26 per cent in select areas of the defense industry. Some of the key non-PSU industry participants supplying defense equipment and services include Mahindra & Mahindra, Tata Group, Kirloskar Brothers, Larsen & Toubro, Ashok Leyland, Jindal Group, Max Aerospace & Aviation, and Ramoss India.

Public-Private collaborations are increasing in this sector. The defense industry is gradually liberalizing and the public sector is facilitating greater private sector participation in the area of defense goods production. There are about 5,100 companies supplying around 20% to 25% of components and subassemblies to state-owned contractors and the market size is expected to be around $6.20 billion in 2005-06. More than 30 per cent of India's current defense procurement of capital items, is imported, however, this is expected to change with the creation of more public-private partnerships.

India's Offset Policy in defense infrastructure development encourages domestic production. The policy is that any purchase from a foreign supplier in excess of $70 million will require a reinvestment of 30% of the total purchase amount in terms of components and services from India. The offset policy applies to imports by defense PSU's, ordinance factories, and private participants of the industry. India's offset policy for defense goods has been designed to leverage the country's position as a large buyer and exporter. The offset policy is also expected to create market-entry opportunities for mid-rung companies, which are looking at investing in research and development and manufacturing of defense goods. It is conducive for private companies to have a larger presence.

The Government of India has shown keenness in allowing international collaboration for the production of weapon systems, which are purely used for non-lethal purposes. The production of the following weapon systems are expected to be promoted in the future: Technologies & equipment for counter terrorism, Surveillance Communication equipment, and sensors for border management, Cyber security synergies in the field of information technology, and devices to neutralize improvised explosive devices (IEDs). Suppliers and manufacturers of these weapon systems are expected to be some of the chief beneficiaries of the increased indigenization of the production process in the Indian defense industry.

Key areas of growth identified within the industry are expected to arise from the upgradation of the production capacity expansion, technology transfer, and modernization of defense infrastructure.

In the Department of Defense Production (DDP), the vision for the Indian Defense Industry is to be globally competitive while ensuring self-reliance in key areas of defense production. The mandate for the DDP has the following objectives:

(i) Develop with the help of Defense Research & Development Organization (DRDO) and produce a wide range of equipment for the armed forces—on time, of good quality, and at competitive prices.

(ii) Create a diversified, self-reliant and self-sufficient defense-industrial production base.

(iii) Enter into co-development and co-production agreements with other countries.

(iv) Facilitate a meaningful role for the private sector.

(v) Promote defense exports.

To achieve these objectives, India has eight defense public sector undertakings (DPSUs) and the Ordnance Factory Board with 40 factories under it. These are: Bharat Electronics Ltd. (BEL), Bharat Dynamics Ltd. (BDL), Bharat Earth Movers Ltd. (BEML), Hindustan Aeronautics Ltd. (HAL), Mishra Dhatu Nigam Ltd. (MDNL), Mazagon Dock Ltd. (MDL), Goa Shipyard Ltd. (GSL), Garden Reach Shipbuilders and Engineers Ltd. (GRSE), and Ordnance Factory Board (OFB).

Experts in the Ministry of Defense (MoD) deliberated on the global practices in offsets and studied offset programs from a number of countries to formulate the 'Offset Policy' for India defense infrastructure. The experience of HAL, the first Indian DPSU to have dealt with offsets for a long time further substantiated. The Offset Policy as outlined in DDP 2006, and released in August 2006, offers direct offsets best suited as of now to the large defense sector in India.

The offset clause is a recent innovation, initiated by former Defense Secretary Shekhar Dutt while the Transfer of Technology in major deals was mandated by former Prime Minister Rajiv Gandhi in the mid-1980s.

Offset would be applicable in all defense acquisition cases with an indicative cost of over Rs. 300 crores. The Indian defense industry is capable of absorbing the full value of the offsets, which would roughly amount to Rs. 5000 crores per year. A foreign vendor would find the policy simple to implement in practice as MoD would find easy to monitor compliance.

The methods to meet the offset obligations are either direct or indirect offsets. India's policy is to accept direct offsets only for the time being. Indirect offsets of Multipliers, credits, additional weights to offset offers or preferred types, banking and other types of offsets have not been included for the present.

Direct Offsets

A. Contractual Agreements involving Defense Products in the form of:

- Buy Back and Market Access • Co-production • Licensed Production.
- Joint Development and Joint Ventures • Investment (FDI) in Indian Defense R&D and/or infrastructure.

B. Services:

- Repair, maintenance and Overhauling facilities.

C. Software: India has developed a co-terminus application for fulfilment of offset obligations along with the main contract, with provision for extensions on special grounds. As per the DDP 2006, 30% offset obligations are mandatory. This obligation is to be discharged through direct purchases or by executing export orders for defense products and components manufactured by, or services provided by, Indian defense industries, both public and private. Direct foreign investments in Indian defense industries are included for discharge of offset obligation both for infrastructure investments and R&D. In fact, investments and participation in these areas are encouraged. (India strategic India's offset policy Kiran Chadha Aug. 2007.)

Raytheon International President Torkel Patterson says that the radar could be sold to India along with its technology so that it could be integrated on Indian jets like the Tejas Light Combat Aircraft (LCA) but for that there has to be a Transfer of Technology between the Indian and US Governments. The radars are adaptable to any platform, he pointed out. The Active Electronically Scanned Array (AESA) Radar is regarded as a key to modern and future warfare systems. Raytheon's new revolutionary AN/APG-79 AESA radar provides F/A-18 E/F aircrews with powerful new capabilities (India strategic Sept. 2007 New Delhi). Further, Raytheon is in joint venture with L&T for defense equipment production.

IAF expects to induct the new Combat Jets by 2012. The tender has been given for the US Boeing F18, Lockheed Martin F16, Swedish Gripen, European Consortium's Eurofighter,

Russian Mig 35 and French Rafale. Their representatives were invited to the Ministry and handed over the tender documents, technically called Request for Proposals (RfP). MoD spokesman Sitanshu Kar said that the manufacturers are to give their response within six months.

There is a 50 per cent offset clause, under which the winning company will have to invest that much value of the contract in the defense sector in India towards building indigenous capability under Transfer of Technology (ToT). IAF will buy the first lot of 18 aircraft direct from the manufacturer while the remaining 108 aircraft would be gradually assembled and manufactured in India under the ToT agreement.

Representatives of Boeing, Gripen and Lockheed Martin issued statements to say that they would do their best to match and exceed the requirements in the tender, while Boeing's Vice President for Global Strike Systems Chris Chadwick said that his company would develop an economic and technical partnership with Indian companies as part of the offset requirements.

Terms of the RfP are secret but sources said that the new aircraft have to be multi-role that is capable of action against hostile air, surface and maritime targets. They should also have capability for reconnaissance and electronic intelligence roles as well as for midair refueling. Sources said that as far as the F16 is concerned, only comparable models to its Block 60 version with Active Electronically Scanned Array (AESA) radar would be considered. Only the UAE Air Force F16s, acquired from 2004, have this capability.

For the first time, private sector companies in India will be given a substantial role in defense equipment manufacture. The RfP gives a free hand to the six manufacturers to choose their partners from among the public or private sector companies.

Hindustan Aeronautics Limited (HAL) has been mandated as the lead systems integrator, which will finally assemble the aircraft from imported and Indian-made components. The $2 billion HAL has been producing an assortment of Western and Russian aircraft and missiles.

According to a survey published by the India Strategic, India needs to invest $35 to 40 billion by 2025 on military aviation, as it needs to replace and upgrade nearly its entire combat fleet, except the SU 30 MKIs.

IAF has had a very high incidence of accidents, due to lack of training equipment, trainer jets, and new aircraft to match the demands of modern warfare. The new trainer aircraft, BAE Systems' Hawks, will be coming over the next few weeks after a 23 years wait.

The acquisition process over the induction of new systems was crippled in the Ministry of Defense over allegations of bribe in the Bofors gun deal. V.P. Singh, who succeeded Rajiv Gandhi as the Prime Minister, virtually put a stop to all acquisitions and the process of buying new systems began only after Pakistan occupied parts of Indian territory in Kashmir, leading to the 1999 Kargil War (Gulshan Luthra India strategic Aug. 2007).

India will build advanced attack Helicopters. Helicopters are playing an increasingly significant role in military aviation due to their versatile capability in reaching tough terrain and being able to land and lift material without forward motion.

India does not have the required number of helicopters, and most of whatever are available with the armed forces, are 20 years or more old. There is a severe shortage of attack helicopters, particularly those which can operate at high altitudes.

The Indian Air Force (IAF), Army and Navy, as well as the Coast Guard, all need newer and better helicopters for a variety of utility, surveillance and attack roles.

According to HAL Chairman & Managing Director, HAL had invested $40-50 million on expanding its production facilities to help speed up deliveries of aircraft and various systems to the Indian armed forces. HAL's turnover is expected to grow three to five times over the next few years from its current $2 billion figure because of offset advantages and the transfer of technology that would come from arrangements with foreign companies.

Global aerospace majors like Raytheon, Boeing, Lockheed Martin, BAE Systems, Northrop Grumman and EADS are setting up partnerships with the Indian industry to supply and manufacture vital equipment ranging from aircraft and helicopters to long-range detection and attack systems.

There would also be collaboration between the state-run and private industry to create a supply chain for various aircraft and helicopters (Gulshan Luthra, India strategic July 2007).

The army may scrap a 600 million dollar deal for 197 helicopters from an EADS unit because of complaints about the bidding process and the role of agents, an official said. Defense Acquisition Committee is expected to issue a fresh tender for the helicopters in the next financial year, said an official with the committee (3 Dec. 2007).

Boeing Integrated Defense Systems has a rich portfolio of products and services to offer India, such as the combat-proven F/A 18 E/F Super Hornet multi-role fighter, the P-8A Multi-Mission Maritime Aircraft, the heavy-lift CH-47F and MH-47G heavy-lift Chinook helicopters, C4ISR platforms, airborne early warning and control systems, and the T-45 Naval Training System, which includes the T-45 Goshawk trainer aircraft. Indian pilots are today training on Boeing's T-45 Goshawk trainers under a cooperative program with the U.S. Navy. IDS is also a leading provider of aerospace support systems and network-centric operations that have high relevance to India's requirements.

The U.S. Navy and Boeing intend to offer the Super Hornet to the Indian Air Force for its upcoming Medium Multi-role Combat Aircraft competition. In April 2007, Boeing submitted a proposal to develop and deliver eight long-range maritime reconnaissance and anti-submarine warfare aircraft to the Indian Navy. The Boeing P-8I multi-mission maritime aircraft, a variant of the U.S. Navy's P-8A, is currently under consideration by the MoD for India's maritime requirements.

The Hyderabad-MTAR Technologies, which provides machinery to space, defense and nuclear sectors, has received a

$65 million investment from the Blackstone Group. MTAR is looking to expand its highly skilled workforce as it gears up to meet the challenges of achieving significant growth while innovating constantly in these sectors. The company wants to use the funds to build capability to meet the growing demands from the aerospace, nuclear and strategic sector.

The New York-based Blackstone's investment could well signal a trend in the possible inflow of private equity funds into Indian private sector vendors in the country's strategic sectors. The equity investment by Blackstone would be subject to regulatory approval. Under the terms of the transaction, the funding will be a mix of primary and secondary equity.

Lockheed Martin and Wipro Technologies of India will set up a Network Centric Operations Centre in India to develop new network enabled capabilities for the world market. Wipro and Lockheed Martin are committed to build modeling and simulation experimental lab in India—'Ambar Jyoti (Sky Light)', "the lab will develop, demonstrate and experiment with emerging network-enabled capabilities and applications", a Lockheed Martin statement said. Ambar Jyoti provides an opportunity for indigenous development and experimentation to identify future capabilities and requirements in network-centric operations for potential civil and military applications.

"This experimentation and demonstration center is the first of its kind in India, the Indian market gets easier access to such advanced network centric based architectures and concepts as a result of this project", said Chief Operating Officer of Wipro Technologies.

The center is designed to leverage Wipro's embedded, telecom and enterprise expertise in creating data centric solutions for the future. Lockheed Martin and Wipro Technologies will utilize cutting-edge technologies and real environment emulation to develop net-enabled capabilities and solutions to employ against current, real-world problems.

The lab will be networked with Lockheed Martin's other such facilities around the world so that an increased number of more complex, real-time, real-world demonstrations can take place in this Indian facility (India Strategic Aug. 2007).

Space Research Infrastructure

International prestige in science and technology is critical. This is Soft Power. The Indian Space Research Organization (ISRO) has a strong partnership with the Indian industrial sector for space programs execution. Over 500 small, medium, and large-scale enterprises work with ISRO, supplying hardware, undertaking fabrication jobs, and establishing fabrication and test facilities. The Indian industrial sector provides all raw materials and high-tech electronic items required by ISRO and has also contributed toward developing systems for launch vehicle spacecraft, remote sensing, and ground equipment. Around 231 technologies developed by ISRO were transferred to the Indian industrial sector for commercial use. ISRO also undertakes technical consultancy projects for industries.

The Indian space program achieved a major global dimension when, at the end of 2006, the Indian scientific community made a unanimous suggestion for India to undertake a manned space mission as well as an unmanned moon mission. India's moon-dream marks a fundamental policy change in respect of its space program. The scientific community has become more confident about the potential of carrying out such projects successfully. It is also an indication of India's confidence in its economy where it can invest vast amounts in these projects.

NASA is looking forward to the launch of Chandrayaan-1 in June 2008. Not only will it mark the first occasion Indian space launch vehicle but will be carrying advance United States technological payload as well. It is a scientific investigation. The payload is synthetic aperture radar that will help find the presence of water, ice on the moon and the poles.

Cooperation between India and USA in space can be useful for both sides because Indian technical community is superb. Both the countries also signed a framework agreement to institutionalize the possibilities for cooperative activities in successive missions. It will also signal the sustained US-India cooperation in outer space.

During the last few years, ISRO has emerged as a useful agency for the developing countries to launch their satellites. It has so far provided countries like Argentina and Indonesia etc. to launch their satellites. Recently, it launched a spy satellite for Israel. This activity is also helping India in revenue generation and it is expected that in the years to come, India may be able to manage 10% share of this fast growing market.

Recently, India's first commercial rocket was fired into space, carrying a 776-pound Italian satellite that collects data on the origins of universe. The success of this launch is likely to give a major boost to India's brand image in the launch sector. ISRO has already given India a brand image in space research and capabilities.

INSAT series satellites are capable of performing communication, surveillance, reconnaissance functions for armed forces and IRS and The Cartosat imagery is particularly expected to help the armed forces. The knowledge gained in rocket science for missile developments is useful. The space infrastructure plays a major role in establishing an Aerospace Command by the three services to ensure the country's security. The Indian Space Research Organization (ISRO) has a strong partnership with the Indian industrial sector for space programs execution.

The Indian Remote Sensing (IRS) satellite for earth observation, INSAT for communication and powerful launch vehicles like Polar Satellite Launch Vehicle (PSLV) and Geosynchronous Satellite Launch Vehicle (GSLV) for orbiting the satellites have demonstrated the power of indigenous technology and skills of home-grown scientists.

Above all, India is a leading country in harnessing advanced space technology for benefiting the common man. The national resource planning, utilization for agriculture, forestry, fisheries, etc., as well as reaching out to people in far-flung places by providing tele-medicine and tele-education services are some of the finest examples of space applications.

Nuclear Power Infrastructure

India does need nuclear power both for civilian and military nuclear programs. There is interest by international powers and industries to help India set up Nuclear Power Infrastructure.

The California-based Dauvergne Brothers Inc. (DBI), an American company, anxious to enter the Indian market, has offered to build commercial nuclear power reactors in the country. While India is still debating how to make the Indo-US nuclear deal work.

These reactors will rely entirely on India's thorium resources—except at the start—and thereby remove the objections of critics. Its novel type of thorium breeder reactor is fuelled with fissile material like uranium only once when it is started. It runs for its full operational life on Uranium-233 (or U-233) bred in its core from thorium. India has plenty of thorium. It cannot be directly burned in a reactor. It has to be converted into fissile U-233. India's own thorium utilization strategy hinges on reprocessing—a contentious issue between India and the US. The DBI claims its design is tailor-made for the Indian situation.

According to the company, its reactor "starts up using conventional uranium-based nuclear fuels, and incrementally converts to an all thorium fuel cycle over a period of 10 years, using India's abundant supply of thorium ores to maintain energy independence".

"International agreements between India and uranium-source nations to use proliferation-resistant fuels in the DBI Reactor Program, subject to IAEA monitoring, could serve the link between civilian and military nuclear programs in India, without adversely affecting India's ability to scale up the DBI Reactor Program using native thorium in future generations," the company said (K.S. Jayaraman India Strategic October 2007).

On participating in nuclear power projects, White of GE said, "We are open to entering the Indian market as an owner or an operator." Eyeing the huge scope for nuclear energy in India after the nuclear co-operation agreement with the US goes through, White said the company was open for either setting up new plants or participating in expansion of existing facilities. He added that GE would be able to provide new reactors with their technologies—Advanced Boiling Water Reactor (ABWR) and ESBWR. To be successful in India, GE would need to tie-up with local Indian companies in the field turbines, and so on, and even in managing nuclear plants.

Tourism Infrastructure

The infrastructure for tourism includes basic infrastructure components like airports, railways, roads, waterways; amenities like electricity, water supply, drainage, sewage. Though they do not form a major share of tourist consumption; several infrastructure sectors like power telecommunication, water supply, roads and some production sectors like travel items, sports equipment, photographic materials, medicines and cosmetics are included in this category. The tourism industry also includes establishments, whose products are mainly sold to visitors, tourism infrastructure focuses on expansion of facilities like hotels, restaurants, tourist coaches, cars, air taxis, entertainment and recreational facilities and so forth. These activities make demands for goods and services, and the establishments which provide such services are considered as part of the tourism industry.

National Strategy: Tourism

Planning for sustainable development of tourism, therefore, involves a national strategy for the development of tourism that has recently been developed for synergizing the activities of different infrastructure sectors, the state governments and the private sector for tourism development. The specific components of the strategy include:

Infrastructure development, product development and diversification including development of mega-tourism resorts; entrepreneurial development and promotion of self-employment opportunities; enhanced tourist facilitation; research and computerization in all kinds of tourism; environmental protection and cultural preservation; promotion and marketing; and monitoring, evaluation and strengthening of tourist organizations.

Tourism has varied focuses from historical, cultural, religious-pilgrimage, wildlife, water sports, mountaineering, trekking and sports, health oriented tourism, cruise tourism, rural tourism and rail tourism, etc.

Tourism is a Versatile Sector

Indian tourism offers one of the most diverse products on the global scene. India has 26 world heritage sites. It is divided into 25 bio-geographic zones and has wide ranging eco-tourism products. Apart from this, India has a 6,000 km. coastline and dozens of beaches. India's great ethnic diversity translates into a wide variety of cuisine and culture. India has a vast and beautiful coastline and hence the potential to develop cruise tourism.

India also has a large number of villages, plantations and adventure locations. India is home to a great variety of wildlife and its reserves are well known throughout the world. It also has one of the world's biggest railway systems opening possibilities for those interested in rail tourism.

India also has excellent hospitals offering affordable medicare and traditional healthcare systems like Ayurved and promoting medical tourism also through latest and advance medical treatments and technology. The Ministry of Tourism has taken several initiatives, in partnership with the private sector, to promote India as a destination for medical tourism and make it a global health destination. Several promotional measures like road shows and developing publicity material have been undertaken for the same. Some of the main advantages that India has are as under:

(i) It has world class doctors and hospitals.

(ii) The cost of treatment is 1/5th of costs in the west.

(iii) Eastern healthcare wisdom along with the expertise of western medicine is available.

A concept of rural tourism has been developed for showcasing the art, crafts and culture of rural India and for creating gainful employment in villages with tourism potential. Rural tourism holds immense potential for India, where 74 per cent of the population resides in its 7 million villages. Thrust is being provided to rural tourism to spread tourism and its socio-economic benefits to rural regions.

International Convention Centers of the global standard are considered to be one of the important segments for promoting India as an attractive tourist destination in the global market. Ministry of finance has already identified New Delhi, Mumbai, Bangalore, Goa and Jaipur for opening of world-class convention centers. Several initiatives have been taken up by way of public-private partnership to develop small convention centers of high standard. India is undoubtedly a unique Convention Destination as it offers cultural and heritage sites, the exotic and mystical, excellent facilities of beach and adventure holidays which can be combined as pre- and post-conference tours.

In addition to this India organizes numerous fairs and festivals, which are quite attractive to foreigners. Tourist facilities are developed accordingly and people both domestic and foreign visit them according to their interests. People may visit independently or go with group package tours.

The globalization has increased the foot falls not only in world known monuments like Taj Mahal—the wonder in marble, Kutub Minar—the highest Minar and the super artistic Temples of Khajurai; but people even enjoy and visit traditional culinary art and cuisine of different regions. Certain modern business spots, hubs, metros, dams and industries attract people from around the globe to visit India with the slogan 'incredible'.

Versatile sectors of tourism offer varied investment opportunities such as in Hotel industry, Service apartments, Adventure Tourism, Health Tourism, Convention centers, Rural Tourism, Wildlife Tourism, Highway Tourism and Amusement Parks, etc.

National Tourism Policy

Responsibility for tourism development is a common endeavour of all agencies vitally concerned with tourism at central and state levels, including public and private sectors enterprises; airlines, railways and road transport systems;

municipal and local bodies as well as cultural and educational institutions.

It further provided an action plan based on a "travel circuit" concept to maximize the benefits of tourism. The plan proposed to achieve intensive development of selected circuits, dispel the tendency of concentration in a few urban centers, encourage the diversification of tourist attractions and open economically-backward areas which have many tourist attractions. The strategy for achieving the national objective is to establish all inclusive "Special Tourism Areas" and undertake intensive infrastructure development for identified circuits and destinations. Tourist attractions have to be affordable for all class of people; therefore varied infrastructure development would be mixed—from luxurious to basic facilities but clean and safe.

The National Tourism Policy was formulated in the year 2002. Broadly, the "Policy" attempts to:

(i) Position tourism as a major engine of economic growth;

(ii) Harness the direct and multiplier effects of tourism for employment generation, economic development and providing impetus to rural tourism;

(iii) Focus on domestic tourism as a major driver of tourism growth;

(iv) Position India as a global brand to take advantage of the burgeoning global travel trade and the vast untapped potential of India as a destination;

(v) Acknowledges the critical role of private sector with government working as a pro-active facilitator and catalyst;

(vi) Create and develop integrated tourism circuits based on India's unique civilization, heritage, and culture in partnership with States, private sector and other agencies; and

(vii) Ensure that the tourist to India gets physically invigorated, mentally rejuvenated, culturally enriched, spiritually elevated and "feel India from within".

Development Schemes: Tourism

Since most infrastructure elements and the delivery systems are within the purview of the state governments or private sector, tourism infrastructure is being developed mainly with financial assistance to state and U.T. governments and by providing various incentives to private entrepreneurs.

Specific schemes for which financial assistance is provided to the states include the following:

(a) Construction schemes, Forest lodges, Tented accommodation, Tourist complexes/tourist lodges, Wayside amenities Motel/restaurants, Tourist reception centers, Pilgrim sheds/dormitories, etc. at pilgrimage places. Public conveniences.

(b) Tourist transport: Mini-buses, jeeps and elephants, etc. for wildlife viewing, cruise boats, ferry launchers, etc. for water transport, tourist coaches in selected circuits and special tourist trains.

Under this pattern, the Central Department of Tourism meets almost the entire expenditure, except the cost of land and interior decoration in the case of construction projects. Funding is given by way of grant-in-aid towards project.

Incentives to private entrepreneurs hotels and tourism-related activities have been declared as a priority sector for foreign investment. As a result, foreign equity participation in tourism projects is automatically allowed up to 51 per cent, and higher percentages of foreign equity can be approved on a case-by-case basis. Tourism industries are also eligible for a number of incentives, such as interest subsidy, income tax exemption, reduced customs duty, etc. Specific incentive is given for approved hotels up to the 3-star category and heritage hotels outside the four metro-cities which are eligible for an interest subsidy for loans from the Industrial Finance Corporation of India.

In order to encourage the owners of heritage properties to convert palaces, forts, havelis, etc. of any size into heritage hotels, a capital subsidy scheme was introduced since May 1993. Under the scheme, a capital subsidy of 10 per cent of the project cost or Rs. 500,000, which ever is less, is available for developing any structure of 75 years or older as a heritage hotel.

Domestic travel agents and tour operators are given assistance to develop markets abroad. Assistance is given for market research, promotional visits abroad, and so forth. Travel agents have credit ratings and they organize group package tours through land, water and air travel. Travel agents, tourist establishments, hotels, restaurants, resorts and other products are registered to safeguard them for safety and authenticity.

Indian Tourism as an Engine of Economic Growth: Tourism sector holds immense potential for Indian economy. Tourism sector has the potential to stimulate other economic sectors through its backward and forward linkages and cross-sectional synergies with sectors like agriculture, horticulture, handicrafts, transport, construction, etc. Recognizing the importance of this sector, the provision for building tourist infrastructure has been increased in country's budget from US $95.6 million in 2006-07 to US $117.5 million in 2007-08. According to the World Travel and Tourism Council, India's travel and tourism (T&T) industry is expected to contribute 2.1 per cent to GDP in 2006 (INR 713.8 billion or US $16.3 billion).

In the first half of the Annual Plan period of 2005-06, the Ministry of Tourism has taken several initiatives in the field of infrastructure development and positioning Indian tourism as a major engine for economic growth. These include emphasis for developing the existing and new destinations to world-class standards; and thus developing the traditional and modern together. There is focus on improvement of connectivity to important destinations by road, rail or air; and identifying 10-15 new destinations or circuits by each state and Union territory for development to world class standard with all the required infrastructure components.

Entertainment Economy

The India's entertainment sector can be divided into two broad areas: film and television; and the leisure industry. Cable television is the largest revenue earner with television broadcasting and television production. Beside cable TV, other modes are direct home broadcasting through satellite, Dish TV and IPTV through broadband. Next is film.

Film: In 2001, film was accorded 'industry' status by the Indian Government thus making it eligible for film financing from banks and financial institutions while the Industrial Development Bank of India (IDBI) set up the country's first film fund worth 100 crores. Prior to that many times the producers have to get the big funds from the underground parties and have to be dictated by them and few times even film people have been murdered when there was difference of opinion. Therefore, getting loans is a big welcome change.

In the entertainment segment, the films sector has been given the industry status by the government. Estimates show that the entertainment industry is currently generating revenue of Rs. 100 billion and this will be able to increase by Rs. 315 billion by the year 2005. These measures include allowing listing a company with 10% public ownership akin to the information technology industry. The FM radio broadcasting has been privatized. The current size of film segment, according to the latest estimate, is worth Rs. 22 billion. The average growth budget for the films has been increasing by 15% per annum.

The Indian film industry has experienced significant growth over many years, evolving into a fully-fledged economic sector marked by large-scale commercialization. Industry reforms and liberalization has attracted foreign investment and allowed foreign companies to enter the market quickly, bringing innovative technologies. India has the world's largest film industry and the following information shows the scale and trends of the industry. India has produced more than 70,000 feature films and thousands of short documentary films in 52 different languages and dialects.

There is a greater focus on state-of-the-art technologies in cinematographic equipment, post-production, and exhibition since government allows import of these equipments. Now even many Indian reputable companies further these endeavours such as Applause films of Aditya Birla Group and Adlabs films of Anil Ambani Group. These lend more credibility to such endeavours with funds and good management practices. According to a PWC-Ficci report (2007), the film-making and distribution space in India is increasingly being supported by corporates; with more than half of the total film releases in 2006 being funded by corporates. The domestic box office market is expected to grow at a CAGR of 13% and double to an estimated Rs. 11,900 crore over the next five years.

Approximately 1000 films are produced annually with an average of $2.36 million spent on each film with a combined turnover of around $1.9 billion annually. Nationwide, more than 20 million people watch a film daily in over 13,000 theatres. Changes in the preferences of the Indian viewing public have prompted a shift towards modern cinema houses with Dolby sound systems and facilities for 3-D animation effects. This has driven an increase in demand for capital equipment and infrastructure.

All the cinema houses with latest technology and architecture are situated in urban areas and none is in rural areas. Many of the films produced are about rural life and documentaries are on village related topics. But the ruralities are not exposed to them as there are no cinema houses to screen. Earlier, some of the prize winning documentaries used to be screened in villages through mobile cinema but no longer. Actually, there is greater interest among the ruralites to view these. These days they are able to watch these through TV and DVDs. It is high time that India's private sector should invest in rural cinema houses infrastructure—one cinema house for a cluster of villages.

Entertainment companies are trying to follow the Hollywood studio model, where a company owns the entire value chain of film-making. While companies like Adlabs and UTV have entered into film distribution and exhibition, exhibitors like PVR are entering the film making space. In a bid to transform themselves into complete studios, movie distribution companies; home video players are also joining the bandwagon and want to control IPR.

The films produced in many regional languages are watched by Indian diasporas around the world with English subtitles. They have access to these films since the Indian Government allows distribution to foreign companies or setting up their own distribution system. Moreover, Indian films expose them to the changing lifestyles, problems and issues in socio-political life and the changing scenario of cultural lives in Indian society. It brings them nearer to home as many of them may not have visited India for years. This communication medium binds them.

According to the PWC-Ficci report, the current size of the total film entertainment business in India is Rs. 8,450 crore in 2006 and expected to grow to Rs. 17,500 crore by 2011. Shemaroo which started as a film distribution company owns the satellite and cable rights for over 700 films, VCD and DVD rights for over 1000 films and the terrestrial television rights (India and rest of the world) for more than 150 films. The company is now making Hindi and regional movies and is also quiet bullish about its animation business. Venus Movies initially produced non-film albums and gradually bagged worldwide rights of Bollywood film music. The company then evolved into producing motion pictures and has become one of the top production houses in Bollywood. The company has an integrated business model covering the entire value chain from motion pictures production and record label to distribution worldwide. Moser Baer in 2007 has entered production of Tamil, Hindi and other regional language DVDs on special photovoltaic CDs. This will produce a film DVD in the range of Rs. 5-10. These DVDs cannot be recorded again. People will not rent rather they would buy them.

Television: Another high growth segment of the entertainment industry is the television broadcasting. The present size of this segment is estimated to be Rs. 35 billion. The subscription revenues of the television channels are estimated to be around Rs. 25 billion currently. There are thirty-five million households having access to about seventy channels the cable networks. The penetration of cable TV, particularly in the rural segment is expected to grow by 12% in the coming years.

In the television and cable industry, broadcasters are investing in the latest technology and additional services driven by the growth in subscription rates, percentage of ad spend and the customer base for satellite and cable television.

Despite jarring economic inequities, TV has provided diverse people with a sense of national community during a period of economic, social and political transformation. It is medium through which people have been sharing the experience of new aspirations and new anxieties.

The future primary drivers for the entertainment industry will be growth in GDP, changes in demographic and the adoption of digital technology by the industry.

Indian filmmakers are already working with Australian post-production companies (and vice versa) in film and television production, as well as television commercials and music video production. Many programs from around the world are exchanged and beamed through Indian TV; especially from UK, USA, and Pakistan, etc. These facilitate to understand their ways of life and we can react to many of the issues. Government should develop exchange program infrastructure to ease these.

The music industry is dominated by music cassettes sale rather than CDs. The music industry in India's expected growth rate of 18-20% in the coming years.

News in Media: Earlier, till 2006 Indian Government has been allowing expansion of entertainment and news channels. In 2007, India is trying to curtail the number of news channels and allow only a smaller body of news channels. Since a greater number is only wasting media space, repeating the same news again and again, false reporting like sting reporting to create sensationalism.

The News Broadcasters' Association of India echoed the sentiment, decrying both misuse of sting operations by a few broadcasters and the government's intent to utilize such misuse to tighten control over the media, amounting to censorship. "IBF has noted a series of highly arbitrary & coercive punishments that the ministry has delivered during the last year to a number of broadcasters at its will. All these punishments have been meted out without following any transparent procedure and violating the basic principle of natural justice," said the strongly-worded statement by the foundation.

The IBF also stated its intention to develop and enforce a socially-relevant code of ethics among its members. However, it will not accept arbitrariness, lack of transparency and stranglehold on media. The NBA unequivocally condemned any attempt by anyone to fabricate news and attempt to gain popularity at the cost of journalistic integrity.

However, this does not mean that sting operations are wrong in principle. "The NBA believes that sting operations are a legitimate journalistic tool and means of investigation, but like all powerful tools, they have to be used with care and responsibility." News Broadcasters' Association also criticized the recent instances of suspension of licensed TV channels.

Walt Disney is planning to expand its presence in India. Sources said that they want to raise their existing stake in UTV. Analysts said that business wise, it seems a perfect fit because UTV is involved in production and is going in a big way in that domain, with UTV Motion Pictures. It has just got a listing for that subsidiary. They are also into animation and have made two acquisitions in that space. Walt Disney has to look at production in India in a big way and the animation segment, which are already in the US. This would seem like a business fit for them as well.

Leisure Industry: With investment in new entertainment parks (amusement, theme, water parks) and family entertainment centers, the Indian amusement industry is likely to become a multi-billion dollar industry in the 21st century. The specialty park segment—which represents only a fraction of the fast growing leisure industry—has secured investments in the range of A$45-50 million and is set to grow almost 100 per cent annually in the next five years. Corporate players in the Indian leisure industry are developing facilities in key cities including Delhi, Chennai, Bangalore, Mumbai and Ahmedabad. Many sports clubs, resorts, and games facilities, such as go-kart tracks, are being established in major cities and are gradually extending to larger towns. The number of indoor facilities for golf and cricket, bowling alleys, video games parlors, water parks, and other recreation centers are also on the rise.

Opportunities exist for multiplex cinema design, construction and management, the provision of telecommunication and broadcasting equipment, film studio management, and post-production facilities. Opportunities exist to provide special purpose technology and equipment for such facilities, and construction and management services.

Several companies are developing multipurpose entertainment and leisure entities that include, amusement parks, recreational facilities, games, food courts and multiplexes. With increasing reforms and opening up of the sector, opportunity exists for foreign companies to invest in infrastructure development in this sector. Top industrial houses such as Modi Entertainment, United Television and Sony Corporation have already expressed their interest.

IBM and Crest Communications, the leading company for computer-generated animation in India, announced that IBM will provide and implement an end-to-end open standards-based technology infrastructure for Crest's next generation digital animation studio. The first of its kind in India, IBM will create an integrated solution for Crest based on IBM hardware, software and services and supported by IBM Global Financing offerings.

The recreation and leisure industries are promising areas for investment with India's rising incomes and living standards, and significant expansion of the middle class, creating a large potential market. The existing facilities are inadequate to service the target 350 million customers.

Entertainment companies need to think of consumers as social networks. Media literacy is important. Restricting a child's TV or computer time is fine but totally banning is overreaction. Kids use media in both constructive and destructive ways. Why not have them as empowered participants in the new media landscape.

When it comes to cutting edge media issues, it is important: how we absorb, influence and generate pop culture content in today's multiplatform marketplace; how the entertainment industry keeps pace with changing behaviors and technologies, how educators may approach teaching media literacy, and how fans communities are rewriting the rules for all of these.

Postal Infrastructure

Postal service is important infrastructure for any growing economy; which needs extensive and quick services and reasonable price. In India postal service is owned by government and it has not grown with the boom. The private courier services have stepped in and they are doing remarkably well in delivery of the letters, parcels, etc. in matter of hrs locally, nationally and internationally. Therefore, all business enterprises and individuals patronize them and the delivery is quick and charges are low and service is excellent. This has cut down in the postal revenues considerably but government is not able to boost it rather in 2007 government wanted to curtail the private courier services by not allowing it to carry certain kind of letters and parcels but a country wide agitation by couriers and business enterprises did not allow this rule to operate.

The Express industry today is an important one and is among the major driving forces of the country's economic growth. With manufacturing emerging as a star industry in India, we see huge opportunities to support the global commerce needs of Indian companies.

Courier Services: Express industry remains one of the fastest growing segments of the Indian logistics space, due to the exponential growth of banking products and e-commerce. "Our segment is moving at a rapid rate. We were the second fastest industry for a long time after information technology sector. Now with the slow down in IT, this industry is the fastest growing, said a Mumbai-based player. Courier companies also piggy ride on expansion of banking activities. Even increasing use of cards—credit cards, debit cards, smart cards—have provided courier services a platform for growth which was not there before.

Big players such as Blue Dart, DTDC and AFL WIZ have revised their charges by 15-20% on account of the rise in fuel prices in 2008 and there are indications that courier rates are likely to be hiked yet again by at least 3%. Transportation constitutes 50-60% of total cost for the express industry.

"Express cargo delivery companies are rapidly ramping up their operations to take advantage of the opportunities thrown up by the massive growth in retail and manufacturing segments. The timing, therefore, is right, and we believe that UPS Jetair strategic tie-up with AFL, with its well established extensive domestic network in India, will allow us to reach out to a wider customer base," UPS Jetair Express managing director said.

Postal telegraph system does exist but it is losing its value because of easy and less expensive and quick telecom connectivity especially by mobile telephones and Internet is another facilitator for it. Postal services' focus on small savings is no longer lucrative for people as many other reliable instruments of investment for small savings have come up and it is time post office should give up this for banking and other services.

The Indian Postal (IP) system is a vast infrastructure providing ultimate "access" for poor people to basic services, the last mile connectivity, both literally and along the development path, to a billion people. This precise connectivity with billion people can be leveraged by the postal department to spread other value added services of government like development programs, implementation of schemes and instituting change in the grassroots level. No other organization in India can boast of such large connectivity with huge mass of people and bear such large influence on Indian masses.

Government has been thinking of revamping the postal infrastructure by curtailing certain services, introducing new and privatizing some in order to raise revenue. Even the department of post is looking to sell space in over one-lakh post offices to retailers.

Since 2004, post offices have been selling insurance and mutual fund schemes of private sector players like Reliance and UTI. And now the department hopes it will earn at least 10% of its revenue by leasing space for other products too.

Since so far in the economic boom scenario and changing business and consumer lifestyles, it is a losing proposition.

Hence, there is need for adequate costing structures for activities and services undertaken by the IP department in order to measure profitability and analyze from that perspective as to understand profitable and loss making services. With adequate costing structures and managerial control IP can transform itself into a viable profitable organization like private courier services.

Even structural changes such as more decentralization and greater decision-making authority to regional centers to make them viable and profit making regions would help and provide adequate incentives to grow and reach wider audience. Postal bureaucracy to function effectively requires effective management control structures, a commercial focus and incentive schemes.

Energy Sector: Power, Oil, Petrol and Gas

How do we build, run or even maintain these physical infrastructures. These demand energy, i.e. power, oil, petrol and gas. We focus on the energy resources—we do produce some of these indigenously, some we import and also make efforts to expand our own resources. We also need financial resources to create energy resources. We have focused on this in Chapter 6.

Power

We focus on power generation, transmission and distribution. There is hydrothermal electricity production through hydro projects such as Bhakra-Nangal, and Neyveli Lignite Corporation's principal activities are exploration of lignite mines and power generation. It generates power by using lignite as fuel. Tata Power Company generates, transmits and distributes power.

Power Grid Corporation of India (PGCIL) owns and operates most of India's interstate and inter-regional electric power transmission system. Power Finance Corporation (PFC), Power Trading Company (PTC), and Rural Electrification Corporation are lending institutions in the power sector. PTC principal activity is to provide power-trading services through purchase from surplus utilities and sales to deficit ones. It catalyses the development of power projects and is also the identified nodal agency for cross, border trading and exchange of power with the neighboring countries. It has cross-border operations in Nepal, Bhutan and Bangladesh.

Some of the companies, Tata Power, NTPC, L&T, Lanco Infratech, Essar Power, Sterlite Industries, Jindal Steel and Power, Reliance Power and Torrent Power are involved in distribution and transmission of power. There are many other big and small Indian companies which are into power generation, transmission and distribution.

Punj Lloyd Company and many other companies provide engineering, designing, procurement, construction and project management services for energy industry and infrastructure sector projects.

Bhilwara Energy is firming up plans to set up 200 MW geothermal power plants in the country at an investment of around Rs. 2,500 crore in the next 4-5 years. It has entered Nepal's hydropower sector in collaboration. It is executing two projects in collaboration with Nepal-based Triveni group. The work is likely to be completed by mid-2010. Bhilwara also plans to undertake 14 more hydropower projects with a total capacity of 1500-2000 MW in Nepal.

It has tied up with Iceland-based investment bank Glitnir for the geothermal project, which would be an equity partner. They are in the process of identifying sites where we can put up geothermal plants. Ladakh, Chhattisgarh, Arunachal Pradesh, Himachal Pradesh and the Andamans are considered potential areas where investments could be made. "A high load factor of 80-85% in geothermal compensates the higher initial capital expenditure compared to hydropower. Plus, there is hardly any operational cost in running geothermal plants."

The India's growth story has attracted investors across the world, but can the energy sector provide enough power to sustain this boom? Addressing such crucial issues has become almost imperative, given that the country is still dependent on large-scale imports to meet its energy requirements.

Currently in 2007, what are the demand and supply scenarios in various energy segments—from power to petroleum and alternative fuels? What is government's initiative towards energy conservation? This is highlighted in the integrated energy policy of government.

According to the Integrated Energy Policy (IEP), for a sustained growth rate of 8% till 2031-32, India needs to increase its primary energy supply by three-four times, and its electricity generation capacity by five-six times as compared to 2003-04. By 2031-32, power generation capacity must increase to nearly 8,00,000 MW from the current capacity of around 160,000 MW, including captive plants. Petroleum, gas, coal, renewable energy are among the issues that need immediate attention.

Economic times organized 'Energize India 2007'—a one-day summit—in the Capital on October 5, 2007 to deliberate on some of the crucial issues that need to be addressed if India were to sustain its double-digit growth in the years to come.

The summit focused on discussions on the role of government in making policies to energy conservation techniques and the pricing issues; and on the energy policy in India in the light of the IEP. The panelists discussed the issue of energy security and its relation to GDP, the challenge of achieving electricity for all, exploring new potentials of sectors like coal and the challenge of capacity addition.

Referring to energy policies, Deputy Chairman, Planning Commission, said that the current oil pricing policy is 'unsustainable'. He added that the rise in energy cost must be passed on to users. The fuel subsidy phase out could represent the government policy in the future. Prime Minister also emphasized that it is important that subsidies be restructured. Infrastructure development is critical for 9% growth, he said.

Energy pricing, would focus on market dynamics and constrains, given the different market conditions under which each energy commodity operates. As highlighted in the integrated energy policy, while some energy segments like the hydrocarbon sector have moved ahead, with market-determined prices kicking in at least partially, some others like power still continue to be completely regulated. In some segments, like auto fuel, the government has failed to implement even stated policies because of political compulsions.

The government's goal of electricity power for all by 2012 seems to be a bit of tall order and look around and you will know why, the cities power cut are facts of life, so you can imagine the plight of the villages.

Sixty years after the India's independence, 56% of rural India is without electricity. It took 50 years for the country to produce one lakh megawatt of power, now the government is hopeful of generating another one lakh or 90,000 megawatt of power within the next 10 years. Is this target attainable? To add just 10,000 megawatt calls for an investment of around Rs. 40,000 crore plus every year and additional money has to be invested in transmission and distribution. Where do we get this kind of money? Look at the State Electricity Boards, they continue to bleed, the reason being huge subsidies and power thefts. Even though we hear of private sectors' ambitious plans, there's still a bit of hesitancy.

The installed capacity in India is 1 lakh 35 thousand megawatts, peak load in India is 100 thousand megawatts, service peak load is 85,000 megawatts. So actually we have more installed capacity than we need at the moment, yet we can't service the peak load. We can service just about 85% of that.

What the power sector needs is the kind of reforms one has seen in the telecom sector. Reforms and funding are crucial for the growth of the power sector. A serious power shortage could jeopardize India's plans for double-digit growth. So what can be done to make things better?

Why we do not have enough power? There are two issues. One issue is that power is there, but it gets bottled up. There are power stations but they cannot be run efficiently; either for lack of money to buy coal, or for spares and pay wages. Second issue is lack of adequate investment in other infrastructure that is transmission and distribution. The country has been rather over focused on the generation capacity and under played these two.

Getting finance for power investment is not a problem and power sector today is a very attractive investment. Plenty of funds are available both in India and abroad. But we are not creating the right type of investment climate. We have to build investors' confidence and give right signals to developers and investors through institutional development, administrative and policy reforms and policy review on continuous basis.

The serious commitments of the promoters, as also of the government can add to their confidence. In fact, private equity is getting interested in the power sector companies where they find the linkages especially for the procurement of coal is strong.

We had a target of 45,000 MW and about 25,000 was added in 10th plan because some of the projects did not go through. There was some hesitation on the private developers. Presently, the private developers have shown additional interest in the electricity sector. There is a change in the attitude of the private sector also. Some of the public-private participation is showing signals of positive response. The advantage of public-private partnership is that the general public expects the private players to perform and the performance comes as a benchmark rather than a government owned entity. To make one lakh megawatt additionally by 2012, both public and private sector investments and the third one public-private participation should co-exist.

Ultra mega power project is a good initiative, the response for the ultra mega power projects has shown that the Indian investment climate and the capital inflows is booming and there is a greater interest by the developers and that's a positive signal, which we have to tap.

Case I—Bidding in ultra mega power project, the project is being offered to the best or most competitive bidder. By and large, most of the landmark has been done by the initial entity that is Power Finance Corporation. After winning the bid, the private investor walks into that company and starts rolling forward. In this case, state or center sector, develops a project and offer on competitive bidding.

In Case II—Bidding, private sector is required to bid against the tender from distribution companies. Here no project is being given, developer has to develop his own project, and developer has to find a way of reaching the power to remote ends. If somebody has a plant in Chhattisgarh or Orissa, he has to find a way of reaching the power there. In Case I bidding, developed project is offered and also the off-taker guarantees the transmission.

Among Ultra mega power projects; Tilaiya project is the fourth in a row after Sasan, Mundra and Krishnapatnam projects. While the Sasan and Mundra projects have already been awarded to Reliance Power and Tata Power, respectively, price bids for the Krishnapatnam plant were opened recently in Nov. 2007. Reliance Power has emerged as the lowest bidder for the Krishnapatnam Project, outbidding engineering firm L&T and Vedanta Group firm Sterlite. Thirteen companies are bidding for Tilaiya project—Tata Power, NTPC, L&T, Lanco Infratech, Essar Power, Sterlite Industries, Jindal Steel and Power, Torrent Power, GVK, AES and Dian Wijaya (Malaysia), sources said.

The issue of fuel availability is crucial for power generation. The country has a lot of coal resources. However, by and large, these have been reserved for the public sector. There is shortage of coal. Coal India is not able to take out enough quantity of coal; the coal blocks are not being allotted to the developers; an allocation of coal blocks to the private sector in enough quantities can help. Otherwise developers are left with the alternative of importing coal. The government itself has issued the advisory that coal based plants should import coal.

Government has planned massive addition to the power generation capacity in the country, besides, keeping with the goal of providing power for all by 2012, the government will give 90 per cent subsidy for providing electricity to 1.34 lakh villages in the country, the government has decided for capacity addition of 78,000 MW. There will also be some addition taking place on account of non-conventional energy as well as power produced from lignite. There is estimated power shortage of 22,000 MW in the country at present. Orders for generating 56,000 MW of power has already been placed, while that for the remaining capacity would be placed by March 2008. However, there are difficulties in procuring equipment required to generate power. The capacities for equipment like boiler and turbines have been booked till 2012. The government is also trying to get technology for supercritical machines. "Power situation should ease over the next few years and people would get power as easily as they get telephone these days".

The power ministry has recommended income tax exemption limit hike to Rs. 1,50,000 vs Rs. 1,00,000 for a tax relief window for investment in power sector only.

It suggests that investments to decentralized power projects, micro- and mini-hydropower projects would be treated as investments in priority sector. Ministry has also written to RBI that the banks should include lending to mini- and micro-hydropower projects as priority sector lending, banks under RBI guidelines, have to set aside 40% of their loan portfolio for priority sector obligations.

"There are three snags in the energy policy which are likely to slow down distribution and transmission of power: first, the transmission projects such as Accelerated Power Development and Reforms Program (APDRP) and Rajiv Gandhi Grameen Vidyutikaran Yojana (RGGVY) are being implemented by the government with a view to improve the transmission and distribution systems in the country. This, along with the restructuring of the distribution sector in the states, has led to an increased demand for downstream products such as meters, power factor correction devices, distribution transformers and switchgear, etc. These projects have been delayed as the government has been slow in sanctioning funds. Thus, the companies have lost confidence to invest heavily in the equipment manufacturing," said Indian Electrical and Electronics Manufacturers Association (IEEMA) secretary general. The government has to be consistent and inform the equipment manufacturer of delays.

The second snag is that despite the repeated requests from various organizations and institutions in power sector, the government has not yet awarded infrastructure status to the transmission sector. Such status suggests lesser tax burden for companies in the sector. Currently, roads, ports and airports, which have the infrastructure status, are enjoying income-tax concession under Section 80 1(a) of the I-T Act.

The third snag is some of the electrical products for the power industry fall under the Packaged Commodities Act. As these products are not directly used by consumers, the system creates operational problem. Under the Act, it is mandatory that the products should be packaged, weighed and priced. The additional efforts increase the cost of the products, said an official in a power equipment company.

As India has free trade agreements with countries such as Thailand, Nepal and Sri Lanka, the electrical equipment can be imported from these countries at zero duty. Indian companies, without the benefit of tax waivers, are facing unfair competition from the products imported at zero duty. The government has already noticed re-routing of electrical products through the countries with agreements to claim zero duty. "Our duty structure is still not streamlined. In addition to the excise duty, we have central and state taxes such as sales tax, octroi and entry tax, which make Indian products expensive and uncompetitive."

To match the mega investments in power generation being planned, there should be a boom in power equipment sector. "The well-conceived APDRP program and passing of Electricity Act 2003 have given hope to the industry. Almost all sectors of electrical equipment industry are indicating fast growth now. The Rs. 50,000 crore Indian industry is also finding a good response for its products in the international markets. The companies are improving the design and capabilities of Indian products to make them more world class," said IEEMA senior consultant.

The bulk transmission infrastructure in the country has increased to more than 300,000 km. now. For supporting the generation growth plan and the ambitious mission of the government 'power for all by 2012', the electrical equipment industry needs to be equipped with the support of policy changes.

D-Link India unveils India's first environment friendly technology for networks in Nov. 2007. It introduced its innovative green Ethernet technology gigabit switches to help reduce power consumption and provide energy costs savings without sacrificing operational performance or functionality.

Juergen Schubert, managing director of Siemens Ltd. also referred to the need for local manufacturing of power equipment. He said "the lack of local manufacturing capacity in the power sector has been a major bottleneck. There is an urgent need for locally produced high quality equipment at competitive prices".

According to some analysts, the government wants to get out of the key sector like power since the government needs immense amount of resources and this is good news for private developers.

The paucity of fuel—coal, power generating equipment, and paucity of downstream products such as meters, power factor correction devices, distribution transformers and switchgear, etc. for distribution and transmission can affect the power status. There is an urgent need for locally produced high quality equipment at competitive prices, and use of Ethernet Technology for producing the equipment for maximum functionality and performance.

Oil, Petroleum, Gas

Oil, petrol and gas are other essentials for infrastructure development. As Chapter 3 on global business expansions has highlighted India is making efforts to produce these at home, in joint ventures and consortium partners with other companies and countries. India is also consortium partners with other domestic and foreign companies to explore oil and gas and other related activities. Beside the government owned ONGC,

ONGC Videsh, other notable private players are Reliance, Lakshmi N. Mittal, Essar Oil, Jaiprakash Associates and L&T.

A number of public undertaking Indian companies are in oil and gas exploration, marketing, distribution, and transportation activities. Activities focus for 2007 and future prospects of a few companies are cited and snapshot of other enterprises is given in Appendix 2.

Indian Oil Company (IOC) business focus is on refineries, oil and gas exploration marketing and distribution of gas, and LNG import. The Company is planning to set up a refinery in Ceyhan Turkey, having a capacity of 15 MMTPA. The project involves a cost of Rs. 200 bn. IOC may have to rework its strategies on equity partnership and forge new alliances. The key to success may depend on IOC's ability to get the state oil companies of both Azerbaijan and Kazakhstan and ENI of Italy as consortium partners. The Turkish authority had also offered provisional approval to two other joint ventures: A collaboration between Azeri state oil company SOCAR and Turkish Turcas and joint venture of Turkish company Petrol office and Austrian OMV.

IOC plans to set up 15 MMTPA refinery-cum-petro-chemical complex in Paradip. It plans to invest around Rs. 430 bn. over the next five years to upgrade its refineries, with bulk investment in Haldia & Koyali, as well as expanding the pipeline capacity. It is also planning to set up a naptha cracker at Panipat refinery and expand the refinery's capacity to 15 MMTPA. IOC is likely to tie-up with Petronet LNG (PLL) for its proposed liquefied natural gas (LNG) import and re-gasification terminal at Ennore.

The Company is planning to form a JV with Reliance Industries (RIL) to market RIL's gas from the Krishna-Godavari Basin. In addition, it is also planning a JV with Coal Bed Methane (CBM) producer Great Eastern Energy Corporation for city gas distribution in West Bengal. IOC and RIL are likely to join hands for exploration in the latter's oil block in East Timor. They have been in talks for a possible tie-up to acquire oil and gas assets abroad as well as exploring farm-in opportunities. IOC was looking at farm-in opportunities which would give it participating interest in RIL's asset. Farm-in activities are very common among global oil and gas exploration companies. To come in as a farm-in partner, a company is not required to acquire the asset directly, but develop the property by taking participating interest in the block.

IVRCL Infrastructures & Projects has entered into a share purchase agreement on 2007 to acquire 100% shares of Alkor Petroo (Alkor)—an unlisted oil and gas E&P company. Alkor had five exploration blocks in the Republic of Yemen and Arab Republic of Egypt along with Gujarat State Petroleum Corporation (GSPCL) and other ONGC's principal activities include exploration, production, refining, transportation and marketing crude oil, natural gas, liquefied petroleum gas, natural gas liquid, ethane/propane and other products.

BPCL focuses on oil exploration, LPG bottling plant and contract farming in Brazil for bio-diesel. BPCL, in collaboration with Videocon Industries, acquired 50% stake in EnCana Brasil Petroleo Limitida for USD 425 mn. The deal will help the company in its exploration business. The company signed an agreement for acquiring 20% participating interest in Australian block for USD 1.42 mn. It, along with Premier Oil, has made the largest onshore gas discovery in Assam.

In order to expand its global reach, the company is planning a bid of USD 350 mn. to acquire 10% interest in Congo fields. It is planning to form a JV with Matrix Marine Fuels LLC (US based company) for expanding bunkering business. The company plans to set up a 44 tmt LPG bottling plant at Fatuha near Patna with an investment of around Rs. 310 mn.

Gail India Ltd. business focus is on LPG and propane gas transmission services, natural gas trading, petrochemicals, LPG & liquefied hydrocarbons.

Gail expanded the capacity of its petrochemical plant at Pata to 410,000 TPA by setting up HDPE plant (100,000 TPA capacity). The company has signed MoU with BPCL and HPCL for promoting CNG and city gas projects in various states. It has signed a deal with ONGC to set up a JV for transporting, processing and marketing gas from ONGC's KG and Mahanadi basins. The company has formed a JV with China Gas Holdings for tapping opportunities in CNG and Coal Bed Methane (CBM) areas.

It completed Dahej-Uran pipeline and the first phase of Dabhol-Panvel pipeline. Four other pipeline projects were also completed. The company plans to raise Rs. 70 bn. from domestic and foreign markets to expand its pipeline network to 12,000 km. by 2011.

It plans to set up a mega USD 2.3 bn. petrochemical plant in Iran. The company is likely to have Reliance Industries Ltd. (RIL) and Iranian Government as its partners. Hundred per cent FDI has been allowed in laying pipelines business, which can increase competition in the industry and thus negatively affect the estimates.

HPCL undertakes downstream petroleum activities including development of infrastructure and marketing of LPG and other petroleum products. Both OIL-HPCL would like to pursue upstream and downstream opportunities in India and abroad. While Oil India Ltd. (OIL) has expertise and resources in oil and gas exploration, development and production, and transportation, HPCL is well established in petroleum refining, marketing, transportation and distribution of petroleum products. OIL is currently looking at partnerships with small companies for acquiring assets in Russia, Africa and Europe. For acquiring larger assets, it has a tie-up with Indian Oil.

It has teamed up with the steel baron Lakshmi Mittal to explore the prospects of setting up a refinery-cum-petrochemicals project in Visakhapatnam, Andhra Pradesh. Besides Mittal, three other companies—Total of France, Oil India Ltd., and Gail India Ltd. have joined HPCL for the project. Mittal has 49 per cent stake in HPCL's Bhatinda refinery.

Mittal is eyeing to buy half of Hindustan Petroleum Corp's exploration arm Prize Petroleum. Besides Mittal, Essar Oil, Jaiprakash Associates and L&T are other firms interested in buying a stake in Prize Petroleum. HPCL holds the balance 50 per cent in Prize. Prize operates Cluster-7 field of Oil and

Natural Gas Corp. (ONGC) and won two exploration blocks in fourth and sixth round of auction under New Exploration Licensing Policy (NELP). The Company plans to produce about 50,000 barrels of oil per day from Cluster-7 fields. Its NELP-VI block in Madhya Pradesh holds three trillion cubic feet of gas reserves.

Power Grid Corporation Ltd. would invest about Rs. 55,000 crore on transmission infrastructure during the five-year period, including in 45 projects that the company is currently implementing. The Rs. 4,200 crore transmission project is for evacuating power from Maithon-Bokaro, in view of the 2010 Commonwealth Games, being hosted by Delhi. Power Finance Corporation (PFC) and Rural Electrification Corporation (REC) are the nodal agencies for these projects.

Petronet focuses on LNG terminal at Kochi. Kochi refineries are crude oil, natural gas and coal producers. The 2.5 million ton terminal to be completed in mid-2011 will be fourth such project in the country and first in South India. It is also the first terminal to be located in a major port.

Cairn India's principal activity is to explore crude oil and natural gas. It is developing an oil field in Rajasthan from which it has targeted peak production of 1,50,000 barrels per day. Malaysia's Petronas owns 10% of the company. The field is expected to produce oil for 25 years from 2009. Cairn India owns a 22.5% stake, while ONGC, Videocon Industries and Japanese firm Marubeni are the other stakeholders in the Rajasthan block.

Indraprastha Gas Ltd. focuses on production and expansion of compressed natural gas (CNG) and piped natural gas.

Kalpataru Power Transmission Ltd. is one of the leading companies in the field of Turnkey projects for EHV Transmission Lines up to and including 800 kV in India and Overseas. As an EPC contractor, the scope of work includes design, testing, fabrication, galvanizing of towers and construction activities from survey, civil works/foundation, erection to stringing and commissioning of EHV lines, besides procurement of items such as conductors, insulators, hardware accessories, etc. It also participates in Substation projects on a partnership basis. And also provides EPC services for distribution projects of 11/33 kV and also construct cross-country pipelines besides Telecom Towers.

Recently, private sector has entered into the oil exploration and gas sector. Reliance Industries (RIL) business focus is on refining and petrochemicals, and oil exploration. The company has been actively pursuing petroleum exploration activities in the middle fast, particularly in Oman and Yemen, besides India, Asia Pacific Region and South America.

Its refining and petrochemicals segment sales have increased due to higher demand for petroleum products due to increase in prices by 3%. RIL's production (including toll conversions) increased by 15.3% to 3.6 MMT due to new PP plant at Jamnagar as well as new PTA plant at Hazira. Company was able to pass on the increase in cost to the consumers. Other segment sales increased driven by higher production from Panna-Tapti-Mukta (PTM) blocks. Oil production from the PTM blocks increased by 25% yoy to 148,617 tones and gas production.

RIL plans to invest USD 8-9 bn. in Jamnagar over the next 3-4 years. The facility will be the world's largest Integrated Combined Cycle Coke Gasification Complex (IGCC) with a capacity of 6 MMTPA and is expected to complete by 2012. Further, the Company is eyeing 15% share of the global paraxylene capacity and thus is expanding its capacity from 1.9 MMTPA to 4.5 MMTPA.

It is planning to expand its oil exploration and production business globally and is in talks with four global players for partnerships to explore new regions in the US, South America and West Asia. In addition, the Company is also eyeing hydrocarbon assets in Columbia, Yemen, Egypt, East Timor and Russia.

The Company has undertaken extensive geological work in 2006 year in the Kurdistan region. It has executed two production sharing contracts with the Kurdistan Regional Government

(KRG) covering petroleum exploration activities in the Rovi and Sarta blocks in the Kurdistan Region of Iraq.

Petro Kuwait Petroleum (KPC), the national oil company of Kuwait, has said it is in talks with Reliance Industries (RIL) to set up a greenfield refinery-cum-petrochemical complex in India.

Company's new petrochemical plants at Hazira and Jamnagar fully operational petrochemical business will further rise in the near future. In addition, gas and oil will start to flow in from KG block from FY09 onwards, which will further contribute to the increase in revenue.

Reliance Industries has drawn a blue print to lay 8,700 km. natural gas pipeline grid across the country that will rival state-run GAIL India's network. It plans to build a Pan-India pipeline network and connect to (GAIL's main trunk line) HBJ from eastern side to form a national gas grid. It is currently laying a 1,385 km. pipeline from Kakinada in Andhra Pradesh, the landfall point of gas it plans to produce from its eastern offshore KG-D6 block, to Barauch in Gujarat. The company has secured approvals for 820 km. Jamnagar-Bhopal pipeline, 651 km. Hyderabad-Goa line and a 600 km. Kakinada-Chennai pipeline. The network would transport natural gas produced from KG-D6 and other blocks off the east coast as well as gas to be produced from below coal seams (CBM), would be completed in 5-7 years.

Iran on 13 Nov. 2007 gave India a four-month deadline to formally agree its participation in a multi-billion dollar project to transport Iranian gas to India via Pakistan. The warning came after Iran and Pakistan finalized the content of the 7.4 billion dollar gas export deal—originally a tripartite project. New Delhi would still join the much-delayed project, under which energy-poor India would receive 30 million cubic meters (one billion cubic feet) per day of Iranian gas. On 29 April 2008 India finalized the Iran gas line project since it was concerned that Iran had been asking China to partner and India needed gas urgently.

India also invests its expertise and money in oil rich countries in return for oil supply. Their expertise and money investments give them priority to oil supply in those particular countries. The oil rich countries benefit by such investments and have ready export markets to earn revenue.

Renewable Energy Sector

Renewable energy sector is concentrating on wind power, solar power, ethanol, bio-ethanol, bio-CNG, CNG gas, bio-gas, bio-fuel—bio-diesel, Hydrogen-blended compressed natural gas (HCNG) and geothermal energy. These are some of the alternative fuels being produced and used in India. Some of the countries are even experimenting to produce energy from algae and woodchips.

Wind Power: Suzlon Energy and Wind Power focuses on wind power production. It is wholly owned subsidiary of Hansen Transmissions International NV, Belgium, a leading global gear box and drive train designer, manufacturer and supplier to the wind turbine and other selected industries. Company plans to increase the turbine, gear box and REpower manufacturing capacity over the next two years. It has orders from Horizon Wind of Houston, US wind power developer, Servtec Instalacoses E Sistemas Integrados Ltda, Brazilian utility, order from Ayen Enerji Co. Inc., Turkish utility. Driven by its presence in all the key markets, access to world-class technology, and a fully backward integrated model, it is well placed to capitalize on the growth opportunity in wind power sector.

Indowind Company generates wind power, undertakes turnkey operations for windmill projects and operates and maintains wind electric generators. There are many other big and small companies getting into this sector. India is going ahead in renewable energies through use of advance technologies, and joint ventures. Corn, Soya, rapeseed and sugarcane can turn into energy crops.

Solar Energy: At high-tech companies and hospitals, executives with a special concern about power disruptions are looking at fuel cells to supply clean and reliable power on site. Solar cell, Solar panels, Solar Photo voltaic panels (also known as solar cells), which convert the sun's energy directly into electricity, grew by 37% last year.

Tata BP Solar India Ltd. is joint venture between Tata power and BP solar one of the largest solar company in the world. It produces wide range of solar products for home and industries and institutions such as solar home lights and street lights, solar aids for roads and highways, solar water heating systems and water pumps, solar power packs and power systems for various sectors. The company also provides reliable and cost-effective solar power to a wide range of sectors from education and banking to healthcare and telecommunications. Solar road safety aids and building integrated photo voltaic also form part of its constantly growing portfolio, integrated photo voltaic and solar lanterns are its few products which are exported to 27 countries across five continents. It provides customized solar solutions.

Tata BP Solar's manufacturing facilities for solar photo voltaic and solar thermal products and systems are the largest of their kind in the country. With a 42 MW module line, its module manufacturing facility is one of the largest of its kind in the world. Its world-class polycrystalline solar cell manufacturing plant is India's first and most modern plant of its kind. NRV Power Technologies Ltd. in India is manufacturer and exporter of solar inverters and solar charge controllers. NEPC India has also developed a wider range of models with higher capacities using revolutionary technologies. The product range has tremendous market potential to cater to high capacity requirements of solar dual power system.

Moser Baer Photo Voltaic (MBPV), a wholly owned subsidiary of Moser Baer India on 30 November 2007 signed a MoU with the Government of Rajasthan for setting up a large solar power project in the State with an estimated generation capacity of 1-5 MW. The project will be the largest grid-connected solar farm in India and entail an investment of around US $25 million (Rs. 100 crores). Moser Baer is also evaluating various options for setting up large sized solar farms across the SAARC region with strategic tie-ups with some of the leading global solar PV companies and clean energy funds. Moser Baer Photo Voltaic plans to emerge as a leading technology driven PV equipment manufacturer in the world by implementing a capacity of 500 MW by FY10 through a mix of technologies in the crystalline silicon, concentrator and thin film domain. The company's photo voltaic equipment manufacturing capacities for crystalline silicon, concentrator and thin film technologies are coming up in SEZ in Greater Noida.

A start up Indian company, 'Square Engineering', has signed an agreement with Green and Gold Energy (GGE) of Australia to build a 30 megawatt (MW) facility in India for the manufacture of 100,000 Sun Cubes per year. The Sun Cube is a significantly simple product, though it works on a similar process—solar concentrators focusing the sun's rays onto a small solar cell with microchip-controlled motors that keep the concentrators pointing to the sun.

Another solar concentrator revolutionary product is 'Sunflower'. The revolution aspect relates to the fact that this device moves all its concentrator panels to always point to the sun. Sunflower is likely to be in the market in 2008, it will cost only $450 and will be mass-produced in China. The Sun Cube does have a head start though, and may be its manufacturing in India will help it bring down prices substantially. Whatever the result, the competition should be good for solar power as a whole.

The most focused applications of solar energy in India is likely to be rural electrification, water pumping for drinking water and irrigation, harvest processing and cooling in rural areas.

Since long, government has started with solar power initiatives in India though it has been on low key due to higher cost affordability. Recently, many other Indian private companies are getting into solar power generation and allied products in joint ventures with domestic or foreign companies.

The Australian Government has recently awarded UNSW A$5.2 million to train next-generation solar energy engineers from Asia-Pacific nations, specifically from India and China, as part of the Asia-Pacific Partnership on Clean Development and Climate. APP and certain other programs are designed to target development of rural solar usage.

Use of Renewable Energy in Villages in 2007: The Haryana Government has decided to implement Integrated Rural Energy Program (IREP) in 40 clusters of villages in all the 20 districts of the state that will cost the state exchequer Rs. 4 crores in the current financial year. The program would be implemented in the state by involving panchayats in the 40 clusters in which 2,538 families living in the rural areas would be provided with renewable source of energy like solar lanterns, SPV LED street light, etc. to meet their lighting needs. The State Department of Renewable Energy had launched the scheme with the assistance of the Government of India and 188 villages of 38 clusters and two cluster of a district would be included under the program, the main aim of the program is to encourage the rural people to adopt renewable energy technologies for meeting their cooking, heating, lighting and irrigation energy needs.

Another Innovative Plan to Use Renewable Energy in Villages in 2008: A recent innovation in 2008, Rice Husk power system is being used to generate electricity in villages in India. Propriety technology is used to burn Rice Husk to generate three valuable products: electricity, waste ash which can be used as an ingredient in cement production, and reduction in carbon emissions. These three products bring revenues which can break even the cost of this mini generator in 2-3 years; whereas the Rice Husk is waste product. The technology provides off-grid power to villages of 200 to 500 households.

Earlier electrification projects have generally provided intermittent power for an hour or so as it was being provided from distant power plants and traveling over miles of wires to the villages. It was challenge to get electricity to houses, irrigation pumps, water purification units and small businesses. Husk power will provide continuous power and will solve this challenge. Other strategies are developed in this context: pre-payment for electricity consumed, an average household is likely to consume of $15 to $18 per year. The wires will be double insulated so difficult to illegally tap them. Husk power will use circuit breaker for $1 instead of meters costing $10 to $15. Circuit breaker would distribute electricity to branch line serving 4-5 households.

A Husk power employee in the village will conduct electricity audit to determine how much electrical load branch of houses will need and installed circuit breaker would allow only that much, any illegal tap or excessive consumption will trip the circuit breaker.

So far since early 2008, two Rice Husk generators are providing power to about 10,000 villagers. But the business plan calls for rapid expansion that will put miniature power plants in hundreds of villages soon. This innovation and its business model are developed by two Indian-American students who are currently using two Rice Husk generators in their own and other villages in eastern India. There are 480 million Indians with no power and 350 of them live in villages concentrated in eastern India's rice belt where the villagers are rice rich but power poor.

The 2007 scenario is: Praj Industries Ltd. is producing bio-ethanol. Indian sugar mills will produce 'bio-CNG' from cane biomass with European aid. Three sugar factories from Maharashtra, India, have decided to produce 'Bio-CNG' from sugarcane biomass as a transport fuel. The projects will be set up with finance from the German Investment and Development Company (DEG), one of Europe's largest international development banks, which has earmarked 15 million for lending to the factories. German firm Biogas Nord and Enersearch—a European research institute engaging in renewable energy solutions will provide technical know-how.

There are environmental hazards of producing some of these bio-fuels. Cellulosed ethanol uses different kind of waste including municipal garbage to produce fuel. Bio-diesel fuel is a clean-burning diesel fuel. Palm oil is a key ingredient in bio-diesel fuel. Demand for palm oil could encourage deforestation in tropical countries and unsustainable demand for palm oil.

Expanding corn production for bio-fuel would deplete water resources and pollute soils with added fertilizers and chemicals. It would also require huge volumes of traditional energy for farming equipments and ethanol-conversion. This could nullify gains from the less polluted fuel.

In India, compressed natural gas (CNG) has been the fuel of choice in large metropolitan areas for autos, taxis, and buses to reduce environmental pollution; and major auto-makers now offer CNG models.

A bio-based alternative made from agricultural waste will make biogas available in rural areas. This represents an interesting case of energy 'leapfrogging'—rural communities jumping into a cleaner and renewable future, beyond what is already the cleanest alternative currently in use in the rapidly modernizing mega cities.

Biogas can be produced efficiently from any type of biomass via anaerobic digestion. The renewable gas contains around 60 to 70 per cent methane (CH_4) with the remainder being CO_2 with minor amounts of contaminants and trace gases. For it to be used as a transport fuel in vehicles as a replacement for CNG, it has to be upgraded, with the CO_2 scrubbed out. The fuel then becomes 'bio-CNG', a very clean, renewable gaseous energy source. The fuel is already being used on a relatively large scale in Europe, most notably in Sweden, Austria and Germany.

Hydrogen-blended compressed natural gas (HCNG) for vehicles is being produced by Indraprastha Gas Ltd., Bajaj Auto, Ashok Leyland, Tata Motors, Mahindra & Mahindra and Eicher Motors have come together to develop hydrogen-blended compressed natural gas (HCNG or Hithane)-run vehicles. It will reduce emissions, improve fuel efficiency and work in existing vehicles. Tata Motors is teaming up with the Indian Space Research Organization to produce the country's first fuel cell car. Another alternative fuel—Ultra-low sulfur diesel (ULSD) easily beats CNG on costs and delivers equivalent reductions in "toxic" particulate emissions, according to India's Tata Energy Research Institute (TERI).

Bio-fuels: In February 2006, BP global group announced the funding of a $9.4 million project to be jointly implemented with TERI in India to demonstrate the feasibility of producing bio-diesel from Jatropha Curcas, a non-edible oil bearing crop. Jatropa a weedy grass is grown in arid lands in large scale to produce fuel.

The project, which is expected to run for 10 years, will cultivate 8,000 hectares of land that is currently designated as wasteland, and install equipment for seed crushing, oil extraction and processing to produce 9 million liters of bio-diesel per year. As part of the project, we will complete a full assessment of the environmental and social impact of all elements of the supply chain, as well as a life cycle analysis of greenhouse gas emissions. Reliance Industries is also getting into production of bio-fuels by cultivating Jatropha.

Ethanol is another renewable energy source. In India, ethanol production is concentrated in Uttar Pradesh, Karnataka, Tamil Nadu, Andhra Pradesh, Maharashtra, Gujarat and Bihar. India is the world's second largest producer of sugar after Brazil. Ethanol in India is produced from molasses, a sugar by-product. Government has allowed Ethanol and glycol to be produced in large scale from sugarcane by sugar companies. It is being used currently as mixed with Petrol for transport fuel.

The government plans to introduce mandatory 10 per cent ethanol blended petrol from October 2008 has hit a roadblock with both the automobile and oil industry expressing reservations about the proposed roadmap. "We would like to bring to your notice that a 10 per cent ethanol blended petrol (E10), would impact vehicles designed before 2002 and reduce fuel efficiency unlike the 5 per cent blending that is currently mandatory, would impact vehicle performance, if the percentage of ethanol varies significantly."

While some of the recently produced vehicles are E10 compliant, the impact of E10 blends on older vehicles produced before 2002 needs to be examined. "It is believed that there may be issues relating to drivability and many of the models in the market may have to change components that come into contact with the blended petrol, as these vehicles have not been designed for the 10 per cent ethanol blended fuel. The oil marketing companies, on the other hand, said that it was necessary to remove inter-state trade barriers on ethanol before the blending ratio is increased."

Recent Salient Renewable Energy Efforts for Automotive Fuel in India: The world's first and only three wheeler solar taxi has come to India; it is a taxi with a difference. The compact electric car runs purely on solar energy. The car's gearless electric motor runs on twin 380 volt batteries that are charged from solar cells panel attached to the car. That allows it to accelerate up to 90 kms per hour.

To tackle the problem of rising pollution, the pilot project will use CNG with different blends of hydrogen ranging from 12% to 30% in different vehicles. These vehicles—small three-wheelers, trucks and passenger buses—will be supplied by these manufacturers. Bajaj Auto's three-wheeler will be the first one to be tested in Nov. 2007, while Tata Motors' LCV will run on the new fuel in December 2007. After the tests, which are expected to end by mid-2008, new vehicles running on this fuel (HCNG) will be introduced by these manufacturers. Subsequently, the existing CNG fleet will also be covered.

IOC facility at Faridabad in Haryana, which has the necessary infrastructure to develop hydrogen as an automotive fuel, will be utilized. IOC will also set up a second unit for hydrogen blending in Delhi and later all the existing 138 CNG stations in the capital will be made HCNG compliant.

Geothermal Energy: Gunnar Palsson, Iceland's Ambassador to India, said that the 30-member business delegation from Iceland have come to learn and orient themselves with business opportunities with India.

The delegation is focused on finance and energy. Geothermal energy and hydropower are the major area of concern for Iceland and the country is keen to partner with India in the energy sector. Iceland is one of the few European countries to nearly match India's growth rate, he informed.

A vital part of the growing bilateral relationship between

Iceland and India is trade in services and bilateral investment. An MoU was signed between Glitnir Bank, Iceland and CEO, Bhilwara Energy Ltd. to cooperate in the area of geo-thermal energy exploration and development.

India's vast demand and leadership position in the development of renewable energy technology provides numerous opportunities for energy cooperation between Iceland and India. Currently, almost 80 per cent of all the energy use in Iceland comes from renewable energy with 100 per cent of the electricity production deriving from clean energy resources, hydro and geo-thermal. In recent years, both Iceland and India have experienced a boom in their respective financial sectors which provides a scope of cooperation in the field of finance and investment for both the countries.

The Government of India has announced that it would open an embassy in Reykjavik, Iceland in 2008. The Government of Iceland had opened an embassy in New Delhi in 2006.

International Oil Policies: Oil Puzzle

Globalization politics and superpower politics create oil puzzle to create oil resources, maintain and protect for their own use by the super powers. Globalization plays further impetus as it gets open to other players who want to play the game differently with different stakes to get advantage over others.

Stage 1

Superpower wants to procure oil for their economic growth from outside sources at affordable prices. They want to dictate the affordability of the prices because it is their technology that is creating the resource. They want to control the oil resource by military dimensions and create dependency dilemma rather than interdependency loop.

- Oil demand leads to military zeal to protect energy resources, military security needed for oil fields, gas pipelines, refineries and tanker routes.
- Oil politics is to give the oil resource country capability by: (i) Setting them up against other countries' union,

(ii) weaponry capability to make them independent and strong, (iii) those challenging American supremacy—may be suppressed by imposing sanctions and or probing their weaponry, and (iv) this creates discontent among the local population.

- Discontentment of enraged local population is expressed in rebellious attitude, terrorism, terrorist attacks to avenge. (i) Terrorist attacks are supported by discontent and cultural revolts by the host countries' local population to alien values of Americans, (ii) when local population do not benefit by employment and other development benefits such as physical infrastructure or health care facilities, and (iii) the luxury of American lifestyle in host countries in juxtaposition to dismal living of local people creates discontent.
- Discontent and their restlessness gives vent to creating special zealots like Taliban, Arab-Afghan band, Al Qaida. These have the weapon capability and access. These create young religious fanatics who are even willing to be suicide bombers in the name of Jihad.

Stage 2 & 2a—Oil as an Import Commodity

- USA needs to import to meet its energy requirements and keeping its own oil reserves. Oil enriched countries need to export to earn revenue. At stage 2a the oil import countries USA, Russia, China, India invest their expertise and money in oil rich countries in return for oil supply. Their expertise and money investments give them priority to oil supply in those particular countries. The oil rich countries benefit by such investments and ready export markets to earn revenue otherwise they would have the oil resource but no benefits without other countries input. There is interdependency for mutual benefits.

Some Interesting Comments

Hugo Chavez PM of Venezuela said in an interview broadcast on state television in 13 Nov. 2007 "I would sell oil to a rich country at $100 (Euro 68.50), and to a poor country perhaps at US $20 (Euro 14) a barrel, that breaks with the schemes of capitalism.... OPEC could do it, although there are hard positions on it, but I'm taking the issue to discuss it at a summit in Saudi Arabia this weekend to consider a plan to aid poor countries struggling with rising oil prices."

He said Venezuela is setting an example by selling oil under preferential credit terms to various Latin American and Caribbean countries. The world crude prices near record levels, oil producers all have a moral obligation to help the neediest countries with below-market prices. "How are you going to sell oil to Haiti, one of the poorest countries in the world, at US $100, the same price that you sell it to the United States? It's not right ethically." "We're going to try to obtain the support, if not of all OPEC countries, of some of them, and of other major producers to design a formula thinking of the coming years," Chavez said. OPEC supplies about four out of every 10 barrels on world oil markets. Chavez said he believes it is time for the cartel to "raise its level of political action".

In short, our discussions above have highlighted that physical infrastructure development is the key for global transformation dimensions, viz. transforming India. As we begin our road to growth and transformation for tomorrow; we realize the importance of world class physical infrastructure and focus on these developments—from power plants, highways and expressways, good roads and transport system of rails and airlines to new ports and shipbuilding; to telecommunication, and safe water, etc. on the one hand; on the other hand space research and defense infrastructure is of importance in global transformation contexts. We definitely need other supporting infrastructure of tourism, and entertainment economy. A boost in energy Sector of Power, Oil, Petrol and Gas is the driving force for infrastructure development and viz. India's transformation and economic growth. We do reiterate:

For any nation to maintain its Competitive value, Proposition and Improve, it will need to go through Constant reforms.

Infrastructure for Human Resource Development

5

Infrastructure for human development facilitates quality of life for people. In this context we focus on health, education, employment and employability. Real estate and Retail, tourism and entertainment infrastructure have been growing fast to demand more manpower along with earlier sectors of IT products and services and manufacturing. The emergence of competition is very challenging but it is very healthy and brings out the best in people. ICTs contribute to competitiveness in all business sectors including education, health and human resources. In these contexts manpower needs, development and procurement are necessary and crucial for economic growth. The physical infrastructure and human infrastructure go together to contribute to economic growth.

Health Infrastructure

In India, you need health infrastructure to take care of health needs—preventive and curative care of millions of people in villages, small towns. It is provided both by government and private sectors. Government plans for universal free health care through its various schemes.

The basic infrastructure requires (i) trained doctors. There are well trained and dedicated doctors. (ii) Primary care dispensaries and referral hospitals for villages and towns are needed. The medical facilities and equipment is provided initially, but it is poorly maintained. Moreover, due to low resources, the essential medical supplies are missing most of the times. By the time if patient's caretakers buy it from the market, the patient may be dead. (iii) Hygiene and general cleanliness is lacking. That creates more infection. (iv) The poor patients overwhelm the doctors since patients need urgent attention in cases like cancer, tumor, etc. and they can only give improvised surgical treatments. Patient to doctor ratio is very high. The quality of treatment given is mediocre due to these limitations.

On the other hand in the private sector, highly trained doctors are available to treat from cancer, cardiac problems, and other complicated diseases to general health problems. Trained paramedics are hired, latest equipment is imported, update buildings with update operation theaters are set up. Cleanliness and good patient and doctor hygiene is maintained. But it is expensive and it caters to two categories. At home, rich patients can afford this private but good treatment. Secondly, they are encouraging patients from abroad to come for treatment—since it is world class and immediate attention and medical procedures are given by the best trained doctors. Those patients can afford it. Thus, these medical facilities infrastructure is encouraging medical tourism and bringing cash, fame and name for them.

How do they do it from globalization perspective? From globalization point of view they are buying the latest medical technology, doctors are being trained and exposed to the latest medical techniques. Pharmaceutical companies are doing very well to do research and development and bring the latest medicines and appliances to treat the patients. The patients from world around are aware of these facilities and come over for treatment. Thus, globalization has transformed the medical infrastructure for rich and global patients.

Government needs to streamline its healthcare—medical facilities infrastructure particularly for those who cannot afford to pay and to raise a healthy nation. Government needs cash resources to treat the poor. But infrastructure for the poor needs development which is the government onus. Though more and more is being divested as well as share by corporate social responsibility (CSR) initiatives from domestic as well global corporates. There are rising expectations of the poor for medical treatment when they are exposed and made aware to the latest medical technology and techniques through media and awareness campaigns. The medicines are not affordable for poor or middle class patients and poor have to rely on what government will provide through public hospitals and dispensaries. Here lies the challenge. Spending on healthcare will witness the highest growth rate among all spending categories over the next two decades, a McKinsey & Company study has found. Healthcare grew from 4 per cent of average household income in 1995 to 7 per cent in 2005 and is expected to grow to 13 per cent by 2025, it said.

The factor of health is important for a healthy society and nation. Factor of food, nutrition, safe drinking water and clean environment, clean housing is associated with health. People should enjoy good health. They should have access to both preventive and curative medical services. Overpopulation in countries and worldwide is bane and problematic but even population control through medical techniques if available to poor will make life livable for them. Healthy nations are prosperous nations.

It must focus on delivery of affordable health services, creating health awareness for people, enforcing hospital standards, devising health insurance system and supporting medical education system. Social programs of healthcare in controlling overweight and obese population should be through dietary control and fitness programs as a matter of food policy, health policies and IEC programs and through school curriculum. Environmental health cut across infrastructure sectors, e.g. water supply, water storage, latrines, improved drainage; private goods, e.g. cooking stoves, ventilation in houses, bed-nets; and behavior change, e.g. hygiene practices and hand washing.

Wellbeing of People

According to a study of the Asian Development Bank, 'International Comparison Program in Asia and the Pacific: Purchasing Power Parity Preliminary Report' 2007, India and China account for 64 per cent of GDP in 23 Asian countries included in a study but rank quite low when it comes to benefits percolating to their people. While India ranks 18th, China ranks at 10th when it comes to benefits to the people in terms of living conditions.

Every healthcare system around the world is constantly working to meet with three objectives: Equitable access, high quality and low cost. For care providers, these are often competing objectives, with the tradeoffs among these goals usually ridden with economic, social and political implications. The inherent challenge in reconciling the three objectives is common to every healthcare system, and not unique to any particular country. Traditionally, for healthcare systems, health and wellness are personal matters, while access to care and its financing are more political ones. This view has to be modified considerably to help build an infrastructure to support basic levels of hygiene, and to encourage healthy lifestyles among individuals.

The second measure we need to adopt to bring down healthcare costs is to improve finance mechanisms. If we need to insure one billion Indians through a sustainable form of health insurance, we would do well to have a segmented approach to the population. Private health insurance could address the needs of all segments of the society other than the poor in both urban and rural areas. The latter segment will need a public-private partnership approach, and some form of support or subsidy from the government.

Talking about the role of public hospitals in delivering cost-effective healthcare, we must remember that the country's public health efforts have brought in commendable results from the time of the country's independence 60 years ago.

Life expectancy has doubled since that time, infant mortality halved, small pox eradicated, and cases of leprosy and polio have been drastically reduced. But with changing disease patterns, particularly in the form of rising instances of diabetes, hypertension and cancer, and the growing millions who are afflicted with HIV/AIDS, India's public health challenges are surely growing.

The fundamental deficiency in the public health system lies in the gross understaffing of the system rather than in the infrastructure per se, which, in reality, is far more robust than what is available in several other countries.

The public health sector in India is unique in that it must take responsibility not only for producing a steady supply of professionals but also for stimulating demand for them. Optimizing costs is largely dependent on the production, acquisition and management of labor resources, and then on the productive delivery of services.

Healthcare providers say that innovative funding models are the need of the hour. With public spending in health is now less than a per cent of the GDP, which compares poorly with the US healthcare spending of more than 15% of GDP, this potential solution for the gaps in healthcare delivery needs more attention.

Preventive Healthcare: A study by ICRIER (2007) on 'Impact of preventive healthcare on Indian industry and economy' reveals that higher incidence of illness among employees is costing India Inc. dearly with some companies losing as many as 51 working days in a year, a study has revealed. One can expect an equal percentage of loss in their productivity and profits which is a cause for concern, says the study. The study reveals that absenteeism was mainly due to acute diseases like diarrhea, influenza, malaria and dengue, followed by lifestyle diseases like cardiovascular diseases, diabetes, stroke and mental disorders. However, chronic infectious diseases like tuberculosis and HIV/AIDS do not seem to be a major burden for the companies surveyed, it added.

Suggesting a positive correlation between preventive healthcare and profits of companies, the ICRIER study said, 'In an era where competitiveness and profitability are determined by intellectual capital, promotion of employee health is crucial for the organization'.

Employee wellness demonstrates a real contribution to company bottom lines since promoting employee health is a means to controlling healthcare costs, the study said. As regards the financing of healthcare, the ICRIER study found that more than half of the respondents supported the idea of vouchers as an effective delivery tool to encourage preventive healthcare measures. The survey also suggested that given the dismal state of affairs of public health spending and the non-existent insurance system in India, the voucher system for financing preventive healthcare should be given a serious thought both by the private employers and the government. Depending on the proportion of employees in different management grades that availed of sick leave, blue-collared workers were at a high risk of disease compared to the medium and senior level employees since the former spend a lesser proportion of their income on healthcare.

The survey covered 81 companies in 15 states and covering a wide range of sectors. The companies included Maruti, Bajaj Auto, Alcatel, TCS, Citibank and Genpact among others. Almost 82 per cent of the respondents (including many of those who do not provide preventive healthcare facilities at present) agreed that such measures increase firm productivity and profitability.

Healthcare informing the poor about government provided health, educational, and social services they are entitled to, could go a long way towards improving the healthcare and education scenario in the developing countries like India, a new study in the current issue of the *Journal of the American Medical Association* has said.

Healthcare needs watch dog. The government views that small—and medium-private sector healthcare facilities have mushroomed across the country. Lack of regulations, high profit margins, huge demand for healthcare services have led to every doctor becoming an entrepreneur and a businessman.

Doctors or medical practitioners may have to meet stringent regulatory provision before being given license to run neighborhood health clinics. The Centre is planning to create a regulatory body to set up minimum standards for different kinds of healthcare providers. The proposal is likely to be announced in December 2007 as part of the medium-term health policy of the government. The provisions of the new legislation would be applicable for all clinical establishments including diagnostic centers and private testing labs.

Once the Centre puts in the place the new legislation, it would be left to states to adopt the model in their state legislation. Every state government would be asked to set up state-level oversight body for accrediting agencies in the health sector and develop minimum practice standards on both infrastructure and service delivery.

Healthcare Initiatives by Private Entrepreneurs

According to sources, Reliance Industries (RIL) plans Rs. 25,000 crore healthcare initiative over 7-8 years. The healthcare initiative will integrate with Reliance Retail foray, reports CNBC-TV18. Reliance plans to set up 1,500 healthcare units in B, C towns. But, Reliance officials have refused to comment.

This is one of the biggest plans that RIL has formulated on the lines of its retail foray. RIL has said that it will probably be able to effect a change in the existing healthcare scenario in the country. RIL plans to set up its own primary healthcare centers in B and C class towns, which will have all the facilities required by the locals to sell their goods. All this will be at the initial stage, but the final outcome is not known yet.

RIL plans to replicate all the existing primary healthcare centers of the government that don't offer good services right now; which probably is not giving the right kind of service that is needed to service the healthcare needs of the rural population

There is a pilot project, which is already under implementation at Jalandhar and it will replicate all the existing primary healthcare centers of the government.

That is where Reliance is focusing and over the next 7-8 years, the plan is to invest up to Rs. 25,000 crore in rural healthcare population.

Apollo Hospitals group and Lavasa Corporation recently signed an agreement to set up an integrated healthcare and wellness destination at the Lavasa Hill town near Pune. Lavasa is a modern hill town being developed by Hindustan Construction

Company group and is spread across 12,500 acres of land, about 65 km. from Pune.

Initially, the plan is to establish a multi-specialty hospital with a capacity of 50 beds which would be ready by 2009, a company statement issued here said. Eventually, services shall extend to wellness activities, long-term care and research and development, amongst others. The integrated hospital and wellness centre would have four major service verticals—medical cluster, wellness cluster, long-term care and education-R&D zone.

Medical cluster would have a higher secondary care hospital and medical and surgical ICUs for key specialties like cardiology, neurology, orthopedics and pediatrics. Support services like radiology, imaging and a diagnostic laboratory would be set up alongside, the release added. The wellness cluster would comprise facilities ranging from complementary and alternative medicine to medical spa, etc. Long-term care would include rehabilitation services for patients who have undergone orthopedic surgeries or have neurological disorders.

The education and research zone will have a medical convention centre, training for nurses and technicians and clinical trials facilities, the release said. The integrated healthcare centre is expected to create 2,000 jobs and would also bring in revenue to the region in the form of medical tourism, the press release added.

Recent initiatives for telemedicine networks by leading hospitals—healthcare providers to reach out to the masses in far flung areas of the country using cutting edge technology appears to be gradually making headway again these days after the initial hype about telemedicine.

Corporate hospital chains, big and small, are increasingly investing in telemedicine infrastructure and are finding technology partners to conquer distance in a country that stretches from Himalayas to offshore islands of Andaman and Lakshadweep.

That is very important considering the poor state of affairs in rural areas. Consider this, 80% of towns in the country have a facility compared to 24% in rural areas, with 90% of the facilities there manned by sole practitioners. Only technology can bring access to healthcare to a comparable status in towns. Healthcare industry players say they are committed to make telemedicine a viable option.

"Telemedicine is yet to get its due as a healthcare delivery system the world over. The main reason for the slow progress in this area is lack of connectivity in medically under-served areas. Lack of easy availability of low-cost treatment and diagnostic technologies that are telemedicine-compatible and lack of regulations that are crucial for patient security and information sharing between two parties are also responsible. The low acceptance of telemedicine by both patients and even doctors in certain locations is also a reason. The good news, however, is that things are changing", Apollo Hospitals group's strategic initiatives president Ashvani Srivastava said.

Apollo Hospitals is one example of the private sector using telemedicine to reach out to medically inaccessible areas to bridge the sharp rural urban divide. It developed India's first model telemedicine village at Aragonda in Chittor district.

The village has gained repute for using telemedicine for curative and preventive healthcare, said Mr. Srivastava. Apollo telemedicine provides hospitals in remote areas with specialist care for second opinions and diagnosis. "Our doctors use telemedicine to review and follow up the care of patients from other cities and states. It has been of great help to our international patients for review consultations."

"We have over 140 telemedicine centers across the country and in other countries like Maldives and Srilanka, Pakistan, Nepal, Sudan and Muscat. We plan to expand this network to about 500 centers with private and government partnership. We are already a partner to the government for providing telemedicine in their community centers. All our super specialty hospitals have telemedicine specialty centers providing consultation", he added.

Wockhardt Hospitals, another leading corporate hospital chain, are aggressively venturing into telemedicine projects. It is setting up a telemedicine network for connecting rural and semi-urban health centers with its hospitals in tier two towns. The hospital group will focus on providing critical care solutions to health centers and hospitals, both government and private, in the rural areas.

"We are already in talks with Indian Space Research Organization to use satellite connectivity for telemedicine, which will help in doing away with the limitations of broad band based telemedicine. Satellite communication is needed more for remote areas where internet connectivity is absent," CEO Wockhardt Hospitals said.

The group plans to take the number of hospitals in tier II cities to 8 by March 2008. It already has hospitals in Nagpur, Surat and Rajkot from where it plans to connect with surrounding rural areas through telemedicine networks. The group will also link its hospitals with those in southern, western and north-eastern states. While north-east will be served from its upcoming Kolkata hospital, the Southern region will be served from Bangalore and Hyderabad.

"It is true that there was a lot of hype about telemedicine a few years ago and it did not take-off. For this reason, one has to identify a niche area where this technology can be used to provide healthcare. Wockhardt has selected critical care because serving the entire gamut of problems may not be feasible for something which is not profitable from the revenue perspective."

Care Hospitals, a low cost hospital chain in Andhra Pradesh has been using telemedicine to reaching out to rural areas in the state for some time now. It now uses this technology to connect with the University of Arkansas in the US for continued medical education, consultancy and for doctors and students to share information. "This is the second phase of our project where the technology is being used for education and research," Care Foundation director Arun K. Tiwari said.

"The technology took some time to take-off. It was considered as a one time solution for providing round the clock connectivity with a doctor. However, with time, it was realized that it is a tool for transmitting medical reports, images and seeking consultation for diseases," he added. Kamineni Hospitals, which is connected to Nalagonda district in Andhra Pradesh is now stepping up its connectivity with other districts.

"We are partnering with companies like the Vizag Steel Plant to provide super specialty telemedicine services," said Gautam Naha, group vice president of Kamineni Hospitals. The hospital is also providing classroom sessions to Gulf Medical College Hospital at Ajman near Dubai.

Not only the cost of expert opinion but also of non-medical cost of treatment such as travel and lodging are expected to come down significantly as telemedicine as a viable mode of delivery gets more acceptability. The productive manpower days are also expected to go up. However, cost of infrastructure is a major handicap. While infrastructure projects like roads and ports get a lot of support from the government, healthcare is yet to get similar treatment.

In an attempt to pull in India's 25-million strong Diaspora to assist in rural development, the sixth Pravasi Bharatiya Divas (PBD) will focus on education, healthcare, empowerment of rural women and knowledge economy. "The focus will be on social areas and issues with special emphasis on women including rural women," Minister told a press conference here. He said the focus of the last five PBDs had been to attract investment from the overseas Indians rather than their ideas and skills. "The investment or money has not been forthcoming. Therefore, we decided that we will not ask for any investment this year but seek partnership from NRIs for philanthropic projects."

The ministry has mooted the idea for establishing 'India Development Foundation' (IDF), which would act like a "single window clearance system" to channel the investments, both small and large, ideas, skills and technology for around 6,000 rural blocks across the country. "The potential investors, could be anyone who wants to do something for his or her village or district, could approach the IDF and it would guide him to implement the plan without going through the red tapes." The PBD, being organized jointly by MOIA and the Confederation of Indian Industry (CII), will focus on micro-finance institutions at the block level and the health sector. "After much thought and research, we found that these were the sectors that could attract a lot of interest from the NRI community," he told media.

India's premier medical institute, AIIMS, is set to become the first government hospital in the country to get a helipad and start an air ambulance service to deliver urgent medical attention to critically ill patients.

An application by AIIMS is being processed by the ministry of civil aviation and permission has been sought to construct a helipad. Senior doctors say close to 50% of critical patients in India die on their way to hospital.

"Keeping in mind the dense population and heavy traffic in Delhi, air ambulances could be a great help," said a doctor, though he pointed out that the expense involved in airlifting patients will have to be underwritten. The service won't come cheap. Transferring a patient, say from Chandigarh to Delhi, could cost close to Rs. 1.5 lakh.

The helicopter ambulance will have paramedic staff and a doctor trained to handle critical patients. The staff on board and on the ground will be given special training on transporting patients in these choppers.

The service will be available at the AIIMS trauma centre which has been operational for the past 10 months. While some private hospitals across the country and in Delhi have air ambulance service, AIIMS is the first government hospital in the country which has made a provision for a helipad at its newly constructed trauma centre.

Salient Alternative Healthcare Initiatives

Anthropological data to be used to formulate personalized medicine based on DNA technology for treatment of complex diseases is expected to come into use in India in the next ten years. Anthropological Society of India (ASI), as a partner of a consortium, has started gene mapping with anthropological data on 500 volunteers from certain areas of Andhra Pradesh, Mysore and Jodhpur in Rajasthan for people suffering from type two diabetes. ASI director-in-charge V.R. Rao told reporters. anthropological data collected since 1946 have provided useful information as to why people of a particular area suffer from a particular disease and need special medication and line of treatment. For instance anti-malarial drug used on patients of some North Eastern states cause fatal jaundice for the simple reason that they have 'G6PD' deficiency in their gene since their ancestors started agricultural practice 10,000 years ago by blocking off an area to collect water.

Medical Colleges of these areas, where the disease is rampant, are the other partners of the two-year project, drug manufacturers are also likely to participate in the consortium.

Biotech firm Actis Biologics India has signed an MoU with Malaysia-based Melacca Bio-tech to develop a 300 acre plot in Malaysia into a biotech city that will offer skilled scientists, technocrats, machinery and real estate facilities to entrepreneurs. Actis, a group company of the California-based Actis Biologics, USA, has been identified by the Malaysian government as its partner in its attempt to become a regional biotechnology hub. The country is targeting the biotech market, which is expected to rake in $1 trillion by 2015.

Actis Biologics has a worldwide license for Angizyme, an anti-cancer drug from Sirna and Chiron, which could be developed with Actis. It is learnt that the cost of development and commercialization of the drug in Malaysia would be less than 20% of its cost in the west. Actis has set up Malaysia Telesta Diagnostics Centre, a medical device company, focusing on computer-aided diagnosis for breast cancer. Telesta is also willing for a technology transfer to Malaysia.

Actis Biologics has already invested a Rs. 100 crore in India which includes a Rs. 15 crore research centre at Saki Naka near Mumbai. Company managing director said the clinical trial for various drugs will be conducted in India as well as Malaysia.

Medical Devices: The government will bring in a new law to regulate the Rs. 15,000 crore medical devices market in the country and curb dumping of substandard equipment here. "We are going to come up with a new legislation to enforce uniform and effective standards throughout the country. The legislation will help India regulate medical equipment from other countries. Since 85 per cent of medical equipments are imported in the country, some mechanism should be in place to check the quality of equipment coming to the country. The medical devices market in the country is worth Rs. 15,000 crore and growing by 12 to 15 per cent per annum." The minister said the bill proposed a regulatory authority that would seek to establish and maintain a national system of certification relating to quality, safety, efficacy and availability of medical devices. Science and Technology Minister Kapil Sibal told reporters here (2007).

About 80-90% of the medical equipments used in the country are imported. Industry officials said once global companies started full-scale manufacturing in India, prices of medical products could fall 15-50%. Hospitals spend a large chunk of their investment in procuring equipment. In the case of top specialty hospitals, medical equipment account for as much as 35% of their total capital investment.

In a bid to tap the booming healthcare market, global medical equipment manufacturers are now setting up plants in India. While companies such as Aloka Science and Humanity of Japan and Starkey of the US have recently set up their units, others like Philips Medical Equipment are scouting for partners.

Japanese ultrasound manufacturer Aloka has entered into a 60:40 joint venture with Chennai-based Trivitron. The joint venture will invest Rs. 50 crore and manufacture 1000 ultrasound equipments annually. Trivitron said it would soon form similar joint ventures with 3-4 more foreign companies to manufacture various medical equipments with an investment of Rs. 250 crore in a medical equipment manufacturing park in Chennai.

In the past six months, Japanese ophthalmic company Hoya, Nova of Brazil and Chinese company Mind Ray have set up assembly units in India. Niche player Starkey, the No. 1 hearing aid maker in the US, has also set up a manufacturing unit in India "As there is a good demand, companies can now break even in 2-3 years, compared with 8-10 years some years ago. It is now much more viable for companies to set up units in India," said Starkey India managing director. However, all these units will mostly manufacture low or middle level segment products and require relatively small investments (2007).

GE has a tie-up with Wipro, which manufactures diagnostic equipment in India. Philips Medical Equipment has said it is looking for suitable partner to start manufacturing in India. "The country has never seen such kind of growth. Companies, which want to cash in on the boom, would like to be close to the centre of action than just depend on imports. The country's healthcare industry could see a boom similar to the one it is witnessing in the auto sector today," said Philips Medical Equipment senior director (Indian Subcontinent).

US-based healthcare IT and technology provider PekinElmer Inc. is also looking for partners to develop its products in India. "Besides the cost advantage, the Indian healthcare industry is a large market and has the right skill set. We plan to make India the center of our exports to unregulated markets such as the Middle East, Asia and Africa," said the company's chairman and CEO. However, he added that the company would develop its sophisticated equipment for regulated markets such as the US and the UK from its global centers.

Medical equipment maker Opto Circuits India has entered into a technology transfer agreement with Italy-based Elpro Srl to develop, manufacture and market different variants of electro cardio graphs machines (ECG Machines). The agreement covers four variants of ECG machines and would give Opto Circuits the ability to market the new variants of stand-alone electro cardio graph machines in the domestic and international market. The Bangalore-based company offers medical devices such as pulse oximeters, pulse oximeter sensors, fluid warmers, cholesterol monitors and stents.

Government is planning to set up an export inspection agency for Ayurveda, Unani and Siddha (Ayush) products to put an end to frequent rejection of Indian exports. There have been instances of Indian herbal exports being rejected due to metal toxicity and microbial contamination. China is a dominant player in the global herbal drug market.

IT for Healthcare

There is great potential for IT to be used for patient care and follow-up after surgery or even to reach patients through telemedicine, most hospitals in the country use it only for business management or administrative work, a recent study has found.

The study was conducted by Bangalore-based IBM Healthcare Business Solutions. The objective of the study was to explore the current state of business in various hospitals and their usage of IT, to explore if IT could help in increasing the objectives of healthcare. The study, carried out in 127 mid-sized hospitals across 12 cities.

The fact that healthcare has to be networked for patients' care with good referral system seems to have lost its relevance and information technology is mostly used as a revenue increasing instrument. Study found that the use of personal computers was driven by the need of institutions to handle more patients and was more focused on business processes like finance and administration, instead of healthcare-related ones.

According to the study, significant scope continues to be unexploited in the core work practices that impact delivery of the healthcare services—like patient care, follow-ups after treatment or surgery.

Cisco and Satyam Computer Services announced a new venture (2007) with a focus on healthcare. Cisco announced an additional investment of $100 million targeting Indian innovation. Beginning with an emergency management—a 911 service across India, the venture will move onto healthcare applications, said Mr. John Chambers, Chairman and CEO of Cisco. Satyam developed a health IT framework—'Distress to Discharge'. The company works with 1,000 hospitals and will build healthcare solutions with the capability of virtual delivery, said Mr. Ramalinga Raju, Chairman and Founder of Satyam. Applications that can be delivered as software as a service (SaaS) model will be developed. Cisco has invested in the venture; "There is a need to bring communication technologies and applications together," he said. Cisco's Unified Communications

System and Unified Contact Center have been integrated with Satyam's customized software applications to make the services citizen-friendly. The integrated health network that will spawn in India might be used in the future in West Europe and the US.

Fortis, a leading healthcare provider entered into an agreement with Microsoft India to deploy solutions and services based on the Microsoft platform aimed at enhancing knowledge management and productivity.

Indian healthcare investments sector will require an investment of nearly 60-70 billion dollars over the next five years to ensure that quality services are made available at affordable prices. In India, we have one bed for 1,120 people which is way below the global average. We need to invest 60-70 billion dollar over the next five years in hospitals and healthcare education to expand this sector and reach out to as many people as possible. In the last 10 years, nearly 80 per cent of the investment in healthcare education has come from private sector and it's time the government started making investment in the sector. The government needs to contribute significantly to this amount especially in healthcare education sector, industry chamber CII's Healthcare Committee Chairman Pratap C. Reddy said. Renowned cardiologist Naresh Trehan said though quality of healthcare delivery was improving, affordability of these services was still a concern.

Indian drug makers have already become a formidable force in bringing out generic forms of chemically-synthesized medicines, especially in the US market, and now are gearing up to break into the follow-on biologics segment. As biotechnology products go off patent, generic drug makers will make similar copies of those drugs and bring them to market at a fraction of the cost of the innovator drug. This 'biosimilar' drug market promises to be more profitable than the chemical generics market. However, the road ahead may be long for Indian companies like Wockhardt, Dr. Reddy's Lab, Biocon, Sun Pharma, Shanta Biotech, Panacea Biotech and Ranbaxy Lab, longing to tap the exciting biosimilar market.

Indian biotech companies are also vying for the biosimilars opportunity. Smaller Indian biotech companies have also entered this segment. "We are working on some value-added products and hope to be able to file these products soon," said Panacea Biotech joint managing director. "We have cleared all the hurdles, on the side of the drug controller of India. A large number of companies are working in biotech and clinical research. So, it is just a question of time," said Analjit Singh, Chairman, Max India.

Medical Tourism

There are 50 million folks in the US, that don't have medical insurance. Part of that is a readymade market for providing care in India. Obviously, there is a huge cost difference. The idea is to work directly with the private players and with insurance companies and see if we can move some of the care provision back to India.

A report by Swiss Re forecasts that medical tourism covers will eventually become available in the West—a move that would boost manifold the inflow of foreign patients seeking treatment in India. In its Sigma report on Global Trends in Private Medical Insurance, Swiss Re has observed that in view of the significant savings potential, some experts believe that health insurance plans covering medical tourism will eventually become available and revolutionize healthcare delivery. "The globalization of healthcare is expected to have a significant impact on the strategy of health insurance companies.

A recent study shows that if one-tenth of US patients travel abroad for treatment, savings of $1.4 billion could be realized after taking into account the cost of travel," the report said. The report pointed out that many hospitals in low-cost countries like India are already getting international accreditation such as Joint Committee on Accreditation of Healthcare Organizations and often employ medical and nursing staff with American or European professional certification.

"Medical tourism will lead to an overall improvement in healthcare services. Once the market expands, everybody benefits. Today, there are hospitals working at 110% capacity and the ones who are suffering are the insurance companies," said ICICI Lombard managing director. According to him, what was pushing up costs was that those with health insurance choose to go to a handful of leading hospitals even though there was capacity available in smaller centers. "In the short-term, it could result in a shortage of beds in high-end hospitals," said Bajaj Allianz General Insurance CEO. But in the longer-term, I expect this to result in more investments in healthcare. This could also result in a reversal of the brain drain, with medical professionals returning to their homeland, he added. He said that the cost of healthcare for Indians is unlikely to go up on account of the influx, as hospitals in any case have a differential tariff for medical tourists.

"India, considered one of the leading medical tourism providers attracted five lakh foreign medical tourists in 2006. Revenues totaled $350 million and the annual growth rate for such services was 30%," the report said. Although Thailand got less than a third of medical tourists into India, its revenues have been far higher at $1 billion. At present, the obstacle to insurers providing cover for treatment in India is a lack of network with service providers.

Also, policyholders need to understand that they stand to gain by agreeing to be treated abroad. These benefits will come in the form of lower premiums or more comprehensive services. Indian providers would have to provide better protection and guarantees in case of malpractices and complications. But not all treatments are suitable for medical tourism. Most suited are elective procedures as well as non-acute complex surgeries such as joint replacement, cardiac surgery and cosmetic surgeries. It is also required that patients can travel without major pain and procedures require minimum post-operative follow-up. There is also need to develop good post-operative/treatment after care medical rehab programs which is almost negligible even for the domestic patients. That mars even the good operative treatments that patients may get. Medical rehab programs need specific development programs of training the Paramedic staff.

Sports Infrastructure Development

The objective is creating awareness about fitness for better healthcare among general public. For this government is making efforts to set up play grounds, fitness and gym centers and yoga centers at no cost for everyone. These are offered in public parks by trained instructors and gyms and fitness centers are equipped with update exercise and health equipment. On the 2nd tier, local sports clubs and gymnasiums are encouraged to expand the scope of their activities. This would also generate substantial self-employment and employment opportunities for our youth. These are subsidized by government but not totally free. Third tier is high level and expensive fitness centers, weight loss clinics, specialized massage centers like Ayurveda massage.

Government create various kinds of sports infrastructure like play fields, indoor and outdoor stadium, swimming pools, and sports hostels, district level sports complexes and State sports training complexes. Sports Authority of India (SAI) has set up training centers all over the country, and efforts are being made, on a continuing basis, to strengthen, expand and upgrade the infrastructure and facilities in these centers. Facilities need to be developed and made available for practice and training to our National Athletics on Synthetic Surfaces.

The second objective need is to bring about a major shift in the present scenario and take sportspersons to the highest possible levels and professionalism in sports, this needs to be evolved so they can compete better internationally also. With this view in mind, various public and private sector business organizations have been approached by the government sports ministry and SAI for setting up national and regional academies in specific sports disciplines to nurture and develop Indian talent. Various public sector undertakings and business houses have extended their help to set up such academies and many more are expected to come.

Delhi has a number of sports complexes in and around Delhi which is being run and maintained by DDA. Sports in Delhi cannot be said to be of world standards but it definitely has facilities that are helping young talents to groom. Sports facilities in Delhi include stadium and training academies for popular sports in India like Cricket, Golf, Tennis, Soccer, Basketball, Badminton, Swimming, etc. Siri Fort sport complex offers the best of facilities. Delhi's only international venue,

Firoz Shah Kotla for cricket matches has been the host of many historic clashes between top cricket playing nations of the world. Other new stadiums are coming up in Delhi which will be used in the Commonwealth Games, 2010. There are other clubs and sports complexes in different parts of the city whose membership varies from corporate membership to temporary membership.

The Federation of Motor Sports Clubs of India (FMSCI), national sports federation recognized by the Government of India for the promotion and control of motor sports in India, affiliated to the prestigious Indian Olympic Association, and to the Asian Motorcycle Union (AMU), over the years it has been able to involve leading manufacturers like JK Tyres, MRF Ltd., Indian Oil Corporation, Indian Tobacco Co., UB Group, McDowells, Birla Tyres, Popular Automobiles, Ceat Tyres, AVT, Goodyear, Maruti, TVS Motor Company, Escorts Yamaha, Hero Honda, etc., actively in motor sport, and their association has benefited the sport immensely. Further, it has brought almost all the major four and two wheeler manufacturers within the fold of motor sports by 'homologating' their vehicles, which is basically the technical registration of the vehicle with regard to its gearbox, suspension, etc. to ensure a level playing field in national competition. The international race track located at Chennai owned by Madras Motors Sports Club has international quality transponder and automatic timing equipment implanted at start and finish line of the track.

Delhi had the privilege and honor of hosting the Asian Games in 1982. During that time many stadiums and other sports infrastructure was built in Delhi and around Delhi but were never maintained well nor used extensively for sports and training; rather for a while they were show pieces and then were in disuse. It is only in recent years that Siri fort complex is developed well. It has once again got the chance to host the mega sports event, the Commonwealth Games, 2010. This will be the first time when India is hosting such a big event after Asian Games.

The process of development, improvement in infrastructure and revamping Delhi is under progress. Commonwealth Games village is being constructed on a 40 acre site in east Delhi. The proposed village would have the capacity of around 8,500 athletes and officials. The new and existing stadiums in Delhi would be used to host games like Aquatics, Athletics, Badminton, Boxing, Cycling, EAD Events, Gymnastics, Hockey, Lawn Bowls, Netball, Rugby Shooting, Squash, Table Tennis, Weightlifting and Wrestling.

The sports infrastructure, sports training competitive sports have developed negligibly in the country. But surprisingly lots of sports equipment, apparel and accessories are manufactured in India and exported. Foreign companies like Nike, Adidas for shoes and sportswear, etc. have set up manufacturing units in India either for Indian market or as hub to export to other countries. Indian companies themselves are into sports equipment business also either individually or in joint ventures with foreign companies. India is allowed to import sports equipment but it is replacing this more and more by manufacturing in India itself. Their manufacturing is of high quality.

Other Health Concerns: In general, health concerns in these upcoming sectors lead to attrition as well as loss in productivity. A sharp rise in lifestyle diseases such as heart problems and strokes, coupled with a lack of adequate preventive healthcare, threatens India's future growth prospects, a research study said. Experts warn that the country's hugely successful outsourcing industry could be the hardest hit. Heart diseases, strokes and diabetes are estimated to have wiped $9 billion (€6.5 billion) off India's national income in 2005, but the losses could total a staggering $200 billion (€144 billion) over the next 10 years if corrective action is not taken quickly, according to a study released in Nov. 2007.

The study by the Indian Council for Research on International Economic Relations, a New Delhi-based research group, said India's rapid economic expansion has boosted corporate profits and employee incomes, but has also sparked a surge in workplace stress and lifestyle diseases that few Indian companies have addressed. Long working hours, night shifts and a sedentary lifestyle make people employed at information technology companies prone to heart disease and diabetes, the report said. There have also been growing reports of mental depression and family discord in the industry.

Health Minister (2007) said his biggest concern was the country's information technology industry that has grown rapidly, riding on the outsourcing boom in recent years. It's the fastest-growing industry in our country, but it is most vulnerable to lifestyle diseases. Its future growth could be stunted if we don't address the problem now. Minister said he was in touch with the information technology ministry to persuade companies to conduct health checks on their employees and take measures to minimize risk.

Infosys Technologies Ltd., India's second-largest software exporter, has a 24 hour hot line for employees suffering from depression to access psychiatrists, and for marriage counseling. Infosys introduced a work-life balance plan. But not many companies in the outsourcing industry conduct regular health checks or provide similar support to their employees.

The ICRIER study (2007), said corporate initiatives are crucial because of low levels of public health spending and poor insurance coverage in India. India's per capita health spending of $7 is one of the lowest in the world and is a fraction of what the United States spends $2,548, according to a 2006 WHO report.

EDUCATION INFRASTRUCTURE

Education System: Structural Changes

Government thinks primitively about education sector so crucial for the country's growth. This could have dramatically altered an average Indian's life. It needs drastic change in policy formation as well as implementation. The purpose of real education is not to let people be only well versed in reading and writing or producing technical or academics but the real purpose is to make them creative, widen their horizons and inflame their intellect. But we have not even reached our first target of making people literate; school educated and vocationally trained fitting the job employability. Our second target is of course higher education for all again with employability curriculum and training. These would change periodically according to the demands of the job market not only nationally but globally where Indians are in demand and they compete.

Government takes onus of formulating the educational policies and providing resources and funding for elementary to higher education both general and technical, and supported by vocational training programs periodically. Government through its educational subsidies makes it affordable for lower and middle segments of population to educate themselves. Besides this, the private efforts and public-private partnership does create sound educational institutions both at school level and higher education; and for technical programs and training but not affordable for the lower strata of society. In 2005-06, the aggregate government spending on education stood at around Rs. 1,20,346 crores; but main concern is how well the funds are being spent for implementation of these policies and to face the barriers for universal education for all.

Our educational system needs structural change. There is lack of quality education and skills, lack of technical and vocational training and low implementation of policies. A negligible percentage of children who complete the primary level of education continue to the diploma level and even smaller ratio goes on further. The discontinuation of education leads to the accumulation of job seekers in the bottom of the education pyramid and the immediate fallout of this is the low skill levels among the working population.

We need systematic and consistent education and job policies matching the manpower forecasts. It is necessary to expand and upgrade education system, adopt new educational models and skills training programs focusing on emerging practices; and to change the long term and short term educational curriculum accordingly. It is important to initiate structural changes in the educational policy and vocational training programs to create a skilled workforce.

"Action plan for education must hit, the action plan for opening 6,000 schools in every village block, 30 central universities and a network of vocational training institutes across the country will be ready in two months. It is only then that the common man will have faith in our ability to deliver our promises; the prime minister told in a meeting on education at the Planning Commission, we cannot discuss options endlessly we need to work with a sense of urgency and in fixed timelines if we have to see action on the ground. Otherwise, we will continue with a theoretical exercise within these four walls for some more years," he added.

He told the meeting "that the outlay for education during the 11th Five Year Plan, which runs from the current fiscal to 2012-13, represents a four-fold increase over the previous plan and stands at Rs. 2,500 billion. The share of education in the total plan will correspondingly increase from 7.7 per cent to 19.4 per cent, adding that it represented a credible progress in enhancing public spending for education to six per cent of gross domestic product" (July 2007).

Reforms in higher education are needed. Directing the Planning Commission to work on the proposal to hike the fees for higher education, Singh favored roping in private sector in both secondary and higher education. "We should also seriously look at the proposal for fee increases to reasonable levels in a graduated manner accompanied by a scheme of extensive scholarships and loans" to ensure that no student is denied education because of financial constraint, he said.

The contribution of institutions of higher education to lifelong education for all must be encouraged by adopting diversified class schedules and designing relevant formulae. Access to education and quality education must be thought of as interdependent and inseparable needs and rights. All of these steps must benefit in priority the poorest and most marginalized populations.

Universities in India are seeking to contribute to 'ICT for Development' efforts, the impact of their efforts upon society and universities, and the internal and external challenges they face in realizing a productive and meaningful place in the ICT for development movement. In other words, it is important to have affordable and widespread access to ICTs, locally relevant content in local languages, offline and online forums for discussing ICT applications, e-commerce services, and human resource capacity, a culture which embraces innovation, investment capital, and cooperation between multiple stakeholders.

People should have higher levels of general, professional and technical education. Such talented and educated manpower create as well as avail of better employment opportunities. With higher levels of education they are able to create innovative ways of doing things in different domains of life and may be in innovations of ideas, products and services. Well-educated manpower not only understand how to control the hurdles for health, environmental pollution, bad food, but through talent and innovative ways it creates as well as supply the employment market both in the country and worldwide.

Technology is a great facilitator for health, education, employment and in fact for procuring BMN as well as additional added values to them to improve the quality of life.

It made the case that secondary education for women and girls had been shown to translate into improved economic prospects, better reproductive health, improved AIDS awareness and more enlightened attitudes toward health practices.

Providing quality of education to enhance learning and develop critical thinking to benefit from knowledge created by relevant and timely information is imperative. The Internet and multimedia tools must not cause us to lose interest in traditional knowledge sources such as the press, radio, television and, above all, the school. Most of the people in the world need books, school textbooks and teachers before computers and Internet access.

Other Initiatives

The Millennium Schools will be set up across Indian cities by independent trusts and societies. These will incorporate unique blend of global best practices in education and inherent strengths of Indian education system with the added advantage of MLS, the Educomp solutions company's cutting-edge software, proprietary learning system for schools.

Millennium Schools will be founded on—a culture of innovative thinking, modem application of technology in traditional systems of education and a pioneering zeal in fashioning students for an increasingly competitive world of the future. It will introduce for the first time in India—a unique and structured talent development program that will seek to nurture the inherent talent in each child in the early part of their schooling life, expanding and upgrading education system, adopting new educational models and skills training programs focusing on emerging practices.

Global internship programs are on the rise and companies are experimenting with fresh talent by hiring Ivy League students to work in their organizations and exposing them to the Indian work culture. Indian students also work on exchange internship programs abroad to gain the experience of global demands, work ethics, work culture and above all what kind of educational and training programs will fit them to these global emerging jobs.

Information infrastructure solutions for human development: EMC the world leader in information infrastructure solutions, announced 25 new information infrastructure products and solutions in India, and demonstrated the increased momentum that its India go-to-market strategy has delivered. This is EMC's largest software development facility in Hyderabad outside of North America. This includes strengthening the India leadership team and announcing that 75 educational institutions in India have entered the EMC Academy Program. The EMC Academy Program is an academic partnership with leading educational institutions in India, aimed at building a resource pool of skilled, industry ready information management and storage professionals in the country.

The products announced include high-end and mid-range storage arrays, data protection software, information security software and content management solutions. Grouped in the four categories of Store, Protect, Optimize and Leverage, they offer customers in India the tools they need to build an intelligent information infrastructure.

"With the explosion of information quantity and complexity, Indian organizations of all sizes are looking to store, protect, optimize and leverage this information. EMC and our partners are there to help them build an intelligent information infrastructure for competitive advantage."

According to EMC estimates, in 2007 the market for EMC's information infrastructure products and solutions in India across the Financial Services, Telecommunications, Media & Entertainment, Public Sector, Healthcare, Discrete Manufacturing, Retail and Energy verticals exceeds USD 603 million. EMC estimates that the information infrastructure solution needs are growing at more than 12 per cent annually. Globally in 2007, EMC estimates the total addressable market for information infrastructure to be USD 61 billion.

Premji of WIPRO advocates ICT can facilitate improvement on several of these dimensions. To him use of ICT for literacy is almost intuitive, given the challenge of reaching out to large numbers which a country like India faces. ICT provides us an effective tool for connecting with a large number of remotely located learners at a low cost.

His perspective on the use of ICT for education and literacy is based on their interaction with the parents and schools in over 1300 villages in 2000, through the Azim Premji Foundation. Through these interactions they gained the following perspective: Parental feedback indicates strong demand for computers; they also consider computer interface as an enabler for knowing English; ICT can strengthen our efforts for universalizing primary education and; ICT could also be the solution to a uniform high quality of instructions without replacing teachers. But more than that, they learnt that ICT also has a huge role in attracting children to the school, and creating excitement in and around the school. ICT is not about the computers or the educational CDs or the Internet or the specific device or medium we use. It is really about a different process that we deploy for the purpose of enhancing the quality of education. It is about providing alternative learning experiences to the children who currently do not have options other than textbook as a learning tool.

The basic issues of quality, equity and access to education still remain unresolved. The policymakers are still apprehensive of the real value of integrating technologies in education to address these critical issues. Again decision-making in technology integration in education is often affected by lack of adequate information on the demonstrated value of technology in enhancing the quality and reach of education. Where technology has succeeded in influencing the education outreach and quality, supporting processes and frameworks that can sustain such efforts have not emerged. A lack of adequate knowledge sharing among key stakeholders has also delayed the process of using technologies as enablers of learning.

EMPLOYMENT

Human Capital Development

Human development in context of 'workforce' for employment contribute to economic growth, change in quality of lifestyles both for individuals and society in general. In India, we have abundance of people of workable age and this could be turned to advantage if appropriately developed, otherwise it becomes liability. The software of human development is to promote education, healthcare, and end caste and gender discrimination in jobs.

Manpower development could have two dimensions: developing workforce in general with sound education, appropriate vocational skills, upgrading the work skills through training and new skills. Over and above, the skills of the work force should match the current demands for such workforce so there is full employability as well meeting work requirement whether industry of otherwise.

Manpower development in a business organization focus on defining talent needs, discovering talents and then developing those talents. The crucial point is to then deploy right people for right job. If companies are able to master these four capabilities, they can be talent powered organization, multiplying their 'talent' for high performance and thus significantly increase its value and competitiveness over long term. Its long term objective could be developing next generation of manpower workforce, talent pool and industry leaders.

Therefore to develop the workforce, we need sound education, employability skills both in local and global contexts. Finances and investments are needed for developing human resources to match the demands of globalization for manpower needs through expanding and upgrading education system, new educational models and skills training programs focusing on emerging practices. Development of local human resource is of utmost importance for glocalization.

The domestic finances for manpower development may be provided by government, private enterprises and institutions, universities and academic foundations. Foreign funding may be invested by such foreign counterparts.

Manpower Development Decision

In India, the major manpower development decision is taken by the government by formulating the educational policies and providing resources and funding for elementary to higher education both general and technical, and supported by vocational training programs periodically. Governments through its educational subsidies make it affordable to lower and middle segments of population. In turn, this investment creates employment for a larger number of people and thus giving good ROI.

This is the base on which different enterprises both business and academic develop workforce talents capabilities according to the rising demands and deploy them efficiently for better organizational performance. More of these rather than government contribute to developing and matching the talents according to globalization demands as many of the Indians are working worldwide in different capacities either when these enterprises set up their own business subsidiaries such as Infosys Technologies, TCS, etc. abroad or they need the Indian software engineers, managers, etc. to manage businesses of Indians abroad such as oil companies using such personnel. On the lower levels also there is increasing demands for even skilled and unskilled labor for construction and turnkey work. Since India has policy of allowing migrants to work aboard. They can have better wages when trained well. The global MNEs develop the local Indian talents when they set up manufacturing or servicing units in India such as Nokia and Motorola for production of cell phones and IBM for computer production and others for semi-conductor businesses. They train and develop technical workforce according to the needs of the industry.

Thus, developing human resources in glocalization, global and local contexts are multi-level and multi-source. It is public-private, government-business, and government-business-global enterprises. It may look complex but not since every entity streamline their efforts and investments to meet their demands.

Employment and Skill Development

India's 11th Five Year Plan is proposing to create seven crores jobs with a view to check the rising unemployment rate and making growth more inclusive during the plan period (2007-12). The challenge to meet this target is to initiate structural changes in the educational policy and vocational training programs to create a skilled workforce. An aggressive public-private, government-business, and government-business-global participation is needed in these efforts.

Despite a projected annual growth rate of 12 per cent, the nation faces a grim future in the face of an acute shortage of skilled manpower, warned Confederation of Indian Industry. "There is an urgent need to create more skilled labor in the country. Unless the private sector is involved in development and education to create more skilled personnel, it would be difficult to meet this demand. We have been caught unawares by the sudden spurt in demand for skilled manpower. Even as the Indian industry has grown faster than anticipated, the needs of skilled labor also has gone up considerably. But I am confident we will be able to bridge this shortfall within the next two to three decades if the issue is appropriately addressed by the government and the private sector jointly." Our discussions in chapter 3 about business expansions in India reflect the urgent and expanding need of skilled, trained personnel in various disciplines and in various technologies in local, glocal and global contexts. If we have skilled personnel we cannot complain about unemployment, low incomes and poverty; and the expanding youth demographics becoming problematic.

It is not only important that economy grows at a pace that absorbs all the job seekers; but it must also expand in activities that generate jobs whether in manufacturing, services, tourism, etc. IT firms and BPO provide jobs to only a million out of 1 billion. In terms of employment, the IT and IT-enabled services sector in India is a rapidly expanding industry and continues to draw significant pools of talent and energy, despite the current economic downturn globally. India seems to have cemented its position as the "outsourcing centre of the world"; and Indian software, services and content companies are gearing up to move up the value chain from basic services to products. In addition to tapping the global software market, having a sizeable domestic user base means India can sustain a lot of local infrastructure, content, foreign capital investment and an online market in general—unlike other, smaller countries that need to focus much more on overseas markets.

We need systematic and consistent education and job policies matching the manpower forecasts; when we will change the educational curriculum and employability skills and training according to the workforce needed ahead.

India Labor Report, 2007 commissioned by TeamLease Services, a human resource and staffing agency highlights the fall outs why the Indian youth are simply "unemployable". Ninty per cent of employment opportunities require vocational skills. But 90% of our college and school output has only bookish knowledge, says the study. The India Labor Report estimates that repairing this skill deficit could cost Rs. 4,90,000 crores, or 10% of our GDP over the next two years. While current budgets facilitate for 25% of this amount, merely allocating more funds is not the solution.

While only 8% of the youth are unemployed, 53% have some kind of skill deprivation. This becomes critical, as nearly 90% of jobs in India are still skill based, with the bulk of employment coming from farming, fisheries and other related work.

Youth un-employability is a bigger crisis than unemployment as poor quality of skills or education show up in low incomes rather than unemployment. Fifty-eight per cent of graduates make less than Rs. 75,000 per year, the report says. Little wonder then that India's per capita income continues to be among the lowest in the world, despite being the fastest growing economy in the world. A degree-driven Indian society treats education as a proxy for skill levels creating strong supply-demand mismatch, says TeamLease Services chairman. Barely 9-10% of India's graduates are found employable. Over 90% of India's 18,064 colleges and 68% of its 378 universities fall under poorer B and C grade "This isn't about funds and resources," says CII, HRD committee chairman. In 2005-06, the aggregate government spending on education stood at around Rs. 1,20,346 crores. It is about how well the funds are being spent.

That is also the reason, economists say, while India will grow to be among the richest countries in the world, its citizens will not be as wealthy as the average American and European citizen. The math is fairly simple. Between a little over a billion people, even a marginal increase in their earnings can propel the country's GDP into a different league. For the people who put it there though, things will change only marginally. Women lag significantly behind males in terms of work participation and employment.

Self-assessed people are ready to make use of their strengths through opportunities available, and through demand. They demand training programs to develop their weaknesses into strengths. This is excellent for human talent development programs.

Despite fears of an economic slowdown in India and a slump worldwide, the country's employers are looking for workers actively. India has topped a global employment outlook survey, powered mainly by service industries such as IT, realty and financial services. The latest quarterly survey of about

5,636 employers—part of a global sample of 55,000—by multinational human resource firm Manpower Inc. says that India's Net Employment Outlook for the July-September quarter 2008 stands at 45 per cent, the highest in the world. "The strongest hiring intention is seen in sectors such as the services, finance, insurance, real estate, media and tourism, Manpower Hiring intentions are weakest in the wholesale and retail trade industry sector and the manufacturing sector where employers have indicated a decline in their hiring plans." The IT and IT-enabled services sector—which accounts for call centers and back-office services have the most active hiring outlook. Employers in all four zones of the country have shown positive hiring intentions.

Education System—Structural Changes

Our educational system needs structural change. There is lack of quality education and skills, lack of technical and vocational training and low implementation of policies. A negligible percentage of children who complete the primary level of education continue to the diploma level and even smaller ratio goes on further. The discontinuation of education leads to the accumulation of job seekers in the bottom of the education pyramid and the immediate fallout of this is the low skill levels among the working population. Absence of vocational training in the regular curriculum hits the poor hard. In fact plenty of graduates and post-graduates too realize that their soft skills help them more than their grades to land a job. Due to sharp supply-demand mismatch at the top of the pyramid, the wage differential between primary and higher-level educated workers is rising rapidly. "Poor are stuck in low-skilled services with not much upward mobility," says Crisil India chief economist.

India, a relatively smaller economy with a far bigger workforce, faces a crisis perhaps far deeper than any other nation in the world today. Its demographic trends (300 million new workers by 2025), its archaic education system (barely 9-10% of graduates are employable) and economic structure (agriculture contributes 18% to the GDP and employs 56%)—

all of them have converged to make the crisis difficult. India is not a sequential economy with linear growth, farm to non-farm, rural to urban, analog to digital, manual to tech-driven and domestic-focus to exports—multiple transitions are happening simultaneously here. ***We have a de-skilling economy without a re-skilling workforce.***

Lots of things are changing about the job market. Women, from all economic backgrounds, are entering the workforce in big numbers. Aspirations, irrespective of social background, are surging. Talent mobility is in, lifetime employment is out, attrition is high and future certainty is low. Constant training, update re-skilling to remain in demand is a reality which both corporates and job seekers need to realize. India will have to work hard to turn its demographics into advantage. As the world's youngest nation in the tech-edged global world, the fast momentum of the economy will demand these fast and update changes. Its education crisis peaks with the demographic trends. In the next five years, one in every four new global workers will be Indian. Alongside, India's working age population (15-60 years) will swell in the next two decades. It is absolute time to act and address the issue now in terms by 300 million and in percentage terms from 58% in 2001 to 64% by 2025.

To create a sustained cadre of 'knowledge workers', India needs to make its education system more demand driven to meet the emerging needs of the economy and to keep its highly qualified people in the country, suggests the research report. "This means raising the quality of all higher education institutions, not just a few world-class ones, such as the Indian Institutes of Technology."

Some ways of making the system more demand driven are to allow the private sector to fill the burgeoning demand for higher education. Increased university-industry partnerships to translate research into applications can yield economic value. Lifelong learning programs can be used to meet the learning needs of all, both within and outside the school system, including using distance learning technologies to expand access to and the quality of formal education and lifelong training programs.

The knowledge economy system requires an education system that is flexible—starting from basic education that provides the foundation for learning, to secondary and tertiary education that can develop core skills, including technical skills; that encourage creative and critical thinking for problem-solving and innovation and to a system of lifelong learning. Lifelong learning system encompasses formal training, non-formal on job learning and informal learning from family members and people in the community.

Tackle Employability Crisis

Manpower supply in general is likely to improve due to various initiatives taken on talent and workforce development by NASSCOM, companies themselves and various engineering colleges, and management institutes and business schools. Now even CII is focusing attention on educational reforms, India Inc.'s attention and lobbying will help enormously (2007). Here are five reasons why employability crisis may get better.

India Inc. Feels the Pinch

So far they focused on restructuring themselves, technology, plant productivity, government policies and other external issues. Now, amid hyper growth, they have begun to worry about skilled talent. It began with the IT industry at the top end. Now virtually every sector—including sectors like construction requiring thousands of masons—are worrying about it.

Unsustainable Workforce Pyramid

Looking at the economy, the workforce pyramid is not sustainable. Manufacturing is growing but services will remain the mainstay of the economy. Agriculture contributing 18% of the GDP and employing 56% of workforce is in crisis and not sustainable. Pushed by poor farm incomes, lured by a talent-starved corporate sector and helped little by the governments and NGOs, the change in the workforce pyramid has begun.

A Political Time Bomb

Inequality is rising, especially in urban India. The social stress combined with surging aspirations in a sizzling economy is a potent combination. After the debacle of 'Incredible India' campaign, issues around education, training, employment—those that directly impact the lower strata of the society is far more sharply in focus. There is geographical skew also. More new workers are in BIMARU states whereas jobs are being created elsewhere will worsen the stress. Demanded by the industry, the government will find good reasons to reform educational system.

Skilled talent needs a critical mass of public-private partnership.

Education-focused companies like Educomp and NIIT are rapidly scaling up and spreading into myriad areas like retailing, banking and finance to cater to the growing talent needs. Universities and premier colleges like Manipal University, IIMs, Symbiosis see good business and growth opportunities in tying up with companies like TeamLease, RPG, L&T, ICICI to offer customized training programs. Firms like Sterlite and SeaKing are exploring full-fledged universities. Amid all this, not-for-profit sector—independent or run by corporates are rapidly evolving and scaling up to connect needs of companies, government and deprived sections.

Manpower training offered by Adobe systems India announced the launch of new site licensing options, curriculum and certification programs to encourage digital communication in schools and technical institutes. This revolutionary offering for the Indian education sector is a unique software licensing program to distribute creative software products cost effectively among schools and other higher educational institutions. The new resources will make it easier for schools to deploy Adobe's new offering of tightly integrated, industry-leading design and development tools into the curriculum, as well as into career and technical education programs.

NITT Asia's largest trainer and leading Global Talent Development Corporation and Adobe Systems Incorporated have entered into a global alliance to create talent pool for Design, Web, Mobile and Interactive Media. Through this strategic partnership, NIIT will offer training programs on Adobe's software tools and technologies used in business, entertainment and personal communication, across its network of 32 countries. Global leader, Adobe will provide access to its software tools and technologies in the emerging creative space, and enable the large software developer community and creative professionals to skill themselves for the Media, rich interactive Web 2.0, and Animation & Gaming Industries.

Adobe and NIIT will also jointly set up showcase centers in key Indian metro cities. NIIT will also offer the training programs in emerging markets such as China and Vietnam, in addition to 30 other countries in its global network.

There is a requirement for 3,00,000 animation professionals by 2008 and the market for gaming development in India is expected to reach USD300 million by 2009, at a CAGR of 78 per cent according to NASSCOM Study on Animation and Gaming Industry (2006). Indian entertainment and media industry is witnessing a phenomenal growth and is slated to grow at 19 per cent by 2010 according to FICCI PWC report—2005. It is also a reboot time for Indian advertising industry with predictions that the online segment is likely to cross the 100 million dollar mark by 2010, according to a study by MSN. Besides this, India is set to become the largest pay-TV advertising market by 2010 with total ad spends on pay-TV channels touching $1.8 billion by that year, as per a study by the Cable and Satellite Broadcasting Association of Asia (CASBAA).

While Adobe will provide access to its latest software development tools and technical resources, NIIT will leverage its inherent strength in curriculum design and expertise in education process management. NIIT will offer training on Adobe's enterprise products with rich internet applications.

Employment Generation & Marketing Mission (EGMM)

EGMM is a government-managed scheme linked strongly to private sector needs. Companies help identify training areas and put together course modules, which makes them better attuned to what the market needs. The program is a novel public-private partnership that addresses the employability issue among the underprivileged rural youth.

What's so special about the EGMM? First, this is a government-managed program linked strongly to private sector needs. Second, companies help identify training areas and put together course modules, which makes them better attuned to what the market needs.

The mission targets poorest of poor rural youth, many of them illiterate; it screens them and then depending on their capabilities and the industry's needs, puts together a program to train them and help them get jobs. Private sector is actively involved in developing and supporting the program. For example, illiterates are put through a program to land jobs in the construction and textile sector; whereas 10th, 12th pass and graduates are trained to be employed in the services sector.

In November 2006, EGMM set up a Rural Retail Academy and has already trained 5000 plus. They are put through 45 day training sessions. While 10th and 12th class pass have been trained for customer care positions, graduates are groomed for supervisory roles. Course modules are developed in-house with the help of industry.

Job Opportunities Diversified

Business expansions in various domains and in diverse directions are creating job opportunities and as we discussed we make efforts to grab them by sound education and matching and updated skills but also we have to move from conventional job areas to others:

Farm-to-non-farm jobs for ruralites: Lured by growing job opportunities in urban India, cajoled by a talent-starved India Inc. and compelled by a crisis-ridden agriculture sector, farmers and their children are beginning to think non-agri jobs. In any geography, at any time, this farm-to-non-farm journey has never been easy. But it is particularly so in India. The contrast between rural and urban life is dramatic. Urban India, with rising consumerism, technology and media explosion feels closer to the developed world. Rural India, many with no power, no schools, and little entertainment and poor communication are closer to sub-Saharan Africa.

Finance Minister suggested providing services like education, healthcare, water and roads in villages to improve the conditions of the rural masses, which he said would be the true percolation of India's 9 per cent economic growth. "I don't agree with the argument that economic growth will (on its own) percolate to villages," advocating pro-active steps to take growth to rural India. He said taking growth to the masses would mean creating jobs that produce goods and services which can, in turn, be consumed by the rural population. Farmers, he said, must be imparted skills which make it possible to wean them away from agriculture to off-farm activities like sheep rearing or dairy and then to non-farm vocations like industrial jobs.

Prime Minister Manmohan Singh has been an advocate of shifting India's large farm dependent population to non-farm jobs to reduce load on the sector, which has been growing at less than 2 per cent per annum. India's agriculture sector supports roughly 600 million people, but contributes less than 20 per cent to the GDP (Sept. 2007).

"Rural workers are natural candidates for government and quasi-government jobs where they can be absorbed easily and transition is easier, says Crisil India chief economist. In fact that has been the easiest route to shift rural workers and create middle class for many nations. But in India the government is not hiring, in fact its role in job creation is rapidly shrinking. In China, the booming manufacturing sector requiring plenty of blue-collar workers has helped. The Chinese factories have been absorbing thousands of illiterate, unskilled farm workers with the lure of better salaries.

There is organized major foray into the blue-collar temping space now. The temping firms have around 3,000-4,000 people on the rolls. But they are focused on certain industrial belts spread over southern and western India. Earlier, temporary blue-collar labor will look for jobs by themselves and would waste many manpower days when not getting jobs or exploited by lower wages.

Adecco India globally, is quite strong in the blue-collar temping space. It has now identified this as a future growth driver in India. "In three years time, we expect our blue-collar temp strength in India will be nearly 25,000-30,000 people. This vertical will also contribute significantly to the top line," added Adecco India CEO.

Adecco will also start training initiatives for upgrading skills of the blue-collar employees. "Globally, we have a 'earn and learn' scheme which will be rolled out in India. We may set up separate infrastructure for this." The company is also going to enter three new verticals in India—retail, hospitality and healthcare. "Our current temp manpower strength of about 40,000 people will grow to 65,000-70,000 people by December 2008 with a bulk of the addition in retail and hospitality."

While temping firms like TeamLease are already big time into the blue-collar segment, others too are now getting into the act with several SEZ projects in the pipeline. Industry sources said other staffing majors like Manpower and Ma Foi have shown interest to be major players in this segment.

However, there are certain grey areas like labor laws. But, there are several smaller firms which are operating successfully and the government too has given indications of liberalization in blue-collar temping. The contract labor segment will become more organized.

In India, the economic growth has been services-led creating primarily a white-collar employment boom. These jobs are at the top end of the value chain in sectors like IT, R&D, banking and engineering services; and the skills these sectors need like communication, customer care, English language fluency are much higher than available with rural folks. Job opportunities are brought by outsourcing and offshoring. The call center has become the symbol of India's newly globalize workforce. While traditional India sleeps, a dynamic young cohort of highly skilled articulate professionals work throughout the night functioning on US time zone, under foreign ID pretending familiarity with culture and climate where they have never been. But this is now changing because India has set up its value. Many in India see the call centers as sweatshops soul-destroying soaking up the talents and energies of youngsters who should be doing better for themselves and their country. But these youngsters enjoy of premature affluence and westernization in Indian setting. Whatever may be the impact; at least they are absorbed in the job market after mere graduation with no skills, all skills provided by the call centers on job training. Large retail outlets meant more jobs in storage and logistics departments.

India's growth story has thrown up immense job opportunities for expats and NRI managers, pilots and other high-salaried professionals, so far. Now it's the turn of cheap and skilled labor from outside India to participate in the growth story. Companies have already started hiring or plan to hire such labor in thousands.

India's biggest real estate developer, DLF, plans to bring 20,000 Indian laborers from the Middle East back home to work for its projects. This follows the move made by Reliance Industries, which hired nearly 4,000 Chinese workers to lay a gas pipeline in the country.

DLF Laing-O'Rourke, a joint venture between DLF and UK-based real estate company which undertakes construction work for DLF in India, wants to hire skilled laborers such as carpenters, bar benders and electricians from China, Indonesia and Philippines. "Chinese labor comes at a low cost and is more productive. Plus, they can be used as captive resource," says a DLF official.

But the UPA government, surviving on support from pro-labor Left ally, has been reluctant in issuing visas. So, the company is now focused on bringing back Indian laborers working in the Middle East.

"There's a large Indian workforce in the Middle East including in projects executed by Laing-O'Rourke. Some workers may want to relocate to India and we could look at the possibility of absorbing them in our projects here," said DLF Laing-O'Rourke India director. The numbers could be close to 20,000.

If the plan goes through, it could be one of the biggest home-coming for Indian laborers, who for the past three decades have been working in Gulf countries to earn higher wages under difficult conditions. DLF's move holds the promise of a better life for these laborers, who are seen as the least beneficiary of India's economic reforms.

DLF plans to match wages and perks the workers currently earn in the Middle East. They would be brought on the rolls of the company, a departure from the current practice where most construction companies source laborers from labor contractors.

Manpower Development

The outsourced countries—India is one of them, have to face the human development challenges because of the widening scope of outsourcing and increase in quantity of outsourcing that would need more skilled and trained manpower in specified areas. These countries must spend more resources on educating, training in focused vocational and professional areas, and ongoing upgrading of these skills and training in new skills to meet the demands of increased outsourcing as well as the new trends in outsourcing. These countries will have great apprehensions about loss of outsource business if trained manpower supply is not timely.

There is need to develop the skills required in a technology services-led economy. This is the foundation for a new discipline that industry and academia are calling Services Sciences, Management and Engineering (SSME). This new field will bring together ongoing work in computer science, operations research, industrial engineering, business strategy, management sciences, social and cognitive sciences, and legal sciences to develop the skills required in a services-led economy.

The ability to use ICTs for human resource development empowers people. There is ability gap which need to be narrowed. Here is where the HRD and capacity building comes into play. Education is the fundamental enabler of the knowledge economy. Well-educated and skilled people are essential for creating, sharing, disseminating, and using knowledge effectively. Government has been very supportive in adopting broadband as an important vehicle for delivery of educational content and is planning to connect all the secondary schools and colleges in the country by Broadband.

The end goal of manpower development is by giving knowledge an unprecedented accessibility, and by engaging in capacity-building for everyone. These could include the behavioral training and behavioral transformation training; and the capacity building and capacity strengthening training.

Closing the digital divide will not suffice to close the knowledge divide, for access to useful, relevant knowledge is more than simply a matter of infrastructure. It depends on training, cognitive skills and regulatory frameworks geared towards access to contents—various rifts observed in the main areas that make up knowledge (access to information, education, scientific research, and cultural and linguistic diversity); From the point of access and participation, there are many knowledge-related asymmetries on a global scale, the digital divide, the scientific divide, massive illiteracy and the brain drain, etc. Gender inequality is a glaring example.

Today learning is redefining the entire process of training and education. It is helping organizations to utilize information technology in enhancing employee skills and increasing their productivity. With the immense competition in the market, companies need to continuously upgrade their systems, products and obviously their employee proficiencies. E-Learning is proving to be of great help in this aspect. Knowledge and talent management are crucial for any organization to meet its business goals; And e-Learning is a means for achieving talent transformation and management. The demand for constant up gradation necessitates this and e-Learning is an extension of the organization's training program.

Learning needs vary from organization to organization. These needs are interrelated with the organization's overall work environment. An effective learning environment works only if the culture and the nature of the organization are assessed initially. The learning solutions are then built based on these findings. For example, in an extremely diverse organization, training might be effective completely through e-Learning; in some organizations, a blend of e-Learning as well as instructor-led training might prove the most effective.

Learning is changing the way the world learns. The fact that the largest universities and well-known institutions like IITs and IIMs are extensively using e-Learning as a mode of learning indicates that times have changed.

New practices in e-Learning suggest broader deployment of conferencing technology in classrooms, to incorporate conferencing technology and other technologies into courses of study. This has made e-Learning more effective. This is happening as there is technology improvement, enhanced functionality, lower pricing and increasing demand for e-Learning solutions. Today's 'media conferencing' approach is integrating audio, video and multimedia tools enabling the use of power point and other desktop applications teaching used in teaching environment now that is available in video-conferencing. The increased functionality, combined with intuitive easy to understand user interfaces, makes it simple for educators to adopt new technology in classroom settings.

India wants its economic development to facilitate human development. It has been focusing on the training and development skills needed for the workforce in demand. As there will be more and more demand for skilled workforce, a mix of focal economic activities would also need mix of skills according to the market strengths it wants to develop.

Globally Integrated Model Jobs

In the Internet process, a new category of work is emerging, the digital factory job. Behind the Internet ad offerings, thousands of human workers are working on data round the clock. Every time you search the Web, the work of such human workers is there; such as the editor, who would do cut and paste digital data, search marketing specialists to type phrases and drive ad traffic, book scanner to flip book pages for digital photos, operator to type put business cards and contact information, and data entry operators.

Companies are going from national to MNC and to globally integrated model. What is the difference between MNC and one having a globally integrated model? In early part of this century, especially the war years, market access was important. Some global operations were multinational operations. The shift in today's world is that it's much less industrialized and much more service oriented. Globally, there is phenomenal intellectual capability and talent in the entire global community. The potential to tap that is huge. This leads to globally integrated model.

The companies doing global businesses must be staffed by international workforce. Any global model needs to be fueled by outstanding local insights. They know the consumers better than headquarters. Indian companies are hiring specialists and local anchors in each country to help reconcile differences and conflicts since they find themselves ill-equipped to tackle diverse consumer and employee cultures in alien markets after the recent spate of mergers and acquisitions. Indian multinationals are now recruiting more locals at the front-end of the business in new global markets. We are hiring talent from international business schools and training our employees to acquire a global mind-set. Indian business schools are also giving importance to exposing students to the elements of international businesses.

Some Instances: Marico, in fact, held a global meet recently (2006) to discuss the relevance of the company values in a global market and expose people to diverse cultures. The integration of international managers plays a big factor in developing global expertise. Understanding how people think, work, eat, and interact in a foreign workplace is crucial to building a successful operation. There are positive aspects also. Cultural diversity has tremendous potential for innovation, arising from the presence of multiple perspectives. "We were initially uncomfortable with the process-oriented systems and a lot of time and planning that people in organizations abroad did before taking on a new project. As Indian businesses, we have the practice of plunging into project head-on and taking decisions along the way."

Tata Motors, which took over Daewoo's commercial vehicle division, continues to let Korean managers run the place. "We decided against placing too many Indian managers at the place so as to let them integrate faster into the system and also draw from each other's strengths. We thought it better to let the company function as a part of the local economy," said a top company official.

Sectoral Job Demands: India is foraying into many unconventional business sectors which are new to India. That needs trained personnel at every level and with speed. A few sectors are mentioned to make the point.

The Aviation Sector Job Demands

The aviation sector is creating more jobs than it can fill, but an acute shortage of skilled staff, especially pilots, has also meant surging salaries which are attracting talent from elsewhere. Industry analysts say India's airlines need 5,000 new pilots over the next five years. Trainers say no other profession, baring financial services and investment banking, offers a starting annual salary of Rs. 24 lakh per year, the average for a freshly-minted co-pilot. It doesn't take too long, either for a CPL, all one needs is to be physically fit, train for 10 months, and be ready for an upfront investment of Rs. 18 lakh if one trains in India and Rs. 25 lakh if one trains abroad. A pilot's job does not require high academic credentials. "Currently, the aviation sector offers the best of opportunities and professionals from different fields are coming forward to be a part of this."

Driven by the aviation boom in India, GCAT Flight Academy, one of the largest flight training schools in the world in terms of customers, proposes to begin operations in India, a market that has been expanding rapidly for three years and is ranked next only to China. At present it has training centers located in London, Stockholm, Copenhagen, Oslo, Riga and Hong Kong. Brian Simpson, chief executive of GCAT Flight Academy commented we will accelerate our growth plans in pilot training with STAR Capital Partner's investment.

There is increasing shortage of trained aviation personnel. "There are existing pilots who have to be certified every six months—their skills have to be tested as per the flying regulations that's a given. And then there are so many young students seeking pilot training; commenting on demands for training," chief operating officer of logistics start-up Avicore Aviation Pvt. Ltd. Commented.

Metro specialist engineers demands development of a cadre of Metro specialist engineers. Delhi Metro Rail Corporation (DMRC) has collaborated with the Indian Institute of Technology (IIT), Delhi, to start a new post-graduate professional course for young engineers. The post-graduate diploma in metro technology (PGDMT) would teach students various subjects specifically connected to the operations and technology of Metro train. IIT academicians and DMRC experts have jointly developed the contents of the course keeping in mind professional requirements as metro engineers. The engineering institute has already started screening process to take first batch of engineering graduates for the diploma course.

According to DMRC officials, there are various aspects of engineering which are peculiar to the Metro and are not taught anywhere. Though engineers are trained in those aspects at the Metro's training school when they join the organization, added officials, with metros coming up in more Indian cities, any prior training and knowledge in those areas would brighten the chances of young engineers in getting better jobs. "The technology being used by the Delhi Metro is quite advanced. Metro's signaling is the most complex signaling system in the world. Similarly, the rolling stock (trains) being used by the Delhi Metro is most advanced, as it accelerates and de-accelerates very fast. The students will be taught all these things in detail. Similarly, train troubleshooting, the overhead electrical system, land acquisition process, etc., are some other subjects which will be dealt in detail in this PG course," DMRC spokesperson Anuj Dayal said.

With Metro system coming up invarious other cities including Bangalore, Hyderabad, Chennai and Mumbai, the demand for trained professionals is set to increase, the DMRC officials said. "We are taking 30 students in the first batch in July 2008. On successful completion of the course, the Post-graduate diploma holders will be absorbed by Delhi Metro as assistant engineers," an IIT Delhi official said.

Logistic Sector Job Demands: There is skilled manpower shortage in logistic sector. While the cross-section of industry players recognizes the critical need for manpower development in this growing sector, little has been done to investigate the core issues and identify initiatives to address this situation.

The manpower requirement for the booming ***industrial and communication design market*** is around 8000 to 10000 per annum against the current overall availability of 3000 qualified designers, National Institute Design Director said. Talent crunch is one of the biggest challenges facing this industry, growing at a healthy 23-25 per cent annually. The industrial consultancy and service market is less than Rs. 500 crores currently and has the potential to grow to Rs. 50,000 crores.

The major segments driving the industrial and communication design market are animation, automotives, new appliances, service designs and retailing. The bane of this growing industry is the disconnect between technology and designing, and brand and designing. The failure of designers to adopt changing tools of technology is also a major hindrance in this field. The adoption of technology to design can bring down the time of designing dramatically. The failure of converting brilliant designing concepts to prototypes is another hindering block. Several young students have some brilliant design concepts but fail to convert them into prototypes, necessary for commercializing the product.

Green Jobs: Can the Transition to Environmental Sustainability Spur New Kinds and Higher Levels of Employment was commissioned by UNEP. The study showed that these are not just green-collar jobs targeted at the middle classes, but that opportunities abound for workers in areas ranging from construction, sustainable forestry and agriculture, engineering and transportation. Delhi in India is introducing new eco-friendly compressed natural gas buses and vehicles that will create 18,000 new jobs while Brazil's ethanol program has lead to half a million new jobs, quoted a new study.

The United States environmental industry in 2005 generated over 5.3 million jobs, 10 times the number in the country's pharmaceutical industry. Eco careers are hot; climate change industry is hiring officers to run Clean Development Mechanism projects.

Customer services jobs are quite widespread since they are needed for enterprises in all domains big or small; and the success of any enterprise also depends on the Customer service. The employability is great in this sector but it needs matching skill development to fit in the role.

Since the businesses are varied, the customer service orientation will also differ. It is crucial for small businesses hoping to compete with chain stores, larger companies, and even the small business next door. The large enterprises need to have good impact on customers and those of the competing businesses and customer service personnel are their business asset. To offer world-class customer service, it is important that your front-line employees feel respected and valued, treating them with the utmost respect, honesty, and trust. They need to know that you are committed to their well-being. They are your most important customer service asset. When they feel happy they unleash their enthusiasm and passion from within, it transmits to everyone around them, most important, the customers. The easiest way to make your front-line employees happy is with positive feedback.

The critical parameters of a customer service role are personalized service, persuasive service and helpful service. Sound education, fluency in language, pleasing personality and the aptitude to interact with people is important for such jobs. The basic orientation towards the job are basic soft skills which a person can hardly acquire through experience and then on job periodic orientation and experience thereof. Since customer service roles are becoming critical, companies need to focus much more on their selection process.

Jobs in IT Sector: Poor skills in English language have been handicap for people to fit into varied jobs in IT sector. It will no longer be a handicap to gain IT proficiency for about 900 million Indian masses, due to novel software, developed by an Indian institution and an Israeli company, which has been formally launched here. Lekhika 2007, a software application, developed by the Centre for Development of Advanced Computing (C-DAC) under India's IT ministry and Israel's FTK Technologies, covers ten scripts and 3,000 characters and supports Windows, MAC and Linux. The application is expected to enable masses in India, who do not know English, to gain computer skills in their own language due to its user-friendly, comprehensive, cost-efficient format.

The country's population is its biggest asset. With new emerging sectors and new training, Indians are honing their skills to follow their dreams.

The Retail sector will create millions of jobs, Aditya Birla retail offering 55,000 jobs in Dec. 2007. Reliance Retail is planning to increase its workforce to one million within the next four years. There are increasing job offers created by many big retailers. Large retail outlets meant more jobs in storage and logistics departments. Since retail is also in varied sectors from food groceries to leather shoes and pharma, it needs varied skills to create employability.

Investments in Real Estate have a multiplier effect on income and employment. HUDCO-IIM Ahmedabad study estimates that every rupee invested in this sector adds 78 paisa to the state's GDE. The study estimates that for every direct job created in the industry, eight jobs are created indirectly. Many jobs are coming up in the Real Estate sector right from construction workers to the top level managerial jobs and the professional to create the Real Estate Industry.

Furthermore, the share of manufacturing which is important due to its potential to create and sustain relatively large number of jobs remains 16-17% of GDP. No doubt, the annual growth in manufacturing output has been accelerating. But can we be complacent? Are we globally competitive to ensure sustainability of the manufacturing growth process in the long run? What about the business climate? Is it comparable with many emerging countries? Our Enterprises Snapshots in chapter 3 itself highlights the diversified jobs that we would need in this sector. But all jobs need specific skills to enter and to make it success on job orientation and training.

Paramedic jobs in health related area are in short and we do need to create sound training programs to fit in the ever increasing demands in the health front at home and for medical tourism to deliver good medical rehab programs. Great awareness is being created for health and fitness. Local sports clubs and gymnasiums, fitness centers and high level and expensive fitness centers, weight loss clinics, specialized massage centers like Ayurveda massage could also generate substantial self-employment and employment opportunities for our youth. As we emphasized all needs training to fit in.

What one needs is to create the employability for these sectors—the Retail, Real Estate, paramedic, customer services and in BPOs, and call centers by imparting the right kind of specialized skills to the personnel, matching their jobs before start of jobs, on job orientation and training. This business era demands befitting skills for the specific job area to deliver the results, success and enter competition. There is great focus on the vocational and professional skills needed to enter a specific sector and specific jobs in that sector. Not only that, periodic on job orientation and training is important as the business scenario, the climate, demands and competition change due to national and globalization demands. Further the flexibility and mobility to switch over to related or diversified career is important in this era of fast changing business scenario, and what a country's economy could or would like to aspire for and deliver. Therefore re-inventing the talent with new skills, and re-tooling is necessary.

Global Employment Generation

Indian Manpower Demands Abroad: The Indian Cabinet has approved the establishment of the Council for Overseas Employment Promotion. Members to the Council will be appointed soon. The members, in consultation with the respective Indian embassies, will study the living conditions of workers in the Gulf. They will also study the future employment opportunities for trained Indian manpower in the Gulf. The

Council will advise vocational training centers in India on the types of courses which are in demand in the Gulf. Nearly five million Indians work in the Gulf region and provide USD five billion of remittances to the country every year. The ministry of Overseas Indian Affairs is allocating funds to state governments to help job seekers upgrade their skills.

The minister of Overseas Indian Affairs also warned that with India registering a GDP growth of nine per cent, only those companies in the Gulf which offer very high salaries and enhanced work conditions will get qualified personnel from India. Ministry's mission is to ensure a legal, regular and transparent flow of Indian workforce to the Gulf. With many Indian housemaids facing problems during work abroad, the government has asked all domestic workers to register with the embassies so that their interests could be protected. All domestic workers, including women, should have a written agreement and should inform the embassy regarding their employment and whereabouts (2007).

European Union demand for Indian manpower is increasing in 2007. The Blue Card proposal, which the European Union has recently adopted, is set to dramatically change the work permit and residence procedure for immigrants in the member countries in a couple of years. The EU countries, which have so far lost out in the race to attract skilled immigrants in a big way, are now trying to send out a clear signal that highly skilled people from all over the world are welcome.

With the EU hoping to attract around 20 million skilled workers, it could become a highly attractive destination for applicants from India, which has the world's youngest workforce. "We feel that once the new scheme gets going, young and highly skilled workers from India will find Europe a very attractive destination," European Commission vice-president Franco Frattini told ET in an exclusive interview from Rome. The proposal is aimed in a big way at qualified workers from India.

"Our new policy will not just facilitate geographic mobility across our 27 member countries, but will also provide easy passage for the spouse and other family members of the skilled immigrant. The procedure for granting the work permits will be fast-track for the immigrants and their families. Further, family members too will be permitted to take up jobs in the EU," Mr. Frattini said. He felt that as a package, the Blue Card scheme that would come up trumps over the coveted US Green Card—which ran into serious problems over family reunification of immigrants as they were often forced to stay away from their immediate family for a number of years after moving to the US (2007) or if in country are not able to take jobs as in case of HB1 visa spouses.

EU in 2007 has adopted two major proposals in this direction. The first is about the EU Blue Card, which aims to harmonize the admission procedures for highly qualified workers; the second provides for a general framework to be applied in all cases, a single application procedure for a single work and residence permit as well as a common set of rights for third-country nationals.

The Blue Card program, which is being pitched to make the EU more attractive for skilled workers than destinations such as Australia, US and Canada, will give individuals geographic mobility across the EU countries.

The new immigration policy that the EU nations are unveiling also addresses the problems faced by member countries and corporates in filling up job vacancies, especially with highly qualified workers. The aim is to provide states and companies with additional 'tools' to recruit, retain and better allocate (and re-allocate) the workers they need. By doing so, the European Commission intends to increase the competitiveness of the EU economy by enhancing the contribution made by legal immigration.

Canada wants more skilled workers from India. Recognizing India as a "key source country" for skilled workers, Canada on Nov. 2007 announced opening of a "referral office" here to scout for talented people who could contribute to its economic growth. Further in April 2008, they announced the policy to give work permits to students after finishing their studies.

Beside these initiatives, the IT sector generates substantial jobs abroad for Indian workforce in their offices abroad; same applies to manufacturing and other service sectors. Since many Indian companies are entering into joint ventures with other global companies abroad or serving as experts in those ventures; there is plenty of scope for highly professional jobs in this globalize scenario.

HR Dilemma

The job market is booming in some sectors, with that attrition in enterprises is a problematic issue particularly in BPOs. The enterprises spend considerable amount of money to train them. But the employees job hop for better pay packets. Attrition happens for better salary, better job environments but also when employees are stressed by night-shift jobs and when they do not see any career growth or future career loss. Retaining employees is important since not only the cost of recruiting and training is high but there can be productivity loss also. Attrition happens at all levels.

Strategies for BPOs to retain employees are to re-look at people strategy to re-invent the talent with new skills and re-tooling. Many BPO have given options to pursue employees for free higher educational courses in different institutions so that they can opt for future careers in other industries or choices of higher options in the BPO company itself. Since the nature of the job does not allow shifts of night hours, the change of morning shift work in the company after few years is being envisaged.

Attrition rate is comparatively low in IT product and services companies. Mainly they leave because of higher salary, career promotion and diversified in work promotion and different challenges of IT or change in geographic placements. IT talent pool does need expansion as the IT companies are expanding their scope and presence both in the country and globally. The crucial requirements for IT industry were high quality professionals. Even these days industry would plan shift to where talent was available. To retain workforce, it is important and necessary that they remain competitive, re-inventing the talent with new skills, and re-tooling is necessary.

Enterprises do continuously train their employees in management positions in leadership, global business strategies, financial infrastructure and development through in-house training programs and work shops and even joining extensive specialized short academic courses. Top management in enterprises also plans to cadre a group of their employees by developing their capabilities and talent over the years for future positions. The employees look forward to future growth rather than jumping the wagon to different business. Other strategies may be retention and performance bonuses, ESOPs (employee stock options) and clauses that forbid staff from quitting to join the competition.

Attrition may spoil KPO sector; over $2 bn. revenue is at stake. The high-flying knowledge process outsourcing (KPO) industry in India, estimated to employ 2.55 lakh people by 2011, may lose over two billion dollars of potential revenue gains due to the job-hopping syndrome. This promising industry is facing unprecedented level of attrition, up to 30 per cent, and this is threatening to spoil its success story, according to a leading KPO and international analytics firm Evalueserve.

Besides attrition, issues like intense competition from countries like Poland, China and Philippines are also casting shadows over the industry which is projected to be worth 12 billion dollar by 2010-11. "In the last four to six months, attrition has touched alarming proportions in the range of 25 to 30 per cent. Such a trend is really worrisome for the industry and might even discourage many players from entering the market." Currently, the sector employs a total of about 1,06,000 people in the country in 2007. In a recent study titled "Career Opportunities in India's KPO sector", Evalueserve had predicted that India's KPO industry might not able to generate more than 9.9 billion dollar (by 2010-11) if attrition continued unabated.

Though switching jobs would not help candidates in strengthening their domain expertise even though it might result in higher salaries. Unlike in many other industries, climb to the managerial level is swifter here. "This sector is very rewarding in long term and depends much on one's performance and domain expertise. For instance, professionals who joined our firm after graduation three years ago are now managing significantly large teams. Those with 4-5 years of experience are earning between Rs. 3.5-5 lakh per annum with a yearly hike of 12-20 per cent" (Evalueserve).

According to the survey, data management, searching and analytics segment are expected to be among of the best performing in the KPO sector by 2010-11. The segment is projected to generate revenues to the tune of 2,500 million dollar and employment to 60,000 people. In 2006-07, this area raked in revenues of 590 million dollar and employed about 15,000 professionals.

According to Evalueserve study, the KPO industry in India had 75,400 billable professionals by March 2007 (who generated 3.05 billion dollar in revenues) compared to just 9,000 during 2001 (who generated just 260 million dollar in revenues).

In terms of competition from other countries, Philippines is gaining prominence in legal services, it said. Besides, game design and animation services and contract research organizations along with biotech services hold promising prospects.

Others in different sectors adopt various methods to prevent attrition. Take instance of retail sector. Retail recruiting is not quite as easy as buying off the shelf. If finding the right staff is difficult, retaining employees like merchandising and operation heads is just as tough. So retailers have resorted to various strategies. Here's how retail giants are trying to keep their mid-management layers intact and to prevent attrition.

The Birla Group which runs the retail chain 'More' gives a retention bonus of between Rs. 1-5 lakh on the first day. Spencers Retail of the RPG Group offers its mid management ESOPs as the company plans to list its retail arm soon. Reliance Retail has a clause in its agreement with senior management, forbidding them from joining a competitor for 2-3 years after quitting. Retention bonuses, ESOPs and clauses that forbid staff from quitting to join the competition are other strategies to prevent attrition. "These practice will not last long, retailers will have to come up with new techniques and internalize their procedures like training."

Retail companies recruit 400 to 500 people a month, including mid-management and front-end staff. And though the first choice is to poach from other retailers, staff with sales experience in FMCG and telecom firms is sought after for positions in operations and merchandising. But for customer care staff, the industry taps the hospitality sector. Still, the challenge, retailers say, is finding the right people in tier-2 towns, where most companies plan to expand. Consultants say the attrition level is 25-30% in the retail industry and it will take three to four years before consolidation sets in. Retention bonuses, ESOPs and clauses that forbid staff from quitting and join the competition.

In general, to create job satisfaction and low attrition is to match the employment demand with sound education, change in academic curriculum with changing demands, academics to apply their mind to overcome the mismatch between industry requirements and the curriculum for workforce; and development and retooling of skills. In short, reinventing the job scenario from time to time with business assessment, economy assessment and human resources is imperative. National Manpower forecasts should be the essential part of the reinventing process.

In short, there are three important keys for human development infrastructure in India: Healthy workforce, soundly educated with wider horizon and creativity, and education and skills training matching the changing job demands periodically and creating employability. Employment is the targeted key for the workforce depending largely on the employability scale. The way India's businesses are expanding and its economy is burgeoning, it can achieve optimum employment if it targets at creating employability. These three keys are interdependent, India has the young demographic asset; and it will be hard to complain about unemployment and poverty with these three keys in place.

Capitals Development

6

Development of Capitals for Growth

Financial capital development is important for business expansion, infrastructure development and human capital development, i.e. manpower development. We need to develop both domestic and global funding to develop and support these three areas.

The flow of funds globally, flow of talents and skills globally, and flow of businesses globally cannot only interconnect economy but boost economy worldwide. Investments are done by the government, public and private in partnerships in two ways: investment in people, and investment in infrastructure to boost economy of any country. Both kinds of investments need right kind of policies, political will, and flow of funds. What is more challenging is that such investments do help the common person and are not beneficial for elite segment of the society only. In this context, communicating with financial markets befitting a country's economy is important both from the point of opening its economy to foreign investments and joint ventures as well as exporting and investing globally in different countries to boost the domestic economy. The forces of globalization shifts power away from governments to private capital in whatever market it takes place. In India it is partially correct but after 90s economic liberalization, there is more and more shift of power to private capital and that has enhanced the economic growth also.

In contexts of national economy, global economy and globalization contexts, investment in people is important also. The focus is on creating more jobs for people, and development of manpower to match the increasing employment opportunities.

Developed countries gradually democratized capital markets opening them to any foreign traders who wanted to play and then developing countries have been following suit; opening their markets for foreign investments as well as foreign investors are finding these emerging markets lucrative for investments and returns.

There is an element of reweighing going on because in terms of global portfolios, India is still a relatively small portion. As the India story gets more and more accepted, we are seeing a lot of that in terms of the news flows and coverage on India overseas. There could be an element of money chasing in absolute returns and we have seen a revival in markets across the globe. So, India is obviously participating in that and is participating better than most other markets because of its inherent growth story.

Investment: Many of the financial institutions that affect the global economy can be difficult to understand, historically as well as functionally. International Trade policies in particular can be complicated and confusing. Many of these trade policies can be controversial.

Economist Larry Summers (2007) has calculated that if developing countries invest a modest proportion of their forex reserves in global equities instead of gilts, their increased return may be 1% of GDP. In India's case, that would mean an additional Rs. 40,000 crore per year. Many see this as a breakthrough in developing-country financial management, to be emulated by countries like India. It could increase the low yield that countries currently get on their foreign exchange reserves.

This approach has risks as well as promise. The world is currently accumulating an excess of savings on an unprecedented scale, lifting asset prices globally. Will countries investing their foreign exchange reserves in equities be suckers rushing into speculative bubbles? Or will they be wise diversifiers? Central banks are not profit-maximizers. Their mandate is to focus on inflation, exchange rates, the financial sector, and business cycles. So, they have traditionally placed reserves in the safest, most liquid instruments (like US gilts), even if that means low yields.

Through the 20th century, most countries struggled to accumulate enough forex reserves to counter balance of payments pressures. Developing countries were categorized as low-savings nations that needed to attract funds from rich countries to meet investment needs. Indeed, traditional development theory saw developing countries as suffering from a savings gap and a trade gap, the two being inter-related. However, the 21st century has placed that paradigm on its head. For the first time ever, we now see developing countries with enormous surpluses. China is, of course, the most prominent, with $1.2 trillion. But other countries in East and South Asia have reserves totaling almost as much.

Economist Dani Rodrik (2007) argues that rapid growth leads to high savings rates. In India, accelerating growth has helped lift the savings rate from 23% a decade ago to 33% today. China's savings rate is around 50%. A new development is the sudden huge surplus of $1 billion per day in oil exporting countries.

So countries are creating new investment companies, that unlike central banks have the expertise to divert part of foreign exchange reserves into equity, real estate and hedge funds. Singapore, Korea, Qatar and Abu Dhabi are examples. India is going to follow suit.

Equities in both developed and emerging markets have spiraled to dizzy heights. In China, the stock market has quadrupled in two years, with a ridiculously high PE ratio of 50 (it's close to 18 in India). This is reminiscent of Japan in the late 1980s, when its PE touched 80 before crashing and ushering in a decade of stagnation.

Real estate is another possible investment avenue. But here too asset prices have skyrocketed across the world, and many fear a bubble. It is in this context of saturated asset markets that investors are now turning to speculative vehicles like private equity funds, which have replaced hedge funds. Private equity firms pay enormous premiums over the current market price to acquire large companies and take them private, reorganize them, and float their shares again at a huge profit.

Financial Development Decision

India is witnessing one of the most far reaching transformations of this century. Over a billion people are seeking salvation within the framework of an open economy and an open society committed to fully respecting fundamental human freedoms and the rule of law. As a result of economic reforms initiated in the early 90s, India is experiencing an explosion of creativity and entrepreneurial spirit that has unleashed an economic boom.

Who are the important people that take financial development decisions for national economy and such decisions in context of global economy; and which market forces would facilitate these. In India, in government set up, finance minister, and ministers dealing with other economic and commerce sectors supported by bureaucrats and planning commission, which plans ahead the programs for the country through five year plans, take the policy decisions and its formats. Parliamentarians, political leaders, and members of civic society debate these policy decisions for implementation or non-implementation.

These decisions are equally debated by business institutions such as confederation of industries, FICCI and other sectoral associations of entrepreneurs; and financial institutions such as Reserve Bank of India, Central Bank, and SEBI Securities. Government set up may decide about the pattern, ratio and sectors of foreign investments in the country; and also allowing Indian businesses to invest abroad for revenue enhancement and product and services growth of the sectors. Business institutions will endorse these decisions through business investments by such business models of collaboration, joint ventures and M&A. Financial institutions will set up the rules and regulations for implementations of policy decisions. Foreign Political and financial stability in general and of particular sectors of the country are significant market forces.

Foreign Direct Investments (FDI) in India are done in three ways. These investments are done in manufacturing of products, providing services such as computer software and hardware, building infrastructures of roads, dams, bridges, flyovers, metro rails, etc., telecommunication, and other transports on BOOT system (buy, own-operate and transfer). Second is investing in collaboration with businesses such as oil exploration, refineries, acquisitions and mergers. These are stable and long-term investments. Third is short-term investment in stocks and bonds which are more liquid in nature through foreign institution investments (FII).

Role of media is important to inform the participating parties about the political and financial stability of India in general and the particular sectors where the other countries can invest for growth and good revenues. Identifying the other countries investing in India would further influence the scope of country 'A' to invest in India. Since investments of others will also indirectly Influence ROI (return of investments) of country 'B or C'.

It is equally important if both Indian media and global media highlight the direct gain country 'B or C' will get if it invests in upgrading people's skills or upgrading the infrastructure of telecom, roads, ports, etc. Even global media channels, or of other countries may even caution about the bureaucratic hassles and corrupt practices of doing business in India. This provides scenario to country 'B or C' about the feasibility of investing in India. Both national and international media set an agenda to inform, discuss, give feedback and guide the participants. In these contexts, it is important for Indian media channels to project positive and correct image of the political and financial stability in general, rules and regulations and bureaucratic and governmental setups. Equally important is that the foreign media channels shed the earlier stereotypes and negative images though at the same time reflecting on the realities.

Efficiency in economic management which can be instrumental for economic reforms and liberalization, planning strategies for direction and pace for economy, remedies for structural and resource backwardness and functional welfare model for all can impact achievement. This requires involved efforts of the governance, businesses and people.

Investments are needed to create world class infrastructure in roads, bridges, flyovers, highways, airports, air travel, airlines, railroads, power, etc., and business structures not only to expand domestic economy but also to participate in global economy. Inviting global partnerships and global investments require world class basic infrastructure to let it function. Political stability and favorable economic policies, economic reforms and liberalization have created credibility for the investors to invest in India. These foreign funds flow has facilitated India to create infrastructure needed for global partners to do business in India. On the other hand, the economic liberalization policies allowed Indian businesses to collaborate with global business partners to expand their businesses as well as tap the innovative trends in those businesses. Such openness of global investments is expanding Indian economy and consumer facilities such as housing, healthcare, education, food, insurance, retail, transportation, tourism, etc. It is creating more and more jobs, higher incomes, higher consumerism and raising standards of living.

The more significant and crucial point for India, in this instance, and for other emerging markets also is that more jobs, higher incomes, higher consumerism and raising standards of living are created for majority of its population, not just the urban but rural populations also, for the lower income strata and for even the absolute poor. Such an endeavor calls for investments and finance spending for all segments of society. India will invest the global finances to give better connectivity to people in all segments of society by providing good infrastructure. It makes efforts to give people quality of life by providing employment, higher income and availability of both basic and luxury affordable goods and services within the country.

This did need the change of stance and the changing communication practices of making people responsible for their own prosperity and not dependency on government. It needs collaborative efforts between the government and people. Here government is telling its people, we do not borrow global funds—we invite global businesses to invest in India. For this, we create credibility through the people of India who has to work hard, work diligently, with innovative ideas and skills which such partners may seek in us. The success lies in national public and private partnerships, global and national public and private partnerships. The result is better quality of life for you people. You can take it or leave it, the choice is yours, and the government is ready to guide you, support you with open and liberalized economic policies, transparency and accountability (Narula 2008a).

Narula further advocates that globalization of capital flow, foreign fund investments, and trade are likely to create mutual economic benefits for the participating countries, enhance their economic growth; and in the event of financial crisis there may be mutual support. These changed practices will not only create economic empowerment to specific countries but would result in global empowerment in general.

According to the biennial Business Environment Survey for 2007 by the Commonwealth Business Council, India is the most reformed among emerging markets owing to the economic reforms undertaken by the government. The availability of free-flowing funds for investment from countries such as India and China means access to finance is no longer a critical issue for developing countries. "India's economic reforms are taking place on various fronts, ranging from privatization, deepening the financial sector, tax reforms and pricing of goods and commodities."

The survey found that the Indian corporate sector had become more externally focused by acquiring foreign firms in advanced economies as a way of gaining access into certain markets and also to pursue technology transfer. It says, the business environment in India, with its low leverage has enabled companies with high profitability to easily acquire the finances necessary for buyouts, unlike in East Asia where leverage was high. It identified the favorable factors that made this new boom of overseas acquisitions attainable as international efficiency of manufacturing companies and low production costs.

Government sets up 13th Finance Commission on 14 November 2007 under the chairmanship of former finance secretary Dr. Vijay Kelkar. The FC is a constitutional body set up every five years to recommend efficient ways to share resources between states and the central government and suggest measures to promote efficiency in the economy. The commission will cover recommendations for the period of five years from 1 April 2010 to 31 March 2015.

FINANCIAL CAPITAL

Foreign Direct Investments

India's foreign direct investment (FDI) policy has undoubtedly played a significant role in taking the Indian economy on a high growth path. From an era when foreign investment in most sectors of the economy was restricted or not permitted, India has moved to a situation where foreign investors can freely invest in most sectors on an automatic basis, i.e. without seeking any prior regulatory approvals.

These reforms ushered since 1991 have enabled the country to harness the potential it has. India today is one of the most favored investment destinations for foreign investors. With robust FDI inflows, and economy growing at more than 8% over the past few years, India is clearly in the reckoning. While the present FDI policy is liberal, investor-friendly and forward looking, there are certain issues which if addressed would assist in further stimulating foreign investment into the country.

Foreign direct investments are done in three ways: these investments are done in manufacturing, services, infrastructures of roads, dams, bridges, metro rails, airports, power generation plants, etc. on BOOT (buy, own-operate and transfer). Secondly, the investments are in collaboration with businesses, acquisition and mergers. These are stable and long-term investments.

Thirdly, the short-term FDI investments are done in stocks and bonds which are more liquid in nature.

Global investments are done by government, public-private partnerships in two ways: primarily to do business in product and services and secondarily investing in people to develop the talents and skills to fit in the upcoming business roles, and investments in infrastructure to create better environments to do business and investments. Both kinds of investments need positive policies, political will and flow of funds. In global economy and in globalization contexts, investments in people is important and of utmost priority. What is more challenging is that such investments create more empowerment for the common person since it boosts its earning power, purchasing capacity and consumerism to change lifestyles.

FDI flows and patterns, and investment patterns and cycles in India have been changing due to market forces and also as and when India is expanding or squeezing FDI norms and equity percentage in certain sectors and regulations for foreign equity.

These inflows into India have more than tripled in the first three months of '06. And these originated not only from the top 20 countries, but also from non-traditional nations like West Indies, South Africa, Nevis and Iceland. There is no difference between the old and new economy as far as FDI into India is concerned, simply because investors find them both equally attractive, given their vast potential.

In '05, the favorite sectors for FDI inflows were services and cement. In '06 the investment cycle in the economy seems to be gaining momentum, with the manufacturing sector leading the way. The steady growths in non-food credit, as well as strong internal and external demands have kept overall investments in the economy strong. Rising interest rates have not curbed project investment activity as yet. The ability of domestic corporate to obtain low-cost funds from abroad has facilitated the overall amount of investments in the economy, and has, to a certain extent, nullified the rising interest rate scenario in India. However, there is a certain degree of moderation in investments in the infrastructure sector.

The share of infrastructure investments in total project investments has fallen from about 26% in the previous year to 23% in June '06, while investments in the sector have grown by 6-7% during the same period. Increased investments in the infrastructure sector are necessary to facilitate growth in the industrial sector, and also help in improving the overall employment scenario.

The western part of the country seems to be the preferred destination for project investments in the economy. The lure of being closer to the financial capital and some of the faster growing service sector, metros seem to have attracted capital investments in the West. Maharashtra is the leading state for project investments in the economy. There has also been a slight change in the pecking order as on June '06, where Gujarat has edged Orissa out to take the second spot. Karnataka and Tamil Nadu rank fourth and fifth respectively. The real bit of good news is that project investments have started to pick up in lesser-developed and poorer states like Bihar, Assam and Madhya Pradesh.

Capital Investments: India's Equity Market

Former RBI governor Reddy has said that global liquidity changes have obscured assessment of risks. The manufacturing sector growth has remained robust. Reddy thinks that there is need to assess risks to inflation from high oil prices and from if global developments persist. India is not immune to risks from global financial markets, Reddy warned.

Global investment bank HSBC is of the view that one of the best ways to capitalize on the growth in India is through the somewhat under-recognized consumption story. It is bullish on sectors like healthcare, education, finance, telecoms and real estate, and the outlook for these sectors over the next few years looks remarkable. Chapter 3 on 'Business Expansion' reflects, oil exploration, gas and refineries, steel production, insurance, have been the preferred sectors by investors in '07. Even the Indian businesses have invested abroad in joint ventures in oil, gas, refineries, steel, etc.

Kamal Nath India's Commerce Minister (Nov. 2007), defending the protection of intellectual property rights, emphasized that it is important, as India graduates from user to producer of intellectual property. It is aimed at coming generations of entrepreneurs who through their innovation would create new products. Besides, he said, it improves the credibility and standing of India in the international community as it fulfils the commitments made and translates into investments with the investors realizing that the country not only has laws but implements them too. It is credibility of India which is bringing in investments in various sectors. Observing that the comparison between India and China is "misplaced", Nath said there is need to see where China was 15 years into the opening up process. India, which started economic reforms 15 years ago, is now getting double the investments China got at that point of time.

Referring to India's stand on WTO trade talks, Commerce Minister told investors and entrepreneurs; India only wants multilateral trading systems that corrects the existing structural flaws in the global trade rather than perpetuate them. The rules of the game are very important for India as it engages in the global trading system more and more (2007).

Private Equity Investment Sectors in India: IT, manufacturing, banking and engineering undoubtedly are still the favorites as far as private equity investors are concerned. However, over the past nine months "shallow sectors" like agriculture, energy, hospitality, telecom and media are gaining importance among investors.

Energy sector is attracting private equity (PE). Power and power utility services are the most vibrant sub-segments of energy sector. The growth of energy sector would be fueled by government initiative to increase competition, consumers choosing cheaper power, and players' interest in a sector with higher returns than in regulated plants. PE parties have invested close to $252 million across 11 deals over the past nine months.

Hotels and resorts is another upcoming sector that is attracting a lot of PE interest. The booming hospitality sector in

India is seeing rising interest from domestic and foreign players keen to invest in hotels, resorts and serviced apartment development. The Federation of Hotel and Restaurant Associations of India (FHRAI) estimates that as compared to the present 97,000 hotel rooms in the country, India will need 30,000 additional rooms in various categories over the next three years. "Lured by 20-25% return on investment, foreign banks like Citigroup, Morgan Stanley and Goldman Sachs are investing heavily in the Indian hospitality sector. Through five deals, PE players have invested close to $259 million in hotels & resort chains in 2007.

Telecom is another sector that is slowly gaining the favor of PE investors. During the nine-month period, the sector has received $136 million through six deals. The most luring aspect of telecom sector is demography. India's mobile phone subscriber base is growing at a rate of 82%. Agro products and agriculture-based research companies are attracting investors, $29 million by way of three separate deals.

The Indian real estate and infrastructure sectors have been a key contributor to rising foreign fund inflows. Out of $10 billion PE fund that India attracted so far, $5 billion came in these sectors. Real estate emerged as the favorite segment with 26% share in all private equity investments in value terms, receiving $2.6 billion in 32 deals, closely followed by telecom with 21% share, investment touching $2.1 billion; real estate and infrastructure have emerged as the most attractive sectors to invest globally also. Global real estate private equity funds have raised $72 billion in 2006 and $50 billion in 2007. A large portion of these funds will be invested in emerging markets such as India and China.

Movie distribution companies like Shemaroo Entertainment and Venus Movies are in talks with PE players for raising funds for expansion. Shemaroo Entertainment is looking to raise an estimated Rs. 100 crores through private equity. Adlabs, Zee Entertainment, Sony are expecting good FDI deals.

Currently in '07 broadcasting sector, FDI up to only 20% is allowed in FM radio and direct-to-home (DTH) services, in television news broadcasting segment 26%, and 49% in cable services, and 74% in telecom sector. In case of internet service providers, and non-news television broadcasters 100% FDI is allowed.

According to government estimates, India will require around $500 billion investments in infrastructure sectors like road, energy, ports and airports. This will create a huge opportunity for foreign investors. Indian infrastructure's is favored because of predictable investment climate and a strong entrepreneurial culture (Nov. 2007).

Some of the major PE funds, which are active in Indian market, are Temasek Holdings, investment arm of Singapore government, Blackstone Group, a global private equity and investment management firm, Warburg Pincus, Carlyle Group, Washington and Actis Capital.

The Eleventh Plan draft (current plan) document has built a strong case for relaxing Foreign Direct Investment (FDI) norms in key sectors like insurance, private banking, single brand retailing and broadcasting. "The progress regarding elimination of FDI limits in key sectors also needs to continue in order to increase FDI flows and stimulate transfer of technology, which is critical for improving competitiveness, reveal the 11th Plan draft document. The sectors with comparatively higher FDI cap of 74 per cent are atomic minerals, private sector banking, telecom and establishment and operation of satellites at present. Given the current scenario, the document says FDI could increase significantly during the 11th plan period. It also suggested that while containing the trade liberalization, government should take steps to consolidate the gains from FDI by reducing delays in State level clearances.

Insurance sector in India has attracted over 540 million dollar of FDI and is poised for tremendous expansion, Minister of State for Finance said at a meeting of Insurance Australia Group. As on March 31, 2007, the entry of foreign partners has resulted in attracting $543 million FDI. The private companies have created a niche for themselves, as they have been able to increase their share in the insurance market in competition with their counterparts in the public sector. As per the current regulation, 26% foreign equity is allowed in this sector.

The growth in recent years has been significant in this sector; India is far behind the world averages and ranks 78th in terms of insurance density and 54th in terms of penetration. Though there are potentialities for growth opportunities. India offers a stable investment climate as well as a huge market with a growing middle class. The world averages are $469.6 in terms of insurance density and 8.06 per cent in terms of insurance penetration against this, in India insurance density was only $19.70 and insurance penetration was 3.17 per cent in 2003.

Besides, there is opportunity in the micro-insurance regulation notified by IRDA facilitating insurers to tap the potential of rural markets. It attempts to offer the target specific insurance products at a relatively lower cost, for a lower coverage of amount through NGO, mutual fund investments (MFIs) and SHGs. At present 17 insurance companies are operating in the life insurance and another seventeen in general insurance sector (Aug. 2007).

German re-insurer Munich Re has developed an insurance cover that will boost renewable energy projects in India by guaranteeing polluters in developed countries carbon credits from their investments in renewable energy projects in developing countries such as India.

The insurance cover—the Kyoto Multirisk policy is expected to lead to more investments into renewable energy in countries such as India. Under the Kyoto Protocol, there is a facility, where polluting companies, instead of improving their carbon dioxide output, invest in renewable energy projects. In return for their investments, the polluting companies receive emission credits. The Kyoto policy goes beyond the traditional cover. If it is a solar plant or wind energy, we are guaranteeing a minimum level of electricity generation. We are also covering at providing political risks, said Ludger Arnoldussen, member of the board of management, Munich Re.

He added that companies are willing to invest in such projects because in many cases, it is cheaper than optimizing their own facility. The investor could be anybody; it could be an electricity producer in Japan or Germany or anywhere else in the world.

Swiss firms have stepped up investment in India. Indian companies are also actively buying into Swiss companies, particularly in the biotech sector. A number of companies have begun to look at Switzerland as an investment destination. Its strategic location in the heart of Europe, long-term stability, legal security, dedicated professional labor force, liberal market conditions, reliable and highly developed financial centre, high-tech infrastructure and modest tax system are attracting more and more Indian firms towards the European country in terms of foreign direct investments into India.

Petrodollar for Indian Investments: Taking into perspective, the business of petrodollars and the kind of inflows the country may see, it has been seen that the FII flows are domestic driven. Can this actually shift further into the Middle East and can we see more money coming in from there? Giving his perspective, R. Seetharaman, CEO, Doha Bank said, that there is huge momentum in terms of bilateral trade over the years in India and GCC. He foresees not less than USD 20-25 billion of foreign direct outflows from Middle East and inflow to India in the next three months. Real estate, telecom and the basic parts of outsourcing will be the immediate investment sectors. Increasingly the focus from the gulf countries is not the developed markets but the emerging markets like India and China particularly, and a few other Asian countries. Most analysts cite Indian economic growth prospects and the fact that more firms are Shariat compliant in India than elsewhere in Asia. The petrodollars seem headed particularly for India (Nov. 2007).

National Security Screening

Foreign investors have started facing new hurdles across the globe since 2005. China, Russia, Canada grow vary of acquirers. These governments have imposed restrictions on foreign purchases of companies, factories and real estates in their countries. Could this harm global economic growth if they proliferate? Measures include bureaucratic and legal barriers to direct foreign investments in which a country buys physical assets such as mines, steel factories, real estate, rather than investing indirectly in stocks and bond markets. Barriers are rising and this could be of concern to Multinationals who conduct majority of their businesses through foreign affiliates rather than sale of exported goods made in the USA. Foreign affiliates produce products locally, relying on local production sited and labor, as well as easy access to local customers. Countries block acquisitions if these are threats to economic security, national security and reciprocity. It proponents the fear that this could disrupt the decade long trend towards more open global economies that has helped spur economic growth. Thus, the greatest challenge is investment protectionism.

India is considering national security screening processes for proposed foreign investments. India has already rejected proposed investment for a Chinese Telecommunications Company. Other countries are getting conscious of the need to protect their own national security and also to make sure that overall substantial investment is for net benefit of the host country. Since 2005 these restrictions are tightening. Against this, it is being argued that while national security is important, erecting barriers will chill investments in their homelands and potentially impact their ability to invest abroad. However, investments takes place within a broader political context and the degree to which (e.g. American) companies are afforded access to investment opportunities in those countries will depend on opportunities available to their (other countries) companies in US. Thus, reciprocity is the third factor.

Issues in Joint Venture Investment: Foreign investors with existing JVs (existing on January 12, 2005) face hurdles under Press Note 1 (2005 series) if they intend to establish a new venture in the same field. Essentially, they require the consent of the existing Indian partner if they intend to set up a new venture in the same field. Earlier, the consent of the Indian partner was required even if the investment was to be made in a similar field. This placed limitations on fresh investments by existing investors, the government diluted the earlier Press Note by issuing Press Note 1 (2005 series).

There are some relaxations through this PN, but not many. For instance, foreign investment in certain sectors such as information technology, mining, etc., has been excluded from the applicability of this Press Note. Additionally, PN does not apply where the participation of the Indian investor/s in the JV is less than 3%. There is, however, no minimum threshold stipulated for foreign participation for applying this PN.

This PN was introduced with the intention of protecting the interests of the Indian JV partner at a time when the Indian economy was in the process of being liberalized and the Indian industry was not fully geared to take on the foreign investors. It was, therefore, found prudent that foreign investors should route any additional investment into India through the existing JV, and the consent of the Indian partner would be required where they intend to establish an independent venture in India. The present status has undergone change.

RBI Enhances Overseas Investment by Indian Companies and Mutual Funds

The Reserve Bank of India (RBI) on 25 September 2007, raised ceilings on overseas investment by Indian companies and mutual funds in order to check the appreciating rupee and move towards fuller convertibility of the rupee in the capital account.

As per the measures announced by the RBI, individuals can now remit up to $200000 against $100000 without RBI's permission. Companies are permitted to invest up to 400% of their net worth overseas as against 300% till now.

Partnership firms are now allowed to invest 400% of their net worth overseas. Ceiling on portfolio investments by companies have been raised to 50% of net worth from 35% earlier. The requirement of 10% reciprocal shareholding in listed Indian companies by overseas companies for the purpose of portfolio investment abroad by Indian listed companies has been scraped. Companies are now allowed to make prepayment of external commercial borrowings (ECBs) up to $500 million as against $400 million earlier. Mutual funds are permitted to invest an aggregate of $5 billion overseas as against $4 billion.

Foreign Institution Investment (FII)

Developed countries and even developing countries are investing in emerging markets in areas of their interests where they can consolidate their own strengths by acquisitions and mergers. Recently in 2006-07 business groups of India such as Tata, Aditiya Birla Group have invested in other countries in steel, copper mines and hotels, etc. Other countries have been investing in India in steel, petroleum, natural gas, power generation and automobiles, etc. The enhanced and diversified trade and commerce markets usher countries into new economy. The convergence of communication technologies, political and economic liberalization has transformed the way people live and communicate, and trade and invest.

Investments are done by foreign institutions and businesses in other countries including emerging markets of India, China, Brazil, Russia, etc. for three reasons: (i) Because they find foreign markets profitable. (ii) They acquire raw material for their businesses from those foreign markets, and they acquire and expand the small foreign companies to expand their businesses. The percentage of foreign investments are regulated by particular countries to expand as well as protect domestic economy from foreign domination and exploitation.

Outlining advantages of investing in India, Chidambaram, Finance Minister India, commented that India, as an investment destination, provides a stable political climate, rule of law, large and educated manpower and the welcoming attitude of governments at the national and state levels. It also offers one of the safest investment opportunities in terms of country-risk also. Indian economy is currently the world's fourth largest in terms of real GDP (PPP) and second fastest growing major economy in the world, adding there is very little political risk in investments. If one looks at the Indian market in the context of Asia, it is one of the most sensitive markets to people's perceptions of global interest rates and inflation. The reason behind this is that unlike a lot of Asian equity markets, India has a big current account deficit. So if people are worried about inflation and interest rates, then they are worried about India.

The risks for India or what we call the 'liquidity plays' in emerging markets would be when there is another bad inflation number in the United States or if suddenly something happens in the bond markets, that would send bond yields moving higher or if oil prices go up. If that occurs then the risk would grow for these liquidity plays, at least in the short-term. To a certain extent, some of the flows that India has benefited from, in recent years, are simply because people are looking for Asia and when they look closer, they discover that India is a place that delivers on earnings. In the past also, economies with their own independent drivers have normally outperformed other markets at times of slowdown in the US. While valuations could come under pressure from any meltdown in global markets, it would be temporary as long as the country's domestic growth story remains intact.

India will remain a relatively safe haven for investors in the event of a possible global correlation in the medium to long-term—notwithstanding its dependence on foreign funds and a high correlation with the world markets, the analysts believe. The domestic equity market is unlikely to under perform on a multi quarter basis even if there is a global correlation triggered by economic slowdown concerns in the US, equity.

Destination India Shines on Investors

India has emerged as one of the most attractive investment destination in the world. Merchant bankers and analysts feel this trend is likely to continue. According to the Morgan Stanley Capital International (MSCI) Equity Indices, which compares the returns from various markets, India has given the second highest annual return at 38.36% among the BRIC (Brazil, Russia, India and China) countries in the last five years. The low returns from the developed stock markets, have made the investments from these countries to flow into emerging markets. India has provided a huge opportunity for foreign investors, resulting into large inflow of funds. According to SBI Cap, India received FII investment to the tune of $4.27 billion till June 28,

2007, which is the second highest in the Asian markets. Taiwan received $7.47 billion during the period.

The main reasons which have enabled Indian market to attract investors are its strong fundamentals and good returns being earned by the companies. On top of this, appreciation in rupee has further increased the return in dollar term in the last six months of year 2007. The return from Indian stock market has gone up to over 57% in the last one year, resulting into foreign investors rushing to invest. India has become a must destination in almost all foreign investors' portfolio. This has led creation of huge liquidity in the market and has provided further momentum to the upward movements of the stock prices.

Chinese economy is growing at 10.7%. But, the stocks prices of Chinese companies are quoting at 41 times of the underlying profits, which are almost double that of India. Therefore, Chinese stocks are being considered as costlier than Indian stocks. Therefore, a senior analyst with a foreign fund argued, Indian stock market, at present, looks the most attractive one.

FII are urging the government to raise the cap on their investment limit on debt investments; having nearly exhausted their limit for investing in Indian debt market within the first quarter of the current fiscal year. This spurt in FII investment is largely explained by widening US-India interest rate differential and a strong and stable rupee.

Many emerging markets suffer the inability to borrow abroad in local currency as financial markets suspect them of using inflation to reduce the real value of the debt. Consequently, the borrowers are subject to a currency mismatch—earn in rupees and repay the debt in dollars. Moreover, raising the cap on FII investment would bring in the much-needed funds in areas like infrastructure, which prefer debt as a way of financing.

Despite these benefits, raising the FII limit is likely to generate several concerns for monetary policymaking. The increased foreign capital inflow through the FII route would introduce excess liquidity in the market, which tends to be inflationary. RBI can mop up the excess liquidity by selling government bonds to the banks, thereby sterilizing the impact of foreign exchange intervention. Nonetheless, given that bulk of India's reserves are parked in low-yielding securities, such sterilization has a huge fiscal cost, measured by the difference between the return on the foreign exchange reserves and yield on government debt.

Alternatively, the RBI can refrain from intervening in the forex market, which will result in further appreciation of the rupee and pose a threat to Indian exports in certain sectors, which have already taken a hit in recent months. Hence, until ways to mitigate these costs are devised, the government should hold off raising the cap on FII investment (July 2007).

Widening Areas of FII Investments

Industry chamber FICCI has suggested that India should neither enter into an FTA with China, nor grant it 'market economy status' for the time being.

The chamber has said that the idea of a full-blown free trade agreement with China is much ahead of its time, and India must wait before considering 'market economy status' for its eastern neighbor, who is characterized by a different operating environment for business and range of subsidies. It is imperative to have a level playing field between the businesses of the two countries before embarking on negotiations towards a possible bilateral trade agreement.

The Chinese industry enjoys 'unfair advantage' over their Indian counterparts due to several factors like an array of tax exemptions and artificially undervalued Chinese currency. There is also massive across-the-board state support for domestic companies.

The practice of managing the Chinese Yuan at a low level and preventing it from moving upwards amounts to an "effective export subsidy" and consequently Indian business is put at a relative disadvantage *vis-à-vis* supplies from China. Because of government support, industry estimates that the Chinese products could enjoy a price advantage up to 30 per cent over Indian manufactured goods (Oct. 22, 2007).

Managing Capital Flow Challenges

Participatory Notes

The Stock market regulator Securities and Exchange Board of India (SEBI) banned investments through participatory notes issued by Foreign Institutional Investors (FIIs) to curb the inflow of foreign funds into the stock market that has risen sharply in recent weeks. SEBI on 25 October 2007, tightened investment rules for unregistered FIIs by clamping down on issuance of indirect investment instruments known as participatory notes (P-notes). It banned fresh issuance of PNs with derivatives and it has also directed to wind up such PNs in 18 months, besides putting curbs on such issue of PNs in the spot market. Foreign investors are liquidating their security holdings in their countries and investing that money elsewhere. Therefore, according to Finance Minister, it is necessary to moderate the flow of funds into India. However, there is no intention of imposing control on capital flows or keep out certain kinds of funds. Many hedge funds that are not regulated in their home country will find it difficult to invest in the Indian market now.

Participatory notes are bilateral contracts between FIIs and investors for taking exposure in specific stocks without registering themselves with SEBI. This helps hiding the identity of the real investors. Currently, 51 per cent of the FII investment in the Indian stock market is through participatory notes. The abundant flow of funds in the Indian stock market has forced the securities SEBI and RBI to tighten controls.

On 26 Oct., Finance Minister said the government wanted to moderate capital inflows without hurting growth of the country's economy. SEBI also changed the eligibility criteria for certain categories of investors that do not qualify as FIIs but want to register with the regulator directly. These entities include pension funds, foundations, endowments, university funds and charitable trusts or societies, which do not come under any regulatory authority in their respective countries.

Chairman SEBI commented on the need for banning PNs, one of the issues is a question of registering. For several months,

SEBI had been inviting investors, from outside India, to consider that the India growth story was truly worth investing in and participating in; to come directly through the front door after registering themselves as FIIs. The response has been less than lukewarm until a short while ago. It was perhaps believed that there was no special merit in registering as FIIs and you could continue to be the entity that you were and access the Indian markets indefinitely, in the same manner that you had accessed it, until recently. That scenario is in the process of undergoing a change.

We will seek to expedite the process of registration, as well as resist the content of regulation, to see what other categories of investors, that were until now kept out of the registration process, can be facilitated to access the Indian market, by being included.

The SEBI chief met domestic brokerage houses on 23 Oct. 2007 to clarify the regulator's position on participatory notes and discuss developments in the equity markets. Earlier, he had held conference with foreign institutional investors (FIIs) on 22 October 2007, wherein he provided partial breather with respect to proposed restrictions on use of participatory notes and said, new P-Note regulations will take effect immediately and SEBI would speed up regulatory clearance for foreigners keen to invest transparently.

Finance Minister while addressing the ICICI Securities global investors' meet in New York on 28 October 2007 clarified that there would be no further measures to curb capital inflows, and India would ease procedures for foreign institutional investors (FIIs) to register and do business in the country. The FM would urge SEBI to meet potential FIIs to explore ways and means to make registration simpler.

While delivering a speech in the Norwegian School of Management on 24 October 2007, he observed that India's healthy economic growth has brought forth the challenge of abundant international capital flows and their impact on the domestic economy, particularly on prices and the exchange rate. He explained that on the demand side there is higher growth in foreign reserves, which were estimated at over $239 billion at the end of September 2007, and robust credit growth have exerted pressure on prices. He further observed that from time to time, our economy is faced with a mismatch between supply and demand in the case of primary commodities, including food articles. High capital inflows impacts exchange rates and inflation.

Market regulator SEBI streamlines the functioning of PNs in the country. A blueprint is prepared for all future foreign inflows in the capital markets. Sources added that the blueprint will focus on three aspects of FII investments in India: access, product and know your customer norms. Access regulations will define just who would be eligible to invest in India through the FII route. Sources say only those, who adhere to the Money Laundering Act, may be eligible to invest. SEBI may also allow different types of products to be accessed by FIIs. Future traded products of even one-year maturity may be allowed to be accessed by FIIs. Besides, KYC norms will be strengthened for FIIs.

Addressing the Economic Editor's Conference on 12 Nov. 2007, Finance Minister, said that the surge in capital flows has led to market volatility and higher reserves. He added that credit growth at 23.5% shows some moderation. The current account deficit is of USD 4.7 billion and the capital account surplus is at USD 15.9 billion. He also stated that the government has no plans to introduce further measures to stop capital flows. Overall macro-economics are still strong.

The biggest threat is from capital flows, especially from unregulated private entities who invest in equities and real estate. These, with a lag, can increase aggregate demand and impact inflation. The central bank's thrust therefore is to control and sterilise flows; hence the hike in CRR periodically.

SEBI focuses on market surveillance. The formal decision is taken that the stock exchanges will be mandated to constitute a committee of board that will focus on surveillance. The broad level attention through the focused efforts of this specially constituted committee would enhance surveillance and ensure that it is consistent with SEBI's interests and with the intentions and interests of the market place. The market will become a safer place for investors and SMEs to access risk capital better than they have been enable to do so far.

Former RBI governor Reddy while addressing the Peterson Institute of International Economics in Washington on 18 Oct. 2007 highlighted that managing capital flows is a challenge for the Indian economy and with the opening of trade it has become more difficult. India allows unrestricted movement of currency on current account for trade and business transactions. It has recently liberalized even the capital movement abroad but retains controls on full capital account convertibility.

According to the governor, India will go in for full capital account convertibility and liberalization once the pre-conditions for a liberalized currency regime are fulfilled. However, certain risks have to be tackled before moving to the full capital account convertibility. An official panel, called the Tarapore Committee, has drawn out a roadmap for the capital account convertibility. On 13 Nov. 2007, Finance Minister said his government would gradually introduce fuller capital account convertibility in line with the recommendations of the Tarapore Committee. Even then there will always be some degree of capital control.

The government admitted that managing plentiful capital inflows without endangering growth and price stability is indeed a challenge in the short term. The problem of abundant inflows is very much a part of the successful capital account liberalization and has to be actively managed as it is likely to persist, due to strong macro-economic fundamentals and the prevailing interest rate differentials. "While there are international experiences in this regard with some successful and painful adjustment processes, the specific Indian context requires innovative policy responses. Going forward, this would be a major challenge," said the mid-year review trends in receipts and expenditure.

Foreign money has been flowing into Indian stocks. More than $16 billion has come in so far in 2007. This had boosted the rupee by about 12% and made it difficult for the RBI to manage the inflows. The currency strengthened by more than 15% between Oct. 2006 and Oct. 2007, thereby hurting exporters. The policy options involve trade-offs and appropriate mix of responses, each of which has its costs. The fiscal cost of sterilization of the inflows, which was envisaged at Rs. 3,700 crores in last year's Budget, is now being supplemented with Rs. 4,500 crores.

The economy's capacity to absorb huge capital flows has not risen as fast as the inflows. Therefore, the management of capital inflows will remain an important issue. The central bank's overall policy would factor in the objectives of price stability, reducing inflationary expectations, supporting growth and ensuring regular credit flow, the study reported.

India, the world's fastest growing economy after China expanded at an average 8.6% over the past four years and is likely to grow at a similar pace in the current fiscal year ending March 2008. It grew 9.4% in the last fiscal year, its strongest in 18 years. In the first half of 2007-08, the economy expanded at 9.1%. RBI sees growth at 8.5% this fiscal, the review said, while emphasizing the need for a more inclusive growth (mid-year review study 2007).

Other analysts think the solution cannot lie in controlling flows of global capital into the stock market. It starves the engine of growth and sends out the most regressive signal to the world; even if it is done, as in this case, under the guise of seeking more transparency.

According to analysts at CNBC-TV18, apart from expediting the FIIs' registration process, and also allowing proprietary sub-accounts to operate, there are other important, but technical regulatory issues. Some of them are: The first issue related to new funds and AMCs is that SEBI has said that there should be at least one-year experience for any fund or AMC to operate in India between Oct. 2006 and Oct. 2007. But there are new fund managers that have come into business, where they were working under FII or hedge fund, but they have experience of over 4-5-10 years. Now, the point is how do you differentiate between a fund that has experience of less than one year and a fund manager who has an experience over 10 years?

The second issue is the hedge fund regulation. Some of the hedge funds are not registered under the SEC, but regulated under the SEC. This poses a big problem and SEBI will be watching this very closely and the solution could be a bit more complicated if they have to allow some of the funds which are not regulated in the home country, to operate in India.

The third issue is related to the third party accounts. This is how it works, there are FIIs and under that, there are sub-accounts; and under sub-accounts, there are third-party accounts, which invest their money via sub-accounts to FIIs. The problem is, most of the times, FIIs have the sole discretionary powers regarding what to buy and what to sell. But now, for the last 2-3 years, the sub-accounts are having control over the FIIs to operate their own accounts. With the SEBI present move, FIIs will have a direct control over these third party accounts. This may be an important question to address.

The fourth issue is related to the foreign corporates. These are broad-based investors, which have at least 20 investors and no single investor should have more than 10% of corpus. If the funds can't satisfy these criteria, will they be considered foreign corporates?

The fifth one is related to deemed FII status. Considering that the India-based AMCs are operating in India and have some offshore clients to invest in India; as the entity is not registered in India, they (offshore clients) can't put money directly into India via the Indian AMC. How will they come? Maybe they can operate through P-notes (some FII-registered P-notes) and indirectly enter into India. The question is, whether SEBI will allow a deemed FII status to these India-based AMCs so that they can get their money directly into India now.

Hedge fund industry is valued at close to USD 3 trillion. Most hedge funds do not want to be regulated across the world. There are 15,000 HFs across the world and about 70% are situated in and operated out of the United States, adding Europe to that, it becomes close to 80%. Every year 40% hedge funds go bust and an equal number are set up. HNIs with big muscles are major investors in hedge funds that obviously do not want to be regulated. The US Securities and Exchange Commission have also been trying to regulate hedge funds for over a decade now, without any luck.

Unidentified money will still continue to come into the Indian equity markets, into stocks and derivatives. Most of the P-notes in India are issued to hedge funds. The question is, will these monies find alternative routes to invest in India or will the business move outside India. If data is to be believed, there are already some signs of this movement.

Baruah Oct. 2007 argues that a lot of money is coming into FDI, particularly in the real estate sector. There is also quite a bit of private equity inflow. The buzz is that portion of those private equity inflows is really sort of regulatory arbitrage, which is trying to circumvent the recently imposed curbs on ECBs and are more complex ways of getting in that money. Broadly, it is a combination of FDI and private equity flows which could be quasi-ECB. Genuine flows do not have problem with regulators. But where there is a case of regulatory arbitrage, then central bank and the regulatory apparatus as a whole will prevent this arbitrage. There have been media reports that the RBI is seriously looking at the issue of trying to impose some restrictions on FDI in the real estate sector, they are looking at other flows as well.

A section of the market does see some slowdown in foreign fund inflows in the near-term, as absence of further rate cuts would make "carry trade" less attractive in a market that is already expensive. Also, curbs on participatory notes may further slow such inflows into India. Carry trade involves borrowing in countries with lower rates and a weakening currency and investing the proceeds in high-yielding assets elsewhere, for higher returns. Analysts partly attribute the glut of foreign institutional inflow into emerging markets, especially India, to this trade, which gained significance after the 0.5% cut by the US Fed in its benchmark rate (5 Nov. 2007).

The US-India CEO Forum in Mumbai (Nov. 2007) discussed the key points of economic growth, capital flows and investment in infrastructure sector. Henry Paulson, US Treasury Secretary, addressing the forum said that he is aware of new P-note regulations for FIIs. But capital control by monetary authority will lead to distortions. “India has also taken administrative steps to adjust the pace of capital outflows and inflows. As recent experience has shown, administrative restrictions of capital flows are instruments, that can have unintended consequences. They tend to inhibit efficiency and lose their effectiveness over time. I encourage India to continue liberalizing such restrictions. Steps to broaden and deepen the domestic financial sector will also help mitigate the risk posed by greater capital flows,” said Paulson.

Earlier, FIIs’ intense selling pressure used to create upheaval in the stock markets; but now the direction of the market is no longer determined solely by FII inflows as was the case in the past, but also by domestic institutions like mutual funds and life insurance companies which have ample cash to invest in the market; and due to deep domestic liquidity.

These domestic institutions are one of the prime reasons why the market remains stable, despite FIIs being net sellers to the tune of $2 billion during July-August ’07. Hence, the domestic stock market is no longer as dependent on ‘foreign funds’ as it used to be, since Indian institutions themselves are now of a size to be reckoned with.

Domestic Financial Institutions (FIs) are fast emerging as the pillar of support for the Indian equity market. At a time, when inflows from Foreign Institutional Investors (FIIs) are dictated by global factors like interest rates and Sub prime crisis, Indian financial institutions are providing the much-needed fillip to keep the indices in good spirit.

While mutual funds have been scaling up their activity in a gradual manner, the real thrust, according to market participants, has come from insurance companies led by LIC. It is believed that around 80% of the new-premium money has come through unit-linked insurance policy or ULIPs.

A surging economy, coupled with healthy corporate numbers, domestic consumption, capex cycle and the Indian outsourcing will set the market to reach new highs. Political tensions can create volatility in the market at times.

Hedge Funds: Like many other emerging markets, India has been benefiting from significant foreign fund flows in recent years as investors' quest for yield has led them to look farther from their home markets. Hedge funds have been a less significant and undoubtedly somewhat nascent conduit thus far. However, a combination of several factors, including continued economic strength at the macro level, increasing visibility and interest from investors and favorable developments from a regulatory standpoint, have arguably positioned hedge funds to become a far more influential and integral force in the market in the future.

The Indian equity market has several features that create an ideal playing field for hedge funds. The market comprises over 5,000 listed companies, providing an extremely broad universe of potential opportunities. At the same time, institutional ownership and research coverage is quite thin and limited to a handful of large-cap names, providing a real opportunity for hedge funds to bring its sourcing abilities and depth of research to bear on an investment.

While the current investment climate in India is undoubtedly favorable for all equity managers, hedge funds are arguably best positioned to exploit the opportunity. This can be ascribed to several factors, including the ability to invest across a wider cross-section of the investment universe (given their typically smaller size), the latitude afforded to run more concentrated portfolios (since they are typically not measuring themselves against a benchmark) and the flexibility to use tools to gain short exposure (single stock, single stock futures and index futures).

SEBI has lifted the embargo on hedge funds in a regulated way; in the past fortnight, six hedge funds have been allowed to register with SEBI. However, the funds that have been permitted to come in directly must fulfil following criteria: The fund must be registered with and regulated by the financial market regulator in its home country. It must have at least a year track record. The funds, registered, as a sub account of FII will have to fulfil conditions that apply to foreign institutional investors as well. They will have to follow documentation norms applicable to other overseas investors (Oct. 2007).

Many asset managers and hedge funds are taking to Direct Access Market trading or DMA for the last few years. DMA trading helps investors access markets directly without the intervention of the broker. Speed and control are the driving forces in DMA. The DMA has now hit the Indian markets.

Data security tops hedge fund company's priority list. A hedge fund typically consists of a handful of shrewd fund managers and hence they need third-party administrators to run their regular, non-critical functions. This means that most of these entities have access to sensitive information about investors in these hedge funds.

Investors in hedge funds like having these third-party, independent reviewers; the growth of hedge funds has led to a mushrooming of many third-party administrators. Availability of English-speaking workforce and flourishing capital markets have led to many global firms setting up their offices in India. GlobeOp, Fulcrum and Viteos are some of the large third-party administrators that have set up their Indian businesses in the past couple of years. Third-party administrators of hedge funds in India are beefing up their systems and trying hard to shed the stigma of being porous organizations. The administrators have been working hard to reassure clients that sensitive information cannot be leaked from their network, according to a report on Hedgeweek, a research website.

International Mutual Funds: Until 2006, not many were aware of the existence of funds that give you the opportunity to invest in international stocks like Apple, Nokia, BMW and L'Oreal. But RBI's has enhanced the aggregate ceiling on overseas investment by mutual funds from $2 billion to $4 billion in a span of just six months.

Mutual Funds are now flooding the market with their products that seek to invest either a part or whole of the investment in international bourses. And by doing so, these schemes aim to provide their investors the benefits of global diversification and gain from the rising opportunities worldwide. The number of schemes in this category has soared four-fold since March '07, and as an increasing number of investors become aware of this opportunity, more and more money is pouring into these funds.

India-based international mutual funds are foraging for opportunities in emerging markets to deploy their funds profitably. According to industry sources, most overseas funds would be skipping European and American markets and shopping in growth markets. Most fund managers are placing their bets on stocks listed on high-return emerging markets like Mexico, Brazil, Hong Kong, Poland and Korea, as emerging markets have a favorable demographic profile. They account for about 50% of the world's GDP and command 7% weightage over world market-cap with lots of potential upside. The most impressive fact is that emerging markets have consistently outperformed European and American indices over the past few years. The focus is on markets with a minimum GDP growth rate of 5-6%. Most India-based funds follow the same investment rationale as Indian investors have high appetite for growth. China, Indonesia, Vietnam, Taiwan have high-value stocks. We have seen phenomenal capital flows into emerging markets and into India.

If the earnings continue to be good, we could hope to benefit. We must also worry about political scene and the absolute level of prices. The Indian markets have shown maturity, it has periodically got corrected for one reason or the other. Earnings have driven the markets over the last three-four years and that's what has always driven the markets. The central risk to the market is more domestic politics than global turbulence at this point. Global impact may be to the extent of rupee strengthening very fast and the impact of it on several popular sectors in the market but otherwise it is largely the local issues like the execution risk, cost rise, interest rate fluctuations, and politics.

Globalization makes decoupling impossible. Latest in 2007 is the decupling theory where they believe that all global cues cannot directly impact the financial markets. Decoupling theory suggests that "Global growth will decouple from US growth to a greater extent than in the past." Goldman Sachs said in a report, the US is a less important destination for world exports, domestic demand is on solid footing in Europe, Japan and key emerging markets. The underlying shock driving the US slowdown is not global in nature, but is linked to a slowing US housing market.

"A sharp slowdown in the US economy in '07 is unlikely to drag the rest of the global economy down with it," Merrill Lynch said last year. "The good news is there are strong sources of growth outside the US that should prove resilient to a consumer-led US slowdown."

Asian countries' dependence on the US consumer has fallen since the tech bubble burst. Goldman Sachs economists recently reiterated their confidence in decoupling, saying BRIC countries remain "key to global decoupling" (Sept. 2007).

Rising economies Brazil, Russia, India and China (BRIC) have decided to gradually intensify cooperation beginning with consultations at the ambassadorial level and then moving on to political level. Consultations will focus on issues of mutual interest in the international arena as also those relating to trade, development and financial system. The decision was taken during a ministerial meeting of the four countries on the sidelines of the ongoing United Nations General Assembly session (25 Sept. 2007).

China has taken steps towards establishing a $200 billion sovereign investment fund, and there are estimates of $2.5 trillion in such funds worldwide. Another key difference this time is that emerging market countries are no longer hampered by a widespread inability to issue debt in their home currencies, a problem known widely as "original sin".

Having to borrow abroad left them open to exchange rate squeezes, where the cost of their external debt could rocket in local terms if their currency fell against dollar. But many emerging issuers can now sell debt in local currencies, often at long maturities. This has both reduced supply of dollar debt and cut back on the chances that emerging markets themselves will face repayment shocks.

So, the next time we face a real market shock, the old order of who gets punished could be fundamentally reversed. "Emerging markets (are) no longer where default risk lies, given the balance sheet improvements that have taken place in the past several years," said David Lubin, an emerging markets economist at Citigroup.

"So if credit concerns are primarily located in the US, then market response to those concerns is to sell US assets, so the dollar weakens, and what does it weaken against? Emerging market currencies..." (Dec. 2007).

European Union is India's largest trading partner and the second largest FDI source is already well poised to take advantage of these gigantic transformations. India PM's Opening Statement at 7th India-EU Summit October 13, 2006, Helsinki, Finland addresses the concerns.

We want EU to look at India as a safe, secure and profitable trade and investment destination; as a hub for high technology R&D, manufacturing and for services. Not just for the vast Indian market but for adjoining areas with which India enjoys close ties—South East Asia, West Asia and Central Asia. We want you to take advantage of the vast pool of quality scientific talent and a young skilled workforce in the manufacturing and service sectors.

We recognize the interest of the EU on measures that India will take to further liberalize FDI in areas such as Telecommunications and Retail; efforts to improve infrastructure; opening up our financial sector and relaxation of labor laws. These issues continue to receive the attention of our government. We want EU to look at the expanded opportunities offered by our Special Economic Zones.

Achieving energy security to provide for safe, secure, affordable and sustainable energy supplies is our common concern. We must also look to alternatives to our dependence on fossil fuels through non-polluting sources such as nuclear energy.

We hope that the European Union will be in a position to support forward looking approaches to enhance international cooperation in the peaceful uses of nuclear energy. This will enable countries like India to expand the share of nuclear energy in their national energy baskets.

Banking

Banking Architecture is Changing

In the past two decades, the banking architecture has changed in India. The automated teller machine (ATM) has been a big innovation. Credit and debit cards have created new financial spaces. Some banks have experimented with rural agents. Yet the bank branch has remained the bedrock of the banking system. You need a bank account in a branch before you can use an ATM or credit card.

Net banking through computers may be about to change. It is still early, but technocrats now view cell phones as the new architecture of virtual banks. This has the potential to make bank branches obsolete, or at least non-essential. Cell phone banking looks especially relevant for India, since it can penetrate the Indian countryside cheaply and effectively where there are not even any banks.

The world over, cell phones are spreading at a phenomenal rate. In many developing countries, more people have cell phones than bank accounts. In India, new cell phone connections are growing at the rate of six million a month, a rate of customer expansion that no bank can dream of. Many Indians still don't use banks. A global consultancy study says India has the second largest number of households that do not access the banking system.

Banks have evinced considerable interest in the mobile-payments banking space. The central bank has mandated that SMS be used for small-ticket payments up to Rs. 1,500, thus making it possible for even the most basic mobile phone to be used for mobile-banking. It has also asked banks to make their mobile-banking services available across all phone networks. Further, RBI has said that the long-term goal of the mobile-payment framework in India would be to enable funds transfer from and account in one bank to any other account in any bank on a real time basis, irrespective of the mobile network the customer has subscribed to.

Banks have evinced considerable interest in the mobile-payments space over the past couple of years and the top players have already rolled them out. However, most of these are restricted to certain mobile-service providers or to high-end users with GPRS-enabled instruments. The central bank's move of making the mobile-payments space operator-agnostic is being perceived by many as an attempt to broad base the service (June 2008).

Rural cell phone towers did not exist in India to permit services in the deep countryside till now. But those towers are now coming up rapidly, and cell phone companies expect to get hundreds of millions of rural customers in the next five years. For the first time in history, villagers will have instant connectivity. This has implications for every sector, including banking. In some countries, cell phones are already part of the financial architecture. All cell phone companies have pre-paid schemes, giving each customer an e-account from which the cost of his telephone calls is debited. Cell phone companies have a wide network of agents—shopkeepers of all sorts who accept money to recharge the SIM card when you have used up your phone time. The same shopkeepers can become virtual tellers of a virtual bank.

Rural banking is a goldmine says global consultancy report. After RBI made out a case for using mobile phones to settle transactions, a new report by consultancy firm Boston Consulting Group (BCG) has recommended that banks collaborate with telecom providers to increase banking penetration in rural India.

With barely 34% of its population engaged in formal banking, India has the second-highest number of financially-excluded households in the world, about 135 million. But the real rate of exclusion, according to BCG, is measured not just by ownership, but also by frequency of use of an account, which it terms as the 'Next Billion'.

The report titled, 'The Next Billion Consumers'—a road map for expanding financial inclusion in India highlights the need for innovation by banks and a change in their approach towards financial inclusion. The report notes that a comprehensive solution for the unbanked can come only from viewing these billion customers as through a prism of opportunity rather than obligation (The government has made it mandatory for banks to provide no-frills bank accounts to such customers).

BCG managing director said, "Innovative business models, backed by government initiatives and regulatory reforms, could reach an additional 30-million households by 2010". To engage the excluded customers, financial institution must first understand this segment's financial needs and aspirations, along with barriers that give rise to exclusion and the impact of India's rural-urban divide.

'The Next Billion' are discerning consumers, the report says. They value speed, flexibility, simplicity and smaller product sizes. Because of their experience with the informal financial sector, most are accustomed to fast-processing and minimal paper work. Low income, poor proximity to financial services outlets and lack of formal employment make it difficult for these consumers to join the formal sector. They also find formal channels intimidating and have a poor grasp of financial offerings.

Given this, the mobile handset could become the sole banking channel for many consumers in India, particularly the billion unbanked. For banks, this possibility is as much an opportunity as a threat. A consumer, in this segment, is unlikely to have a strong relationship with a financial services provider, but may already (or soon) have a relationship with a telecom provider. Among 'The Next Billion', mobile phones already outnumber bank accounts.

'The Next Billion' consumers in India will not necessarily see banks as the only possible providers of payment and transaction services, particularly if another industry can offer those services through a more convenient and accessible channel.

Despite the growing threat from telecom players, banks should not see them as adversaries. A smart model for banking through mobile phones has the potential to create advantages along the entire banking value chain from product development to collection and to radically alter the economics of serving 'The Next Billion'.

It is only a matter of time before banking through mobile phones gains momentum in India. Banks should explore opportunities to collaborate with telecom providers before they find themselves competing against what could become the 'Next Billion's' channel of choice.

The microfinance legislation has been tabled in the winter session of Parliament in 2006. This would provide a regulator for the banking needs of more than 400 million Indians, who are currently out of the banking system. The emphasis will be given on development and nurturing of the microfinance movement in the country.

Another emerging practice upcoming in microfinance in India in Nov. 2006 is to set customers overdraft facilities as opposed to conventional loan. Banks in India have now announced some rather unique ways in microfinancing to get them to deposit savings.

Citibank has launched the Pragati saving account for its microfinance customers. This account is similar to a no frills account and does not require any minimum balance. The bank will provide services through a biometric ATM that will also speak to customers in Hindi, Marathi, Tamil, Telugu languages. "As the customers start saving, there will be ability to sweep this money into deposits so that they earn better interest than the conventional saving account. As we start getting imprints of customers in terms of deposit behavior we may be able to set them overdraft facilities as opposed to convention loan," says Business Manager—Global Consumer Group, Citigroup India. What's unusual about the Citi product is that it is offering micro-savings, while most banks offer microloans. Other banks like Andhra Bank and Bank of India, ICICI. Banks also offer biometric ATM facility to their microfinance customers. In fact banks see this untapped segment not as philanthropy but as sound business, at a time when cheap deposits are hard to come by (Nov. 2006). Microfinance has helped millions reach a better life through their own initiative. It has also given them valuable skills as well as crucial financial back-up.

The upswing in the Indian economy is younger population, the low penetration of banking services in the country and a host of other factors; the Indian banking sector today stands on the threshold of exponential growth. According to Price Water House Cooper (PWC) report, India may well be the third largest banking hub in the world by 2040.

A host of foreign banks have either applied to or are in talks with India's banking regulator, RBI, for licenses; attracted by the idea of servicing a fast growing economy and the promise of a liberalized scenario in 2009. The Royal Bank of Scotland, The Royal Bank of Canada, Credit Suisse and Switzerland's UBS AG are among the many banks reported to have evinced interest in being part of the Indian banking sector. India today offers one of the fastest growing markets for financial products and services across the globe; any banking and financial services company seeking growth can afford to ignore India. Further, within the E7 group (seven emerging market economies which include China, India, Brazil, Russia, Indonesia, Mexico and Turkey) India is likely to be the fastest growing of the E7 economies in the long run, according to the report.

Citibank had asked for permission to open 37 branches but RBI has given clearance to only three. Other banks like American Express, Bank of America, and JP Morgan Chase have also filed applications with RBI to open more branches in India. But Finance Minister has indicated that the permission granted to Citibank may be the last unless more Indian banks are allowed to set up branches in the US.

Perhaps as a result of this tough talking ICICI Bank's application for branch license has just been cleared by the US authorities. Sources said the Fed is not too keen on granting branch licenses to Indian banks because of weak regulations relating to money laundering. But the Finance Minister said,

India has already passed the Anti-money Laundering Bill in 2006. For record, 52 branches of US banks are operational in India while only 6 Indian banks branches function in the US. This issue is likely to generate a lot more discussions.

Infosys Technologies has announced the launch of Finacle bank-in-a-box (BIAB), a pre-configured and fully integrated framework for banking transformation. Finacle BIAB has been developed on the powerful architectural foundation of Finacle and brings a fully web-enabled application and process stack in a ready to deploy state. The global expertise in powering close to 100 banks across 55 countries has enabled Finacle to offer this specialized framework for various regions. At this time, the regional framework has been developed for three regions Europe, Middle East and South East Asia (25 Oct. 2007).

In short, Capital flow, both from domestic and foreign resources is important for India. Since Capital is needed to expand businesses, its infrastructures and to achieve transformation in various domains. Equally important is to be selective about the channels of capitals as well as to manage them well for optimum utilization and benefits.

7 Connectivity

Mankind has deep desire to build bridges figuratively and literally. They like to know people and what is on the other side of water and land, how they live and who they are and to know them well. Telecommunication is the bridge that links them. Connectivity is the buzzword.

We are entering a new hyper-connected age where consumers are demanding more applied technology than businesses. As older technologies fall by the way side, new ones are poised to take their place in bigger and better ways. The focus is on creating better connectivity through telecommunication development, transport development, television and radio. Wireless technologies and digitalization are changing everything.

Telecommunications in modern version comprise wire and wireless telephones, Internet—broadband. Internet gives instantaneous connectivity through email instant messages, and product ads, etc. It widens the information and knowledge instantaneously on any subject. Internet technology is dependent on computer connectivity. Broadband technology creates better quality of Internet. Thus local, national, and global connectivity is dependent on the quality and access to these technologies.

Despite the positive benefits these technologies can have for economic development, many people in developing nations are held back by a diverse set of factors—such as low connectivity in rural locations, duties and taxes imposed by governments, the costs of handsets and computers and the cost of services.

Usage costs can play a large role in determining the purposes for which, and the frequency with which, people use these facilities.

It is often claimed that access to telecommunication facilities is a propeller of economic prosperity in developing countries. Mobile phones in particular are considered pivotal in encouraging growth. Prahlad (2004), in Fortune at the Bottom of the Pyramid asserts that defining change in the world's poorest economies will be led by access to communications and not through the evolution of IT as was the case in the advanced countries of the world.

Narula (2004) highlighted that such changing practices in late-90s and 2000 decade created mobile access boom in developing countries for the lower strata of people and created social change in India. The revolution in cellular phones in India has brought social change and given connectivity and business enhancement to the lowly placed in the society. This has changed the way these people communicate about themselves socially, vocationally and professionally.

Businesses are built on developing the capacity of the poor. There are 300 million cell phones in China or 40 million cell phones in India and they are adding 1.5 million subscribers per month. They are not all in the hands of the rich. In fact, in developing countries, the poor skilled or unskilled in business of plumber, electrician, carpenter or vegetable vendor are utilizing it for connectivity for their business. Diffusion of cell phones is creating business connectivity besides social change. The cell phone businesses are (being) built around the consumer demand and experience of the poor people. In these countries they have the growth opportunity (Narula, 2005).

In India, the transformation in telecommunication is from landlines to cellular phones, computers use in general and low price computers in particular, Internet access through businesses, individuals and cybercafés; and development of broadband for Internet to improve quality. Earlier, this is connected through telephone land lines. Very low density, higher rates and expensive telecommunication software and hardware created poor scenario for telecommunication connectivity. Television has also expanded and created new roles in these two decades. Economic transformation created a progressive scenario or vice versa—a progressive telecommunication will propel economic development.

The information technology model in India has been developed for social and business transformation in the country to give information power to people by diffusing information at grassroots level; and to give information power to business enterprises to compete in the global markets. It is based on three principles of connectivity (social), accessibility to the system and reliability of the system.

We focus on India's progress in telephones, computers—Internet—broadband; and television. During 2000 decades, these have transformed the economic and technological scenario in India and these have widened global connectivity and giving rising expectations economically, professionally, politically, culturally and socially.

Telephone in India

In 70s and 80s, the tele-density in India was low; still the expectations were there that there will be growth through telecommunications services as they replace transport and energy costs in a cheap and efficient way. At that time the telephone subscriber in India experienced problems at both micro and macro levels. The government at that time needed to address these issues, bring costs down, increase availability, and offer incentives to the masses to use the system.

Liberalization started in 1981 when Prime Minister Indira Gandhi signed contracts with Alcatel CIT of France to merge with the state owned Telecom Company (ITI), in an effort to set up 50,00,000 lines per year. But soon the policy was let down because of opposition from leaders of the opposite political party. She invited Sam Pitroda a US based NRI to set up a Center for Development of Telematics (C-DOT), however the plan failed due to political reasons. During this period, after the assassination of Indira Gandhi, under the leadership of Rajiv Gandhi, many public sector organizations were set up like the Department of Telecommunications (DoT) , VSNL and MTNL.

Many technological developments took place in this regime but still foreign players were not allowed to participate in the telecommunications business.

The demand for telephones was ever increasing. It was during this period that the Narsimah Rao led government introduced the national telecommunications policy (NTP) in 1994 which brought about changes in the following areas: ownership, service and regulation of telecommunications infrastructure. They were also successful in establishing joint ventures between state owned telecom companies and international players. But still complete ownership of facilities was restricted only to the government owned organizations. Foreign firms were eligible to 49% of the total stake. The multinationals were just involved in technology transfer, and not policy making.

During this period, the World Bank and ITU had advised the Indian Government to liberalize long distance services in order to release the monopoly of the state owned DoT and VSNL; and to enable competition in the long distance carrier business which would help reduce tariffs and better the economy of the country. The Rao run government instead liberalized the local services, taking the opposite political parties into confidence and assuring foreign involvement in the long distance business after five years.

After 1995 the government set up TRAI (Telecom Regulatory Authority of India) which reduced the interference of government in deciding tariffs and policy making. The DoT opposed this. In India, the Telecom Regulatory Authority of India (TRAI) is functional since January 1997, with a view to provide an effective regulatory framework and adequate safeguards to ensure fair competition and protection to consumer interests. Presently, the main role of TRAI is that of an adjudicator and arbitrator, TRAI monitors and enforces mechanism checks.

Department of Telecommunications (DoT) looks after policy making, licensing and coordination. TDSAT is independent entity for telecom disputes settlement. The political powers changed in 1999 and the new government under the leadership of A.B. Vajpayee was more pro-reforms and introduced better liberalization policies. They split DoT in two, one policymaker and the other service provider (DTS) which was later renamed as BSNL. The proposal of raising the stake of foreign investors from 49% to 74% was rejected by the opposite political party and leftist thinkers. Domestic business groups wanted the government to privatize VSNL. Finally in April 2002, the government decided to cut its stake of 53% to 26% in VSNL and open it for sale to private enterprises. TATA finally took 25% stake in VSNL.

This was a gateway to many foreign investors to get entry into the Indian Telecom Markets. After March 2000, the government became more liberal in making policies and issuing licenses to private operators. The government further reduced license fees for cellular service providers and increased the allowable stake to 74% for foreign companies. Because of all these factors, the service fees finally reduced and the call costs were cut greatly.

Initially, fixed lines focused on providing infrastructure within the cities, then to link cities and then connecting internationally. The expansion of telephones and the need for improving quality of voice and connectivity necessitated the telecommunication infrastructure. New technologies are on the scene. Since 90s the economies opened and India could import technologies. We deal with the consumer needs and the technologies available to address this deficiency, including the replacement of copper with fiber optics, full utilization of IP, optical switching, the use of lasers, intelligent networks, etc. Also the need to develop the local loops quickly and intelligently. Along with the technology accessibility, demand-supply and competition increased and setting price structure became the issue. More and more cities were connected, and prices declined as the demand for telephony increased. Late-90s also witnessed the start and the revolutionary expansion of cell phones in urban and rural India.

In early-90s Urban India experienced the vast network of Public Call Offices (PCOs) in every nook and corner operated by both public and private enterprises. That was revolutionary and gave easy accessibility and connectivity to people. Rural India was still not that connected. Late-90s also witnessed the start of pagers and cell phones and then the revolutionary expansion of cell phones in urban and rural India in 2000 decades. Cell phone revolution was made possible by many private businesses, production and import of technologies and cheaper handset made available by Nokia, Ericsson and Motorola who initially were supplying and then started production in India and catered to variety of clientele affordability.

The pay-phone booths are dying with the affordability of cell phone by common person. Small private entrepreneurs are exiting the pay-phone, it is no longer remunerative but government is still providing this facility through state owned BSNL at public places like railway stations, bus stations and bus stops, airports, post office, and market places or other strategic public places.

The telecommunication infrastructure for both fixed lines and cell phones is handled by government companies of BSNL and MTNL, and VSNL for overseas calls. Many private domestic companies are now on the scene, they invested huge funds in the improved telecommunication infrastructure. Many international companies ushered for telecommunication in joint ventures with domestic companies.

BSNL owns around 85% of India's copper wire local loop networks. The company is the largest telecom operator and the largest public sector enterprise in India, providing basic fixed-line services nationwide, except for the cities of Mumbai and Delhi.

MTNL is India's dominant fixed-line telecommunications incumbent in Delhi and Mumbai. With the market opened to competition in 2001, MTNL has been facing rivalry for its share of the market and declining long-distance call rates. To diversify its revenue base, the cash rich company has expanded into GSM and CDMA cellular services and is developing its Internet related services, including ADSL, Intelligent Network services, call centers and IDCs. The company is expanding beyond its traditional areas to offer Internet services nationwide, and to provide basic services in Nepal. MTNL is considered a likely candidate for further divestment by the government.

The government is planning to exempt fixed-line telephony from license fee to encourage service providers, especially those in the private sector, to go to the rural areas. Currently, telecom operators pay 6-10% of their total revenues, including revenue from landline and broadband, towards license fees. BSNL will be the largest beneficiary of this move as it will save up to Rs. 1,200 crores annually. It has over 90% market share in the fixed-line space. BSNL gets annual revenue of about Rs. 15,000 crores from its fixed-line operations and pays on an average, 8-9% of AGR as license fee to the government. Private operators such as Airtel, Reliance and Tata have minimum presence in the landline space (May 2008).

India's investment in telecommunications infrastructure over the last decade has extended to a heavy involvement in international infrastructure. Under the leadership of International operator VSNL the country has been assembling an extensive infrastructure of gateways, satellite earth stations and fiber optic submarine cables. Billions of rupees continue to be invested in a combination of submarine cables and microwave systems to satisfy India's demand for international bandwidth and high-quality connectivity.

Bharti Tele-Ventures Ltd. controlled by the Bharti group is India's largest non-government telecom company and the largest provider of GSM mobile services. It also provides fixed-line local access, national and international long-distance telephony, VSAT, Internet services and corporate data network solutions.

Many other telephone companies, Reliance communications, Idea cellular, Tata tele-services, VSNL, and Vodafone-Essar, have been in the limelight. We have discussed about some of these in Chapter 3. Many more companies are in the business of manufacturing technology of hard infrastructure and providing soft tele infrastructure services.

India is one of the fastest growing markets for mobile technology. The country's mobile operators have been providing services based initially on GSM, but subsequently a substantial

CDMA presence has been added. While India moves into advanced forms of mobile technology, including GPRS and EDGE, the country has been waiting for the adoption of 3G (third generation mobile). The government was finalizing the 3G licensing process in 2007. However, there have been a series of regulatory battles going on with vigorous participation by the wider market in the discussions about CDMA 2G deployment in India—2006 and CDMA 3G deployment in India—2006. We have discussed this spectrum controversy in later sections.

The dynamic Indian mobile telephony market has seen a number of important takeovers and mergers, resulting in significant shifts in market share among the players. Initially three major private players—Hutchison Telecom, Bharti, and Idea Cellular—emerged from the fray to do battle. The entry of the state-owned enterprises BSNL and MTNL as mobile operators, BSNL in particular, throws a major challenge to the private operators. Finally, we have seen the arrival (through the back door) of the CDMA based services. Amongst these, Reliance has emerged as a serious challenger to the GSM operators.

Telecommunications infrastructure is being developed to provide landline and mobile telecommunication, VSAT, Internet and broadband services in India. There are varieties of broadband technologies being used. Now Wi-Fi and Wi-Max are being developed. Public cybercafes become ubiquitous in India from metros to small towns to give Internet connectivity to people at affordable prices. The update of cybercafé profile in metro or smaller cities is providing facilities of Internet, pay-phone for long distance domestic and international calls through Internet or otherwise, fax, and word processing/and printing through computers. Rural areas still remained inaccessible through cybercafé.

The future of Internet, its mobile applications, video and text, and the continuing drive for a single network capable of carrying all types of traffic; and VOIP telephony is also being focused by Indian entrepreneurs.

GSM and CDMA services for mobile telephone are being developed more in 2007. In Oct.-Nov. 2007, government has released more spectrum as subscriber base is expanding. Still to overcome the limitations of spectrum, cell towers are being constructed; optical fiber capacity is expanding to cater to high bandwidth applications.

Sterlite Optical technologies company will expand and double its optical fiber capacity to 12 million km. for telecommunications. This state-of-the-art facility would be capable of manufacturing the company's existing range of optical fiber products as well as have the intrinsic capability to manufacture products as per evolving international telecom standards that are being introduced to cater to high bandwidth applications required by global markets (Nov. 2007).

Telecom companies are growing their presence in rural circles for mobile telephones as wireless telephones are easier and cost efficient to set up in rural areas of India than landline wires.

As there are so many private players in the telecom area, the government in Nov. 2007, has made the telephone number operability in all metros initially and then plans to spread to wider areas. Telephone number operability allows persons to keep the same telephone number even they may switch to different telecom company. Telephone number portability for telephones will initially be in the four metros. Mobile number portability will be operationalized from Q4 2008. In India, the consumers can easily switch among networks by popping SIM cards—the memory chips that store mobile numbers in and out of their phones. The cell phones roam seamlessly among different carrier networks.

A new technology would integrate both CDMA and GSM. LTE (long term evolution) 4th generation wireless telephone technology is on the anvil. LTE is expected to boost download speeds of tens of mega bites per second. Vodafone Group has opted to go with LTE technology that might eventually let wireless carriers offer interconnections at speed equal to or faster than existing wire-line DSL or cable services. It sees lucrative growth prospects in speedier Internet access and related services. LTE promises higher quality of video, music and mobile games. These can be streamed faster on the cell phone. It is intended to connect digital cameras and gaming services. This would mean more business for the equipment vendors. Wi-Max is also 4th generation technology but not compatible with LTE.

Cellular Phones: The Indian telecom market was opened to privatization and competition in 1992, but the regulator, Telecom Regulatory Authority of India (TRAI) was set up only in 1997. It has also been entrusted to find solutions to other issues such as policy initiatives, the transition mechanism that is best suited for the migration, the requirement for a national test bed and dividing the transition cost among the stakeholders. Subsequently the New Telecom Policy, 1999 was promulgated and under this policy, operators could use any technology. The competition has brought sharp drop in call rates and handset subsidies and promotional schemes have fueled the phenomenal growth of subscribers during the last two years. Cellular operators are upgrading their networks to provide services beyond basic voice connectivity.

Major part of mobile subscriber growth now comes from the emerging markets and understanding this has enabled the mobile operators to prepare business models according to needs of this segment. Low tariffs, low cost handsets, new content, sharing of infrastructure are leading to developing of new business models. Competition is the key driver of explosive growth of wireless cellular communication. Mobile cellular competition has brought innovative pricing and service offering.

Some Lessons for Other Emerging Markets

Priorities, pattern of governance and needs of different countries are different, but lack of infrastructure is the common handicap in all developing countries. Some of the lessons that could be helpful in formulating policies, regulatory issues and implementation of plans for providing telecommunication services to the masses at affordable prices are as given below:

A sound competitive environment by providing a fair playing field is necessary for the market to develop. Emphasis on better quality of service gives better customer loyalty and increase in revenue due to maturing of more calls.

One of the factors responsible for faster growth in developing countries is the availability of low cost handsets through large volumes. Companies like Motorola, Nokia, Sony Ericsson and Samsung have set up their handset manufacturing plants in India and China that supply low cost hand-sets to neighboring countries in the region as well.

For doing business in developing countries, foreign companies' partnership with local telecom operators and service providers is helpful to both partners. This helps in bagging big projects. The foreign companies should establish necessary infrastructure in the country with long-term market perspective to support the operator proactively.

China and India combined have a population of nearly 2.5 billion people and both the economies are doing exceedingly well by recording the highest all-round growth in the world. India has an added advantage of a large number of technically qualified manpower available at low cost and this has attracted a number of multinational telecom companies like Motorola, Ericsson, Nokia, Microsoft and Intel to set up it research and development in telecommunications centers in India. India like China offers a huge opportunity for mobile vendors evolving the global telecom markets and reshaping the technology landscape. Using wireless to provide voice and data communication to many outlying remote areas will help bring the people into 21st century faster. Mobile communication is not simply about replacing wires or upgrading existing 2/2.5G mobile services, but in developing countries it means connecting the people through voice and data, where there were none before.

Mobile Telephones

The mobile communications technology is evolving rapidly in the world as more and more people demand mobile services with larger bandwidth and new innovative services like connectivity anywhere, anytime for features like TV, multimedia, interoperability and seamless connectivity with all types of protocols and standards. While the 3G services are yet to fully come up, serious discussion on 4G has started. WLAN hot spots have made inroads along with 3G to offer an alternative form of mobile access.

Every hour as many as 10,000 mobile phones are sold in India, thanks to the ever-increasing mobile services' market and availability of entry level handsets that has brought phones well within everyone's reach, an IDC India report said.

At present, India has over 270 million mobile users and is adding over eight million subscribers every month. Out of the 560 million mobile users, about 53 per cent or about 298 million subscribers would use mobile Internet, while China would have 40 per cent or 320 million mobile internet users. Mobile Internet for an increasingly large and attractive consumer segment is an important distinction for marketeers to keep in mind.

According to the report; BRIC region represents the next great growth curve for both mobile and interactive marketing industries and forms the core of an emergent global middle class population that would cross one billion by 2015.

India has shipped close to 85 million mobile handsets between April 2007 and March 2008, compared to fewer than 66 million units shipped in the previous fiscal, registering a year-on-year growth of around 29 per cent.

Technology Challenges

Recent worldwide explosion of mobile communication systems can lead to a most effective key technology for solution of telecommunication issues in bridging digital divide in the developing world.

The single biggest phenomenon that is transforming the global telecom industry is convergence. Internet users are now exposed to different modes of communication as against the basic voice telephony. Communication now includes pictures, videos and is not limited to person-to-person communication, but communities and user groups are being created and information exchange is not limited to and from people known to each other. Content is driving the service subscription and identifying the right content, in the right format at right cost and delivering it in secure manner to any kind of business model for communication industry are the main issues. Unless convergence reduces the cost of communication for the common masses and provides content in local languages, convergence will remain restricted to enterprise segment for another two to three years.

'Communications Convergence Bill' is pending before the Indian Parliament for the last few years but its enactment is likely to be delayed. This is due to experiencing of difficulties in launching of convergence of technologies introduced through law in some of the Asian Pacific countries. One of the aims of this new proposed legislation is to establish a licensing framework for carriage and content information in the scenario of convergence of telecommunication, broadcasting and multimedia and other related technologies and to establish a single regulatory authority as 'Communication Commission of India'.

New Application and Services

Airtime rates have already hit the bottom and now the focus has shifted to Value Added Services (VAS) to increase revenues. The handset has become an entertainer, an informer, a secretary and an undeniable part of users' lives. The world over, voice revenues are reducing and this is forcing operators to focus on non-voice revenues. The initial change is towards SMS and then progressing to other data services like ring-tones, sports updates, film gossip and astrology. While browser and voice-based services are expensive and require expensive handsets, operators need to reach out to the masses through SMS with compelling India-specific content in local language.

Multimedia Messaging Service (MMS) and other 3G services will become common by the year 2010 and Indian market share is expected to be 7 per cent of the world market. The predictions are that due to MMS experience in Japan and South Korea, Asian countries will become leaders in 3G MMS. Availability of low cost handsets is an important factor for the fast growth of mobile communications in India. Entry level cheap handsets are now available at a price of US $30 and soon a handset with basic features is expected to be in the market for US $15.

Improving Profitability

Mobile entertainment industry is another area where potential is huge and with recent introduction of Java color handsets in the Indian market there is an immense scope to improve revenues by mobile operators. For mobile gaming to become popular and enjoyable, quality of content and gaming concepts that users can relate to are the drivers. Java games will increase GPRS and WAP usage on GSM as well as on CDMA 2001-1x networks. Other important issues that need to be addressed are promoting emerging technologies quickly and aim at lowering ARPU further. Operating expenses in India are still higher at $4 per subscriber as compared to $2.41 in China. Infrastructure sharing and flexible tariff rates are other areas that need special attention and innovative approach to meet the affordability of vast Indian population.

Tele-density in India: Tele-density, the number of people owning a telephone out of every 100 people improved. According to TRAI, gross number of telephones crossed 248.66 million by the end of September 2007 compared with 241.02 million in August this year. A total of 7.64 million telephone connections were added in September 2007. The tele-density reached 21.85% in September 2007 as against 21.20% in August 2007. A TRAI release stated the subscriber number has already crossed 250 million which was the target for December 2007. Hence, the expectation of 500 million by 2010 is by no means ambitious. Indian telecom market still has a huge potential for growth.

In the wireless segment, there was an addition of 7.8 million subscribers in September 2007 compared with 8.31 million additions in August 2007. The total wireless subscribers (GSM, CDMA and WLL(F) base touched 209.08 million. However, subscriber base in the wire-line segment, with the lowest tariff in the country, declined by 0.16 million to stand at 39.73 million end August 2007.

Bharti Airtel, the country's largest mobile service operator, added 2.03 million new users, taking its number of subscribers to 50.90 million as on 31st Oct., 2007 and reaching a market share of 31.88 per cent, the Cellular Operators Association of India (COAI) said in a release. Vodafone-Essar, formerly Hutch-Essar, added 1.52 million new users, which pushed its total subscriber base to 37.18 million. It had a market share of 23.28 per cent.

BSNL and MTNL added 727,855 and 53,739 new users, respectively during the period. Birla Group's Idea Cellular reported 750,108 new additions and a total number of users at 1.94 million. Reliance Communications, primarily a CDMA player, registered a total subscriber base of 5.03 million users with a 3.15 per cent market share.

Development of Cellular Telephones

There was steep growth of cell phones, almost 96 per cent over the previous year. Driven by the introduction of full-mobility CDMA cellular services and stiff competition among GSM operators, 2004 broke all records for growth in the Indian mobile market. Volatility in the cellular market was expected to continue until at least 2006 as the main operators carved out their future market positions and some other players attempted to establish their niche positions. Samsung and LG enjoy an early mover advantage, working with local operators such as Reliance, Nokia and Motorola have started to make their presence felt in the CDMA and WCDMA market.

At present, India's telecom operators are unable to roll-out third generation services such as high-speed Internet on mobiles, interactive gaming and mobile TV as the frequency bands in which these services operate are occupied by the defense forces. The expansion of 2G services in several key circles have also been hampered due to non-vacation of spectrum by the armed forces.

Government is working directly with the armed forces to solve this problem. The Wireless Planning and Coordination (WPC) wing, the national spectrum management agency is entrusted to work with the Joint Communication and Electronics

Staff (JCES), which coordinates the spectrum needs of the services, to help the later vacate frequencies in 1700 MHz—2000 MHz bands.

The defense ministry troposcatter methodology of using spectrum was highly inefficient, unreliable and was an obsolete technology that has been discarded globally.

The communications ministry has also said that the global trend was to replace wireless links between fixed locations with physical medium like the optic fiber cable and has added that this would enable the services to have a more secure network, better signal quality and carry higher traffic. Besides, the ministry has also asked the armed forces to take a look at international practices followed by countries such as the US, UK, France and Germany.

India, the fastest growing country in wireless telephony, now has over 200 million mobile subscribers, going by industry estimates in Sept. 2007. "We have one of the most contemporary networks. Most of our networks are 3G ready and should be ready to launch services once the government comes out with the policy."

Other cellular operators including Bharti Airtel, Vodafone Essar, and BSNL are also gearing up for launching 3G mobile services for offering advanced voice, video and data facility to its subscribers. Apart from offering new services, this technology will also allow operators to use spectrum more efficiently.

Idea Cellular also announced that it has joined the Asia Mobility Initiative alliance in which Celcom (Malaysia), MobileOne (Singapore), Excelcombindo (Indonesia), Telstra (Australia) and DTAC (Thailand) are other partners. However, being a part of this alliance does not bring any reduction in roaming rates to Idea subscribers. It is aimed at bringing better quality of service to the users.

The government committee that analyzed TRAI's recommendations on third generation (3G) telecom services has concurred with the regulator's stand and suggested an auction mechanism for awarding spectrum for such services in 2.1 GHz band.

It should have, however, been more forthright in allowing new players in 3G services. While the committee has broadly endorsed TRAI's recommendations, it has suggested some changes; an increase in reserve price, a maximum of three players and one slot for BSNL and MTNL. These modifications are largely warranted if, as per the committee's understanding, adequate spectrum may not be available for supporting more players. So while the number of players has been reduced to three, higher reserve price would ensure the government gets the expected revenue from the auction.

Reserving one slot for state-owned BSNL and MTNL also appears reasonable since security considerations are involved. Moreover, that they would have to pay the same spectrum charge as other successful bidders make the suggestion more equitable. Where the recommendations are wanting is with regard to a clear stand on the entry of new players (including telecom majors currently not in India) in 3G services. The committee has recommended that all existing basic and cellular mobile services, unified access service license holders, as on a specified date prior to bidding, be eligible.

However, TRAI, in its suggestion on 3G services, had noted that '2G services will have spectrum for their present and medium-term needs'. That gives the government the headroom to work on a 3G policy without worrying about the implications for the predominantly voice services on current 2G networks.

Though the expected high price of the 3G spectrum would ensure that the business model would predominantly be a value-added-services-based, 3G would have to also offer voice. The increased competition would benefit the consumer and encourage systemic efficiency.

In May 2008, stung by the BlackBerry mobile telephone controversy, the government has made it mandatory for telecom operators to furnish details about value-added services in advance so that security agencies can keep track. "It has been brought to the notice of the Licensor (DoT) that telecom service providers are not meeting the legitimate monitoring requirement of the security agencies which has serious implications on national security," DoT said in a letter to all cellular and basic service providers. The department directed that service providers must inform it about the launch of any new service/facility in their network 15 days in advance as per earlier instructions, failing which will be treated as breach of terms and conditions of license agreement and appropriate action will be initiated. The required information, in the prescribed format, with regard to monitoring arrangement is made available by all the operators for each service that is being offered or proposed to be offered; to the respective cell of the department on quarterly basis. Upon furnishing of information, DoT would inspect the nature of monitoring arrangement that have been made available by the service providers for the services offered by them.

DoT also said that an amendment was made in the license agreement in 2002 with regard to VAS that *inter alia* provides that "the licensee should make arrangements for monitoring by government security agencies." However, this has not been implemented by most of telecom service providers. The licensees are also directed to ensure that no new services are launched until appropriate systems for monitoring of this service are put in place.

The government has taken this step in the backdrop of the controversy over BlackBerry services in India, which have allegedly posed a major security threat in absence of monitoring of information transmitted through the device.

The government may soon find a solution to the BlackBerry security issue. San Jose-based Cain and SS8 had approached the DoT offering their interception solutions after security agencies here had raised concerns over the BlackBerry services. DoT, after consultations with IB, had invited both companies to demonstrate their equipment and solutions.

Cain Technologies and SS8 Networks will be demonstrating their interception equipment to the DoT and Intelligence Bureau (IB) on 16 May 2008. DoT sources said if the demonstrations are successful, the government will direct Canada's 'Research In Motion' (RIM), maker of BlackBerry smart phones, to install the interception solution on Indian mobile networks expeditiously. "The cost will have to be borne by RIM. It is up to them to discuss costs with the providers of BlackBerry services—Airtel, R.Com, BPL and Vodafone," said a senior government official. At the same time, if the demonstrations are successful, DoT may drop its demand that RIM set up servers in India. SS8 and Cain are developers of voice-messaging communication solutions that meet the US government's requirements of lawful traffic interception.

In a major change of stance, RIM may allow the Indian Government to intercept non-corporate emails sent over BlackBerry. This is expected to solve the row between the DoT and RIM to a large extent, since the government's security concerns pertain more to emails from individual users than enterprise customers.

At the core of the issue is the data encryption technology used in BlackBerry (Encryption means converting data and emails into algorithmic codes that travel through the network and later get decoded into the original form). It uses a very high level of encryption—at 256 bits—while sending data. BlackBerry scrambles messages before sending and unscrambles them at the receiver's BlackBerry. Owing to security concerns, the government wants to be able to intercept and decode the data. However, the government's decryption software can decode messages encrypted only up to 40 bits. India wants RIM to either hand over the decryption keys or reduce encryption to 40 bits.

According to officials close to the development, Canadian High Commissioner David Malone and RIM officials met telecom secretary on 7 May 2008. It was explained by RIM that "it should be possible for the government to monitor emails to non-business enterprise customers. RIM is considering giving access to individual users' email to the government. Details on this will be provided in two or three weeks," sources said.

RIM, which is under fire for violation of Indian regulations by offering services with encryption standards above the permissible 40-bit standards, has pointed out that several other companies in India are involved in similar violations. RIM's stance, therefore, is that the DoT is following a discriminatory approach by targeting it. DoT's communications also add that RIM had named Skype as another service provider whose services in India are above the 40-bit encryption standards.

The issues relate to the fact that data on RIM network flows with the 256-Advanced Encryption Standard, whereas, India's security and intelligence agencies are equipped to intercept encryption standards of only up to 40-bit encryption. Several Internet Service Providers (ISPs) supported RIM's argument that many Indian companies, including most airlines, telecoms, banks and even the Indian Railways' online portals were all offering commercial transactions above the 40-bit encryption standard.

"DoT had earlier asked all ISPs to slash encryption levels from the 128-bit standard to a 40-bit level, but we have been unable to do so. This is because, more commercial portals, some of which are also owned by government departments such as the Railways, Indian Airlines, telecom PSUs all offer services at the 128-bit encryption standards. Before we scale it down to the 40-bit, these portals must rework their facility for online commercial transactions," explained an official with the Internet service providers association of India (ISPAI). Globally, the 128-bit standard is followed for all online transactions.

DoT sources also say that once the BlackBerry issue is addressed, the department will come down heavily on all portals and ISPs whose encryption standards were beyond the 40-bit. This will mean the ultra-cheap Internet telephony services offered by Skype and other such global majors will soon be under the government's scrutiny. The larger implication is, that all commercial transactions over the mobile handset or via the Internet in India will be subject to a mere 40-bit encryption, making them unsafe, when compared to the standards followed globally.

DoT is still struggling to resolve the BlackBerry controversy to the satisfaction of the security agencies and in the process it has asked the service providers like Bharti, Vodafone and Reliance Communications not to offer services unless the

BlackBerry vendor RIM deposits the master key to decipher the information with the government.

The direction would have serious implications for the growth of VAS, which is contributing nearly 25 per cent to telecom operators' profitability.

Spectrum Policy in India

Mobile communication is one of the most important developments in the recent times. The current technological developments promise high speed data services based on Internet Protocol (IP) as well as greater capacity and efficiency. The 3G platform provides converged voice, data, Internet and multimedia services supported by high data rate. The single global standard for third generation wireless technology and network, based on ITU initiative is International Mobile Telecommunications—2000 (IMT-2000). In India CDMA-2000-1x EVDO and WCDMA are accepted as Universal Mobile Telecommunication System (UTMS) for 3G services.

For the spread and growth of mobile services, spectrum (radio frequencies on which mobile services operate) is most vital and scarce resource. Spectrum below 3 GHz is most suitable for mobile applications presently. But shortly mobile technologies using 3-6 GHz band are expected to be available. India with its highest growth rate in mobile services, lowest tariff and huge market potential is in a leading position for this development effort. A sound spectrum policy and efficient utilization of available spectrum are the key points while dealing with spectrum issues. At the same time, spectrum policy has to be technology neutral, till the availability of equipment in particular frequency band affects the technology neutral approach. Technology developments like software defined radio, different frequency radio transmitter-receiver (Tx-Rx) on a single chip and demand in the market will very soon remove the restriction of availability of equipment in specific frequency bands. Ultimately, equipment using various technologies would be available in all frequency bands where demand exists. These developments would also help in achieving seamless connectivity among various networks.

European Union in Nov. 2007 approved the proposal to open up the 900 MHz frequency band to telecoms for offering third generation (3G) mobile services, as it is more efficient to run 3G on this frequency, the government cannot replicate the same model here. "3G services are possible in 900 MHz, but in India, we have already exhausted this band by allotting them to GSM operators for second generation (2G) services," explains TRAI chairman.

Spectrum Controversy

Spectrum for Mobile Telephones: Ministry of telecommunication will release 3G spectrum, for 3G and WiMAX, 3G spectrum will be auctioned and will be open to all. They will work out guidelines shortly for 3G spectrum and it will be permitted only in 2.1 GHz band. Government will not permit merger of 3G telecom companies for five years. It will also not permit trading or re-selling of 3G spectrum (Nov. 2007).

The government approved increase in subscribers' base, recommended by TRAI 19 October 2007. It will be the basis for further allocation of spectrum. Consequently, existing GSM players like Bharti, Vodafone-Essar and Idea may find it difficult to get additional spectrum for expansion as the DoT has raised the subscriber base by nearly five times. According to the DoT there would be no cap on number of players in each circle to ensure rapid expansion of telecom services. It is a new twist to the spectrum controversy.

As reported by CNBC-TV18, Tata Tele is all set to apply for a GSM spectrum license in 20 circles. This move comes days after the government allowed telecom operators crossover allocation on the spectrum. Here, why the Tata, which has for long been staunch proponents of CDMA, is now dialing GSM? Tata Tele Services Ltd., will be applying for spectrum in 18 circles; meanwhile, Tata Tele Maharashtra Ltd., will be applying for GSM in two circles where it is operating, namely Maharashtra and Mumbai.

Why GSM especially for a company which has been such a staunch proponent of CDMA technology for all this while? That's because of two crucial policy changes that have happened over the last week. One, DoT has allowed dual technology use. Second is the fact that the subscriber thresholds for allocating GSM spectrum have been increased significantly. This means that none of the existing operators are going to be eligible for additional GSM spectrum, at least not in the near term.

Some amount of GSM spectrum may be available once defense vacates it. Tata Tele also, like R.Com, wants to get into that spectrum queue. R.Com has applied for fresh GSM spectrum in 23 circles on paying an upfront fee of Rs. 1650 crores. Now Tata Tele is following suit.

A day after DoT allowed crossover from one technology to another, it has adopted stricter norms for spectrum allocation. These two changes have enabled R.Com a CDMA player to edge out GSM operators like Bharti Airtel and Vodafone in the race for spectrum, but with a big catch. Players such as Idea and Spice must be cleared to help them expand their footprint on a pan-India basis, before R.Com is granted GSM spectrum. If the DoT was to accept these demands, GSM players may drop their objections to dual technology.

Besides, GSM players have also told DoT that the exercise to arrive at new allocation norms must be carried out separately and simultaneously for operators on both technology platforms. They have also said that the revised criteria must be introduced for both sets of operators at the same time as there was no justification in DoT implementing new norms only for the GSM industry.

Significantly, GSM players also agreed to the two issues the DoT had offered them earlier as part of a compromise formula and want these retained in the new settlement agreement. The first is with regard to number operatability, where they want this to be extended across India and not just the four metros and also that CDMA players be asked to unlock their handsets before this facility be allowed.

With regard to 3G spectrum, they want DoT to drop its initial plan to restrict it to just three GSM-based operators with each getting 10 MHz each. Instead, they want to go by TRAI's recommendations where six licenses of 5 MHz each are issued per circle based on an auction process. This is because, while 5 MHz will make it impossible for a new player to enter the telecom market as it will require additional start-up spectrum, it will be enough for existing GSM players to migrate to 3G.

GSM operators like Bharti and Vodafone which have long been opposing auction of 2G spectrum and wanted allocation according to number of subscribers, find themselves being upstaged by R.Com using rival CDMA technology. This is because the DoT has accepted the telecom regulator's advice making existing players ineligible for additional spectrum if they fail to use the spectrum they have much more efficiently.

In a bid to find a solution to the ongoing spectrum tangle, leading GSM operators have told DoT that they are willing to negotiate towards tightening of the existing spectrum allocation norms, but only in category 'B' and 'C' telecom circles.

"We admit that the subscriber-linked spectrum allocation norms in B and C circles are more relaxed compared to the metros and category A circles. We have indicated that in some of these circles we are ready for an up to 40% increase in the subscriber numbers (from the existing norms) for us to qualify for additional radio frequencies," a top source with a leading GSM player told.

However, with regard to the metros and A category circles, leading GSM players want new spectrum allocation norms to be issued based on the results of trials done on a 'practical' network over a period of time ranging from three to nine months, rather than using a simulation or mathematical model.

Here, they also want the DoT to consider international models of spectrum allocation in cities which have similar population numbers to that of India's metros, and also submissions made by international experts be examined, before any final decision is taken.

Earlier this week, dominant GSM operators, which include Bharti Airtel, Vodafone Essar and Idea Cellular, had turned down an offer from the DoT to accept TRAI's recommendations on subscriber-linked spectrum allocation norms. TRAI had recommended that existing service providers increase their subscriber base between two to six times before being granted additional spectrum.

These GSM players had also turned down the DoT's offer to cap the maximum spectrum allotted to each player per circle at 10 MHz. Here, GSM players have indicated that while existing guidelines entitle them to a maximum of 15 MHz per circle, they are willing to consider a cap at 12.2 MHz, another source from the GSM side said. While DoT during the last meeting had assured telecoms such as Vodafone and Idea that they will be given 4.4 MHz spectrum of priority to launch services in the circles where they currently hold licenses, these operators want start up spectrum quota to be increased to 6.2 MHz per circle, the source added.

The operators under the aegis of Cellular Operators' Association of India (COAI) and Association of Unified Service Providers of India (AUSPI) commented, "We feel that with all these innovations in GSM technology, there is a need to bring parity in the spectrum allocation between GSM and CDMA, the association added."

Spectrum Allocation: It is likely that the current first-come-first-served basis would continue for spectrum allocation even for new entrants and the existing players would get spectrum first, as and when it becomes available. Stating that there is no spectrum to be given to such a huge number of players, the sources said the current norm of existing players getting spectrum first would continue till there was a change in the policy. But there is a caveat. Even among the existing players, a handful of companies who have already got over 10 MHz of spectrum may not be able to get any more. Those who have less than 10 MHz of spectrum would be considered for additional radio waves first.

Government has allocated start-up 2.5 MHz spectrum to new telecom players including Shyam Telelink, Unitech, Datacom and others in Kerala circle. While Shyam has been given CDMA spectrum, others have been allocated GSM spectrum, sources said. Tata Teleservices also got GSM spectrum in Kerala under the dual technology clause. In the GSM space, new players have already been given spectrum in Tamil Nadu and Karnataka.

Earlier, Shyam Telelink was allocated spectrum for 13 circles namely Tamil Nadu, West Bengal, Andhra Pradesh, Uttar Pradesh (East), Uttar Pradesh (West), Himachal Pradesh, Madhya Pradesh, Bihar and Haryana, North-East, Assam, Jammu & Kashmir and Maharashtra (15 May 2008).

Amid differences between DoT and TRAI over entry of foreign players in the 3G telecom services, Communication and IT Minister will discuss with Prime Minister Manmohan Singh and Finance Minister whether participation of more players in 3G, which would fetch additional revenues for the government, should be allowed or we should go by TRAI recommendation. The next generation telecom services (3G) would be reality before May 2009.

TRAI had warned that allowing foreign players in 3G at this juncture would have serious impact on the Indian telecom sector in terms of affordability. TRAI feels that with 12-13 players in each circle there would be enough competition for fetching fair value of spectrum for 3G services. Foreign players are allowed in any case, but in partnership with Indian partner. "It is a question of whether to allow more players over and above the existing operators to participate in the 3G services." While DoT has said that government may get more revenues, if additional players are allowed (May 2008).

While the country's leading telecom players are at loggerheads over grabbing radio waves, India added a whopping 5.71 million subscribers under the GSM segment of mobile telephony in October 2007. The booming telecom sector has fetched Rs. 3015 crores revenues to the government from spectrum fees in 2007-08; while it was Rs. 2090 crores in 2006-07. The sector has now 134 private licensees offering mobile services with a user base of Rs. 20.84 crores till February 2008 with a total investment of Rs. 95,000 crores. Besides, 120 new private licensees are yet to commence operations, said the minister. Government has already issued 126 Letter of Intents for grant of telecom licenses to 17 operators who have applied up to 25 Sept. 2007, out of which 120 licenses have been awarded to 16 operators; 14 operators from this have applied for initial GSM spectrum (May 2008).

Telecom Players in India

A few salient telecom companies are mentioned which are trying to foray into other new telecom areas other than landline and mobile telephony.

Bharti Airtel in 2006-07 is present in only 4,855 towns and 243,584 villages which leaves a large scope for expansion. Internationally also, the company is planning to foray into new markets. Thus going forward, Bharti's subscriber base is expected to increase along with higher MoU. As a result, we estimate the company's net sales to grow at a CAGR of 38.6% for FY07-FY09E.

Moreover, Bharti's plan to demerge its tower business will further provide a push to the company's growth. Recently, Reliance Communications Ltd. (RCOM) sold 5% stake in its tower business for Rs. 14 billion, thus valuing the total business around Rs. 270 billion. Bharti having a much bigger tower base and being a market leader can command a much higher price than RCOM. In addition, the Company's initiatives like the possible launch of DTH and IPTV applications by the end of FY08, will also contribute to its sales growth.

Bharti Airtel is all set to partner IT and telecoms hardware major Cisco for enhancing its managed services portfolio. The Bharti move comes within days of French-US equipment firm Alcatel-Lucent forming a JV with Reliance Communications to offer managed-network services to domestic as well as international telecom operators. The JV has announced that it is targeting revenues to the tune of a billion dollars within the next few years.

With falling tariffs and reduced ARPUs, all major telecoms including Tata Communications, BSNL and R.Com, are now looking at managed services which combines IT services with telecom offerings. Besides, managed services also help telecoms move up the value chain and increase revenues as Indian corporates extend their footprint both within the country and globally.

According to a recent report by Gartner, network IT services are set to become a $7 billion market by 2011. Telecoms are, therefore, looking at end-to-end managed services; installation of the hardware at the customer premises, providing customized software solutions, managing and maintaining both IT and hardware platform.

IT's president for enterprise service David Nishball said that Airtel is collaborating with Cisco to launch managed Multi Protocol Label Switching (MPLS) services. "With Cisco's Tier I certification for the CISCO Managed Serviced Channel Partnership program, Airtel will now be able to offer Indian enterprises end-to-end Managed VPN Services including last mile and customer premise equipment (CPE) management, network design, installation, configuration, and 24×7 monitoring and maintenance support. It will launch a series of managed services on an OPEX model; though he did not divulge specifics; it expects to grow its MPLS business by 50-60% in this financial year 2008-09. The company, which has more than 400 customers on its MPLS network, intends to increase its customer base by at least 30% in the next one year. He also added that the Bharti-Cisco combine would look at partnering other service providers and IT players from time to time depending on the specific requirements of their customers (May 2008).

Bharti is planning to acquire stake in telecom MTN South Africa. Originally the price tag for MTN was quoted at 40 billion dollars for a 100 per cent buyout of MTN but now the figure is up to 50 billion dollars or 25 dollars a share, based on MTN's surging stock price and analyst expectations that Bharti might have to pay a possible 25 per cent premium (May 2008). It fizzled out and R.Com is negotiating now with MTN.

DLF, Unitech, Parsvnath, Indiabulls, Ansal, Jaypee and Omaxe are all Realty companies but they are applicants for new telecom licenses in 2007 as potential telecom operators. The companies have applied for pan-India telecom licenses and claim to be in talks with international telecom operators looking to enter India. But why is there a realty rush in telecom? Experts say there's no real synergy between the two businesses but these companies are sitting on substantial cash reserves that they want to invest in a sector that's giving 30 to 40% returns. Cash flows are robust and the sector has a lot of opportunities still since tele-density is still low.

Experts say that with 6 or 7 players in each circle, it would be extremely difficult for new entrants to make money. New operators will have to spend over Rs. 20,000 crores to set up a basic network; and the new subscriber additions are low-revenue customers. So, returns may not justify the investment. Besides, setting up a pan-India network could take two years. Still, all these players are keen to jump in.

While all these realty companies say they are confident of the potential of the telecom sector, none of them has divulged details about their plans or partners. Considering that all big international telecoms like Vodafone, Singtel, Maxis and Telecom Malaysia are already in India and AT&T has applied for an independent license, the question is who are the other big international players on whom these new entrants are banking to set up a telecom business (Nov. 2007).

Sasken Communication Technologies on 05 October 2007 has entered into an agreement with EMS SATCOM, a division of EMS Technologies, Inc., to provide essential software for the design of a next generation dual-mode satellite and GSM mobile phone for Immarsat. This agreement will see the first-ever integration of Sasken's complete development solution—the GSM and GPRS protocol and supporting application framework into a dual-mode GSM and satellite phone. The new Immarsat phone, targeted for launch in early 2009, will offer remote field and aid operations, and other private and government agencies' unprecedented communications reach and capability across remote corners of the world.

Sasken's key contribution to the development of the handset will be in the protocol software which enables and controls communication between the handset and the base stations or satellites and in the application middleware and user interface, which will be developed to Immarsat specifications. The company made this announcement in October 2007.

Chinese telecom operator Huawei Technologies Co. is mulling over a long-term strategy for research and development in India and will continue to invest in a big way for its existing R&D facility in Bangalore.

The company is exploring new areas to spread its research and development activities, said Huawei Senior Vice-President and Chief Marketing Officer Eric Xu (Zhijun). "We will continue to invest for the expansion of our Bangalore facility," he told media at the company's corporate headquarters in the Special Economic Zone of Shenzhen. Having already made investments to the tune of $200 million, the company plans to spend another $100 million. The Bangalore unit, which currently has strength of 1,300 employees, is expected to recruit 700 more people in the next two years. The company also has R&D facilities in the USA, Germany, Sweden and Russia besides China. Ten per cent of its revenue is invested in research and development.

About manufacturing plans of networking equipment in India, Eric said: "Indian telecom industry is a rapidly growing market and our decision on manufacturing will be based on the growth and the opportunity, the Indian telecom market will offer, adding Huawei has no current plans for setting up manufacturing terminals in India. According to him Huawei's good cooperation with Vodafone in European markets might help it in India. We supply network equipment and UMTS handsets to Vodafone and going by this strategic relationship, we plan to carry this association to the Indian market too, and to achieve this, we will make all efforts to grab the opportunities."

Verizon US-based telecom has received Letters of Intent for International and National Long Distance licenses for offering advanced communication services to India-based multinational companies (Nov. 2007).

Vodafone Essar has decided to outsource its IT operations to International Business Machines (IBM) India in a five-year deal designed to boost efficiency and enable faster roll-out of network infrastructure and services. IBM will develop and maintain key applications such as billing, business intelligence and financial systems for Vodafone. Under the deal, IBM will assume the responsibility of managing both the hardware and software side of IT operations with the exception of network service platforms, a communication from Vodafone said.

Vodafone claims that the agreement has an innovative structure based on risk and reward. "As per the agreement, IBM's revenue from the deal will be linked to the commercial performance of Vodafone Essar. This will ensure the agreement continues to deliver value to Vodafone. The deal builds on Vodafone's existing outsourcing agreements with IBM in Spain, the Czech Republic, Australia, New Zealand, Portugal, Ireland, Greece, and Italy.

Analysts believe outsourcing of non-core processes is a pressing industry need owing to the fast-paced growth of the telecom sector. Hiving off non-core functions such as network design and network management to third-party vendors has now become a very important business model to gain competitive advantage, said a telecom analyst.

For IBM, this is the third engagement with a telecom operator in India. It has had similar engagements with Idea Cellular and Bharti Airtel in the last three years.

Reliance Communications, in addition to its telecom presence in landline and mobile telephony in big way and telephone towers will foray into remote network management services, reports CNBC-TV18. It will tie-up with US-based Glasshouse for managed IT services and will set up new network operating centre for remote network management.

VSNL global launch of Tata Communications as the new corporate identity for VSNL; is a national player in the retail Broadband and Internet market was the first company to commercially roll-out WiMax in India for enterprise customers in Bangalore in May 2007. Over the next two months, VSNL plans to commercially roll-out WiMax services in Bangalore to retail customers as well.

WiMAX enables wireless infrastructure deployment in a cost effective, decentralized and effective manner in places like India where the entire country is not covered by wire-line infrastructure. In the future, WiMax will also allow for Mobile Internet access at much higher speeds than what is experienced at present.

BSNL has decided to expand its mobile phone service to the Himachal villages having a population of about 1,000. The machinery and equipment required for the purpose is being acquired, BSNL's Chief General Manager (CGM), Himachal Telecom Circle told reporters on the eve of World Telecommunication and Information Society day. He said that this year the theme is connecting persons with disabilities and providing opportunities for all through communication technologies.

HP Telecom Circle would expand its broadband service for the people living in the remote and far-flung areas so that they could have contact with the outside world. The retail outlet would supply SIM and also cheap handset to the consumers. The department had tied up with a company which would supply cheap laptop to the consumers who are interested in having e-mail. The company would supply laptop on installments also.

HP Telecom Circle has declared Year 2008, customer care year and many initiatives have been taken. He said that single integrated billing service would be launched soon in 160 stations that the customers could deposit the bill at one place. First phase would cover Shimla centralized call centre and grievances and upgradation of service through web self-care service would be available.

BSNL in May 2008 launched a scheme with LG Electronics India Ltd. to provide LG handsets with BSNL mobile connections in attractive schemes to its customers. Under the scheme customers would get free talk time worth Rs. 100 for 15 months. The package would be available both in post-paid and pre-paid categories. The scheme will get converted to general pre-paid scheme after the expiry of 15 months or to any other pre-paid scheme desired by the customer.

VSNL Lanka Ltd. has been renamed as Tata Communications Lanka Ltd., following the global launch of Tata Communications as the new corporate identity for VSNL. Tata Communications Lanka Ltd. is a part of the 29 billion dollar Tata group, one of the India's largest business conglomerates. Sri Lankan subsidiary, like its parent company, will focus on the new world of IP, MPLS, Ethernet and managed services. "We will strive to leverage the global capabilities of Tata Communications to create a new world of communications in the Sri Lanka market. Tata Communications Lanka Ltd. will leverage the Tata Global Network which is one of the most recent and advanced submarine cable and IP networks to meet the demand for converged IP solutions," the company said in a statement. In Sri Lanka, company offers wholesale enterprise as well as retail solutions, including international voice, international IP bandwidth for Internet service providers and international private lease circuit.

The Tata Communications brand integrates the former VSNL, VSNL International, Teleglobe, Tata Indicom Enterprise Business Unit (TIEBU) and Cipris brands worldwide.

Bharti Telesoft acquired Jataayu Software in Dec. 2007 to bolster its portfolio of Internet and VAS applications for mobile operators and handset manufacturers. As a result, the company also made a headway into markets like the US, UK, Singapore, Taiwan and South Korea. However, Bharti Telesoft's primary focus has been on the emerging markets.

Now in May 2008 it is looking at acquisition opportunities in Eastern Europe and Latin America. Bharti Telesoft wants to buy mobile VAS firms with niche technologies. The company is eyeing firms with a valuation of $20-100 million. "We are scouting for an acquisition with a two-pronged strategy—to grow our presence in Eastern Europe and Latin America or develop technical expertise in areas of mobile commerce and mobile entertainment. We have identified these as future growth drivers."

The promoters—Bharti Enterprises, Sequoia Capital and Cisco Systems have already given their green signal to infuse additional funds in the company to finance the deal. Bharti Telesoft CEO said that the company had formed a separate team to identify targets.

Telecom Hardware—Recent Trends

In 2006, many global players in telecom and IT giants have set up manufacturing and research facilities in the country. These include reputed names such as Alcatel, Aspocomm, Ericsson, Cisco, Flextronics, Foxcomm, Microsoft, Motorola, Nokia, Samsung, LG, SemIndia-AMD, Intel, etc. These global telecom and IT companies have together committed investments of over USD 8 billion in hardware manufacturing or chip design or R&D or to develop software products.

GSM Lines Hardware: Bharat Sanchar Nigam Ltd.'s controversial GSM project has run into more trouble. BSNL's GSM project, initially envisaged for 45 million GSM lines, had been in limbo for more than a year. The contract initially got stuck in litigation when Motorola challenged the PSU's decision to disqualify it from the bidding process. It hit another major block when the Communication Ministry intervened and asked the company to revise the contract both in terms of size as well as price. Later, BSNL decided bidding for 22.5 million.

Swedish major Ericsson has decided against accepting the entire contract of 22.5 million GSM lines from the state owned company. Ericsson, being the lowest bidder, was given the full contract after the second lowest bidder Nokia Siemens walked out of the project citing pricing issues.

Ericsson has now decided to take up only 60 per cent of the contract as was planned initially. BSNL will have to find another vendor to set up the balance 40 per cent of the network.

Bharti's GSM Network: Bharti Airtel the country's largest mobile operator in July 2007 awarded a two billion dollar (Rs. 8,000 crores) contract to Swedish equipment supplier Ericsson for expanding its telecom network. The two-year deal is one of the biggest contracts for Ericsson. Under the contract, Ericsson will design, plan, deploy and manage Bharti's GSM network across 15 circles and its pre-paid platform across 23 circles in the country.

In addition, Ericsson will also deliver pan-India integrated device management solutions, enabling usage of advanced data services by all mobile customers of Bharti across retail and enterprise segments. This contract is an important part of realizing Bharti's vision of a converged network and of expanding coverage in rural India to launch innovative voice and data services for Indian consumers, Ericsson India Managing Director Mats Granryd told reporters.

Bharti Airtel has initially launched 8 megabits per second (mbps) broadband Internet access in Bangalore, Chennai, Pune, Kolkata and Delhi NCR region. Later on, it will also launch the service in Mumbai and Hyderabad. The speed would enable customers to download heavy files, streaming videos, enjoy online gaming, and browse on multiple windows at the same time without compromising on the performance of any application, company said. The service is primarily targeted at home users and small—medium businesses.

Bharti Airtel in India (Aug. 2006) announced a strategic tie-up with Microsoft to provide the latter's Windows Mobile 5.0 platform, enabling Airtel subscribers to access corporate e-mail through direct push technology. The service will deliver powerful business applications and multimedia experience to all enterprises and SME (small and medium enterprise) customers. This new service will benefit Airtel users to access a host of Microsoft Office applications and other multimedia products on their mobile phones, besides allowing them access to corporate e-mail.

Spice Mobile has introduced the Spice Dual Phone. Inbuilt with the option of two SIM cards, the Spice Dual is a technological first from Spice Mobile in the Indian market. The Spice Dual comes with two variants—D-88 which supports both GSM + CDMA active connections at the same time and Spice Dual D-80, which supports two GSM + GSM active connections. Spice Dual enables the user to make or receive calls from any SIM at anytime as well as receive and send SMS. The phone is targeted to all who have two cell phone numbers and have been looking for a convenience of carrying just one phone.

Nokia in a bid to capitalize on the booming mobile value-added services market, handset manufacturer, it is planning to expand its focus from mobile devices to offer a range of Internet-based services in India early next year. The company is all set to bring its services arm—Ovi which was launched globally in August 2007.

"Ovi is an important initiative for Nokia in its efforts to bring the power of communication to the consumer. Ovi, meaning 'door' in Finnish, enables consumers to easily access their existing social network, communities and content, as well as acts as a gateway to Nokia services. We should be in a position to roll-out this in India by June 2008 or earlier".

As part of Ovi, Nokia will bring its Music Store and N-Gage that will enable mobile users to buy music and games from a range of artists and publishers, including exclusive content only available through Nokia. Nokia Maps is also under the Ovi umbrella. It is a navigation service that offers maps, city guides and more directly to compatible mobile devices. The company plans to charge a fee from users for the service though India's specific plans are still being worked out on this front. "In India everything is free. TV is free and so is Internet. So we have to find a way to monetize the services being offered by Ovi. It could be a mix of free and paid content".

The Nokia 770 is basically Wi-Fi connected Linux computer. Nokia designed it to be a portable Internet-browsing machine. The latest update to the operating system running on this device comes with support for voice over IP and the SIP protocol. As a result, users of this device can use it as a VoIP phone whenever they land at Wi-Fi hot spots. The OS on this tablet now comes loaded with the Google Talk application, which has both instant messaging and VoIP capabilities. A client for the Gizmo Project phone, by SIPP phone, will be available shortly to make calls to regular phones possibly using the Nokia 770 (July 2006). It plans to add navigation to half of the phones it sells within a few years to find new revenue streams amid decreasing handset prices, a senior official of Nokia said.

'Nokia Satellite design studio' is set up in India. The world's leading mobile devices maker Nokia Corporation has set up its first satellite design studio in India at Srishti School of Art in Bangalore. Design and Technology together is being used here to create designer handsets for Indian and global markets. The India's satellite studio, the first of four such facilities the Finnish multinational plans to locate around the world, will explore a range of design trends and themes, including colors and materials.

The second studio is being set up at Rio de Janeiro in Brazil. A third design studio has been set up in 2007 at its global headquarters in Espoo, Finland and another one is coming up in London soon. "Globally, we have about 300 designers representing 34 different nationalities, Nokia design head for Insight and Innovation, Hannu Nieminen disclosed. Its other studios are located in Helsinki, Beijing and Tokyo. The global teams consist of researchers, psychologists, anthropologists, engineers and technology specialists besides designers."

A team of top Nokia designers will engage students of Srishti in studying the use of the Internet on mobile phones and its implications for design and features of the next generation handsets. "As one of the hotspots for the increasing usage of mobile phones, India is a strategic location for us to work on new design trends that will meet the aspirations and changing lifestyle of customers in the subcontinent and the world over," Nokia chief designer Alastair Curtis said. Over the last four years, Nokia has been outsourcing design work from Srishti to meet the aspirations of handset users in South Asia. Going beyond the look and feel of handsets, Srishti students will be trained to incorporate designs that are not only ethnic, but also trendy to complement the features of new generation devices that will be extensively used for voice, data, music, videos, images and navigating the Internet.

With clear leadership in the world's fastest-growing mobile market, Nokia's game plan is to connect the next one billion in the subcontinent by using local talent and resources for distribution and sales, research and development, manufacturing and design. India is the third biggest market for Nokia after China and the US (2007).

Nokia launched a theme design competition, 'Art Meets Intelligence Design Festival' for consumers across India in association with magazine Elle Décor on 18 July 2007.

Motorola Inc. plans to set up a plant in India to manufacture mobile devices and network infrastructure equipment, the plant is to be located near Chennai in southern India, where Finland's Nokia and Taiwan's Foxconn are building plants for telecom equipment. Motorola has tapped India's software skill base for years and employs over 2,000 engineers in development centers throughout India, including an applied research lab in Bangalore.

Motorola unveiled the first phone of the series, MOTOZINE ZN5, a five-mega pixel camera phone with built-in image correction in June 2008. It has entered into a ten-year agreement with Kodak as per which the companies would develop phones for the Zine series, Motorola Inc. Corporate Vice-President (Mobile Devices Marketing) Jeremy Dale said. The phone would be launched in China in July before the Olympics and later, will be introduced in India. "India is an important market for us. The country has a strong blogging community. There has been a massive rise in content creation by the users who want to blog. Sharing of user generated contents is going to be the next generation application which will drive the growth of mobile devices across the globe," he said, adding that today people don't just shoot photo but want to share it with the peer groups.

Other top phone manufacturers like LG, Samsung, Nokia, and Sony Ericsson already have launched mobile phones with five or above five mega pixel camera. ZN5 has features like 350 MB of available memory with an option of adding a micro SD card up to 4 GB in size, FM radio and MP3. ZN5 is optimized to work with Kodak's EasyShare and provide access to Kodak gallery or other web sharing sites. Users can also share images with Edge or Wi-Fi connectivity and can also print photos via Bluetooth Wireless technology and Kodak printers.

Bharti Airtel and Vodafone will launch the 3G version of the much talked about iPhone in India this year. In addition to the regular features of the iPhone, the new device will support 3G—a mobile telephony standard that enhances network efficiency and allows faster data transfer rates over mobile and has yet to come into operation here. The new device also has GPS a satellite-based technology that enables users to identify his location on a map.

Apple's iconic iPhone is in the market in 2008 and soon to be in Indian market.

Reliance Communications will formally launch a mobile video streaming service today, reports Business Line. Mobile video streaming is similar to a webcast, except that the events can be viewed on mobile phones. The service has great potential in providing online video footage of popular events to mobile phone users. The company estimates the size of the video streaming market in India to be around Rs. 2.5-3 billion a year.

TELES India, a telecommunication manufacturer, has launched TELES.iPBX, a multifunctional and scalable Soft PBX for IP telephony controlled by SIP and H.323 protocol providing the better utilization of IP complete security. It allows organizations to add extensions in local LAN, at branch offices or at home office using the Internet. It provides comprehensive PBX functions to small and medium businesses, enabling them to leverage the power of IP and VoIP. The solution provides advanced least cost router mechanism to optimize cost savings and the voice network efficiency.

It can extend the network with additional voice features, which is normally available with big PBX systems and provides n-way conferencing, IVR, call attendance, voice mail and call forwarding.

The government has revised the norms for merger between telecom companies within a circle, making consolidation among existing players more difficult and expensive, and, in the process, facilitating entry by new players that have not acquired a license so far. Specifically, merger conditions have been made more stringent in four areas: pre-approval by DoT is required for any merger; the threshold market share of merged entity beyond which a merger will be prohibited has been lowered from 67% to 40%; a licensee must complete three years of operations before it can contemplate merger; and, finally, the merged entity will have to pay extra for spectrum.

Interestingly, the new guidelines deviate from regulator TRAI's recommendations in two ways. The regulator had ruled out M&A till roll-out obligations were met. In the revised guidelines, there is no mention of roll-out obligations, they seek three years of operations, and the word acquisition has been dropped. Omission of the word acquisition, according to an industry insider, paves the way for some ambiguity on whether these norms seek to make a distinction between merger and acquisition (May 2008).

Telephone Towers

Bharti, Vodafone and Idea have come together and combined their tower business in 16 circles. This JV is Indus Tower Company. What this tower business joint venture would mean for the companies and the industry as a whole? Bharti will start a tower joint venture with 70,000 towers. Bharti is looking to add another 50,000 towers. They will be starting about 70,000 towers at inception and expect extensive roll-out in the next coming few years, whereby they can take mobile telephony to every nook and corner of this country. At the moment, it is the world's largest tower company and will become bigger with add ons.

All the funding will be done through Indus Tower Company; Bharti's balance sheet will not be impacted for any other roll-out. So, it benefits both Bharti and Idea and especially Idea, as it gets access to a lot of towers, in which it does not have to invest now. The tenancy for Indus Towers will be between at least 2-3 players. It costs about Rs. 25 lakh for setting up a tower. So, these kinds of savings will happen for all these companies. When they come together, it will lead to a lot of efficiencies in the system.

Managing Director of Bharti Airtel, said that in the proposed tower JV, all telecom companies will be able to use shared infrastructure. The new company will have an independent board, for which an IPO is likely after two years; they are looking at listing the tower business in two years. So, that could lead to value in the future.

The whole construct of the deal is that it's not just for Bharti or Vodafone or Idea. This is going to be a completely independent tower company whereby all the operators would be able to come on to these towers, use this infrastructure in a common manner, share it amongst each other and thereby the cost for each of the operators will come down quite significantly.

UBS also expects that Reliance together with Aircel and some other companies will form a similar joint venture, which could mean that a consolidation in the tower industry will happen sooner. There are 22 standalone tower companies. Eighteen thousand towers are to be set up in rural India to provide mobile telephone.

With the required number of 3,30,000 towers by the end of 2010, operators have come to realize the potential of their tower assets and have begun spinning off their infrastructure activity into separate businesses. This is another ancillary opportunity for the tower business.

Public sector BSNL is in talks with Tata Teleservices (TTSL), R.Com and Aircel for sharing passive infrastructure as it attempts to expand coverage in the shortest possible time. "Discussions are at a preliminary stage. We are talking to operators who have not yet formed an alliance for tower sharing," a BSNL official said. Aircel's GSM expansion to 14 circles gives BSNL an opportunity to have the company as a tenant on its telecom towers while the PSU firm can be a tenant on the towers of TTSL and R.Com and vice versa. However, it ruled out the formation of a tower company on the lines of Indus Towers, as it will not be feasible.

Many of BSNL's towers, however, can't be shared and have been designed for only one operator or two at the most. The capex required for a GBT is higher than that for a roof-based tower (RTT). However, a GBT can accommodate higher number of tenants 3 to 5 while this will be the first time that BSNL will share its infrastructure with private operators. Its policy till now, has been to stay aloof from all alliances in the telecom space.

Tower sharing will help to moderate the tower requirements for all operators. This will facilitate easier, faster and cost effective entry of small or regional operators into new circles turning them into pan-India operators. Players like Bharti Airtel and Reliance Communications which are at the forefront of the tower initiative; run the risk of significant potential competition from these new entrants.

Macquarie Research estimates huge demand for wireless towers as coverage in rural areas of India increases and Indian wireless companies cover more people. We estimate that the industry would need 450,000 BTS (Base Transmitting Station) by March 2010 to support a forecast wireless subscriber base of 425 million. Research firm expect Bharti Airtel to capture dominant market share in this space. Bharti Airtel to have a portfolio of 114,000 towers by March 2010, translating into all-India towers market share of 33%; Reliance Communication is likely to have the second largest portfolio, with 63,000 towers, implying a market share of 18.3%. India currently has total tower sites of 120,000, housing 136,000 BTS of various operators.

Other third-party, independent tower companies are also likely to succeed. However, competing with bigger players with assured captive occupancy will remain the key challenge for these companies. Third-party tower companies are likely to have lower occupancies since they start from scratch, while operator-owned tower companies already have occupancy ratios of 1x or more.

Bharti Airtel has seen nearly 90% growth in their subscribers from 19.57 million in FY06 to 37.14 million in FY07. During the same period Reliance Communication has seen growth of 39% from 20.21 million to 28.01 million subscribers. In FY07, Bharti Airtel has total tower site of 39,281 and R.Com held 13,000 towers. Even with the largest tower portfolio in the country, Bharti has the highest occupancy ratio on its towers with 1.26 occupants per tower. However, all other operators' towers have lower occupancy ratios resulting in average occupancy of the industry being low at 1.13. Macquarie Research expects the tower businesses to add significant upside to Bharti and R.Com's valuations. Bharti Airtel is likely to gain from lower capital expenditure at the parent company level due to outsourcing of their tower requirements.

In the analyst meet held post-deal, Anil Ambani (Chairman R.com) said that the Company is on track to unlock value, in FY08, on four fronts: (1) tower biz; (2) FLAG undersea cable biz; (3) development of SEZ land; and (4) development of a BPO biz around existing contact center facilities. The company may look for another tranche of value-unlocking in towers and RTIL & reiterated plans for overseas listing of FLAG. The company will issue IPO for its tower biz but said there is no pre-committed timeline for this.

According to Citigroup Report, "R.Com's tower plans scaled up to set up 23,000 towers during FY08 (capex of US $1.5 bn.); which could go up if GSM becomes reality leading to higher number of towers and US $2 bn. capex. On the supply side, 80% of the towers will have tenant capacity of 4 plus. On the demand side, management is also factoring tenancy from WiMAX and 3G apart from 2G Voice."

Mobile phone operators have agreed to share seven transmission towers in Delhi and two in Mumbai as part of project MOST (mobile operators shared towers initiative), which will bring down costs of setting up new towers by 50 per cent, de-clutter the city's skyline and reduce call drops. Delhi alone has nearly 6,000 cell towers, each costing nearly Rs. 30 lakh. Rapid growth in subscriber base requires expansion of telecom infrastructure, particularly towers, which are being replicated by nearly every operator. Sharing of towers will bring down infrastructure costs for all operators. This will be the first time that GSM and CDMA operators will share the towers.

In Delhi, seven towers will be shared by six service providers—Bharti Airtel, Hutch Essar changed to Vodaphone, Idea Cellular, Reliance Communications, Tata Teleservices and MTNL.

The operators under the aegis of COAI and AUSPI will also announce plans of sharing infrastructure for the rest of the country. Infrastructure-sharing initiative was suggested in February 2006. Subsequently, a committee was formed under a joint secretary in the department of telecommunications with telecom industry representatives. India's Minister for Communication and Information Technology supported the sharing of "passive infrastructure" like towers by telecom operators, as it would save significant resources to finance further roll-outs, enhance aesthetics of the environment and lower the costs per operator.

The six cell-sites located in different parts of the national capital that were being successfully shared by mobile operators under Project MOST were proof that the concept could be replicated in other parts of the country. Project MOST team had brought together GSM and CDMA operators, public and private sector players and independent infrastructure providers to establish infrastructure on a sharing basis.

"With Indian operators offering one of the lowest mobile tariffs in the world, we in India have to look at all possible solutions to improve our cost-efficiencies and offer increasingly affordable services to our customers. Shared towers would reduce the costs of the operators and the customers would be able to get quality services at affordable prices."

Shared infrastructure for mobile roll-out would be launched shortly in rural areas also. For that, a detailed exercise was being undertaken to identify villages in the rural and remote areas not covered by wireless signals with Universal Service Obligation Fund (USOF) assistance. It was proposed to create shared infrastructure to enable telecom service providers to provide cell phones in the identified rural areas. Between 8,000 and 10,000 towers were likely to be set up and this would ensure that almost 85 per cent of the area of the country was covered by wireless signal after completion of the project. Telecom operators need to extend the concept of shared passive infrastructure to rural areas (2006).

The news that Bharti Airtel may sell a portion of its holding in its tower business to a private equity firm underscores the increasing action in the domestic telecom infrastructure space. A few months ago, Bharti's close rival Reliance Communications had sold 5% stake in its tower company Reliance Telecom Infrastructure (RTIL).

The deal valued RTIL's existing infrastructure of around 14,000 towers at $6.8 billion or close to Rs. 2 crores per tower. RTIL is expected to add another 23,000 towers by FY08 end. Considering this future growth, valuation per tower comes down to Rs. 73 lakh.

Given the same string of logic, one can arrive at a rough estimation of the valuation of Bharti's tower business. The company is expected to have around 70,000 towers by the fiscal-end. This makes its tower business worth over $13 billion or nearly one-third of market capitalization of its wireless business.

The tower business of Indian telecom companies has been in the limelight given the need of these companies to consolidate their operations in the face of increasing competition. As mobile operators compete for the same pie of subscribers in a given territory, it leads to duplication of tower infrastructure. Hit by declining trend in average revenue per user (ARPU), mobile operators are now focusing on reducing operating costs per user to maintain their margins. Given this, sharing of common infrastructure in such a scenario makes sense.

Increasing tenancy rate per tower (the number of players using the same tower infrastructure) is an efficient way of reducing operating costs and increasing efficiency. This factor reflects in much of the current valuations and the market attention enjoyed by the tower companies of the mobile operators.

The government is considering a proposal by which companies using solar or biogas power for running the rural telecom infrastructure (towers) would be subsidized. The Department of Telecommunications (DoT) is also likely to allocate funds for renewable power projects under the Universal

Service Obligation Fund (USOF). "We would subsidize the power projects of companies investing in renewable energy. The subsidy would be effective for the next phase of infrastructure projects which include setting up of 11,000 towers," USOF joint administrator said. The proposal has got the backing of the ministry of new and renewable energy (MNRE). The finance ministry too is supportive of the proposal as it is an alternative to fossil fuel on which the government is paying a huge subsidy bill. The DoT has about Rs. 15,000 crores of unutilized money under the USOF scheme and is finding ways to spend this in a holistic way (June 2008).

New Telecom Features in Cell Phones

The cellular technology is being diversified and updated with different hardware and software features and technology systems from GSM to WCDMA.

Micro Technologies India will launch LMS (Long Messaging Service) in global mobile market. The company has developed an innovative Global Mobile messaging product Micro LMS. This product fulfils the long-standing need for a messaging service that overcomes the barriers posed by a SMS (Short Message Service). It not only overcomes character limits but also enables location identification of the respective users.

While, SMS enables short messages of generally not more than 160 characters, Micro LMS enables longer messages initially limited to 800 characters. Hence, Micro LMS is more useful to transmit information service messages like news, promotional schemes and transaction statements. Another feature, which makes Micro LMS attractive, is the enabling of off-line messaging, where even if the mobile of the receiver is switched off, you can send messages, which may be accessed whenever on-line.

Micro LMS is the easier and more cost-effective option now available to mobile phone users. Application has been developed in Java (J2ME), thus it requires Java compatible handsets to run with GPRS activated SIM. This system has been recently developed by the company for the Global markets and the product has been tested live in US and other western countries and has generated lots of interest. The system benefits various sectors such as the universe of mobile phone users as well as operations involving logistics, transports, marketing, human resources and sales process within organization. This is expected to bring in good international business with the growing mobile communication (May 2006).

Tata Teleservices has launched a Web browser mobile phone 'Samsung Explore' that is customized to access the Internet in Sept. 2007. At Rs. 5,499, the phone has other features such as 0.3-mega pixel digital camera, FM radio, MP3 player, mobile tracker, SOS alert and provision to insert external memory cards. Starter kits and SIM cards would be additionally charged. Tariff plans for Internet access include Rs. 10 a day, Rs. 30 for 7 days and Rs. 99 for a month; all offering unlimited access at speeds of about 156 kbps. Both pre-paid and post-paid consumers can use this phone. The company currently has over 1.9 crores subscribers, about 60 per cent of them access the Internet via mobile phones. The company expects to sell about 4,000 'Samsung Explore' handsets.

Google has unveiled software, which it hopes will power a variety of future mobile phones and boost the web on the move, reports CNBC-TV18. The first phones, using the so-called Google "software stack", will be available in the second half of 2008 (Nov. 2007).

VSNL has launched Tata Indicom's Web Protect, an innovative product that enables users to block access to specific websites in July 2007.

MTNL unveiled the Lost Mobile Tracking System in order to help its customers track their mobile phones when stolen or lost. "The software can be downloaded for free from MTNL through GPRS and can be installed on almost 250 models of mobile phones," a spokesperson for Micro Technologies, the Mumbai-based firm which developed the software said. The software after installation, stores the IMEI number of the phone, a unique number that identifies each mobile phone, as well as the SIM (subscriber identity module) card number being used by the customer, he said. The software then asks the user to provide an alternate phone number and email address which is stored. If the phone is stolen and a new SIM card is being used, the software immediately sends an e-mail and SMS alerting the customer that the phone has been stolen and where it is presently. It also informs the original customer the phone number of the new user. We will be providing upgrades to the software which will allow users to delete the contents of their inbox from the stolen phone," MD of Micro Technologies said.

MTNL will be providing the service to its users at a cost of Rs. 30 a month. MTNL will be introducing other VAS in the near future including steaming video content on phones. The required software will be provided by MTNL and will allow users to watch live video on their phones (May 2008).

The implementation of the Mobile Number Portability (MNP) in India will be delayed if state-owned telecoms BSNL and MTNL don't significantly upgrade their networks. MNP allows subscribers to change their telecom operators while retaining their numbers but it cannot be implemented on the networks of private telecoms alone.

Sector regulator TRAI has already written to the DoT demanding that the government get cracking and ask BSNL & MTNL to upgrade their networks within 6-8 months. Private operators are already directed to do so (May 2008).

MTNL is building a network based on Internet Protocol infrastructure to provide convergent services integrating data, voice and video. The project—MPLS (Multi Protocol Label Switching) based IP network infrastructure would also be a primary source of Internet bandwidth for ISPs, corporates, institutions, government bodies and retail users.

The infrastructure would also allow MTNL to introduce additional services such as bandwidth-on-demand, TV Broadcast with minimum 5,000 channels (SDTV as well as HDTV), VoIP and others over the same network. MTNL sources said that it is poised to offer a variety of high-speed data and video services and for that it needs such infrastructure.

Earlier in 2008, Chinese company Huawei rolled out MTNL's MPLS Backbone Network in India to provide the

Indian users with a variety of quality carrier-class services including Internet, VoIP and IPTV.

The deployment of the MPLS network would help MTNL transform its legacy TDM (Time Division Multiplexing) network into networks which would support more services such as NGN, 3G, VPN (Virtual Private Network). The project is all set to expand extending the MPLS services access to the business users and carry all value added, triple play services, successfully running for select customer on IP MPLS Backbone. Almost all private mobile players have MPLS infrastructure.

With its fixed line subscribers base declining and competition from private players on mobile services, MTNL faces an uphill climb to hold on to its fixed-line subscriber base in the competitive Mumbai and New Delhi markets. To beat all these, it has launched commercial IPTV services in India and is betting on the introduction of triple-play services (June 2008).

Multipurpose use of Cell phone for money remittance in addition to Cell usual role of telephony, taking pictures, web and Internet use, advertisements, locating places, video streaming, music and entertainment.

It can be used to send remittances home through the cell phone-cum-retailer network. When you give the shopkeeper cash, he loads it onto your telephone account by recharging your SIM card, so it's like depositing cash in your e-account. You can withdraw cash from your e-account the same way—the shopkeeper will give you hard cash, and transfer the equivalent sum from your e-account to his own. If you want to pay an electricity bill, you can give the cash to the shopkeeper and he can transfer it to the account of the electricity company. This is not science fiction or futurology. Many Mexican migrants to the US already send remittances home through the cell phone-cum-retailer network. This is faster and cheaper than using banks for money transfer. This will soon give hawala operators in the Gulf stiff competition for sending remittances to India.

Rural Telephony

The government's role in funding telecom infrastructure will be crucial to the growth and spread of telephony in rural India. This is because operators will increasingly look for support from the USOF for setting up tens of thousands of telecom towers in rural India over the next three years, especially in areas where it would not be viable for them to invest in launching commercial telephony. Besides, subsidies from the USOF will also be vital if telecoms are to take broadband and Internet services to rural India. Telecom companies pay 5% of their adjusted gross revenues towards the USOF, which is used for funding telecom infrastructure in rural India. As per DoT, unutilized USOF has already crossed Rs. 10,000 crores.

DoT took the first step towards this earlier in 2006, when it invited bids from telecom operators and 22 standalone tower companies for setting up about 8,000 telecom towers across the country at an estimated cost of Rs. 2,500 crores. This project is estimated to help provide about 50 million mobile connections in rural India. More importantly, after finalizing the contracts for setting up for this, DoT will soon issue a subsequent tender for setting up additional 10,000 towers in rural India. With the tender rules mandating that a minimum of three operators share a tower, rural India will also have a choice of service providers.

At the same time, DoT has also initiated discussions with both private and state-owned telecom operators to utilize the USOF for broadband roll-out in rural India through a bidding process. DoT's plans include providing broadband connections within a 10 km. radius of all block headquarters in the country. It envisages a minimum speed of 512 kbps, where the network connects community centers, primary schools, banks, health centers, panchayats and police stations located close to all block headquarters.

The project also proposes that users are charged only annual rentals with the subscriptions being provided free of cost. In a bid to ensure that the broadband infrastructure created with USOF support is utilized fully, DoT has decided to rope in various other government agencies such as Panchayati raj, health, agriculture and education to jointly evolve a strategy for it. With more tenders in the pipeline, rural India looks set to keep its date of having 150 million telephone users by 2010 from less than 20 million currently.

Union Labor Minister was addressing an Assocham conference in the capital in July 2007, when he said that the government is putting its best foot forward in bringing village farmers closer to mobile phones. The objective being mobile connectivity and Internet accessibility would help farmers enhance farm production, and dictate a fair price for their produce from end consumers. He said the state and privately-owned communication companies will make cheap mobiles available for farmers for Rs. 500 a piece. This will be done through digital technologies that help considerably cut mobile telephone costs.

TRAI says that the rural markets should now be viewed as an opportunity rather than an obligation, and private companies can only be attracted if the government also reduces charges for the license and the spectrum. That would mean a greater use of wireless technology, rather than wiring up rural India. "It is cheaper to take mobile technology rather than wires everywhere, that is why we want to take mobile technology to rural areas rather than fixed lines." Earlier years TRAI has been focusing on fixed landlines through rural exchanges which have not been a success. TRAI says that unless these recommendations are implemented at the earliest, tele-density in rural areas is likely to remain stuck at 3-4 per cent.

The changing communication practice in India should be to provide telephone connectivity as well as to increase tele-density in rural areas through cellular technology. It is cheaper and does not require rural electrification.

Government is in the process of giving a final shape to a scheme for supporting infrastructure for roll-out of cellular mobile services in the rural areas. Keeping in mind the difficult conditions in these areas, it is proposed to provide financial support for land, tower, power and electronic equipment for transmitting, receiving and backhaul. A "plug and play" scenario will be created for the telecom service providers. The emphasis will be on sharing the infrastructure so that capex costs can be kept down and on encouraging adoption of technology which can reduce power consumption and therefore operating costs. The infrastructure thus created will be used progressively for providing broadband connectivity and will be able to accommodate equipment of new and emerging technologies.

Television

The growth of television in India seen from a historical perspective is totally transformed in its growth in the 2000 decades from the point of hardware, and software technology, the wider country areas it is covering, the number of channels, the content—the entertainment and news and other viewpoints analytics, the 24 program availability and of course the media power that it has given to people in general and politicians and subject matter experts in particular.

The direct-to-home television market in India is all set to sizzle early next year, when the Reliance-ADAG plans to launch BIG DTH hoping to repeat the magic Reliance wrought on the mobile phone scene years ago. Industry sources say Reliance-ADAG executives are lobbying hard to get the government mandate conditional access system (CAS) in 55 cities, just in time for BIG DTH launch.

The advent of CAS will force consumers to make a choice between cable TV, Internet TV and DTH, thus helping BIG DTH plays the volume game efficiently. The strategy includes attractive subscription offers that would seek to lure viewers further away from cable TV, the sources said. Reliance executives close to the DTH venture confirmed the move.

IPTV (Internet Protocol Television)

In 2003, R.Com announced that Microsoft would develop a solution for its IPTV services, using the existing Reliance fiber network. IPTV is a technology which enables you to watch television on computers and mobile phones. It is convergence of cable TV, Internet and telephone services. Reliance Communications is understood to have tied up with Microsoft, for several technological collaborations, including software for IPTV, WiMAX and a software development tool kit for the Internet, the personal computer and mobile phones. Reliance Communications would roll-out IPTV by the end of 2007-08, sources close to the development said, adding that Microsoft would provide the technological back up for the venture. Steve Ballmer, CEO of Microsoft, would be in India on 5 Nov. 2007 and both the companies will be finalizing the blueprint for the collaboration. R.Com Chairman had told an analyst in a conference call that the company's IPTV roll-out will happen in two months and R.Com had already finalized the necessary technological back up for the venture.

MTNL announced the launch of IPTV in the Delhi and Mumbai "Initially MTNL would offer 30 free-to-air channels at a charge of Rs. 125 and will also add other pay channels as per TRAI guidelines," said CMD. MTNL has partnered with Akash optical fiber and UT Starcom for the delivery of Internet Protocol Television (IPTV). The service has various features such as video on demand, time-shifted TV—a technology that enables one to watch last one week's television content aired by any available channel at the push of a button—and video conferencing (June 2008). While other operators, including Bharti Airtel, Vodafone and BSNL, are in the process of rolling out the IPTV services.

Mobile TV

Mobile Virtual Network Operators (MVNO) could soon offer virtual mobile telephony in India. MVNOs are mobile service providers who do not own the spectrum or the telecom infrastructure but provide services to customers through the spectrum and infrastructure they share with the traditional mobile operators on a commercial basis. A MVNO buys minutes of use (MoU) in bulk from traditional mobile operator but have their own SIM card, branding, marketing, billing, and customer care operations. MVNOs could actually result in greater competition in the telecom space. It can lead to a correction in telecom tariffs.

"The use of spectrum may have more than one owner and it is time for us to study this and move in that direction," TRAI chief asserted. This implies that companies with spectrum would be allowed to share the resource with the MVNOs. TRAI's recommendations on mobile TV would also be sent to the department of DoT, and the spectrum band for mobile TV would be auctioned. Mobile TV is expected to bring television right onto our palms.

Telekom Malaysia, Virgin Mobile, Mobile ESPN and Value First are among the international players to have shown interest in the Indian telecom space. DoT had also favored sharing of spectrum on commercial basis as it results in better usage of spectrum. TRAI had called for a consultation on MVNOs from different stakeholders around two years ago. Telecom operators had then not welcomed it fearing that MVNOs would eat into the revenue of incumbent operators. TRAI chief also said that with Universal Access Service License offering multiple services, the license gets delinked with spectrum (Nov. 2007).

Digital Media Convergence Limited (DMCL), part of Essel Group, announced the launch of mobile TV application service 'ISEE' in partnership with BSNL in the northern region in July 2007. "With this partnership, BSNL subscribers having GPRS facility will be able to watch Zee group of TV channels on the prescribed mobile handsets," DMCL Project Head (ISEE) told reporters. ISEE, which is a video portal, would offer streamed content from Zee group of channels and it would also allow the subscribers to view current affairs, news and sports highlights, fashion trends and soap operas. "A distinguished feature of ISEE is that one can watch Zee news and Zee sports live with a difference of just 15-20 seconds from the live feed".

Initially, this service is available free of cost for the first 30 days and subsequently, it would be charged at a monthly price of Rs. 150, adding that subscription grants unlimited access to all content within the portal for BSNL customers and does not require the user to pay additional data tariff changes.

During the first phase, this service would be made available to northern states like Punjab, Haryana, Uttar Pradesh (West),

Uttarakhand, Himachal Pradesh, Jammu and Kashmir and Rajastahan. "By December, this service will be available across India," BSNL General Manager (Mobile) said. TRAI advisor said it would submit this month a proposal on 'Mobile TV' to the information and broadcasting ministry to frame a policy on television broadcast through mobile handsets.

Satellite TV

Revolving around the earth in different orbits, satellites perform such diverse tasks as meteorology, navigation, remote sensing and communications. While there have been many attempts to launch satellites into new areas such as the Internet and broadband, its core business remains long-haul bulk communications traffic and TV broadcasting. Currently, the industry is going through a period of change, with large operators consolidating, new operators starting up, and old operators attempting to move into new markets. A new generation of ground equipment, revamped service plans, and the launch of some exceptional in-orbit satellite assets also means that the industry has obtained a set of tools that better positions it to take advantage of a variety of business opportunities.

The satellite broadband market will, however, continue to face stiff competition from terrestrial players in the years to come. Dish TV and DBH and IPTV operations are other opportunities being explored in India currently.

COMPUTER

Evolution of Computing

Computer technology is fast diversifying, converging and updating. To understand the democratization of computing, we must understand the path that has been traversed so far. We can divide the evolution of modern computing into four phases.

The first is the age of the Mainframes provided by IBM and the BUNCH—Burroughs, UNIVAC, NCR, Control Data Corporation and Honeywell. During this phase, computing was controlled centrally and was in the hands of a few people. The systems were designed for professionals.

The second is the personal computing phase. With it, the democratization of computing began. Computing was no longer restricted to a few professionals. The third phase is the Internet phase, which transformed the world. Information access was greatly simplified. People could receive and send information instantaneously and in a manner they wanted. Investment in technology infrastructure gained momentum. The 'dot-com' era led to massive investments in capacity. Communication pipes were laid around the world and Internet access exploded exponentially, leading to global communication and collaboration. The world got connected.

All this has shifted the power from corporates to individuals. This is leading us to the fourth phase of democratization of computing, where individuals and communities hold the key. Individuals are coming together to form communities around common interests through social networks. They are using the power of networking to discover products and services, to collaborate with people they trust, to express their opinions and even take up societal causes.

As the world moves towards greater transparency, individuals have greater access to information. Businesses simply cannot ignore the benefits or challenges of computer democratization.

Personal Computer is here to stay. The business model that created the popularity and affordability of PC will continue to drive innovation and choice in the area of personal devices such as cell, digital players and mobile PCs. The PC is becoming important and key enabler for these new digital scenarios in every corner of the world. This is just the end of the phase one of this evolving technology and it is now as ubiquitous as TV or automobile. It is continuing to expand its global reach, deliver new capabilities, more choices, and new opportunities to more and more people in every part of the world.

Since the dawn of the PC era, this relevance has been fueled by a technology framework that enables any PC maker in any corner of the world to design, build and market its own products based on industry-standard components and software. This technology framework also provides industry-standard ways of connecting all kinds of devices from computer mouse and keyboards to digital cameras and MP3 players. Beside this availability and affordability business model, we would have never dreamed of a billion connected users in mere 25 years; nor would we have made the vision real of a computer at every desk and in every home in so many parts of the world.

PC will be even more important in years ahead. This is because the peripheral devices and the personal computer exist in a symbiotic relationship. Together, they provide greater freedom, choice, flexibility and affordability for our options for communicating, accessing information, and experiencing entertainment where and how we want. PC has expanded beyond its original use of creating documents and spreadsheets. Today, we use it as communication device, a radio, TV, movie theater or a photo-album. It has also become an essential business tool to access World Wide Web and all that information and services that reside there through Internet. Every year, every month new innovations in hardware and software are unveiled and that ensures the enduring relevance of PC. (excerpted Narula 2008).

India's Computer Policy in 80s

In 60s India wanted to computerize functions of banking, insurance, hotel reservations, telephones, libraries and voting in the national elections; but at that time there was neither indigenous hardware nor software to back it up. The country planned to import both but its initiating computerization at that point was not successful because many people feared that it would usurp their jobs. At that time no amount of persuasion could convince and make those people accept the fact that computerization would rather create more jobs in those particular fields; and also that would mean less time being spent on traditional performances.

At that point, India could not initiate computerization against the wishes of majority of the people. But a move did begin to create awareness among the people about the efficiencies of computerization; by attempting to foster computer literacy in the country, and by developing a plan to produce computers indigenously. It also liberalized its policy for the import of computers, transfer of technology for computer hardware and software production, and allowed the indigenous production of computers on a large scale. Various institutes of technology in the country started teaching basic computer courses.

Government started computerization for its national planning forecasts and planning procedures for its National Development plans. Some of the physical sciences and social science institutes used computers for data analysis purposes only. A few large industrial houses notably Tata did import computers and computerize their functions on a small scale particularly for data analysis.

In 80s, government and business organizations attempted to use computer on a large scale. Initial progress in computerization from 1983 to 1987 was good. Functioning of major networks and areas of airlines, banking, insurance, transportation, defense, telecommunication, government, police, space travel, hospitals, hotel reservations, mass communications and scientific and technological applications in the public sector, i.e. government domain; and many big businesses started computerization of their functions.

Computer literacy project CLASS was initiated in government schools. Computer science and engineering courses were offered in the technology institutes and selected universities. These were long term courses. Private organization offered short term courses in computer software and data analysis. Millions of dollars were invested in developing a computer culture in India. This included the indigenous resources, assistance from developed countries, and UN agencies that provided technical expertise, hardware and planners. These projects were all in public sector.

UNDP project aimed at specifically creating a cultural revolution in Indian industries in the use of microprocessor technology. Five regional sectors were set up in Bangalore, Jabalpore, New Delhi, Pune and Ranchi for special sectors such as agriculture, communications, steel manufacturing and mines, electronics and industrial control. Other projects on microprocessor use started in utility sectors such as environment control, transport and aeronautics. Two key projects, microprocessor-based computer-aided learning systems were planned in Bangalore.

A computer controlled system was being developed for satellite-based communication network software. Packages were being developed for graphic terminals, and microcomputer based data acquisition systems. Microprocessor-based agriculture equipment was being developed to complete the green revolution. Further, UN assisted the development of basic healthcare and electro-medical equipment for more than 30,000 primary health centers throughout the country through computerization. Another major UN assisted project was setting up knowledge-based fifth generation computer systems involving artificial intelligence.

India had also been negotiating with both USA and Soviet Union for a supercomputer for defense purposes. The sites planned for supercomputers are Hyderabad and Pune and a central computer site at New Delhi. A national software center was being set up in Bhubaneshwar in Orissa state. This center was later shifted to Mumbai.

At that time the indigenous production of computers was limited to supercomputers. Businesses and individuals were encouraged to import small computers. These were expensive so domestic consumption was low. The above-mentioned projects do highlight India's interest and efforts in introducing computerization in the country in a big way but it has its limitations. The electronic infrastructure, technical, financial, and marketing considerations limited diffusion of computerization in India at that time.

Computer Policy: A new computer policy was formulated in 1986 after reviewing the existed situation and by discussions with computer manufacturers, experts and economists. The government liberalized computer policy to make more computers available, to promote manufacturing within the country at comparable international prices and based on the latest technology; and to promote their applications on a variety of resource-saving uses. The major components of the policy included the following:

- No restriction on industrial capacity for manufacture of micro- and mini-computer systems;
- Reducing cost of inputs that are required for computers manufacturing;
- Simplify procedures to enable users to obtain computers from indigenous or overseas sources;
- Micro and mini-computers can be manufactured by an Indian company with 40% equity whether in private or public sectors;
- Manufacture of mainframe and super mini-computers were reserved for the public sector (ECIL) up to 1988. Since then ECIL will provide horizontal transfer of knowledge in addition to import of transfer of technology in this direction;
- Government will also reduce duty on computer peripherals such as disk drive, disks and printers;
- Reduce duties on source codes for software producers to obtain source codes from their collaborators rather than object codes.

India's Key Computer Projects in 90s

Government aimed at creating computer literacy and computer culture through computer plans at schools. CLASS project (computer literacy and studies in school) was initiated in 1984 to teach computer skills at schools; thereby reducing the knowledge gap and reticence of the students towards computers and technology. The real aim had been to create a human-power base upon which a technologically capable workforce could be built. The school teachers were trained in computer skills to spread computer culture and demystify the technology for the students.

Such schools represented in all geo areas and its student population largely comes from lower socio-economic level. The government did not want to make computer skills as resources of the elite only. Government wanted this to an ongoing project and extended to over 250,000 schools. The project failed as the lack of infrastructural facilities delayed developing computer curriculum and advance level computer training programs for the schools. The indigenous efforts to produce computers floundered, and on the software front the CLASS computers could not keep pace with the imported software. This project was guided by specialists from UK and UK has donated computers for this project.

During this period government did not subsidize private schools to run computer training programs for students and teachers; and on their own these schools could not have afforded it because of high price of imported computers. Thus even the elite students were devoid of computer training at that point.

The project was laudable but the government did not have the requisite number of computers. Government focus was on indigenous production of computers in the public sector only where the resources were limited. The indigenous efforts to produce computers floundered since it did not have the capital and capability to manufacture and did not allow foreign collaboration or private sector to manufacture at that time. This was the flaw in the 1986 policy, since government wanted to manufacture everything. Since importing computer peripherals became cheaper by duty reduction, there was more focus on assembling the computers by importing the peripherals; the private sector was allowed to assemble the computers. This made computers easily accessible to the users; though still expensive. More focus was on development of software as there was no restriction for the private enterprises to do so. Private enterprises were offering short term software development courses.

Government is hoping that the third attempt to bridge the digital divide between private and government schools succeeds where the earlier two endeavors of Computer Literacy and Studies in Schools (CLASS) in the 1980's and revised-CLASS of 1990's failed. Computer literacy programs are likely to benefit from Intel's World Ahead program and Teach to the Future, and Microsoft cheap computers for India programs and IBM's expanding presence in Bangalore, through its technology hub, and building various new software labs and technology centers to develop products and offer client services.

Computer Literacy projects in both government and private schools are necessary for developing workforce but needs inexpensive and easily available home computers and both public and private sectors have to make efforts and fund. Currently, even schools in the private sector are offering computer courses and skill training and even most of the students can afford to buy their own computers.

The government of India's second focus during that time was on to manufacture Super Computers with indigenous as well as imported components. During this period USA provided Cray-xmp for complicated aeronautical designs, defense purposes and metrological forecasts. India also used Cyber-205 developed for USA. A supercomputer from Japan S-1000; its four units were installed in National Informatic System to process data from various government departments. Another supercomputer ELBROS was from Soviet Union.

This suggests that government of India planning to manufacture supercomputers, mini-computers as suggested through 1986 computer policy needed revising as government neither had the financial resources nor the capability to manufacture them. Moreover, it was not ready to open that sector to private enterprises.

Earlier, the private sector was restricted to produce super computers. In 90s computer policies became more open in this regard. In 2007-08 Tata has produced EKA supercomputer in its Pune-based Computational Research Laboratories. EKA, has been ranked the fourth fastest in the world and fastest in Asia. Computational Research Laboratories built the supercomputer using dense data center layout, novel network routing and parallel processing library technologies. "EKA has put India at the forefront of high performance and supercomputing technology globally. It gives the ability to address applications in multiple disciplines including software research."

The Government of India's third focus was Rail Cargo computer project aided by World Bank and Canadian railways.

The computerization was expected to provide dramatic improvement in the railroad productivity in freight movement and increase in revenue.

Fourth focus was computerization of library and information services also funded by UN. But it had slow progress since there was lack of interest. Moreover, adequate computer training was also not available for library documentation professionals in using computers for these services. Some of the larger library and information centers—INSDOC and DESIDOC were set up in this process. They tried to recruit computer specialists but could not attract them for library based computerization activities at that time. So only a very few library professional could be trained for the system.

It may be noted that India's four above-mentioned major computerization projects during the period 1984-90 were mainly supported and aided by foreign aid agencies; as India did not have policy of allowing foreign direct investment or joint venture with foreign companies. (4 Computer focuses are based on Hansen & Narula 1990).

Transformation Point

The efforts to create awareness and computer culture in the country during 80s and private and public efforts to give software training produced software professionals and interest in computerization. The economic policies were opened in 90s and that started 'outsourcing of software programs' from India by developed countries. This was the onset of expanded interest in computerization as it was new field and it was providing jobs to the computer skilled and software professional in the outsourcing companies. Larger Indian companies set up their software program development divisions. Many other computer peripheral related and outsourcing handling companies came up; and thus creating new and well paying job avenues. The demand of such workforce created need for skilled professionals and private funded institutes such as NITT, APTEC and others offered training programs to meet the growing demand for outsourcing of software programs and other computerization related tasks. Even those companies who started software program development divisions; they offered in-house and on the job training programs to meet their supply chain of skilled workforce for their outsourcing contracts.

Outsourcing gave the first shot in the Indian company and growing revenues boosted the economy as well as interest in computerization as career and businesses. Later outsourcing divisions were set up in many countries by big India companies such as Tata, Wipro, Infosys technologies, Satyam computers and others both for handling outsourcing and training programs; NITT, APTEC also set up training institutes in many countries.

The new economic policies allowed joint ventures with foreign companies, it allowed foreign direct investments in Indian companies, and it also allowed the foreign companies to set up manufacturing of computer peripherals, assembling computers and producing low cost computers specially for rural India or for other developing countries; and R&D hub in India. As a result many Indian computer companies could set joint ventures with foreign companies or allow them to invest foreign funds in their companies. In 2000 decades HPL, IBM, Toshiba and Sony have set up their outlets in metros of India to retail sell to businesses, offices and individuals update computers, its peripherals and servicing also.

This was the turning point for Indian economy and step towards road to growth and transformation and there has been no turning back since then.

This provides an interesting backdrop of India's transformation in these areas through its own efforts, in collaboration with other technology giants and other technology companies making India as technology hub for their outsourcing, offshoring products and services. These efforts have contributed to India's transformation in these areas as well as transformation in other domains through these technologies progress and applications.

Cyber Café: People who cannot afford to own personal computers can have access to computers in the urban cyber café set up by private initiatives. It has given easy access to people to computers and its related functions; the primary being Internet and VoIP and many other sites which increase information and knowledge. It has facilitated computer culture among people by self-initiative. This is a big transformation whereas in 80s people totally rejected it for fear of losing jobs and now it is creator of jobs along with global information and knowledge.

A changing business communication practice for PC in developing and emerging countries particularly in India is changing to create accessibility for consumers having lower income and limited access to credit and for rural people.

Global Computer Companies' India Initiatives

Global computer companies are helping Indian population in ICTs initiatives in 2000 decades. Intel, Microsoft, IBM, Advanced Micro Devices Inc. have collaborated with Indian companies, have set up computers, microchips, and semiconductor hubs in India; innovations by Intel and AMD have created low cost and innovative computers for rural areas with diverse applications by Intel, IBM, Microsoft and customized solutions for PCs, etc. have transformed India's computerization scenario.

Intel through its 'World Ahead' program aims to bridge digital divide in developing countries. Intel is working with governments worldwide to develop innovative, cost-effective programs that increase access to PCs and the Internet, improve educational outcomes, grow local ICT industries and develop the skills and infrastructure that nations, citizens and businesses need to thrive. Intel pledges to invest $1 billion over the next five years to broaden access to technology—computers and Internet access, and educational resources in developing countries. Intel and Advanced Micro Devices Inc. are experimenting to bring inexpensive hardware and Internet connections to underdeveloped regions.

The program has three primary goals: to design affordable computers tailored to the needs of the developing countries; to make high-speed Internet access more ubiquitous in some cases by use of WiMAX technology; and to provide training to teachers and students on the use of information technology. Intel is working with governments and telecommunication companies in the regions to design computer system that would start around $300 each. Other companies have also proposed simpler PC or terminals costing less.

Intel through its community computer initiative in India is providing low cost PC in rural India. In March (2006), it unveiled a prototype PC for use in India where dust, heat, and humidity can cause reliability problems. This PC can withstand these. Given the electricity problems in rural India, it can run on alternate power sources including a car battery. Another prototype of a full featured computer notebook is expected to cost less than $400. It has started an initiative 'jagruti' (awakening) in coordination with this technology; with donation of community PCs to help bridge the digital divide. It could have the advantage of exposing children to technology at an early age. It opens up whole range of opportunities for the villagers. Intel sees potential in India and its talented pool of citizens. The low cost, fully featured desktop PCs priced 20% lower than the current Intel configured ones were launched in 2006 and working with Indian manufacturers with HCL, Millennium, PCS, Wipro and Zenith Computers for 'Discover the PC initiative'.

As part of World Ahead Program (WAP), Intel plans to donate 100,000 PCs for use in classrooms in developing nations. The company has already been spending 100 million a year on educational programs. It has trained about three million teachers so far in the use of technology, and plans to train 10 million more over five years as part of the World Ahead Program. WAP of Intel is set to chip in much more in India. Chip maker Intel will boost its story in India with new initiatives planned to accelerate technology accessibility, Internet connectivity and effective education. The initiatives, coming under this program, include low-cost computers, pay-as-you-go PC purchasing models, small learning devices for education and extending WiMAX broadband connectivity in the country.

Intel in 2006 launched its Community PC, a flexible pay-as-you-go PC purchasing model in India. Another product set for introduction is an affordable, rugged learning device for students—code named Eduwise. The notebook to provide collaborative learning between teachers and students in developing countries was designed in Intel's Bangalore platform definition center. We expect to launch it in the first half of '07 priced less than $400, Otellini, the president and CEO of Intel said.

He said that the Indian facility will play a key role in designing and developing computing technologies for the WAP. "The Bangalore centre, along with Intel's platform definition centers in Shanghai, Cairo and Sao Paulo, will work on specialized products for emerging markets; India is one of the five critical markets. Only 2% of India's population having a PC or Internet connection, the potential for increasing PC penetration is immense and challenging. By multiplying the effects of computers, Internet and education, we intend to accelerate the reach of technology benefits in the country over the next five years." He told the media in Bangalore.

Intel will be investing $1 bn. in India in the next five years to grow its R&D, venture capital activities, education and community program. So far, the company has invested about $750 million. Among other programs, in India, Intel will collaborate with ICICI Bank to facilitate loans for PC ownership through the emerging subscription payment model and working with Tata VSNL to bring Intel-based PC solutions and WiMAX wireless broadband connectivity to Tata's RailTel cyber cafes across India.

Intel will focus on customized technology solutions which enable new types of PCs that meet the specific needs of developing countries, such as the recently introduced Intel powered Community PC in India. Intel plans to develop six more geographically tailored PC designs worldwide in the next two years by the end of 2008. These include low-cost, full featured, easy-to-use PCs for home and work, community PCs customized for public access, PC kiosks, and low-cost PCs tailored to the needs of schools and educators. The platform definition centers they have established around the world, including in Bangalore, will play a central role in these efforts. Intel is also continuing its efforts to grow the availability of WiMAX technology for low-cost broadband access.

Intel will also train about 8 lakh teachers in India as part of the 10 million target it has worldwide by 2010. Since 2000, the 'Teach to the Future' initiative has trained about 5.5 lakh teachers in the country.

Intel chip design units which are knowledge intensive have much more value in short term than chip manufacturing plants. However, it is still in talks with the Indian Government as they put together a package for the chip industry.

Microsoft on May 22, 2006 in New Delhi announced computer ownership program for India. Microsoft, chip makers and PC firms aim to increase PC usage in the developing world with a new flexible payment program to lower the initial costs of buying a computer. It is leading a group of technology companies in offering the first-ever "pay-as-you-go" computers in Brazil, India, Mexico, Russia and China over the next several months. The pay-as-you-go model lowers the initial costs of buying a PC by 50 per cent or more and the consumer owns the PC after a set amount of minutes are purchased. Using Microsoft's Flex Go software technology, a customer can buy a computer loaded with the Windows operating system then purchase prepaid cards powered by Microsoft Flex Go technology or pay a monthly subscription fee at a cost similar to using a computer at a local Internet cafe, Microsoft said. When the usage time ticks down, a customer can go online or to a local retailer to buy more minutes.

In India, Microsoft has entered into a tie-up with BSNL, Intel and Lenovo to provide users a complete PC under this offer in India. "The trial service of this product will be launched in June and on the basis of users' feedback, the actual product will be rolled out after 3-4 months." The company has already completed successful trials of this offering in Brazil with various industry partners. The next round of trials would look at countries such as China, Hungary, Mexico, Russia, Slovenia, Vietnam and India.

Microsoft's is working with partners Advanced Micro Devices, Intel, Lenovo, Phoenix Technologies and Transmeta, but it also aims to work with other hardware companies, telecommunication firms, banks and retailers in India (in other emerging markets also) to expand the market to help bring PCs within reach for hundreds of millions of families. The personal computing offer has been designed for fast emerging markets.

IBM management said it plans to use the larger budget to expand IBM's presence in Bangalore, India as technology hub, and build various new software labs and technology centers to develop products and offer client services. "That investment will ensure that we make the most of the opportunities to grow this marketplace, while it also enables IBM to fulfil its vision to be a good global citizen."

With the spread of Information Technology and IT Enabled Services the time is ripe to make India a preferred destination for the manufacture of semiconductors and other high technology IT products including Wafer; Assemble, Test and Manufacture of Semiconductors; Flat LCD/OLED/Plasma Panel Displays; and Storage Devices.

Indian Institute of Science (IISc) Banglore is constituting a team of researchers to see how a fixed-line phone, with a five inch screen and broadband access can help take the benefits of computing to the masses. Both models, from IISc and Microsoft, have a simple interface that is easy to use and not intimidating for the target group—users in remote areas and the poor.

What can good old fixed-line phones morph into if you have broadband and large screens? And if you have computers with audio and text user interface, or computers in classrooms that don't have just one mouse but multiple rodents, does it help anyone?

These are just three different ideas to meet one objective: bridge the digital divide. Such modified machines from IISc, Bangalore, and Microsoft Research India are helping domestic helps find work in housing societies. Children in schools that have one computer to a class can use a device with multiple mice to help up to 10 students work on a single machine.

The computer with audio and text user interface is one of the ambitious projects of Microsoft Research that seeks to take computing to the underprivileged—much like an electronic voting machine enables even illiterates to vote.

Computerization in Rural India

Over time, there is greater realization about the widening digital divide between urban and rural segments and between men and women which is hampering the development process in India. There are both national government and private partnership efforts; there are also international efforts to bridge this digital divide. It is assumed ICTs will empower women particularly in rural areas; and rural segments in general will be empowered more in economy and development through ICTs accessibility. The increased focus is on tele-density, cellular phones, Internet connectivity through broadband access and wireless access, computer literacy and computer accessibility and affordability of these information technologies.

Initiatives in Rural Computerization

Few illustrations will highlight some of the efforts and experiments made to create computer literacy among the rural communities to help them both in farming and their other vocations and life in general.

M.S. Swaminathan Research Foundation (MSSRF) in India is a center for research on sustainable agriculture and rural development which has been in operation since the mid-eighties, bringing much needed insight and guidance to the grassroots rural communities in the region.

Various workshops by MSSRF provide an opportunity for the exchange of knowledge and perspectives between village communities in Tamil Nadu and Pondicherry in southern India and civil societies from developing countries with a specific focus on ICT-enabled development. They conduct action-learning workshops which help participants learn about how to integrate modern ICT effectively in their development projects, provide perspectives regarding various technologies and innovations involved in rural ICT, and help participants to blend ICT in the local knowledge management process. These workshops make efforts in facilitating learning from concrete, on the ground, practical knowledge in the use of ICT for rural development.

ICT researchers at the Pondicherry branch of the MSSRF; specializing in rural women's agricultural network, are helping to develop an information village centre.

"We're linking up twelve rural villages across Pondicherry, providing them with computer and Internet access so that they will have update information to help them in their farming work." Through the Information Village Centre, the farmers can check weather forecasts, bus timetables, crop prices as well as get advice on best practices when it comes to buying seed and growing their produce.

Infothela Project—an Experiment in Computer Literacy

Hope for a better life arrives in poor farming village Bithoor in Uttar Pradesh, India's most populous state, three days a week on a bicycle rickshaw that carries a computer with a high-speed, wireless Internet connection. The bicycle cart is the center of a project called Infothela or Info-cart. Designed like temple carriage during festivals, the brightly painted pedal-cart rolls into the village accompanied by a computer instructor who gives classes to young and old, students and teachers alike.

Conceived in 2003 by the Indian Institute of Technology in Kanpur, about 10 miles southwest of Bithoor, the project is funded by the national government and provides free computer classes in six villages here in Uttar Pradesh state. It aims to use technology to improve education, healthcare and access to agricultural information in India's villages, where most of the country's 1.06 billion people live; with only 12 computers and 4 Internet connections per 1,000 people. Another project to disseminate the latest crop prices and farming methods is also being developed. Young people look for jobs in cities, but often lose out to better educated urbanites. Computers and Internet will open up new opportunities for these villagers.

India has one of the world's lowest Internet usage rates and much of rural India remains oblivious to the sweep of technology as there are no computers and Internet connections. Infothela seeks to break the disparity that confines access to technology and growing affluence to the cities. All the villages involved in Infothela and Pedicab projects lie within a 50 mile wireless corridor created by the Institute of Technology and linked by high-rise Wi-Fi antennae and amplifiers along the highway.

Many Indian villages are poorly wired making wireless technology the most reliable Web connection. The mobility of a cycle rickshaw, which is light enough to cross muddy, potholed roads, ensures that the same computer and Internet connection can be used by people in several neighboring villages. The Infothela cart has a specially designed frame and cushioning to protect the computer and accessories from the bumpy ride. The mobile platform is necessary to reduce cost of ownership because the resources are shared by a large population. It is also necessary to push information to women and elderly people who cannot travel outside their village. The service is free for now, but fees will eventually be charged.

A few miles from Bithoor, another cycle rickshaw carries its high-tech load to Gorahah village, where men and women gather side-by-side for a class on electronic mail. The mix is nothing short of a revolution in tradition-bound rural India, where women are often kept indoors. Rural women are learning computers. "We are now learning computers. There is no point if we cannot use that new knowledge. We have to go out and do something worthwhile, we want to see the world," said a woman who also attends college. The classes teach the basics of computing, word processing, spread-sheets, Internet browsing and Web cameras. Once they learn how to use a webcam the villagers can take part in online classes, something the info-cart organizers hope to implement later. These simple lessons are a big privilege in an Indian village, where half the population can't read or write.

It reflects how computerization aims to use technology to improve education, healthcare and access to agricultural information in India's villages, and provide consultation to villagers through video-conferencing.

Villages are mired in tradition and poverty, information on various topics and sectors through computer learning can help rural women move from tradition and poverty and look beyond the village, household chores drudgery or just marriage at an early age. They can dream of seeing the world by travel and work which they see through TV images.

Pedicab Project

Another computer on a Pedicab is being used in an experiment to help doctors in Lucknow, the state capital of Uttar Pradesh. It provides consultation to villagers through video-conferencing in nearby Saroha village.

Software for Farmers

Centre for Development of Advanced Computing (C-DAC), Bangalore, ITC Research and Training Center in India, has developed two software applications catering to the needs of people in rural areas; benefiting rural communities through appropriate computer software. The first, called Vyapar, is an online trading tool. The second, ECKO, provides a framework for building e-communities through collaboration and knowledge sharing. The software is being piloted with local organizations in India. ICTs can be used to assist small and medium-sized enterprises to increase productivity, efficiency, and participation in the local and global economies.

Video Empowers Villages

Most of the women in rural Gujarati neighborhoods are illiterate or semi-literate; video is a powerful teaching medium. So Aruna and her colleagues make videos around health and education themes covering everything from AIDS and literacy to assertiveness training. They use locations and people from their own community which enables the learners to relate more easily to the content.

"Initially villagers were very suspicious and we had to build up a rapport with the village chief but gradually we were trusted and now the rural women are actively using video to empower themselves." Video SEWA is so competent that they were appointed by the state to document the Queen of Bhutan's visit to the region one time.

Rural e-governance

The slow progress of e-governance in villages was due to low computer literacy, low accessibility of computers and low tele-density in rural areas. With improved tele-density by cellular phones and community computers, many e-governance projects and practices are targeting the rural areas for better governance.

Computer & Microfinance in Rural Retailing

Village households are expected to rise to 153 million in 2009-10 from 135 million in 2001-02, probably making rural India the market with the largest potential in the world.

According to the CII report's findings, an estimated India's rural retail market will grow 29% to Rs. 1.8 trillion by 2010 driven by rising rural incomes and changing consumption patterns. Rural retail includes fast moving consumer goods, durables, agricultural inputs and autos like tractors. Poor infrastructure, supply chain inefficiency, unorganized marketing and product pricing can be the major bottlenecks for the growth of rural retail. There exists no organized marketing and distribution in 87% of India's villages, wherein 50% of the rural population resides. The development of organized rural retail in rural India will create jobs, check rural migration, raise tax generation and improve agricultural efficiencies.

Chapter 3 reflects the efforts of large Indian conglomerates and government's efforts to offer organized rural retail for many products and services. The rural business hubs (RBH) project involving Reliance, Tatas, Coco-Cola, ITC, Mahindra and Mahindra and Microsoft among others. RBH is a P4 model initiative wherein the industry will be involved with rural resources and skills to develop products of internationally accepted quality.

Tata Chemicals launched its Tata Kisan Sansar (TKS) in 2005 in Punjab, Uttar Pradesh, Haryana, Bihar, and West Bengal. DCM Shriram launched its Hariyali Kisan Bazar in 2002 in Punjab, Haryana, Rajasthan, Madhya Pradesh, Uttar Pradesh and Uttarakhand. Reliance Retail's Rural Hubs (procuring-cum-processing hub & one-stop farmer shop) has plans for Punjab, Maharashtra, West Bengal, Andhra Pradesh and Gujarat. Pantaloons also have plans for a similar procuring-cum-processing hub for setting up farm input malls in rural areas. Bharti-Wal-Mart is focusing on rural retailing. Indian Oil Corporation's (IOC) rural retail initiative was launched in 2006 in UP, Madhya Pradesh, Punjab, Tamil Nadu, Karnataka and Bihar.

The self-help groups of companies like ICICI, the ITC e-chaupal, the adult literacy program by TCS, Shakti Initiative of HLL in India have realized the need to work their supply chain backward starting with the rural consumer expectations and experiences. Hindustan Lever (HLL) for one has been continuously strengthening its marketing network in the villages and is producing goods to suit the needs and budgets of rural consumers. Others are Pepsi Foods, Tata Kisan Sansar, EID Parry—the list is expanding everyday. All taking the rural route to expand their market base, as well as to procure raw materials for their agro ventures. Thus rural areas are covered in a number of states for retailing products and services.

Along with rural retailing, computer literacy and training are important to benefit appropriately from these efforts. In due course, both government and these conglomerates are starting these efforts in their rural hubs. It will be easier to arouse computer interest and need for computer training among the rural shoppers who would visit these hubs. Seeking requisite information through Internet and online e-business even may actively interest them and encourage them for computer learning and applications. The companies also offer microfinance to avail of their products and services in retail.

Government and the companies can through such ambitious programs multiply the effects of computers, Internet, education and marketing to accelerate the reach of technology benefits. They believe people in rural areas require the computer education, Internet connectivity and the access to the right technology to meet their unique needs; where consumers must cope with a lower income and limited access to credit.

Simple applications of ICTs in rural communities are helping to reap even the basic benefits of life by adapting these technologies to local environments. Affordability, accessibility, learning, and practical applications give them information and knowledge gain for better living.

Although these initiatives are successful in their own right, closer alignment and engagement with other ICT stakeholders and initiatives could strengthen these efforts in encouraging NGOs to take a more active interest in ICT issues, sustain and expand this interest, and harness the power of ICTs in meeting their development goals.

Until recently, such technology was the privilege of a tiny section of Indians—engineers in the country's software hubs who earn more money while in their twenties than village farmers do in a lifetime. India churns out 300,000 engineers each year and is a growing software power, but farmers are the backbone of its economy.

Urban India has accepted the challenges of computerization and Internet as an important aspect of occupational and personal life of people and the significant role in people's daily routine. Now, government, businesses and rural community themselves aspire for the same and are ready to accept the social technology challenge of computerization by assimilating that as important aspect of their lifestyle.

Earlier discussions are pointer to the fact that there have been integrated efforts towards this for rural communities—education, telephone connectivity through mobile telephones, computer accessibility and affordability through low cost and broadband Internet accessible and affordable through low cost; and television has become the ubiquitous part of their lifestyle through the same process of accessibility and affordability. Government and businesses pool financial resources and subsidies.

Ruralites feel highly connected by cell phone, television exposes them to news and images of world around them and education makes them understand the world and themselves as a component in that. They are equally motivated that computer and Internet will connect them to the world around them and make them understand it as television does. Ruralites accept the integrated challenge and push themselves to achieve it and be on the road to growth as urbanites are.

At one point of time government set up community radio, television, and video, in the villages, to familiarize the villagers with the technology and its utility and advantages. By and by they were accepted in the lifestyle. Lately, cell phone is accepted as important connectivity technology. Now it is the turn of community computer and Internet Kiosk to be set up in the villages or nearby cluster of villages.

Computer through Internet will not only make the benefits of the new "Information Society" accessible and meaningful for people, but in particular to raise public awareness and give deserved public recognition to the highest quality e-content produced all over the world. The following eight categories of content are focused: e-learning; e-culture; e-science; e-government; e-health; e-business; e-entertainment; and e-inclusion. Through this the focus would be on a range of parameters which can be referred to as the 8 Cs of the digital economy: connectivity, content, community, commerce, capacity, culture, capital and cooperation.

Internet

Telecom regulators have done a commendable job in bringing a mobile telephony revolution in the country, by regulating less and less, and relying more and more on market forces. However, telecom policymakers and regulators have not taken similar initiatives, and market-friendly decisions, to stimulate the growth of Internet. They should let market forces regulate the Internet.

Internet adds to information, knowledge and instant messages and connectivity. It provides forum, enables consumers to gather around a topic that are meaningful to them in ways that are impractical and impossible offline. The in-forming makes the world transparent. In-forming by web search through search engines Yahoo, Google and Microsoft. These do not push their products and services on their customers but build collaborative systems that enable customers to pull on their own and then respond to what they pull.

At the same time, Internet growth has been steady, particularly among youths and business professionals in India. The youth—especially in urban areas—are very Net savvy, and the gender divide is narrowing in this segment as well. The total number of Internet users is estimated at around 30 million. The big concern is the shortage of international bandwidth, which NASSCOM estimates will exceed 20 Gbps by mid-2005. Prices of international bandwidth are still not at par with those of neighboring countries. This could hinder Internet usage and the outsourcing business to some extent.

Internet Promotion: National Internet Exchange of India (NIXI) has been set up to improve the quality of service and help in efficient routing of the domestic traffic within the country. Four Internet Exchange Nodes have been set up and made operational at Noida (U.P.), Mumbai, Chennai and Kolkata, and as many as 40 ISPs have been connected with these nodes. Government has installed three mirror Internet root servers at Delhi, Mumbai and Chennai. The root servers form a critical part of the global Internet infrastructure.

Internet Content: Most of the Internet content is in English Language. It is therefore an important barrier. There is increased focus on Indian languages and making packaged software available in local languages. To enable wide proliferation of ICTs in Indian languages, government has taken a major initiative to make available tools and fonts in various Indian languages freely to the general public. It has released in the public domain, various Tamil language fonts, e-mail client, Optical Character Recognition (OCR) software, spell checker and dictionary in April 2005. Similarly, the Hindi and Telugu software tools and fonts were released in June 2005 and October 2005, respectively. Software tools and fonts in Punjabi and Urdu are ready for release. All Indian languages are expected to be covered in the next years.

Cost: Government is making efforts to make Internet and telephones affordable to all. As a first step towards making long distance tariffs more affordable, government in May 2005 made telephone calls within states equivalent to local calls. The second step was taken in November 2005 where the government significantly reduced the entry barrier for acquiring national and international long distance licenses. On January 1, 2006, government allowed Access Service Provider to provide Internet telephony, Internet services and Broadband services. 'One India initiative' enables people to talk from Kashmir to Kanyakumari at a very affordable tariff of Re. 1 per minute. There is focus on lowering the cost of PC at below Rs. 10,000. This will increase PC penetration. The fact still remains that unless content is relevant, use of ICTs will always be constrained.

Internet Access: The urban cyber café set up by private initiatives has given easy access to people. Over the years because of greater demand even these cafés have reduced the charges per hour and providing better services. Moreover, different telephone companies Bharti's Airtel, Reliance Communications and MTNL have been providing Internet to people and businesses at competitive rates for different speeds. With increasing demands and competition, these companies have been reducing monthly charges and giving other value added services; thus making Internet access more affordable.

The aim is to reduce the digital divide by providing Internet access and IT enabled services to the community at large and to facilitate citizen interface with the government by establishing 100,000 web enabled Citizen Service Centers or CSCs in rural areas, which will serve not only as the front end for most government services, but also as a means to connect the citizens of rural India to the World Wide Web. CSCs would extend the reach of electronic services, both government and private to the village level. It is these advances in ICT technologies, which have enabled the government to take concrete steps towards turning citizens' dream of "Government at your doorstep" into a reality.

The Internet Service Providers Association of India (ISPAI) claims that STD calls can be offered at 15 paise per minute and local calls can be free on the same network, if the government permits unrestricted domestic internet telephony.

Search giant Google has revived its plans to set up a server farm in India. The $1-billion back-office, its second facility in India and seventh globally, is likely to be located in Andhra Pradesh, industry sources said. Google's proposal to set up a server farm in India comes amidst a surge in the number of Internet users in the country. A local server will allow users to access the Internet faster and also save on accesses costs from international locations when volumes increase. Google's server farm in India will also boost the country as a preferred destination for competing companies like Microsoft and Yahoo.

Server farms host websites and also act as a storehouse for all information available on the Internet. It will store e-mails, blogs, photos, documents and chat records, and make it available to users when they demand it. Google's earlier plan to set up a server farm in the country was thwarted by infrastructure bottlenecks. Google then went to Taiwan instead to build its farm. The California-based company was in the news recently over its plans to set up an SEZ in India.

India is set to join a select group of countries to adopt IPv6 technology, which is considered to be a long-term solution to overcome the limitations of the present IPv4 Internet regime. In addition to offering almost infinite address space, IPv6 technology is considered as the solution for end-to-end global connectivity and Internet scalability.

"The inclusion of IPv6 as a significant element of a larger national strategy on IT is of critical importance. The subject should be addressed alongside infrastructure issues such as broadband and mobile wireless," said global networking giant, Cisco Systems, in its response to TRAI on the issue.

Wipro Technologies has meanwhile said India has already been left behind in adopting the new technology. It has also pointed out that while India's software community was engaged in product development and services related to IPv6 for overseas market, the country was yet to realize this potential. Bharti too has told the government that migration from IPv4 to IPv6 must be carried out in strict predefined time frame.

Broadband

Internet can be accessed on narrow band or broadband. Earlier in India only narrowband was available till 90s; and gradually it moved into affordable broadband and narrow band has become totally obsolete in India. Narrow band was through regular landline telephones but the Internet software package was marketed by many companies such as Sify, Wipro, etc. It was sold according to the number of hours the consumer wanted. The disadvantage was the double cost of your telephone calls and blocking the telephone till you are using Internet.

There are two types of Broadband—wire-line infrastructure and wireless broadband. Wireless is also of two types, Wi-Fi and WiMAX. Wire-line infrastructure for broadband is through a modem which is connected to your computer through broadband cables specially laid for it. Wire-line broadband is offered by few telecom companies—Airtel, Reliance, Idea cellular, BSNL and MTNL on monthly charges according to the speed required by the consumers. This is mainly available in metro towns and bigger cities.

Broadband is increasingly regarded as a catalyst for economic success in information society. Developing countries are opting for use of wireless broadband technology to leapfrog ahead of the traditional wire-line infrastructure. Wireless Fidelity (Wi-Fi) or the 802.11 family standards have become the most popular standards for wireless LAN solution using 2.4 GHz unlicensed portion of radio spectrum band. Wi-Fi has emerged into the wireless scene in the year 2003. It has put 3G in the back seat, as far as wireless broadband Internet is concerned. Wi-Fi is basically for Wireless Local Area Network or WLAN, and more recently the 802.16 standard has been approved by IEEE, enabling wireless metropolitan area network (WMAN) or WiMAX (Wireless interoperable).

The main advantage of Wi-Fi is that it enables multiple users to share the same Internet connection without cables, allowing full portability using laptop PCs or PDAs. Wi-Fi technology also holds much promise for developing countries who want to achieve universal access to ICTs for the masses in rural areas or regions where telephone or cable infrastructures are not deployed. Computers tailored to the needs of the developing countries; to make high-speed Internet access more ubiquitous in some cases by use of WiMAX technology.

Wi-Fi hot spots are setup in Airports, Malls, certain shops like Starbuck, and restaurants and other public facilities in India to facilitate Internet use. But still they are very few.

In the area of broadband Internet, the country lags behind the rest of the world and is practically at the bottom of the ladder, with just 0.006 per ten people broadband tele-density. China with a figure of 0.268 has more than 40 times broadband tele-density compared to India. South Korea with a tele-density of 2.466 and Hong Kong with 2.335, are at the top of the list. South Korea and Hong Kong have taken policy decisions to promote broadband in their respective countries. In both these countries, Internet Service Providers (ISPs) have played a very important role in bringing the broadband Internet revolution. This has been achieved by unbundling the 'local loop' of the dominant operators, so that the ISPs use them at a reasonable cost, without the need to duplicate this bottleneck facility.

Broadband Policy: There is potential of broadband service in growth of GDP and enhancement in quality of life through societal applications including tele-education, tele-medicine, e-governance, entertainment as well as employment generation by way of high speed access to information and web-based communication, government has come out with a Broadband Policy to provide affordable services to the public. BSNL and MTNL have launched broadband services across the country and people can get access to such connections for as little as Rs. 199 a month in 2006. Airtel and other telecom companies are offering at competitive prices. We have touched a million broadband connections so far. We expect to see 20 million by 2007.

Bharat Sanchar Nigam (BSNL) proposes to set up a Joint Venture with an Original Equipment Manufacturer (OEM) firm for manufacture of the latest generation ADSL2+ CPEs or customer premises equipment like modems to be used on BSNL broadband service, at its Telecom Factory at Kolkata. The proposed JV will Design and Develop a range of models of ADSL2+ CPEs exclusively for BSNL as per TEC/BSNL specifications taking into consideration the market conditions prevailing in India.

The OEM would be responsible for the transfer of technology for setting up facilities for design, manufacture, assembly and testing of about 1 Million ADSL2+ CPEs per annum. The

ADSL2+ CPEs would be launched by BSNL in the market under its own brand name. The JV partner apart from investing in the production line will also be responsible for arranging of funds to meet the working capital of JV Company at competitive market rates. After meeting the requirement of the BSNL, the JV Company would be free to sell these items in the open market or export (June 2008).

Broadband in Rural Areas

The era of mobile broadband has commenced, wireless as access network technology for broadband is the main technology for remote and rural areas. Fixed wireless access in UHF and higher frequency bands is becoming popular solution for rural communication and as point-to-point corporate access. But no clear standards have emerged in this area. 3G evolving with HSDPA (High Speed Downlink Packet Access) is going to soon become wireless broadband standard and will find its extensive use in rural areas due to cost advantage as the incremental cost of extending networks to cover more and more villages will work out less.

In 2008, DoT has also started discussions with both private and state-owned telecom operators to utilize the USOF for broadband roll-out in rural India through a bidding process. DoT's plans include providing broadband connections within a 10 km. radius of all block headquarters in the country. It envisages a minimum speed of 512 kbps, where the network connects community centers, primary schools, banks, health centers, panchayats and police stations located close to all block headquarters.

Broadband connectivity from urban homes and small and medium businesses is extending to villages for e-services to improve the quality of living of vast majority of Indians living in rural areas. Trials for WiMAX technology are going on in number of Indian states to develop a low cost business model for rural applications.

Five years back Wireless Broadband Alliance was created to drive the adoption of wireless broadband technologies and services around the world by developing a common commercial, technical and marketing framework for wireless network interoperability. The WBA is now aggressively pursuing with various other alliances and forums on other forms of wireless broadband roaming like dual mode devices and WiMAX roaming. Tata Communications is the only Indian telecom to be a part of this prestigious forum.

Telephone Infrastructure

India is the world's most dynamic and fastest growing telecom market. All projections state that the country will have 500 million telecom subscribers by 2010 from about 225 million in 2007. But the pace of growth of telecom infrastructure can turn out to be the bottleneck that can slow down the celebrated success story. To put this in perspective, consider this: according to TRAI the country needs about 3,30,000 telecom towers by 2010 from about 1,10,000 currently to touch the projected 500 million subscriber base.

To maintain the current growth trends, India needs to build two times the cellular infrastructure it has created over the last 12 years within the next 36 months. This implies, the country needs massive investments in infrastructure, be it passive, active or backhaul. All major telecoms Bharti Airtel, R.Com, Tata Teleservices and Idea Cellular over the last couple of months are hiving off their physical infrastructure in line with global practices. The move, in addition to increasing operational efficiency, will also enable these companies to unlock value for its shareholders.

India will need to add about 90,000 towers each in FY08 and FY09. At a cost of about Rs. 40 lakh per tower, the total investment required annually is Rs. 36,000 crore ($10 billion). Telecoms have realized that investments towards setting up towers individually, where the assets are completely owned and used exclusively by single players can no longer be sustained. Hiving off their infrastructure arms will make sharing of the active and passive components easier, which is the only solution in sight to bring in return on investments within a reasonable time frame.

Internationally, tower management companies have been highly successful. Globally, this is an emerging business model with cell sites and other related infrastructure being owned by third parties who lease out the same to multiple service providers. At the same time, equity dilution in the tower arms offers a window to bring in both strategic and financial investors on board. While strategic players will extend their expertise in running and managing the tower companies, the financial partners will provide operators with the much-needed capital to build infrastructure of such scale.

For instance, Reliance Telecom Infrastructure, the tower arm of R.Com is divesting a minority stake. According to sources, J.P. Morgan, which is advising R.Com on the stake sale, is estimated to have valued the company's 15,000-plus towers at between $8-10 billion. A 10% dilution will therefore fetch RCOM over $800 million, which it can use to partly fund its capital requirements to set up about 20,000 additional towers this fiscal year.

Similarly, TTSL's services had recently short listed nine tower players to sell or lease out its 6,000 telecom towers across the country. This is set to help the company monetize assets valued at around Rs. 12,000 crores and the proceeds will be used for further expansion of its services.

Infrastructure sharing is a crucial factor to effectively leverage to roll-out services at a faster speed and at affordable costs. Moreover, sharing of infrastructure is likely to increase presence of all the operators and hence more competition. The advantage of such infrastructure sharing will also be passed on to subscribers in terms of faster roll-out of services and greater affordability of services. In terms of the effects on costs, operators are expected to increasingly resort to sharing of infrastructure, thus controlling their capital as well as operating expenditures, justifying the roll-out in the Indian hinterland. Additionally, the falling costs of the unshared electronic components will further benefit the operators' attempt at overall cost control.

"Maintaining such exponential growth calls for creation of huge infrastructure requiring significant investment. The challenge is to optimally utilize available resources while ensuring competition and availability of services at affordable prices. The infrastructure sharing is essential," TRAI recommended that telecoms be allowed to share both passive and active infrastructure, including backhaul.

In addition to sharing the towers, telecoms can also share the electronics located on the tower, which constitutes the active component and include antenna, feeder cable, node B, radio access network and transmission systems. Besides, they can also share their backhaul from Base Trans Receiver Station (BTS) to Base Station Controller (BSC), where such sharing will be permitted both on optical fiber as well as radio medium.

"Non-availability of backhaul especially in rural areas has been a major concern. As the traffic in such areas is likely to be low in the initial stages, there is an obvious advantage of sharing of backhaul. Such backhaul sharing can also help to reduce the load of the backhaul antennae on the tower reducing the cost to set up such towers and increase the possibility of sharing same tower by more operators," TRAI had said in its recommendations.

Another impediment for faster roll-out of telecom infrastructure is the delays associated with SACFA clearance procedures. SACFA clearance relates to approvals from a slew of local bodies before telecom companies can set up their infrastructure. TRAI had recently addressed this issue by mandating that these clearances need to be given in a stipulated time frame. "If no communication is received in the prescribed timeframe, the request may be deemed to be approved," it added.

According to industry estimates, the infrastructure arms of telecoms have a combined value of $60 billion. Even a 10% dilution in tower companies will enable the sector to fund a third of its capital expenditure requirement over the next two years.

The scale of infrastructure requirement over the next couple of years also brings huge opportunities for stand-alone tower companies. Therefore, a number of stand-alone tower companies have lined up massive investments to tap this market.

The liberalization of the Indian telecom sector has been one of the most successful ones and has lead phenomenal growth since the late '90s. Today, the country boasts of being one of the five largest networks in the world, with 20% telecom penetration level and staggering net additions in the range of 6 million mobile subscribers per month.

While the growth has thus far been largely limited to the affluent urban pockets of the country, the next wave of growth is slated to come from rural areas. Riding on this the government and the industry stakeholders expect the country to double its penetration levels to 40% plus by the close of 2010 because of enormous population which resides in these untouched regions.

While the country has one of the lowest tariffs in the world and has witnessed a steady decline in the average revenue per user (ARPU) levels in the past few years, what the effects of further expansion would have on the margins of the operators. At present, large Indian operators can be said to have much lower earnings before interest, taxes, depreciation, and amortization margins as compared to their Asian peers. It is important to highlight the fact that the regulatory impositions including levies such as license fees, spectrum charges, access deficit charge (ADC), service tax, etc. on the Indian service provider stand at a 30% and is much higher than those experienced by its counterparts in the other countries, thus explaining the visible gap.

Hence, the government's intervention by way of rationalizing this burden together with introducing a single levy mechanism could play a crucial role, leading to more affordability of telecom services by the masses by way of tariff reduction. However, if the present situation were to continue for the next few years, the operators could still expect an increase in their margins, owing to the scale of growth and the opportunities available in the vast untapped territories. The volumes of net additions that are expected would negate the effects of falling ARPU coming out of the marginal low value users. The industry expects large Indian telecoms to witness revenue growth at the rate of 20-25% up till 2010, rendering ARPU measurement redundant. Operators would also need to further outsource or centralize a range of non-core activities such as billing, customer relationship management (CRM) and finance functions bringing in more avenues for effective cost-saving mechanisms.

There are growth prospects for the players in mobile telephony; there is the enormous future scope of introducing converged services by way of triple play and ensuring a larger share of the end consumer's revenue. The operators could also capitalize on their assets such as their expansive retail network and call-center functions if outsourced to other non-telecom businesses, as it would enable them to ride on the merits of such well-tested establishments and would be invaluable cost-saving mechanisms.

Other ancillary opportunity is that of the tower business. With the required number of 3,30,000 towers by the end of 2010, operators have come to realize the potential of their tower assets and have begun spinning off their infrastructure activity into separate businesses.

Key Risks for Telecom Infrastructure

- Unexpected failure to execute in the tower-sharing business.
- A change in regulation or restrictions on pricing may have an adverse impact on the business.
- A slowdown in business due to higher competition or otherwise will lead to significant decrease in already poor interest coverage ratio. This could further increase the financial risk for the company and may potentially lead to higher than forecast dilution of equity.
- This is a highly capex intensive business and most tower companies plan to increase their leverage significantly to support their aggressive capex plans. A huge increase in capex could have a very negative impact on the balance

sheets of the companies exposing them to significant financial risk.

- Unforeseen financial burden from likely 3G auctions.
- Unexpected pressure on RoE (return on equities) due to overseas expansion plans.

All these reasons put together have been making progress for the telecom market, which is further supported by the fact that the enterprise multiples of the Indian telecoms are one of the highest in the globe today and are expected to continue being this way in the years to come. Hence, owing to the unprecedented scale of growth available coupled with new opportunities in the telecom space, the Indian sector is now well on its way towards starting its next phase of revolution.

Changing Telecommunication Practices are Empowering People: The changing communication practice in India and elsewhere in other developing countries is to provide telephone connectivity as well as increase tele-density in rural areas through cellular technology. It is cheaper and does not require rural electrification. Cheaper Cellular technology both hardware and software is creating wider and bigger markets even among the poor and bringing better connectivity and social change among the developing countries.

In 1987, Mr. Pitroda was asked by Rajiv Gandhi, the Indian Prime Minister, to help democratize access to telecommunications. His response was to deploy instantly-telephone kiosks in every town and village. In the process, he helped to release the Indian telecoms industry from state control and opened it up to dozens of private companies, paving the way for India's telecoms boom. Through World-Tel, he now promotes similar policies in other parts of the developing world.

To Sum up: India has achieved a high level of connectivity through telephones connecting both the urban and rural India through easy accessibility and affordability. Mobile telephone technology has been on the forefront bringing a leapfrog progress both in personal and enterprises connectivity, bringing social change by bridging the connectivity divide. The policy of allowing the private players to enter the telephones created competition, better services, initiated new technologies, affordability for the customer and thus increasing the subscriber base and tele-density.

Another areas is the computers and Internet bringing much progress in connectivity, and accessibility to information and knowledge gain.

Television has been ubiquitous in Indian homes since 70's; but the wider scope through accessibility to numerous world channels through improved technology. Indian economic policies were open in 90s, the world companies such as LG, Samsung, Panasonic and Sony marketing television in India created competition and the low cost produced or assembled TVs allowed easy access to people in the lower income strata even. Ubiquitous TV created closeness to global scenario through news and images.

People's expectations in India were rising as the three—Telephones, Computer and Television were making tremendous progress worldwide and Indians were becoming more and more aware of them and were recognizing their importance in life and jobs. Exposure to the three gave them information, knowledge and connectivity to the world around them.

Government policies to open these areas with competition, M&A with foreign companies and policy of allowing FDI in these businesses created accessibility and affordability for Indian people.

When resources, national policies, needs and demands interact with one another, the outcomes may be many; such as changing patterns of the economy, occupation and employment, patterns of work, work ethics and organization practices, and infiltration of new values and ideas in the society.

India's rising expectations, and achievements from these three together—Telephones, Computer and Television have transformed the India of Today and Tomorrow.

PART III

Transformation Challenges

8

India imagines its future is challenge in itself.

The Key Challenges Ahead

Earlier than 90s India faced the challenges of low economic growth, and close economic policies. Since 90s the expectations have been rising because of economic liberalization, economic reforms and economic policies opening gradually which paved the way to globalization participation and economic growth.

India faced multiple urgent challenges when its economic policies opened in 90s. India must address several challenges to increase its international competitiveness.

The transformation of India through its rising expectations has posed some key challenges to make it successful. The challenges are in broader context of its participating role in globalization and in particular context of Indian situations.

The ongoing transformation in many domains is challenging and even more challenging is the search for strategies, solutions, policies to transform these challenges for development and economic growth. The biggest challenge is how to give citizens a sense that they can exercise their will not only over their own government, their businesses, and economic choices but also on some of the global forces shaping their lives. The gap between the rising expectations and challenges they pose.

The challenges in the first decade 1990-2000 have been to create visibility for itself on global scenario. The government (since everything has to be routed through government and public sectors) focused on economic growth projects and dealt with the challenges it posed and the intervening challenges, and took policy decisions to make the challenges successful.

These created the challenges for globalization participation. In this context, the first challenge was the decision to participate in globalization by opening up its markets and economy to do business with other countries in various products and services. Second was to take steps to set up its global brand image. A brand image that India's business environment is amenable to do business with other countries, and that it has products and services which can be upgraded for world markets; that it has stable political environment and consistent economic policies; that it is heading towards transformation by revitalizing its industries and trade, political and social environments both by public and private efforts.

The influence of a nation's history, infrastructure, and culture permeates all aspects of life within the country, including the norms, values, and behaviors of workforce in its national companies. Nationally influenced behavioral characteristics become an ingrained part of each company's "way of doing things" and shape its international organization structure and processes. How India's enterprises have been handling this challenge?

Changing world economies, changing prospects of access to world markets, new technologies and its changing implementation can affect the competitive edge. The competitive edge in terms of sharpness, vigor of competition suggests action for growth, innovation and value creation. Indian enterprises have risen to this challenge.

Our discussions in earlier chapters have highlighted the struggle, push and pull and the ongoing efforts to face this challenge which pose other new intervening challenges as the national and global scenarios were undergoing changes periodically and India's global image was upgrading gradually; when India has been trying to create niche for itself among a globalize world through globulation and glocalization; and by accepting the iconoclasm of globalization by re-envisaging the world that arises through the nature of the complex global interconnectedness, the process of time-space compression and action at distance.

The second challenge was to put country on the road to growth by raising people's expectations of expanding economic growth and thus economic boom and thereby improving the quality of life for them. People have to be motivated by the economic visions of high growth, high GDP, and high incomes. They have to be sensitized to the reality of changing their quality of lifestyles and good consumerism through economic growth and for that they have to push for achievements through competitions on varied fronts, strengthen capability, developing skilled manpower for meeting the ever renewed global market demands and facing reality of limited and untapped national resources.

The third challenge was posed by global structure, i.e. focus is on business expansions in key areas of product and services and different geo markets; expansion and development of new business models as applied to expansion, development of new products and services and markets in new geographies. Globalization is further structured through development of human, intellectual and financial capitals.

Before expanding businesses to other geo areas, it was necessary for the government to liberalize its economic and business policies for domestic markets. It was necessary to modify its bureaucratic rules and behavior. At the same time it was challenging to develop the educated and skilled manpower and capital resources to solidify and expand businesses for various products and services. Managing capital flows for short term was a challenge for the Indian economy. The government admitted that managing plentiful capital inflows without endangering growth, its autonomy was indeed a challenge.

The fourth challenge was to have the right attitude to move towards transformation and be on road to growth by government, businesses and its people.

Political consensus is important for transformation policies and programs. The consensus will be taken in the context of economic growth, policies, plans and targets and most important in implementation of these. This is most challenging particularly in a democracy when global concerns or interests are associated with the national interests.

Business consensus is important for business expansions in diversify products and services and to pick its strong areas; to have consensus about expanding to various geo markets and in what products and services; and to create cooperating platform with government for changing business polices and practices to fit the changing times and in globalize contexts.

It was also important for people to be motivated to develop befitting skills, and work ethics to meet the demands of the business expansions at home, in different geo market with different business and cultural practices.

It was important for government to create political, business and people consensus and entrust more power to private sector and people to pursue expansion schemes and models to move the country for growth. The business expansion needed capital and government was willing to approve of policies to allow foreign capital flow in the country with certain restrictions.

The intervening challenge was to provide economic and social opportunities to people by streamlining economic policies. For this, it was important and necessary to develop and streamline skills and resources, develop opportunities and strengths of people and economy, and work out to improve on weaknesses, and threats and vulnerabilities of people and economy.

India took the fifth challenge when it got the opportunity for outsourcing of IT and outsourcing BPOs. The low cost factor, educated and English speaking personnel and trained workforce in software development attracted the developed countries such as USA and UK to outsource software jobs and back offices processes to India. The first hub was set up in Bangalore. Tata Consultancy Services, Wipro, Infosys Technologies took the challenge. It created jobs, revenue and an 'outsourcing image'.

During this period, companies worked hard to expand to be much sought after by countries for outsourcing jobs in competition with China and other Asian countries. These companies worked hard and with vision and strategy for future expansion; expanded the home base and set up software outsourcing consultancy units in these countries where Indians manned these units. Thus, more jobs and revenues were created.

Skilled personnel were absorbed by both types of outsourcing hubs and also created demands for more personnel to be trained on ongoing basis. Some of the Indian expats were joining the outsourcing revolution now and later in its varied formats.

Globalize outsourcing was the start of India's transformation story and its sailing through government and private efforts, policies, planning and actions. National efforts, people's efforts and international efforts were significant and essential for ensuing transformation to take place. This was the first significant contributory factor for economic boom.

The sixth challenge and very crucial one was the availability of technology of telephones, computers and its peripherals, Internet, computer printers, copying machines and fax machines to make outsourcing a success. Government allowed computers, computer printers, copying machines and fax machines to be imported and also its peripherals to be imported and assembled in India by foreign computer companies as well some Indian companies and these assembled computers were available for comparatively less money but still expensive for the individuals to own. As we will note in government's computer policy of 1980, they planned to produce computers indigenously; but they realized it was not going to work for many years because of many practical difficulties. The policy did simplify procedures to enable users to obtain computers from overseas sources; government also reduced duty on computer peripherals such as disk drive, disks and printers; and on source codes for software producers.

These clauses of policy did allow not only outsourcing businesses to own but majority of the big, medium and small Indian companies bought a few computers and computer printers, copying machines and fax machines for their efficient day-to-day working. At this point India did favor the policy of transfer of foreign technology whenever needed to expand businesses.

Outsourcing companies were also developing software packages for Dial-up Internet connectivity in India. Internet has come on the scene in 90s in metros and bigger cities; but still expensive and only businesses could afford it. Earlier in India, only narrow band was available till 90s; and gradually it moved into affordable wire-line broad band and by 2000 narrow band has become totally obsolete in India. Dial-up narrow band Internet was accessed through regular landline telephones and the Internet software packages were marketed by many companies such as Sify, Wipro, etc. It was sold according to the number of hours the consumer wanted. The disadvantage was the double cost of your telephone calls and blocking the telephone till you are using Internet and most of all the unreliable connectivity of landline phones.

India made urgent efforts to improve the landlines by changing the obsolete manual telephone exchanges by automatic electronic exchanges, changing underground telephone wires first to copper wires and later to fiber optics. These needed transfer of imported technology and large financial resources.

The challenge is searching for the best initiatives that accelerate the use of information technology for social and economic benefit of citizens and communities in public administration, culture, health, education, economic development, and environment. These challenges call for changing communication practices. It projects the endeavors for progress in related fields and better connectivity.

The Challenges in the Second Decade Following 2000

After 2000, India was ready to face other challenges since it has created economic boom through its outsourcing projects and business expansions. The economic growth rate is 8.8% as by 31st March 2008. But worrying signs are also that this momentum may not last as both food and fuel prices are rising for the poor and CII said the impact of tight monetary stance on industrial production has been severe (30 May 2008).

India is still grappling with number of challenges to sustain this growth rate including poor physical infrastructure that chokes the flow of people and goods and need to improve human infrastructure as there is shortage of educated and skilled workforce as we are expanding our business resources. Physical and human infrastructure development is equally important for effective globalization participation.

Poor infrastructure is challenging the economic and other development growth. In 2000 decades India is giving more attention to it. As we begin our road to growth and transformation for tomorrow; we realize the importance of world class physical infrastructure and focus on these developments—from power plants, highways and expressways, good roads and transport system of rails and airlines to new ports and ship building; to telecommunication, and safe drinking water, sanitation, etc. on one hand; and on the other hand, space research and defense infrastructure is of importance in global transformation contexts. We definitely need other supporting infrastructure of tourism, and entertainment economy. A boost in energy sector of power, oil, petrol and gas is the driving force for infrastructure development and viz. India's transformation and economic growth.

We have discussed in chapter 4, 'Road to Growth: Transforming Tomorrow', how India is meeting this challenge from various standpoints. Snapshots of oil and energy related companies in Appendix 3 reflect the ongoing activities in this area after 2000 that shows that Indian companies both private and public are forging ahead in big way, investing billion dollars and collaborating with other foreign big companies in this sector to explore oil, to refine and produce gas. Ultra mega power projects are being set up in different states with funding from private, government and international conglomerates.

India wants to develop world class infrastructure, which is need of the day on vast scale and that would need a fair amount of capital and money resources. India needed global financial resources and capital investments; and even global expertise. India has invited foreign entrepreneurs to invest their financial and other physical resources, as well as their expertise to set up such infrastructure. This may be facilitated by collaborative or cooperative business models. These may be built through foreign funding as joint venture or by total foreign investments on BOT (buy-operate-transfer) basis depending on again country's openness of economic policies about the foreign capital flow in without reservations and restrictions or it may levy certain conditions. The other modes could be public-private investments.

India's robust growth in GDP has exposed the grave inadequacies in the country's infrastructure sectors. Committee on Infrastructure Financing, which submitted its report in May 2007, has advised that the target for infrastructure investment should be revised from $320 billion to $384 billion at 2005-06 prices, which is equivalent to $475 billion at current prices. It had been earlier estimated that during the Eleventh Plan period (2007 to 2012), the country would need to invest over $320 billion in infrastructure alone.

India's goal of attaining 10 per cent growths by the 2011-12 financial years would be unachievable unless infrastructure spending moves into much higher gear. The Indian government will pick up the tab for 70 per cent of the infrastructure spending but the rest—around 150 billion dollars—must come from private sources (India Economic Summit, 4 Dec. 2007).

Business expansion challenge is the next challenge during 2000 decades; being further expanded in its diversified and upgraded formats as what was being pursued in 90s to 2000 decade. Business expansion during this decade has given Indian enterprises confidence to move ahead. Business expansion structure sets the stage for transformation and it becomes an ongoing process seeking support from globalization dimensions of connectivity and infrastructure to give it more stability. Rising expectations and stability is necessary for transformation success of India and expanding its global participation to an extent that it is being reckoned as powerful country with its booming economy.

Chapter 3, 'Rising Expectations: India's Transformation' highlights the business expansions in multi-geographies and expanding in volumes and domains which also demands more and more of world class physical and human infrastructures to develop fast, reliable and updated to have easy access to do business. If roads and road transport are outdated, if airlines and airports are not modernized, and if ports are not conveniently accessible and modernized for cargo containers, the developed countries doing business with India may start looking elsewhere and the strongest competitor is China, which has moved much ahead in infrastructure development and is also a preferred destination for businesses.

The second scenario is when country 'B' does want to do business with India because of low cost factor and other expertise and talent workforce and it decides to develop some of the infrastructure—physical or human for business profitability.

India is expanding businesses in multi-geographies and diversifying into varying innovative products and services. It has been changing images of business enterprises of India which reflect India's companies' strengths in smart management, low costs, and increasing ambition to join the elite ranks of multinationals. Globalization structure of business in India focuses on globalization of enterprises and business expansion of products and services, global markets and geographies through collaboration, joint ventures, merger and acquisitions. Collaborative business model focuses on joint ventures in domestic market, with other global corporates in multi-geographies; it could be bilateral or multi-country; with one company or with multi-companies.

India experienced that business success depends on its business models. India did move ahead from its traditional business models to innovative and newer models as it fitted its expansion plans. It reiterated its low end markets and rural markets, and microfinance models to give new lease to these models to boost more economic growth for the low end population; and in return boost more business volume for Indian businesses.

India is experiencing economic growth as businesses are expanding both nationally and globally. The business expansions must be managed well so that economic growth and even economic boom is continuous and remains stable. We find the three essential concepts of globulation, glocalization and globalism conducive to expanding and managing businesses well.

It transformed its business through globalization services, business innovations and opportunities, development and diffusion of technology (or a practice) that is new for the society concerned and competition both at home and abroad.

It is a dominant player in computer software development products and services and manufacturing. Outsourcing strengths expanded in 2000 decade through KPOs, focuses on analytics and research in various disciplines in addition to BPOs for many sectors; the scope of RIM (remote infrastructure management) is widened. Outsourcing is further focused on insurance, health, pension funds, foods, etc. New business models are developed and applied for new products and services, and new geo areas and markets are entered and developed.

Offshoring has also expanded the outsourcing and BPOs. The MNCs started setting their businesses—hardware or software development in India itself such as IBM, Nokia, Motorola, Oracle, Microsoft. Offshoring brought foreign investments, knowledge, expertise and jobs for the country.

Initially, India's globalization participation has started with setting up IT 'Outsourcing hubs' in India itself. Later they expanded their IT service providers' hubs in different countries for better earnings by being closer to the service providing areas such as setting up in Latin American countries to be able to serve USA. They also set up training institutes to train different countries' personnel to work in those hubs and BPO offices. Their motive is also of increased earnings through low cost and cheap labor in those countries as well as less transportation costs. Those offices are manned by their own personnel as well as from host countries. So glocalization principle is operative for better results. More and more Indian professionals are being exposed to foreign countries, their business practices and finding business solutions for them. The business practices need to be the best, assimilating to the business, political, administrative and social cultures of the host countries. At home businesses are developing SEZ zones, retail infrastructure, and realty sector.

Snapshot of randomly selected Indian companies given in Appendix 3 highlights their foray into expanding products and services, new technologies and multiple geographies. Current scenario 2007-08 is that everyday news in the media point that the Indian companies are moving on in various domains to different geographies abroad and at home focusing on varied products. They highlight their product range, operation areas development, geographies and expertise. These tell the story of progress, transformation made by these companies, and getting into diversified businesses that was not the earlier norm before 90s, or during 90s; their developing and growing into MNCs, and conglomerates; and thus giving way to rising expectations among people, experts, businesses, policymakers, and among national and international economic and political leaders.

India is also taking the challenge well of managing global businesses. India could attract FDI through its soft power. It could attract foreign investment funds because it offers stable political environments, stable and consistent economic policies, business and management expertise of its business leaders and a talented work pool. Secondly, it is updating technological needs of businesses. India is able to meet its technology needs both by innovating indigenous technology by research development; and importing advance technologies as now government has open policies for import of such technologies. Moreover, when foreign MNCs are opening their units in India, they are bringing with them latest advance technologies, or setting up research and development units for advancement in technologies and the best part is that they train manpower to operate these technologies. When Indian MNCs acquire and merge foreign companies, they also acquire their operating technologies. Further, the expats returning home bring their expertise and knowledge in advance technologies. Businesses have trained and skilled workforce in updated technologies. Since Indian businesses their up their units in different geo areas, their workforce must manage people with their cultural practices. Business expansion knows no bounds in India and there is rising aspirations and growth.

Chapter 3, 'Rising Expectations: India's Transformation' discusses the challenging dynamics of above factors in details how India is expanding its global businesses.

Energy Challenge: It is necessary that India should be prepared for energy security by focusing: building strategic oil reserves, pursuing civil nuclear options, removing foreign investment barriers to remove develop its own energy infrastructure, developing alternative energy technology like, wind, solar, bio-fuels and cars that run on alternative energies and increase energy efficiencies. India's growing energy demands to support its rapidly expanding economy can be a key factor impacting global energy markets. This growing energy demand is influencing India's diplomatic and military priorities in significant ways. India is the fourth largest energy consumer in the world today and as a nation whose energy security is driving its foreign policy, it needs to engage in energy dialogue with other developed countries to face the energy challenges and find solutions.

There are several policy initiatives that India can take to prepare for future energy shocks. How it would protect to terrorists attacks on energy production and distribution facilities creating energy crisis.

The challenge is developing skilled workforce to meet the ever growing demands in various sectors. The demand for skilled workforce for employment is increasing as businesses are expanding. Developing workforce in general with sound education, appropriate vocational skills, and employability skills both in local and global contexts; upgrading the work skills through training and new skills is necessary. This calls for drastic structural changes in the educational policy and vocational training programs to create a skilled workforce on priority basis.

We are fast realizing our educational policy is outdated. We do need a skill-oriented education system and which can inculcate innovative and creative attitude and capability. We do focus on physical sciences, social sciences, business education and engineering in general education system but not from innovative and creative practices, or creating skills angle to match the changing times. This focus must be applied from school system to higher education, and specialty education. When a student finishes the school level, he should be fit for some kind of job, when he finishes his college or university level, he should again have the employability. The criteria are that the education system at different levels prepares him for employability. But through present education system, his employability is very low and calls for further skill developing; whereas he should come out with certain skills, and innovative and creative capabilities should be in-built in the education system. Our education system should be skill-oriented. The next stage of specialized training should be training his innovative and creative attitudes and capability and skills according to the job sector aspired for. This will be upgraded training program. Focus is on computer education in schools. In June 2008, NIIT bags new orders to impart computer education to 1.9 million school students in Bihar and Maharashtra.

There are three important keys for human development infrastructure in India: Healthy workforce, soundly educated with wider horizon and creativity, and education and skills training matching the changing job demands periodically and creating employability. Employment is the targeted key for the workforce depending largely on the employability scale.

Prime Minister (2005), cautioned that if we focus all attention only on government redistributing incomes and providing employment, while suffocating enterprise and creativity, we will be pursuing an economically and fiscally unsustainable path; hence the need to focus on equity and efficiency. The growth of private enterprise as part of national development is a challenge before the country. An aggressive public-private, government-business, and government-business-global participation is needed in these efforts.

While only 8% of the youth are unemployed, 53% have some kind of skill deprivation. This becomes critical, as nearly 90% of jobs in India are still skill-based.

Youth unemployability is a bigger crisis than unemployment as poor quality of skills or education show up in low incomes rather than unemployment.

Over and above, the skills of the workforce should match the current demands for such workforce so there is full employability as well as meeting work requirements whether industry of otherwise. If we have skilled personnel we cannot complain about unemployment, low incomes and poverty; and the expanding youth demographics becoming problematic.

Finances and investments are needed for developing human resources to match the demands of globalization for manpower needs through expanding and upgrading education system, new educational models and skills training programs focusing on emerging practices.

Business expansions in various domains and even for diverse products and services are creating job opportunities and we can make efforts to take them by sound education and matching with updated skills. The share of manufacturing which is important due to its potential to create and sustain relatively large number of jobs remains 16-17% of GDP. Manpower development in a business organization focuses on defining talent needs, discovering talents and then developing those talents. Jobs at all the levels are constantly being created both for their domestic and international sites.

Our discussions in chapter 3 about business expansions in India reflect the urgent and expanding need of skilled, trained personnel in various disciplines and in various changing technologies in local, glocal and global contexts and changing business focus and practices. Periodic on job orientation and training is important as the business scenario undergoes change, therefore re-inventing the talent with new skills, and re-tooling is necessary.

The essential factor for managing businesses successfully and its growth is a vast pool of skilled workforce at all levels.

India is making efforts, pooling its private and public resources to educate the people and impart vocational skills both hard and soft skills. These skills need constant updating. Thus, with this ever increasing demand, the supporting businesses of imparting training to workforce also expand more and more.

The skills training have to be updated with changing technologies. In India, there is continuous effort to create a skilled and trained workforce but much is needed to take advantage of the young demographics of vast ever increasing manpower. Returning expats and Indian workforce do contribute to this need.

The companies doing global businesses must be staffed by international workforce. Any global model needs to be fueled by outstanding local insights. They know the consumers better than headquarters. Indian companies are hiring specialists and local anchors in each country to help reconcile differences and conflicts since they find themselves ill-equipped to tackle diverse consumer and employee cultures in alien markets after the recent spate of mergers and acquisitions. Indian multinationals are now recruiting more locals at the front-end of the business in new global markets. They are hiring talent from international business schools and training them; they are training their employees to acquire a global mind-set. Indian business schools have not yet paid much importance to exposing students to the elements of international businesses. As employees become scattered around the globe, virtual teamwork has become crucial.

There is increasing demand as well as current shortage for IT workforce as outsourcing and offshoring is growing in this sector. Talented and trained manpower is needed for computer software development, research and analytics trained for KPOs in different areas because of its talent pool and expertise in these areas such as radiology, law and accountancy; trained for RIM and for growing BPOs in many fields. Call center jobs are on the increase; where dynamic young cohorts of highly skilled and articulate professionals work throughout the night functioning on US time zone. These youngsters enjoy premature affluence and westernization in Indian setting. Whatever may be the impact; at least they are absorbed in the job market after mere graduation with no skills, all the skills are provided by the call centers on job training.

Physical infrastructure construction is creating more jobs from low level laborer to designer and architects and at all managerial levels; but all these jobs need skill training with the growing new technologies. The contract labor segment is getting more organized, schemes like blue-collar temping, recalling skilled labor from outside India to participate in the growth of physical infrastructure is increasing. Companies have already started hiring or plan to hire such labor in thousands.

India is foraying into many unconventional business sectors which are new to India. That needs trained personnel at every level and with speed. A few sectors are mentioned to make the point. The jobs are on demand in the aviation sector, logistic sector, industrial and communication design market, ranging from construction, sustainable forestry and agriculture, engineering and transportation, and in the banking sector. Delhi, in India is introducing new eco-friendly compressed natural gas buses and vehicles that will create 18,000 new jobs, Customer services jobs are quite widespread since they are needed for enterprises in all domains—big or small; and the success of any enterprise also depends on the customer service. The employability is great in this sector but it needs matching skill development to fit in the role.

Paramedic jobs in health related area are in short and we do need to create sound training programs to fit in the ever increasing demands in the health front at home and for medical tourism to deliver good medical rehab programs. Great awareness is being created for health and fitness. Local sports clubs and gymnasiums, fitness centers and high level and expensive fitness centers, weight loss clinics, specialized massage centers like Ayurveda massage could also generate substantial self-employment and employment opportunities for our youth. As we emphasized all need training to fit in.

Retail sector needs trained personnel in its thousand skills to make it really remunerative. India needs to adopt multi-format retail model, so it would need diversification of personnel skills on account of this factor also. For rural retailing format they would need different handling skills. Still workforce may not be sufficient for the million jobs that it intends creating both from metro to small towns and rural hubs. These need to focus on offering 'Retail Training Modules' for selected candidates, both in the set areas of retailing like sales, procurement and in new areas of logistics and storage.

The retail sector will create millions of jobs, e.g. Aditya Birla retail offering 55000 jobs in Dec. 2007; Reliance Retail is planning to increase its workforce to one million within the next four years. Since retail is also in varied sectors from food groceries to leather shoes and pharmaceuticals, it needs varied skills to create employability.

Real estate sector would need trained personnel, from sales to design engineers, architects, advertisers, public relation officers, etc. A recent research study estimates that for every direct job created in the real estate sector eight jobs are created indirectly. Many jobs are coming up in the real estate sector right from construction workers to the top level managerial jobs and the professional to create the real estate industry.

Employment generation and marketing mission (EGMM) of government targets poorest of poor rural youth, many of them illiterate; it screens them and then depending on their capabilities and the industry's needs, puts together a program to skill-train them and help them get jobs. Private sector is actively involved in developing and supporting the program, e.g. illiterates are put through a program to land jobs in the construction and textile sector; whereas 10th, 12th pass and graduates are trained to be employed in the services sector.

Chapter 5, 'Infrastructure for Human Resource Development', highlights dynamics of meeting the challenge of manpower development needs in India for economic growth and boom and for employability target.

Transforming Rural Base is Challenging. Government has tried to initiate programs in the 90s to 2000 to develop the economy of rural areas where 80% of population lives and most of them are not economically comfortable. Earlier than 90s, in fact since 60s; the development programs have been mainly rural based such as panchayat raj, green agriculture revolution, white milk revolution. There was increased realization to focus more and more on education, healthcare, water, sanitation and road connectivity and electricity in the villages. Now almost 90% of the villages are electrified.

In 70s rural people were exposed to TV through satellites, though many of the people could not buy them till 80s as they were expensive but government did put community TVs and radio in every village. Many villagers could buy transistor radio as they were inexpensive or many times they were distributed free by national and international agencies. In the sixth five-year plan, VHF sets were installed in five selected states for community viewing in rural areas. After 80s electrified villages could access cable TV and later on many international TV channels.

Satellite INSAT 1B was a unique joint venture between department of space, television services (Doordarshan), All India Radio services in 70s. Two extra powerful S-band channels could give direct telecast facilities to rural areas and remote and hilly areas where development programs needed mass media support. Doordarshan produces television software for rural communities besides other national target groups. INSAT television has two distinct features, direct telecast and nation-wide networking using terrestrial transmitters. The instructional objective of the INSAT television covered the areas of agricultural productivity, health, hygiene, family welfare, formal and informal education, and national integration.

In 90s to 2000 decade besides these development programs, government focused on creating employment for rural masses in farm-to-non-farm jobs. Lured by growing job opportunities in urban India, cajoled by a talent-starved India Inc. and compelled by a crisis-ridden agriculture sector, farmers and their children are beginning to think non-agri jobs. In any geography, at any time, this farm-to-non-farm journey has never been easy. But it is particularly so in India. The contrast between rural and urban life is dramatic. Urban India, with rising consumerism, technology and media explosion feels closer to the developed world. Rural India, many with no power, no schools, and little entertainment and poor communication are closer to sub-Saharan Africa.

To improve the conditions of the rural masses would be the true percolation of India's 9 per cent economic growth. The argument that economic growth will (on its own) percolate to villages is not true; rather advocating pro-active steps to take growth to rural India. Taking growth to the masses would mean creating jobs that produce goods and services which can, in turn, be consumed by the rural population. Farmers and villagers must be imparted skills which make it possible to wean them away from agriculture to off-farm activities like sheep rearing or dairy and then to non-farm vocations. This would check the migration to urban areas.

Telephone revitalization was planned under Sam Pitroda's Telecom Mission plans in 1986. Rural telephony was focused as priority area also. India had taken indigenous production of rural automatic exchange (RAX) and experimented in 1987 in one village. The experiment showed that technology was effective but the cost of the services and receivers would prohibit individuals to have more than one telephone available in the village. RAX project aimed at proper connectivity to 1 billion rural people and 30 million phones against 3 million at that time in 1986. The solution for the government was either to have one telephone in the village and not to invest in RAX or make service inexpensive for ruralites to afford it. Less than 6% of 575,000 villages had public telephones in 2000.

In 1990 to 2000 decade, the government focused on developing rural telephony but it did not take off. That was the time government was revitalizing landline telephony in urban areas, and mobile telephony was developing through private efforts. In 2000 decades the mobile telephone receivers and the services have become inexpensive that rural people could afford it. Government also realized that cell phone is the answer for rural tele-connectivity rather than wiring the rural areas which was expensive.

During 2000 decades, national government and private partnership efforts; and international efforts are being made to bridge the digital divide. The increased focus is on tele-density, cellular phones, Internet connectivity through broad band access and wireless access, computer literacy and computer accessibility and affordability of these information technologies. It is assumed that rural segments in general will be empowered more in economy and development through ICTs accessibility. Many Indian villages are poorly wired making wireless technology the most reliable web connection.

Intel's through its community computer initiative in India is providing low cost PC in rural India; and community PCs customized for public access, MSSRF linked twelve rural villages across Pondicherry, providing them with computer and Internet access so that they will have update information to help them in their farming work. Through the Information Village Centre, the farmers can check weather forecasts, bus timetables, crop prices as well as get advice on best practices when it comes to buying seed and growing their produce.

Indian Institute of Technology, Kanpur in 2003 set a computerization project creating a computer corridor; and provides free computer classes in six villages in Uttar Pradesh. It aims to use technology to improve education, health-care and access to agricultural information in India's villages. The project is funded by the central government.

Software for farmers is being developed by companies in Bangalore. The first, called Vyapar, is an online trading tool. The second, ECKO, provides a framework for building e-communities through collaboration and knowledge sharing.

With improved tele-density by cellular phones and community computers, many e-governance projects and practices are targeting the rural areas for better governance.

Fixed wireless access in UHF and higher frequency bands is becoming popular solution for rural communication.

In 2007, there is increased focus on India's rural retail market which will grow 29% to Rs. 1.8 trillion by 2010 driven by rising rural incomes and changing consumption patterns.

What is significant is that villages have undergone drastic changes in the post-reform era. While the trickling-down effect of higher GDP growth and a low inflation rate have improved the economic conditions of the villagers, the exposure to new products through media especially broadcasting channels has changed their consumption patterns also. The delivery of those goods through the efforts of the businesses in various areas, and in different ways further facilitates those consumption patterns.

Rural retail includes fast moving consumer goods, durables, agricultural inputs and autos like tractors. The most dramatic change has been witnessed in the non-durable consumer goods sector. They would like to buy TV, VCR, DVD, washing machine and refrigerator for personal comforts. They would be equally interested to buy tractors and other agriculture machinery to enhance their agriculture productivity.

The development of organized rural retail will create jobs, check rural migration, raise tax generation and improve agricultural efficiencies. It will be easier to arouse computer interest and need for computer training among the rural shoppers who would visit these hubs; encouraging them to seek requisite information through Internet and online e-business.

Ruralites feel highly connected by cell phone, television exposes them to news and images of world around them and education makes them understand the world and themselves as a component in that. They are equally motivated that computer and Internet will connect them to the world around them and make them understand it as television does. These are pointer to the fact that there have been integrated efforts for rural communities. Ruralites accept the integrated challenge and push themselves to achieve it and be on the road to growth as urbanites are. Now it is the turn of community computer and Internet Kiosk to be set-up in the villages or nearby cluster of village Microfinance. It may be the demonstration effect caused by the opening up of the economy to the global market. But the fact remains that ruralites expenditure on consumer goods, services and consumer durables and non-durables has increased sharply. The significant point in this context is to focus on increasing the purchasing capability of this segment without being exploited. Microfinance is the solution for it. Microfinance is considered an essential tool to lift the poor entrepreneur.

The practice of microfinance has now changed for profit making by making the working model efficient and at the same time financing and helping the poor ruralites for more diverse products without any gender differentiation. This practice created more scope. The other significant practice that has emerged is that microfinance is not only available for the products for starting enterprises and buying technology and machinery for livelihood; but for the consumer goods also—both durable and non-durable to improve their lifestyle.

These emerging practices created markets and increased the business volume for products and services targeted at them. Rural consumer segment is recognized as deserving the goods and services and right to comforts and improved lifestyles. The emerging microfinance practices are lending by profit micro-lenders, national and private banks and through private-public partnerships. Low-cost rural banking ATM with biometric sensor—Gramteller is developed for use in India in 2008.

In 2000 decades the rural population has cell phone connectivity for all, rural retail accessing to purchase and microfinance increasing their purchasing capacity. TV is ubiquitous on the rural scene and exposing them to world around them.

There are two biggest challenges for the coming years to boost rural economy in India: to educate villagers through revitalized education system in village schools and create skilled workforce whether farm or non-farm related. To create high level computer literacy and computerization in most of the villages; and the generation of non-farm employment, as well as creating more farm ancillary jobs such as food processing or cold storage industries around the villages. Thus, education, skills, employment are the targets to develop rural economy and it needs more resources and sustained efforts of both government and private sector than urban sector. Since rural sector has long been away from the mainstream. The next decade must put efforts to bring rural economy at par with urban economy.

More detailed information and dynamics can be had from the focus of challenges of business expansions in both periods, infrastructure from chapters 3 and 4; developing human capital—through workforce from chapter 5; technology and connectivity challenges in chapter 7; the challenges of creating resources through indigenous efforts and foreign capital flow in chapter 6.

Future Envisions

Our opening citation in this chapter suggests that India takes its 'Future a Challenge'. We envision future challenges anchoring from what we have addressed and accomplished since 90s till 2008. The challenges it faces are from combating terrorism, poverty, corruption, and diseases, protecting the environment to expanding businesses, developing physical and human infrastructure, creating jobs, increasing connectivity of people through telecommunications, and developing rural segment on one hand and on the other hand to find the sustainable energy to fuel its explosive economic growth, navigate international and domestic politics to ensure India's security and its status as global power. Overpopulation and density of living space with minimum basic needs, inequitable economic growth and benefits, minimizing absolute and relative poverty and limitation of physical, human and financial resources to achieve the targeted economic growth is challenging.

The urgency of these challenges is spurring innovative solutions. India's transformation from a developing country to a global powerhouse is revolutionary. How this is going to affect the future of India—financially, socially, culturally and politically is challenging?

India's economy is growing, it has to focus to eliminate poverty and ensure substantial improvement in living standards of people across all the sections of the society. The benefits of economic growth, education, employment, healthcare and technology development should reach all. Rural base needs special focus to be brought closer to the main stream.

Challenges of Rural Life in India. Optimum development of rural segment will pose ongoing challenges. In the 2000 decade, rural India is getting special attention for development in various sectors; but we all realize, in the coming years rural segment needs greater and exclusive plans and programs to develop it. Its present development is only a drop in the ocean. At present it has become segregated segment which will need special plans and programs to be brought closer to the main stream of society and benefit from programs planned for the whole society. How do we bring it closer to mainstream society? We need to focus on particular strategies, why it is lagging behind despite the fact rural segment has been the priority sector for development since 50s.

Connecting roads, electrification, safe water and sanitation should have been the first priority even in 50s; but we failed. There have been efforts to provide good healthcare through primary healthcare centers and dispensaries tiers, and barefoot doctor schemes in 70s. We had initiated excellent program of Panchayat Raj to the lowest tier of village level workers. Villages had always been the focus of new agricultural training. Even NBAD—rural bank was set up to microfinance. Many other development schemes were initiated from 50s to 70s; but schemes were ideal, but implementation was poor and villagers' motivation was low. So efforts made did not commensurate with the progress and development expected.

India can no longer afford to ignore the "dualism in the society" wherein the urban areas surge ahead on the path to progress while the rural India lags behind. There is an India which wants to move stronger while there is another which is trying hard to catch on with it. We need to think hard to give rural India a better deal. No government can ignore either challenge.

The challenges of rural life in India before the country currently is to provide better education, provide access to health, safe drinking water and water for irrigation and other purposes, sanitation and a better environment to people residing in rural areas. To develop rural road connectivity is very important. Be it sanitation, education, public health, electricity, roads, public spaces and environment, whatever is the criteria, rural India needs special strategies. The physical and social infrastructure in rural India must catch up at least with that of semi-urban India within the next decade.

The other major challenge is to provide employment within the rural areas so that flux to urban areas is controlled. Developing business bases, BPOs, and outsourcing outlets in the villages, and expanding rural retailing may create more jobs.

Challenge of Environmental Issue: India has to face the challenge of environmental issues particularly environmental pollution when transforming its economy through various industrial and other modes. "Human Development Report 2007-08—Fighting Climate Change: Human Solidarity in a Divided World," the global climate change threatens to undermine India's efforts to improve the well-being of its poorest people. The report, which focuses on the impact of climate change on the world's poor and vulnerable, highlights that the role of energy in human development is reflected in the record of CO_2. According to the report, China and India are the largest emitters of CO_2 among the developing nations.

The report says, in India changing rainfall patterns could result in drops in agricultural productivity, directly affecting 60 per cent of the population, who rely on this sector. The continued retreat of the Himalayan Glaciers could increase water scarcity, affecting 500 million people in South Asia, it adds. The report calls for greater efforts in developing countries to 'climate proof' infrastructure, deepen social protection for those who are most vulnerable, build community resilience and strengthen disaster response. To fund these critical adaptation measures, the report recommends that 86 billion dollars be transferred from developed countries, which bear the historical responsibility for climate change, to developing countries between now and 2016.

Narula (2008b) suggests that quality of life that people enjoy empowers them. Quality of life is affected not only by personal habits and choices but it is also affected by the air that we breathe, the water we drink, the agricultural or dairy products we eat, the climatic changes that we enjoy or suffer, and the fuel energy we use for our daily needs, and driving our business economy—the industries and the technologies. This suggests that environment factors are important variables for the quality of life. India is moving ahead by growing its economy by expanding the growth in various domains but it should not be at the cost of downgrading the quality of life and the clean basic amenities to its people.

These factors are controllable by individuals to some extent by keeping their environments clean and healthy, to a greater extent by governance by making efforts by good administrative practices to control the environment factors. Here good governance and politics are important. But the environmental factors need greatest global control for better quality of life. The geo-politics play important role in this context.

Therefore, it is imperative that awareness, information and knowledge about environmental issues be created locally, nationally and globally by government, people, environment activists and watch groups and by progressive environment policies both at national and global levels. Along with it, it is imperative that people, the leaders in various domains, and the policymakers are motivated to create healthy environment through good practices. For eco-friendly good practices, we need healthy choices of people and supportive decisions of governance.

For India, the biggest challenge is to provide clean basic amenities like water, sanitation and garbage disposal both in urban and rural areas. We need water management schemes, public conveniences and toilets at homes—rural areas totally lack this amenity. Schemes have to plan to control pollution created by humans, and through industrial pollutants. Household garbage collection and recycling schemes in urban areas are not implemented well so creates air pollution. In rural areas no plans are set up for garbage disposal; the rural people must be made aware of the problem and guided how to handle it. Water in rivers, ponds, and lakes are polluted both by the humans by unhygienic practices and industries discharging pollutants in them.

Energy efficiency and conservation are the most challenging. India's current total primary energy supply (TPES) comprises coal, oil, natural gas and uranium, each of which has very different global dynamics. Major factors, dictating the dynamics are current consumption, demand growth and global reserves, apart from transportation economics. The growing dependence on energy imports increases the uncertainty, not just about the price, but the availability itself. Appendix 2 gives details about energy and energy renewable resources, minerals, plastics and polymers demands and supply in India, and Integrated Energy Policy (IEP), and that highlights the future challenges for economic growth and sustainability.

Challenges of Poverty

Poverty in India has become fact of life and is a challenge to deal with. The Planning Commission has estimated that 27.5% of the population was living below the poverty line in 2004-05, down from 36% in 1993-94 according to 61st round of the National Sample Survey (NSS), poverty at 28.3% in rural areas, 25.7% in urban areas and 27.5% for the country as a whole. The criterion used was monthly per capita consumption expenditure below Rs. 356.35 for rural areas and Rs. 538.60 for urban areas. This defines the poverty line. A 2007 report by the state-run National Commission for Enterprises in the Unorganized Sector (NCEUS) found that 25% of Indians, or 236 million people, lived on less than 20 rupees per day with most working in "informal labor sector with no job or social security, living in abject poverty."

Despite significant economic progress, 1/4 of the nation's population earns less than the government-specified poverty threshold of $0.40/day. There are also a variety of more direct technical factors. About 60% of the population depends on agriculture whereas the contribution of agriculture to the GDP is about 28%. High population growth rate, although demographers generally agree that this is a symptom rather than cause of poverty.

The middle class has gained from recent positive economic development, India still suffers from substantial poverty. Although Indian economy has grown steadily over the last two decades, its growth has been uneven when comparing different social groups, economic groups, geographic regions, and rural and urban areas.

Despite this, India currently adds 40 million people to its middle class every year. Analysts "Forecasting International", suggest that an estimated 300 million Indians now belong to the middle class; one-third of them have emerged from poverty in the last ten years. At the current rate of growth, a majority of Indians will be middle class by 2005. Literacy rates have risen from 52 per cent to 65 per cent in the same period.

A study by the McKinsey Global Institute found that in 1985, 93% of the Indian population lived on a household income of less than 90,000 rupees a year, or about a dollar per person per day; by 2005 that proportion had been cut nearly in half, to 54%. More than 103 million people have moved out of desperate poverty in the course of one generation in urban and rural areas as well. They project that if India can achieve 7.3% annual growth over the next 20 years, 465 million more people will be spared a life of extreme deprivation. Contrary to popular perceptions, rural India has benefited from this growth: extreme rural poverty has declined from 94% in 1985 to 61% in 2005, and they project that it will drop to 26% by 2025. Report concludes that India's economic reforms and the increased growth that has resulted have been the most successful anti-poverty programs in the country.

How realistic is the poverty line base? For all of us, food is just one of the things we spend our income on. What about shelter, clothing, transport, fuel, healthcare, education, putting something away for a rainy day? What about paying off a loan one might have taken to buy seed, or a motorbike? All these things need money, take chunks of our earnings. To put this in perspective, let us arbitrarily decide for the purposes of this argument that people at the lower end of the economic scale spend one third of their earnings on food. Therefore, to be able to spend Rs. 540 a month on that basic basket of food, such a person would need to earn Rs. 1620 a month. Less, and she would be unable to afford those minimum nutritional standards. Less, and she would be poor.

The way we distribute food is not according to need, but according to the market. As a result, those who are able to afford food get to eat, while those who don't—starve. This is the inevitable consequence of a world of poverty and markets in food.

Seventy-five per cent of the poor are in rural areas, most of them are daily wagers, self-employed householders and landless laborers. India is a more rural-based country highly dependent on agricultural sector. There is higher concentration of poverty in the rural India as by the given statistics. Government's plans and procedures have failed many times.

The Government of India has taken various steps from time to time to reduce rural poverty in India. The recent steps are as Small Farmers Development Program, Draught Area Development Program, Food for Work Program, Minimum Needs Program, Integrated Rural Development Program, National Rural Employment Program, Rural Labor Employment Guaranty Program and Assurance on Employment. All programs focusing on earnings to survive. Government's policy initiatives for eradicating the problem of urban poverty are as Nehru Rozgar Yojana, Prime Minister Rozgar Yojana, National Social Assistance Program, and Urban Basic Services for the Poor Program.

The main causes of poverty are illiteracy, a population growth rate by far exceeding the economic growth rate for the better part of the past 50 years, low employability, and protectionist policies pursued since 1947 to 1991 which prevented large amounts of foreign investment in the country.

Agricultural research investments have large impact on rural poverty reduction, but in addition have also played a major role in the reduction of urban poverty. Agricultural research investments, increase agricultural production, and increased production in turn lowers food prices. The urban poor often benefit proportionately more than the non-poor since they spend 50-80% of their income on food. Among all the rural investments considered in a research study, agricultural research has the largest impact on urban poverty reduction per additional unit of investment.

Policymakers cannot afford to be complacent about this trend and continued investments are still needed to keep food prices low. Among all government policy instruments, increased agricultural research is still the most effective way to achieve this objective.

Relative poverty happens when people get their basic minimum needs (BMN) at a low level through their low earnings and through the subsidies of government or NGOs charity programs. There is relative poverty when there is low earning or nil for a long period. In sharing their lives, hopes and needs, relative poor men and women highlight other material deprivations but also speak forcefully of social, physical and psychological dimensions and of lacking freedom of choice and action.

This challenge can be handled on the public policy level by guaranteeing education, employment, low health costs and clean environment and affordable living; and better access to basic information or services through technology. The most ambitious approach seeks to exploit the unused entrepreneurial abilities of the relative poor through microfinance. These require the collaborative efforts of both people and other policy stakeholders to aim at reducing the poverty. People have to be highly motivated to reduce their deprivations and authorities must cooperate with them to provide the means for livelihood. Reducing poverty creates purchasing power, stability and security. These are tangible benefits for both the poor and business. It emphasizes the interdependence of all elements of development—social, structural, human, governance, environmental, economic, and financial.

Poverty is still a fact of life in India and that most benefits of globalization have gone to the top 20 per cent of the population. Still, the unabashed pursuit of global connections—through immigration, direct foreign investment, and investment in education and other social capital—has led to growth, job creation and innovations that eliminated poverty for millions.

Higher rates of economic growth, facilitated by periodic doses of liberalization, pushed forward poverty reduction. The policy implication therefore is that more, not less, liberalization fosters and sustains rapid economic growth.

Relative poor in the urban areas do create slum conditions, since they cannot afford good housing so they put up shacks on encroached lands. These lack basic civic amenities. They earn to survive but live in slum conditions and afraid of catching diseases, etc. They do create environmental health hazards but they have no control over it. Government has to provide them organized (slum) colonies as they did many years back in Delhi; basic housing and civic amenities were provided with some leisure and entertainment avenues. The experiment did succeed though it has its limitations of being away from work places and other social checks and balances of castes, etc.

Just as government authorities and corporates and other private sector effort provide education and skills for livelihood to relative poor; they can set up small residential areas near the work places to provide them good living for which they aspire also and it will be a step towards reducing relative poverty since they will spend low on health problems. We reiterate that the challenge of relative poverty can be handled on the public policy level by guaranteeing education, employment, employability skills, low health costs and clean environment and affordable living; and better access to basic information or services through technology. Such policies can upgrade the relative poor to middle class levels and a significant step towards relative poverty alleviation. Poverty alleviation is expected to make better progress in the next 50 years than in the past.

Globalization has contributed in raising the GDP and eradicating the relative poverty to a greater extent in emerging markets of India, by creating job skills, employment, raising purchasing power and consumerism and thus when there is economic growth in the society, there is less of poverty to some extent.

People are absolutely poor when BMN are minimally available. Such people are totally occupied with day-to-day survival of life efforts for hunger. Human deprivation occurs not only in lack of income, but lack of basic capabilities—when people are unable to reach a certain level of essential human achievement or functioning.

Absolute poverty or abject poverty is more identified with beggary and people living on the roads. Absolute poverty is more of urban phenomenon, since the absolute poor ruralites migrate to nearby urban areas; but both kinds of poverty exist in urban and rural areas. In India, it is a big challenge to bring this over to the level of relative poverty. Government, NGOs, Corporates through their social responsibility programs plan strategies for handling absolute poverty by providing night shelters, soup kitchens, health checks, medicines, clothing, etc. and making these poor work so they get interested in employment. But absolute poor people have lackadaisical attitude to work or even life.

Another important aspect which needs to be highlighted is that the there is bunching at the bottom of the pyramid. This means that a large proportion of those below the poverty line are below even the half-way mark, and are the absolute poor. In India, it is estimated that about 350-400 million are below the poverty line, i.e. absolute poor.

Absolute poverty is complex to alleviate. It will be monumental task to lift those who are at the bottom. People are not motivated to work for living even when some unskilled work is provided. It is hard to break this barrier; because of this trait they cannot be trained in any skill. Absolute poor migrate to nearby towns and cities from rural areas in hope of getting charity or government doles of shelter and food; or to be on the roadside and satisfied with people doling money/food, etc. They do create slum conditions whenever they are on the roadside in the absence of any public conveniences and it is hard to check them for diseases and provide them healthcare.

Poverty in India, in general has been reduced by 10 per cent over the last few years. It would be incorrect to say that all poverty reduction programs have failed. The growth of the middle class indicates that economic prosperity has indeed been very impressive in India, but the distribution of wealth has been very uneven.

India has to handle the biggest social challenge of upgrading relative poverty and handling absolute poverty in the years to come.

Thus, India's challenging future envisions challenges of rural life in India, challenges of environmental issues, energy demand and supply, its efficiency and conservation, challenges of poverty, and challenges of young demographics of India. A demographic dividend can become demographic disaster if you do not have education and job for all these young people, you will be creating very combustible social environment. You need to have an environment where more jobs get created. The other overall challenges will be providing quality of life for majority of people, transforming social values and the India identity and creating an innovative India. We strongly believe that Incredible India@60 will show the world a new contemporary-facing India.

Currently, rising inflation is posing challenges for India. In early June 2008 the rate surged to 11.05% due to high crude and commodity prices, putting a question mark on growth estimates and on the ability of the Indian market to absorb any further increase in input costs. Borrowing will become costlier and growth momentum will be affected. Indian companies, large and small, have drawn up large plans to expand capacities. Since borrowing will become costlier, the future of such expansion plans looks uncertain. The high inflation will slow down the manufacturing sector. Although expansion projects will be affected, those that will be funded by domestic debt will be hard hit, while companies depending on foreign loans may be relatively better off.

However, the infrastructure sector may not be affected as deferring such projects would be even costlier. India is scheduled to spend $500 billion to develop various infrastructure projects.

Transformation Revolution in India

Transformation was set in through rising expectations of economic gain through best and changed practices in business and finances. Transformation opened it to world economy and trade to get benefit of increased trade and foreign investments. In the later stages, the transformation is being enhanced by exposure to more and more of emerging best practices in various domains; and India is on its transformation journey by choosing the best practices facilitating its progress in various domains. It is redefining itself and its global stakes through dynamism, vitality, and the energy to transform it. India's explosive growth is due to six factors changing the mind set of India. They seem simple but have far reaching consequences for transformation.

Our attitude towards country's overpopulation has changed. Earlier we use to think overpopulation as burden and problem; but now we think it as human capital and we make efforts to develop human capital, make optimum use of it both at home and abroad. This is more critical as India is going to be the only young country in the world in the coming years including China with its one child policy. In the next 20-30 yrs India would have the largest pool of young people. This is demographic dividend. Not only would they contribute to the internal economy but also to the global economy as they would work in other countries or contribute through outsourcing in many other domain than IT only. Human capital is the core and essence of India's transformation today and root of India's resurgence.

Second change in the mindset is looking at entrepreneur as icon of economic growth. Private sector has large role to play and there is huge entrepreneurial Indian talent at home and even outside USA. Indian entrepreneurs are confident and globally competitive. This happened because the government since 90s economic reforms entrusted the expansion of businesses and diversification to private sector rather than taking care of every business itself.

Third change is attitude towards English language, which is no longer viewed as foreign language not to be taught but to be cultivated as international language for global competition and taught more and more as primary language along with Hindi—our official language and other regional languages. All the political angst is changed against teaching English language; because English language knowing personnel could expand outsourcing, which has created more jobs, and created growth in economy. Today English is seen as language of aspirations. Even more and more people in villages and towns are realizing that.

Fourth, the notion of democracy has undergone major transformation since Independence. There is change in democratic stance. In 50s and 60s it was really a top-down idea. It was vision of leaders that created the kind of country they wanted; it was given or gifted to people who may not necessarily be wanting, or be ready for that, or who understood the value or importance of that kind of country. Leaders rather created learned dependency for its people by planning everything for them. Now democracy is bottom-up. More and more of it is being created by people who understand their democratic rights as well as what is growth for them. People are now not dependent on government to do everything, they want to push themselves in the global arena and empower themselves. Empowerment must start at the village level also—reviving Panchayat system which was planned for them in 50s when they were not ready for it.

Fifth is the leapfrog in technology, we shift from antiquated system to modern applications. Leapfrog applications of technology in India such as use of computers for outsourcing when computers were expensive and we had few talented and trained computer personnel. We experimented, gained confidence and pushed ahead in outsourcing in competition with other countries. Thus, this technology and entrepreneurs confidence has played part in India's internal development as also the 50 billion export if IT. Cell phones giving connectivity and other technology applications are giving quantum jump in productivity such as technology has boosted online trading and revitalized Stock exchange functioning, giving its business much financial transparency.

Sixth, India adopted a progressive view of globalization. The confidence that it gained has made its worldview on globalization very positive. More and more people are becoming comfortable with globalization and open economy and not afraid of liberalization; not even the government who was initially apprehensive about its outcomes.

India has been facing challenges of poverty, corruption, inefficiency in public services and management of diversity by its democracy, free media, energetic human rights groups, and consumerism.

It is equally challenging to create leaders' visions for a transformed India. At this historic juncture, it requires visionary leaders in all walks of life in business, politics, education and society for unleashing prosperity. Leaders must focus on empowering people with meaningful education and heightened awareness, employment, healthcare and providing basic amenities of life essential for prosperity of all. There is need to motivate and give opportunity to young people, having untapped potential.

Currently, India is developing its business power for transforming itself but it needs to develop it soft power for transformation, *a brand-image consistent with reality and attitude towards transforming itself in geo-politics of globalization process.*

Nye Joseph (2008) discussing the Paradox of American Power suggests that there are three ways to get power: coercion (sticks), payments (carrots) and attraction (soft power). Soft power of a country rests on primarily on three resources; its culture—in places where it is attractive to others, its political values—when it lives up to them at home and abroad, and its foreign policies—when they are seen as legitimate and having moral authority. Three types of countries are likely to gain soft power and succeed: those whose dominant cultures and ideals are closer to prevailing global norms—which now emphasize liberalism, pluralism, autonomy; those with most access to multiple channels of communications, and thus have most influence over how issues are framed; and those whose credibility is enhanced by their domestic and international performance.

Whether possession of soft power produces favorable outcomes depend on the context.

Tharoor Shashi (2007) advocates that hard power, i.e. military power is no longer sufficient to guide a country's conduct in world affairs. Informed knowledge about external threats to the nation, fight against terrorism, a country's strategic outreach, its geo-politically derived sense of its national interests, and the way it articulates and projects its presence on the international stage are all intertwined to internal dynamics. A country's role on the world's stage is seen more and more as reflection of its society. At the same time country operates in era of competition with others seeking to promote their security by leveraging their assets. This is where soft power comes in.

India has geo-strategic advantages, its economic dynamism, political stability, proven military capabilities, its nuclear space and missiles programs, the entrepreneurial energy of its people, country's growing pool of young and skilled workforce. Will all this give India super power status? India must determine where its strength lies. *India needs to develop it soft power.*

What does the three ways to get power as defined by Nye means for India? It means giving attention, encouragement and active support to the aspects and products of our society that the world would find attractive and to enhance our country's intangible standing in their eyes. Indian art, classical music, dance, writers, fashion designers, Indian cuisine, sports, science and technology institutes IIT, IIM, India's free press and thriving mass media, and its people's creative energies expressed in many appealing ways raise our culture higher in people's reckoning. Culturally, India is super power and that cultural diplomacy must be pursued for political ends.

But soft power is not what we deliberately show case to others; it is rather how others see what we are such as crimes, rapes of tourists, garbage around, low safety, unsanitary conditions, poverty, and beggars. The religious intolerance and political opportunism undermine the soft power.

Globalization does have two-way impact of geo-politics—the relationships that exist between a country's politics and its geography and population distribution and talents and skills and quality of its people, and the influences that these will have on political and business relations among countries. This is a significant emerging concern. Thus, geopolitics can set up our position in the globalization race. Globalization influences geopolitics in many other ways. They create new sources of pressures on the countries to change how they organize themselves. This would come from the businesses, investments and consumer goods and services and from super-empowered individuals and not from pressures of military incursions of one country to another. *This is invisible invasion of information and private capital.*

The positive attitude for transformation is essential. When Brand India is mentioned, it should conjure the series of associations in the public mind, expectations of how it will perform. The brand can be built up with skilful advertising but ultimately the brand's continued worth is in actual performance of products and services. India transforms and it needs a fresh image to keep up with the transformation.

The brand name for 2006 World Economic Forum session in Davos where India was the guest of honor was "India Fastest-Growing Free Market Democracy" by CII. This suggests India's rapid economic growth is worth drawing attention to, it is free market—we want foreigners to invest and a democracy—that distinguishes us from others and to replace the old images of poverty and despair. We can build images on tourist attractions—the incredible India, and the unparallel diversity of our plural society. *The challenge of brand India continues what matters is projecting reality.*

It is a challenge to face the dangers of transformation process to India's future: threat to India's pluralism; danger to India's democracy; the persistence of poverty, strains of overpopulation, the risks of unemployment, politicization of development, failure to curb corruption, risks of demographic imbalance, limitations of federalism-center rule, and neglecting the software of human development. Economic interdependence is not incompatible with political independence. In fact, geopolitical and economic affairs during the 21st century will require that government at all levels have inspired leaders.

The transformation challenges are impacted by external global factors.

The external factors of external threat of terrorism combined with internal subversions, political conflicts with neighbors and associated countries, economic conflicts with global business enterprises, and religious and social tensions create challenges for countries and societies which are trying to transform themselves for higher economic growth.

The factors accelerating or slowing economic growth can impact the transformation speed in India. In May-June 2008, high food prices and high oil prices are biting into inflation at 8.75% and the economic growth is likely to slow down in India. These two factors and high inflation is likely to slow down world economy also; which has been a significant causal factor of India's progressive transformation.

With inflation and oil prices at highs, and the world economy in turmoil triggered by the US sub-prime crisis, India is no doubt affected by uncertainties all around. But the degree may be less than comparable developing countries. Data from World Bank and other think-tanks suggest that the past decade of reforms and trade growth has put India in a situation less vulnerable than earlier phases of high inflation and oil prices because growth is driven largely by demand and savings in the domestic economy.

India's transformation journey is ongoing with its success and failures and the intervening challenges are posed and the strategies and solutions sought. India is on its transformation journey by choosing the best practices facilitating its progress in various domains. We have surmised that the transformation success and failure of India along with its challenges and the rate of transformation is dependent on the planning, policies and actions of the governance and people.

Global Financial Crisis

9

Global Financial Crisis

The factors of global financial crisis of Sept. 2008 onwards can slow economic growth and can impact the transformation speed in India as its transformation is affected by the globalize factors playing role in growth of business enterprises and economic growth in general and by the spillover of the global financial crisis.

Financial crises are terrifying when underlying economic fundamentals are out of line with established theory, leading to bursts of unjustified optimism and/or pessimism. It is the responsibility of the powers that be to bring sense to the market. Every financial crisis is different, but they do all end. The Lehman Brothers bankruptcy and Merrill Lynch's acquisition by Bank of America is yet another stage in the progression of the financial crisis in Sept. 2008 onwards that had its roots in the US subprime mortgage market and in Nov. 2008 Citibank massive failure.

Key features of this crisis that started in the middle of 2007 has been the lack of clarity on both the nature and number of financial institutions that have indirect exposure to subprime assets as well as cross-product problems involving movement from subprime to prime mortgages with final spillover into derivatives, structured products and counterparty risks.

These are days of extreme and often irrational pessimism. The way to survive this crisis is to stay focused on the fundamentals. From a fundamental perspective, India's financial system has a lot going for it. Indian banks have no direct exposure to G-7 mortgage markets and their indirect exposure is minuscule relative to the size of their balance sheet. This has protected India in the past and will continue to insulate it to a significant degree from the turmoil in global markets. As this phase of extreme pessimism abates a bit, global investors are likely to reward India for the robustness of its system.

Decoupling theory is proving wrong with the emerging economies including India and China being hit hard by the economic recession in US, UK, Japan and Europe. Many major emerging economies are facing capital flow reversals, export contractions and resultant large scale job losses. China has cut production and trying to sell the export goods to non-western countries where also there is consumption slowdown in the aftermath of global crisis. The governments of both China and India are giving fiscal support to their economies in a bid to offset the negative impact of the export slowdown.

The emerging markets may be the sole contributors to the global growth in 2009. The lessons for emerging markets is to learn how to manage the global imbalances, following the Asian crisis, East Asian countries built up huge reserves as deliberate policy of self-insurance. China and India too have built up their reserves. It is this war chest of reserves that has given the emerging economies muscle to withstand the worst impact of the crisis. Emerging economies with younger population have higher marginal propensity to save. Conversely, advanced countries with ageing population have higher propensity to consume. If the demand for and supply of savings at the global level is so well matched how do we prevent recurrence of global imbalances (Seminar Mitigating spillovers and Contagion: Lessons from the Global Financial Crisis Mumbai Dec. 2008).

The enormity of the global crisis disaster sparked distrust among high-street banks, which refused to lend to each other, and panic among investors who sold fearing the worst, forcing some of the central banks to swing into action. People's Bank of China cut interest rate for the first time in six years and lowered reserve requirements for smaller banks, while the US Fed made it easier for bond houses to borrow. It offered bailout packages to Lehman Brothers and Merrill Lynch. It is actually need not be a bailout proposal at all. It's in fact a proposal to try to re-liquefy markets by reducing leverage, by increasing transparency, and by increasing liquidity and by establishing a set of pricing processes that involve the private market.

According to Standard & Poor's monthly stock market review 'The World by Numbers', world's emerging markets have fared even worse than its global peers falling 7.09 per cent in August 2008 and 19.40 per cent over the past three months. With the credit crisis casting its shadow on the international market, developed and emerging equity markets lost ground in August, and have now produced double-digit negative returns over the past three months, it said.

Post-mortems of what went wrong with the global financial system highlight new global economic truths: First rich countries were never rich at all; they were living off the debt generated by growth of powerhouse economies like China. Secondly, the new wisdom that China and at time India save too much. The analysts and economists suggest that real solution to the problem will be if India and China start spending all that they earn instead of saving and financing the debts of Americans and Britons. China and India are not amused at this suggestion.

USA is managing the global financial crisis by offering bailout, financial stimulus packages, rate cuts even to zero level and lower taxes. It has offered $1 trillion package again in Dec. 2008 to salve its economy and jobs. May be USA—the super power is in decline. It can feed, clothe and be self-sufficient and is still capable of those 'dirty' jobs like manufacturing and others that are outsourced to China and India. It has to take the decision on that though decline in outsourcing and offshoring may hit India, China and other emerging countries.

India Financial Scenario Re-Global Financial Crisis

Earlier than 90s India faced the challenges of low economic growth, and close economic policies. Since 90s the expectations have been rising because of economic liberalization, economic reforms and economic policies opening gradually which paved the way to globalization participation and economic growth. India faced multiple urgent challenges when its economic policies opened in 90s. In 2008, global financial is impacting its economic growth and slowing it down due to those global factors which were boosting its higher growth.

Globalization did create challenges for India from various perspectives and it does face more and more challenges as the process, the structure, the dimensions and face of globalization changes vis-à-vis India. India's transformation challenges are impacted by external global factors. The factors accelerating or slowing economic growth can impact the transformation speed in India.

It is being assumed that we in India are experiencing the spillover effects of what is happening in the advanced countries. We are not the cause of the problem but we are being invited to be part of the solution to the problem.

Capital flows is one important factor for Indian economy. Indian policymakers will now have to face up to the challenge of slowing capital flows, which could slide further after the latest developments on Wall Street. The turmoil in the global financial and credit markets had led to capital flowing out at a faster pace. Between April and July 2008, foreign portfolio investors have taken out close to $4.5 billion, going by RBI data. According to SEBI figures, foreign investors have pulled out close to $400 million in August and September so far. For the full year, foreign portfolio investors have sold stocks worth over $7 billion. Apprehension is that India may run out of capital to support growth—significant decline in growth rate which can have serious economic consequences. Sectors like metals, textiles, mining and automotives, cement, real estate, media IT needs capital to fund projects underway. India needs 'fundamental restructuring' to put India back on its growth trajectory (McKinsey & Co., presentation to Planning Commission, Dec. 2008).

Much of the India's current economic problems relate to external sector—exports, rupee depreciation and capital inflows.

What has began as financial crisis is now a crisis in the real economy affecting growth outlook of all economies of the world and India is not exception.

The slowdown in capital flows this fiscal year is in sharp contrast to the scenario over a year ago when the Indian central bank was struggling to manage inflows. The new RBI Governor D. Subbarao now has the challenge of stemming outflows unlike his predecessor, Y.V. Reddy who had to manage the copious flow of capital for a good part of his tenure. The Prime Minister's economic advisory council in its outlook for the economy for 2008-09 has already warned that policymakers "may have to be prepared to face a situation of greater volatility in capital inflows on account of the uncertain external environment".

The Prime Minister's advisory council report, however, adds that even if capital inflows are lower this year, it will be adequate to finance the enlarged CAD, leaving about $29 billion to accrue in the foreign exchange reserves of the RBI. Of all the major sources of foreign capital inflows such as foreign direct investment (FDI), foreign portfolio investment, overseas borrowings by Indian corporate (ECBs) and NRI deposits, only FDI inflows have been strong this fiscal. At the policy level, there may well be measures to boost flows.

Over the next few months, the challenge for the RBI would be to handle outflows. Just as excessive inflows are not good for the economy, even excessive outflows will have an adverse affect on markets. As for other policy measures, it is time to take a look at certain capital controls. The end-use norms on foreign borrowings and the rate cap at Libor plus 200 could be revisited; even the Participatory Note (PN) norms could be diluted to encourage capital flows. The government in order to invite FDI is relaxing some of the norms and regulations such as about Participatory Note. However, assuming that the foreign borrowings window is opened up again, there may not be much of an impact considering that there is hardly any global appetite for debt paper from emerging markets, said an analyst with a private bank.

The problem of capital flows is not confined to the Indian markets alone. According to a recent report by Fitch Ratings, capital flows to Asia have started slowing down given the heightened risk aversion of global investors and the deteriorating economic fundamentals of the region; and to that extent, the central bank should be less worried about the weak currency and its competitive advantage/disadvantage.

Stock Markets to Bring Liquidity in the Market: Money market is volatile and there is liquidity crunch. Emerging economies are bearing the brunt of global meltdown, giving double-digit negative returns in the past three months, even as Indian stocks have managed to perform the best among BRICs in August. Three steps need to be taken: stabilize the markets, fix the problem, and finally prepare long-term rehabilitation. Those three tasks must be accomplished in order.

The economic slump may have slowed down the private equity (PE) investments but more PE deals are being stuck in emerging businesses. Earlier most of the PE investments were in venture capital (VC) deals. Analysts say pre-IPO placements by FDI have dried up as many IPOs (initial public offering of stocks) are not coming up due to slump. FDI used to invest in a company through pre-IPO placements and made money by offloading the stake when the investee company goes public. A number of FDI funds are now adopting the VC way of investing and working in close tandem with the company to make it grow and creating values so that good returns accrue when they exit.

RBI may unveil fresh steps to make money markets efficient through greater coordination between the reverse repo—repo, call and collateralized lending (CBLO) markets. This will put an end to any major fluctuations in the overnight rates which have destabilized the markets in the past. For this RBI is setting up a new technical and committee for money markets and forex. So far corporates have very little role to play in the CBLO markets since the transactions are done only through government paper. SEBI is working towards allowing repo of corporate bonds.

Tightening Outsourcing and Offshoring by developed countries to India can be another significant factor for slow economic scenario. India's outsourcing industry will likely to face pricing pressure and a slowdown in volume growth. Still new deals come as the competence and cost effectiveness of outsourcing through India cannot be ignored. Infosys bags mega deal in multimillion dollar agreement from Astra Zeneca UK in Dec. 2008 to offer applications maintenance services to its global operations including supply chain finance, human resources and manufacturing. Wall Street firms have long dominated the client lists of India's top outresourcers who are now diversifying revenue streams from these troubled financial clients. Infosys has been trying to wean from US clients which account for its 62% revenue.

Global Crisis is Likely to Impact the Business Scenario and Employment: The government is taking adequate steps to bring cash liquidity in the market and avoid credit crunch. As government warns we have to be cautious in investments and business dealings; the growth will slowdown.

The government does not want the country to go into economic recession, people to lose jobs and to make them face credit crunch in taking bank loans for housing and vehicles and other non-durables. It is urging the business employers not to fire people with knee-jerk as that can adversely affect the economy as well as employee's morale. Businesses have agreed not only to fire people but also they are not ready to hire people; thus not generating employment.

On the business front the joint ventures with foreign partners are put on hold and even they are deferring projects on domestic front to consolidate their financial position. DLF has deferred its Mega mall project in Gurgaon, and mergers and acquisitions are also put on hold for better times.

Industry posted negative growth in Oct. 2008 quarter; this is first time in the 15 years. The industrial output decline for October is down 0.4%. Manufacturing, capital goods, consumer spending is worst hit and recorded negative growth. Meltdown is hitting India harder than anticipated. The consensus among analysts and economists is that the trend is likely to continue for some time. Nobody is sure whether stimulus packages announced in bit and packages by government will be able to trigger significant recovery.

Institutes that sprung up a few years ago to fill the talent gap such as Aviation, retail, fashion designing and retailing, finance, banking, insurance, etc. are changing their business model to align themselves with the market realities and ensure that students passing out manage to finds jobs. They are lowering their student intake, diversifying their curriculum, broadening their course focus, targeting foreign and non-traditional recruiters such as recruiters from Middle East, and delay student's entry into the job market.

Risk Management in Global Financial Crisis

India is trying to manage its economic crisis in a way as not to thwart economic growth in a big way. Agriculture is managed well and should grow, adequate liquidity is provided to industry, credit is actually delivered to industry, and individuals, and credit crunch has to be avoided; for that confidence has to be infused in banks to give credit at affordable rates. It is important to pull down inflation rates to single digit.

Finance Minister P. Chidambaram (Nov. 2008) speaking on the effects of the current global crisis on India said that there have been global recessions in the past but added that the current recession threatens to last longer and deeper than before. He said that India does not have a problem but is bearing the brunt of the spillover of this global recession. The world economy has changed more rapidly in the last sixty days than it has over a long time. But this is not the first time in which industrialized countries are going into a recession. There have been recessions in the past in Japan, in Europe and in the United States. This recession of course threatens to be a longer and deeper affecting more industrialized countries notably USA, Japan and some European countries. *We in India are experiencing the spillover effects of what is happening in the advanced countries. We are not the cause of the problem but we are being invited to be part of the solution to the problem.*

The crisis will end some day. We must take note of the structure of economy and the manner in which most Indians live and work. Sixty to sixty-five per cent of India's workforce depends on agriculture and he expects a bumper crop this year and feels it will continue to grow at a robust pace.

"In the last sixty days both the government and the Reserve Bank of India (RBI) have moved swiftly to take steps that will ensure adequate liquidity is provided to industry. However, providing liquidity is not the panacea for the current crisis. Providing liquidity is only the first step, the second is ensuring appropriate price and the third step is ensuring that at that price credit is actually delivered to industry."

Other scenarios are volatile money market that may erode banks profitability. ICRA says that net interest margins for banks in the country are likely to come under pressure and may vary across entities. The firm attributed this to extreme volatility in inter-bank and money market rates.

Government would also try to return to growth trajectory of 9% once the stock market stabilizes. On the whole, the general outlook continues to be one of cautious optimism. Economists agree with the Finance Minister's projections and expects economic growth to improve from the second quarter of next (2009) fiscal year. The global economic scenario will also improve towards the second quarter next year.

Government is borrowing more than originally planned, spending more on welfare schemes and is open to further cut taxes. 'Since there is increased expenditure, government may take one more year of fiscal responsibility management targets' FM said.

The housing industry in India may be going through one of the worst phases but in such times there are enough reasons for making affordable housing a priority. The focus has been mainly on upper-end urban housing and commercial malls and office spaces. But there is greater need for low-end urban housing and rural housing. The additional low-end urban housing free up rental dwellings for migrant populations at affordable rents and thus preventing slumps and ensuring supply of human capital for city's growth. Experts say that to fulfill the unmet demand for affordable housing we need innovative techniques to make lesser use of resources of cement, aluminum and steel, etc. Government is also urging banks to give housing loans at affordable low interest rates. Softening global commodity prices coupled with good domestic harvest is pulling down inflation rates to single digit.

December 2008: Interest rates on home loans and retail will soften soon. Interest rates on deposits have started falling in the last two weeks; this would enable the banks to cut rates on loans also. Lowering of inflation will also help to reduce both deposit and lending rates.

Slowdown in air traffic and real estate crash is impacting the completion of 8,900 crores Delhi airport modernization plan by 2010. GMR backed Delhi International Airport authority (DIAL) have tied up on 4,800 crores for forty-five days only and suggested two ways of raising the balance amount either government give long term soft loans or levy charge on each domestic and international flyer from April 1, 2009 to finish the project in time.

It is suggested that trade within Asia should be taken to tackle slowdown. India will do well to make use of free trade pact with ASEAN countries in certain sectors—automobiles, pharmaceuticals, and electronic components. It should not be merely a transient option but could well be long-term strategy.

Montek Singh Ahluwalia in Dec. 2008 advocates that a set of measures should be taken to minimize the impact of the weak global economy on the Indian economy. RBI announced the monetary and the credit side of the package, there is a significant effort to give a stimulus on the expenditure side. We have tried to look at what additional expenditure, particularly in key infrastructure, rural infrastructure, etc. is possible in the rest of this year and we think that it may be possible to authorize and to implement additional expenditure up to about Rs. 20,000 crores. In addition to this additional expenditure, a very strong effort is being made to make sure that the expenditure that has been budgeted already actually takes place. One of the problems we have had in the past for many reasons is that expenditure that is in the budget tends to be under utilized. *It is a very important spending boost to the economy.*

In addition to the planned expenditure side, there are actions that have been taken on the revenue side. There is an across the board reduction of four percentage point in the Cenvat rate except for some one or two items that would be across the board and that will be an important example of fiscal stimulus. A number of measures have been taken to respond to the concerns of the exporter community. Exporters faced a weak global demand situation. Most of our exporters are also small and medium enterprises, so a number of initiatives have been taken which in our view will make it a lot easier for exporters in the remaining months of the year. We are also putting in place significant new initiatives in housing. On 7th Dec., 2008 the Governor of Reserve Bank announced the special refinance facility of Rs. 4,000 crores for the National Housing Bank. On the government side; we are looking at what can be done to expand expenditure in the Indira Awas Yojana. That will be part of the expenditure stimulus as I mentioned earlier. Public sector banks are coming out with attractive and affordable package for homeowners wishing to take loans to purchase flats or houses.

He mentioned the small medium and micro sector—this is a very critical sector of the economy. Most of the employment in industry comes from this sector and we are very concerned that the weakening of the growth stimulus should not leave this sector high and dry. So, in quantitative terms, announcement on 6th Dec., 2008 of a refinance facility of Rs. 7,000 crores that will go to Small Industries Development Bank of India (Sidbi) and be available for incremental lending by Sidbi or for refinance for incremental lending by the commercial banks. It is a very major step to help the medium and small sector.

In addition, several other steps have been taken like expanding the guarantee cover and also giving instructions to the central public sector enterprises that they should ensure prompt payment of bills for the small scale sector. This is a very important area in the sense that when there is a tightness of credit, the bigger units delay payments to the smaller units. We are in fact taking steps to make sure that the banks will lend and that public sector enterprises should have no difficulty in getting their credit needs met by the banks and we want to make sure that they, in turn, pass on the benefits of this to the SME. There is a package for the textile sector where another Rs. 1,400 crores is being made available to clear the backlog in TUF scheme of the textile sector and also expanding the coverage of the Vishesh Krishi and Gram Udyog Yojana.

A major area for the government to focus on is infrastructure financing. Prime Minister had said several weeks ago that we need to give a contra-cyclical thrust to infrastructure investment. We are doing that in the public sector through some of the measures being taken on the budget side. In addition, many initiatives are underway promoting infrastructure investment in the public-partner mode, particularly, in the area of roads and ports. I know that a large number of projects have now gone through the various clearance processes and are pretty much being put up for invitation to bid. It is very important that the financing environment for infrastructure is supportive.

What is being proposed is that the India Infrastructure Finance Company Limited (IIFCL) which was setup just over a year ago, is being given additional resources of about Rs. 10,000 crores in the form of permission to mobilize tax-free bonds and depending on need, government will in fact expand this permission. The resources mobilized will be used by the IIFCL to refinance bank lending to infrastructure. This will be in addition to what it normally does, which is to provide direct financing. The point about refinancing is that it doubles. If they provide 50% refinancing then it means that this Rs. 10,000 crores will actually come to Rs. 20,000 crores going out into the infrastructure sector. On the whole, taking a longer view, all this cannot be done in the next three or four months but we are really trying to build up an entire program for infrastructure investment. We think, for example, in the highway sector alone, it would be possible over the next 18 months to support or to clear to total investment program of almost Rs. 100,000 crores. That doesn't mean that all that money will be spent in

18 months but we will start and bring to financial closure projects which would get implemented over a period of 2-3 years but which would have a total value of almost Rs. 100,000 crores.

There are some other measures also, for example, government departments being allowed to take up replacement of government vehicles within the existing budget which is relaxation of economy instructions, reduction in import duty of naphtha and also a reduction in the export duty on iron ore lumps and an elimination of the export duty on iron ore fines that would basically provide a stimulus for exports for this sector.

The overall position really is that like all countries, we are facing a world economy that is not in good shape. Fortunately, the Indian economy is in much better shape than most others. But we cannot be complacent. We want to take action in advance of any problems arising so that factors that would otherwise weaken our growth performance are minimized. It may not be possible to eliminate them completely. Growth in the year 2008 will be less than it was last year but the steps that we have taken will make sure that the impact is minimized and also this must be emphasized that this is not necessarily the only thing we are going to do. We watch the situation closely both on the monetary and on other sides and would take additional action if necessary.

He further suggested that Financial Stimulus given by government will be needed in 2009-10 also as global slowdown is likely to continue next year also. Plan panel is working on the allocation estimates for the next fiscal year.

Deputy Chairman of Planning Commission Montek Singh Ahluwalia's address to the press (Dec. 2008).

In the global meltdown of 2008, government is taking stock of India growth story. India story has been road to growth and it must be sustained. There is liquidity crunch. RBI and government are coming forth to reduce the liquidity crunch. Banks have lost confidence in public. But they should not freeze the financial system by their fear factor. They should give credit/loans for investments to individuals and corporates.

Government has been concerned about the impact of the global financial crisis on the Indian economy and a number of steps have been taken to deal with this problem. The forward looking policies of the government and its intervention inputs will counter fiscal crunch. It suggests corporate focus on customers through inter-factoring and micromanaging domestic demand and finance flows back to banks. Government has to reduce cost of transactions and improve infrastructure. It must energize business leadership to improve strength and capability, and deliver high in global meltdown.

The fiscal stimulus package is expected to boost demand. Fiscal policy is an important instrument to stimulate demand. Dec. 7th, 2008, the government has announced Rs. 20,000 crores fiscal stimulus package to industries, banks, textiles to boost the morale of the market. The crucial focus of fiscal stimulus package is on expenditure stimulus, consumer consumption stimulus, creating demand by consumers to produce goods and services and thus sustain employment. The focus is on creating housing demands and credit through housing loans by banks thus helping the real estate sector. The other sectors are infrastructure financing, and stimulus for exports. As RBI Governor Subbarao commented, when there is upswing, confidence is restored and world economies start recovering. India will be the first to recover.

Experts' Opinions: Narula (2009) advocates that three new concepts of global structure which focus on expansion of businesses and development of human, intellectual and financial capital, dimensions of global transformation and transformation challenges for countries participating in the globalization process may be undermined by the global meltdown. The transformation success and failure of India along with its challenges and the rate of transformation is dependent on the planning, policies and actions of the governance and its people in global meltdown scenario.

Current situation in India is going to get better as India is going through slower growth (Peter Hendal Dale, Carngie training), India will see higher growth rate once the current situation settles down, i.e. by end 2009 (Research Analyst, Gartner), India's exposure to global trade is low which will help soften the adverse affects of slowdown. Given the favorable demographics and long-term growth potential we expect India to attract significant foreign investments particularly in infrastructure, which should help improve productivity and competitiveness of Indian industry (Joel Pelman, Copal Partners). There will be significant change in the verticals. The focus will be on the domestic market than exports. In the short run, revenues and margins will be affected but in the long time it will lead to good industry practices as bad practices will be weeded out (Anil Kumar, Quinnox).

Experts are predicting that once India gets back to its feet, things will get better for industries as well as for organizations and their employees. This will also be the time when other industries will also gain in value in terms of availability of other job opportunities for potential gain strength and there will be shift in the focus to core sectors like power, construction, manufacturing and retail. Growth will be stronger in government and industrial sector wherein they would like to leverage competitive advantage through technology.

Education sector is likely to gain momentum as many people will retool themselves to adapt to the changes resulting from crisis. The pressing need will be to make qualified the right talent by looking at pre-hire assessments and other tools to improve the selectivity of the recruits (Diwakar Nigam, Newgen Software, Esawaran, Dexterity).

This will also give Indian organizations and entrepreneurs to expand more in terms of value and supply as they will be entering and playing in a more mature field. There has been tremendous downsizing of the employees because of meltdown but experts say that by the end of this period employees will be better off as organizations will come with rampant policies to help them get better suited to their jobs though salary increases will be modest. Most companies will reduce their HR budgeting by snipping increments, outsourcing work to cut costs and increasing proportion of variable component and performance linked pay.

Infosys CEO said, the company is focusing on additional training and education for employees to prepare them better for the growth and recovery after global financial meltdown (Nov. 2008).

Shankar Acharya, Member, Board of Governors and Honorary Professor, ICRIER (Dec. 2008) sees FY09 GDP growth at 7%. "We will be lucky to see 6% growth in FY10. He feels the speed of the global recession and the huge uncertainty increases risks. The severity of the global recession is not yet fully seen in India. The recession is likely to be longer than that seen in the last few decades. A turnaround in the global economy is likely only by 2010. Commenting on the recent government and Reserve Bank measures, Acharya felt both entities have reacted promptly and effectively. The effects of the recent fiscal package will kick in next year. There is more room for fiscal stimulus in FY10 only if commodity prices stay low. We will see more RBI action in the form of refinancing CRR, repo and reverse repo cuts."

India being cautious at this stage will be cautious to invest FDI in USA, UK through M&A and joint ventures.

It is presumed that *rural spend and housing* may rescue growth. India may buck the global crisis largely based on the buying power of the bottom 80% of population that accounts for 67% of the consumption. These are also the people who are not affected by the negative wealth effect caused by the stock market crunch. Schemes like NREGA, pay commission handouts and farm loan waivers may revive consumption and even boost the stock markets (M.K. Venu).

C.K. Prahalad (Dec. 2008) talks about the current slowdown and its impact on Indian entrepreneurs and suggests how to manage global financial crisis in India. The Indian entrepreneurs learn to increase productivity, build global efficiencies, and build capacity to handle volatility. They should be able to scale up and down rapidly. They may have to relook at the way they make capital commitments, commitment to people and skills. Indian companies have to consider whether they can outsource functions, whether they can use more temporary labor, whether they can be more flexible in their pricing. Basic idea is to spread the risk. Education and healthcare can give highest return on capital today. Agriculture too has a lot of potential provided Indian companies tackle post-harvest issues of wastage, poor preservation of perishable products and inadequate access to markets. Companies like Amul, ITC, Reliance and Bharti are investing to address these issues and it will benefit farmers.

Telecom companies in India have increased telecom density in the country by making mobile phones inexpensively accessible to the low income groups and poor by following a business model; they focus on how much such consumers can pay and then look at the ways to bring costs down to that level and that model has succeeded in India.

Kumar Manglam (Dec. 2008) feels that whatever happens elsewhere is bound to impact India we are no longer isolated. We are still part of the global economy and are not decoupled; though we have very strong domestic market. There is crisis of confidence, liquidity crunch and no demand for any industrial products such as aluminum that is linked to global pricing. But other products which have domestic play such as cement, the demand is impacted by the infrastructure activities and general economic scenario. Industry has its own issues of overcapacity and of lag effect.

China is dumping goods in India as its US market is close but we must protect our domestic industries and act against it speedily.

Companies are reacting with proactive mindset and focusing on making process improvements and cutting costs to the extent possible and focusing on cash flows and not firing people though cautious about hiring new also as that would create employment crunch. Interest rate cut could be a great confidence booster and it could regenerate lots of projects that have been put on hold. Banks have the liquidity and they must start lending.

Several Indian businesses are bucking slowdown. Experts believe that there are other sectors such as education, healthcare, consumer goods and retail, media and entertainment, avionics, auto-electronics and robotics which are likely to do well despite of the slowdown. As for the IT sector, the focus is shifted from pure services to products, and technology in education and healthcare. There are sectors like security, medical science and technology in defense and remote monitoring which are recession-proof. Even energy management will gain in such times.

These are the few steps to be taken immediately in the current financial crisis scenarios. Government is boosting up the morale of the businesses, banks and investors and people in general by taking various steps to safeguard the economic and financial health of the country and assuring that India is not in recession state. The key actions that the government should take are to put infrastructure projects back on fast track as lack of infrastructure is causing 1-1.5% decline in growth. We must invest in education to turn our large demographic factor to advantage.

Call it prediction or hope—this global financial crisis will end. It had domino effect across the globe. For India it may be sooner than the rest, it will be among the very few countries to emerge mostly unscathed and also with a positive outcome.

What would you rather do, continue to discuss the economic meltdown or focus on strategic solutions with innovation gurus.

Terrorism

The external factors of external threat of terrorism combined with internal subversions, political conflicts with neighbors and associated countries, economic conflicts with global business enterprises, and religious and social tensions create challenges for countries and societies which are trying to transform themselves for higher economic growth.

Mumbai Terror Attacks 27 Nov. 2008: The terror attack of this scale shattered some of the transformation dreams of India. There were human loss and tremendous financial loss estimated to the tune of 50,000 crores and $20 billions when the three posh hotels in Mumbai—Taj, Oberoi and Oberoi-Trident were attacked where many global meeting would take place and foreigners would stay and do business transactions. This would affect the hospitality sector, hotels, food entertainment, and tourism and of course disturbing the global meets and conferences.

Post Mumbai terror attacks, there were a few disturbing voices on the geopolitical front that might worry a lot of global investors and local investors. But if the parlays between India and Pakistan get more shrill and global investors get the sense that geopolitical equation in this region is getting destabilized, then there might be some kind of lingering impact on the market because that will be one more reason not to buy into one emerging market like India.

Some experts think that majority of the investors are bullish about long-term prospects of India, based on advantages such as lack of leverage and favorable demographics. Analysts think the long-term impact depends on how India responds to terror threats. A few US strategic and financial investors may prefer strategic alliances with Indian companies, over setting up their own offices in India. The tourist industry may be hit but the general fundamental economics of India remain intact.

Do we have to stop talking about being super power though we may be super influencer in the world economy in the next two decades?

Appendices

Appendix 1

Outsourcing in India

Outsourcing and offshoring: Both of these factors are interlinked to the economies of the developed world. There is interconnecting of markets and knowledge. Such globalization has its challenges though no doubt creating global prosperity and economic growth for themselves.

Insourcing: Synchronizing global supply chains large and small.

Global supply chains: The convergence of technology and events allowed India, China and many other countries to become part of the global supply chain for services and manufacturing, creating explosion of wealth among the middle classes of the two biggest nations and giving them huge stake in the success of globalization.

Outsourcing

Infosys Company provides worldwide comprehensive end-to-end business solutions that leverage technology for its clients, including consulting, design, development, software reengineering, maintenance, systems integration, package evaluation and implementation, and infrastructure management services. It has set up facilities in US as well as China, keeping India as base, outsourcing technologies products and services from there, and research and development.

Wipro provides IT services in India, as well as research and development services and software solutions to companies worldwide. The company also maintains a presence in the Indian market segments of consumer products and lighting.

America's outsourcing to India is approaching a new frontier—outer space. India and US space agencies signed an agreement on 9 May 2006 in Banglore, India. Accordingly, the Indian agencies will fly two American lunar mapping instruments in India's unmanned mission to orbit the moon, scheduled for 2008. NASA is taking advantage of India's more immediate and lower cost plans as the possibility of sending American spacecraft to moon remains possibility in the distant future. The joint space venture is part of Bush administration's efforts to forge close strategic partnership with India.

RIM is long-distance monitoring of computer networks. The workers at outsourcing centers oversee computer systems for clients abroad. Remote infrastructure management includes security, operation management and network management for them. Security is about protecting company's network against virus and hacking attacks. Operation Management ensures adequate capacity of data and analyzes patterns of data usage.

Network monitors overall network and reviewing performance. This is India's latest frontier on outsourcing. This business could be worth billions of dollars as multinationals try to cut costs and Indian outsourcers tighten security check on corporate data they manage. According to Indian industry estimates (2006), market is still small, only $300 to 1 billion though growth is expected. Nasscom India estimates that the market size will grow 60 per cent as the foreign companies cut costs by shifting information-technology services abroad.

So far Indian companies have been hired to do specific software projects, with specific chores on IT systems but have not managed the entire networks or production sites. The multinationals outsourcing this type through RIM will be concerned about the security of propriety information. To reassure potential clients, Indian outsourcers are taking certain steps: They have tightened security check on corporate data they manage. Indian law-enforcement agencies are being trained to detect data theft, and database of employees at software companies is being built for easier track if they commit crime. The data base will include person's biometric—fingerprints, date of birth, education, family background.

RIM units at Indian companies were set up since 2003 and the business is growing fast. HCL Technologies, Wipro Ltd., and Infosys Technologies Ltd. are growing fast with RIM; and more companies are likely to take up.

Business transformation outsourcing (BTO) is another new trend.

TCS Outsourcing

"The other advantage comes into play when I also operate at the transaction level, running the system. In such a case, since I know their system, I can optimize that as well. When I look at infrastructure management offerings, I can optimize a lot more. I not only develop the system, but also ensure that it is doing well. I can also maintain the database, giving information about processes and thus, contributing to business intelligence."

And all these services are further laid on a consultancy model, which can be architectural or governance consultancy. Optimization at various levels leads to better margins in case of a full services play. The current play in TCS is about extending relationships with clients.

Growth for TCS, so far, has come mainly from organic strategy. What is their approach regarding inorganic growth? Talking about inorganic growth, it acquired Comicrom, a BPO firm in Chile, to address the South American market. Hence, it was a regional play. It made an investment in UK's Pearl to enter into UK's life and pensions industry. However, TCS greater thrust is on organic growth and that's how they have grown.

Is insourcing an in-thing for TCS? They do provide BPO services in the UK, Chile and Budapest through regional set-ups. Their approach towards insourcing is need-based. For instance, in order to sort out the language barrier, they acquired Comicrom in Chile. In this case, outsourcing was not feasible due to the language difference.

Appendix 2

Energy in India

Can India achieve the development targets across industries without the crucial input of energy? To deliver a sustained growth of 8-9% through 2031, the country needs to increase its energy supply by 4-5 times and electricity supply by 5-7 times the current consumption levels. Energy remains the most critical factor requiring massive growth, apart from the financial sector reforms for sustaining the growth rate of the economy. What are the challenges to sustain this rate? Energy efficiency and conservation are the most challenging.

India's current total primary energy supply (TPES) comprises coal, oil, natural gas and uranium, each of which has very different global dynamics. Major factors, dictating the dynamics, are current consumption, demand growth and global reserves, apart from transportation economics. For India, the situation is slightly peculiar in the sense that while it can have an independent coal policy, it is closely and inextricably linked to the global market for all other sources of primary energy. The growing dependence on energy imports increases the uncertainty, not just about the price, but the availability itself.

Of the four major fuel sources, coal has the largest share of India's energy requirement at about 55%. Despite globally declining share (down 26%), coal continues to drive the Indian economy and is expected to remain the mainstay of India's growth strategy. Integrated Energy Policy (IEP), the comprehensive policy document says, "Coal shall remain India's most important energy source till 2031-32 and possibly beyond".

For the 10 supply options projected by IEP, coal's share remains between 42% and 65%, indicating its criticality to growth. With an estimated reserve of 248 billion tones and proven reserve of 92 billion tones, the supply is expected to last for at least 80 years. However, the sector is mired with significant inefficiency and productivity stagnation coupled with outdated technology. Apart from policy issues, environmental issues such as huge pollution, ash handling and disposal and logistics continue to act as shackles.

On the positive front, allotment of captive coal blocks to power, steel and cement producers and more recently, decision to allot blocks to private producers, should bring in the latest technology and lead to a competitive market. An increase in imports should also put competitive pressure on domestic coal industry.

OIL: In case of oil, the proven reserves to production ratio stands at 22, meaning the current reserves will last for only 22 years. If the reserves were used to provide the entire requirement, they will last for only around seven years. As a result, the current dependency of around 70% on imports is expected to go up to more than 90%. While acquiring equity abroad and demand substitution are the options available to reduce the dependency, this can have only limited impact.

GAS: While gas holds lot of promise for future, it is facing the most serious problem today, in terms of both availability and pricing. Its share in energy basket, which is only 8%, was expected to go up towards the global share of 24%. However, the hike in price in the past three years turned the situation from bad to worse. The meltdown of the past few months, and expectation of moderation in the near future, has brought some respite.

The current gas availability in India is about 90 MMSCMD, against an estimated requirement of around 150 MMSCMD. India's current reserves are about 30 trillion cubic ft (tcf), enough for only around 30 years, at current production rate. While there are enough reserves globally, the problem here is of bringing it to the demand centre. Another aspect of gas supply is availability of significant gas in neighborhood areas, which needs diplomacy more than economics for harnessing.

URANIUM: As a fuel option uranium holds significant promise in the medium-to-long term. India has a current requirement of 600-50 tons a year of uranium, which will nearly double in the next 15 months. However, a big jump in India's fuel needs will come by 2015, and India's uranium requirement could be more than 3,000 tones a year, if things go as per plans. Current global requirement of uranium fuel is

66,000 tons, against the production of 45,000 tons, the rest being met through inventories. Uranium faces significant demand pressure in about a decade's time, with significant new capacities coming on-line.

However, the good thing is that there are ample reserves for this source, and supply can certainly match the demand, albeit with a time lag. Another aspect, which can change the dynamics of uranium market, is commercialization of thorium as a fuel, which will reduce consumption of uranium substantially. For India, this is of even greater importance as it has less reserves of uranium and high reserves of thorium.

Renewable Resources

Minerals Use: There is an urgent need to develop economically viable processes for the effective recovery of metals from zero wastes like red mud and fly ash; for energy efficient mineral production and that metallurgical industries ensure optimal utilization of available mineral resources at all times. Processing of many natural materials (glass, paper, wood, metals) consume far more energy derived from fossil fuel.

Polymers and Plastics: The fact that plastics are made from hydrocarbons derived from petroleum, which is non-renewable, has raised questions concerning its sustainability. Nevertheless, the consumption of petroleum hydrocarbon for the production of plastics is less than 5%, the balance being consumed as fuels and energy source. Additionally, research and development work currently in progress globally will provide future opportunities to make some of the plastics from biomass and other renewable resources.

Plastics replace several natural materials, which are either scarce, consume more energy for processing or cause damage to the eco-systems during their production. Thus, use of plastics makes a positive contribution to the sustainability of earth's resources in myriad ways.

The long life and desirability of plastics, which have made them a material of choice for many applications is seemingly a disadvantage when it comes to their disposal and their non-biodegradability.

Plastics have the advantage that they can be easily reprocessed and recycled.

The overall eco-friendliness of plastics becomes apparent when one evaluates the total 'life cycle', namely, an analysis of raw materials, energy, effluents, methods of disposal, etc., of a material from its origin to its final disposal.

The Indian plastics processing industry is highly fragmented. Injection molders dominate the Indian plastics processing sector. Polyethylene bag and sheet producers dominate the extrusion segment. India is expected to be the third largest consumer of plastics after US and China by 2010.

Demand for plastic polymers in the next 5 years is expected to grow at CAGR of 15%. Polythene and Polypropylene will continue to dominate polymer demand in India. Demand of all polymers in India is expected to reach 12 million tones by 2011.

Appendix 3

Snapshots of Recent Business Activities 2007

Reliance Industries signs two E&P contracts in Colombia offshore.

Reliance Industries has signed technical evaluation agreement in 2005 which has been converted to hydrocarbon production and exploitation contracts with agenda nacional de hydrocarburos (ANH) of Colombia for two offshore blocks, Borojo (pronounced as Boroho) North and Borojo South. These contracts will in due course be assigned to REP DMCC, a 100% subsidiary of the company.

Signed on December 10th at Bogota, Colombia, the contracts envisage exploration of two blocks located in the Pacific Ocean, west of Colombia in water depths reaching up to 1500 meters. Each block size is approximately 4,000 square kilometers. The company has carried out comprehensive geological studies before selecting these blocks.

December 2007, the seventh round of New Exploration Licensing Policy (NELP) will offer 57 oil and gas blocks. Speaking to newspersons here on Monday, the Petroleum Minister, Mr. Murli Deora, said, "we will announce NELP-VII on December 13".

The round may also see steel baron L.N. Mittal's Group participating for the first time. Of the 57 blocks to be offered, nine are in shallow water, 19 in deep water and 29 are on land blocks. Most of the deepwater blocks would be in the western offshore. Bids close on April 11, 2008 and the awards would be decided by July end.

In the latest round, the intent is to attract more global majors who have the expertise to develop complex deepwater blocks. The seventh round would see change in bid evaluation criteria to give more weightage to companies having experience in deepwater exploration and production. Additional weightage would be given to those involving foreign partners with deepwater experience.

Satyam Computer Services to set up Japan center of excellence. To intensify focus on Japan Kanzen, Satyam Computer Services has announced the setting up of a Japan Center of Excellence (COE), code-named KANZEN, to significantly strengthen its presence in that country. This announcement was made on the sidelines of the inauguration of an offshore development centre (ODC) for Japanese group Inoac Corporation by leading management exponent from Japan and CTO of Inoac. The company has already initiated a process to intensify its focus on Japan by commencing training for Japanese engineering graduates in India, building the bilingual talent pool in India and China and setting up of delivery centers at China, Pune (India) and Fukouka (Japan).

Moser Baer Company plans to rapidly emerge as a leading, global technology driven manufacturer through a mix of technologies in the crystalline silicon, concentrator and thin film domain by implementing a capacity of 500 MW by FY10.

Globally, given the rapid growth of the photovoltaic industry, there is currently a shortage of silicon wafers, a key raw material for the photovoltaic industry. The company has implemented a flexible three pronged model for securing raw material, supply through a mix of strategic investments in silicon manufacturing, long term wafer supply contracts and spot purchases.

The company's photovoltaic manufacturing capacities for crystalline silicon, concentrator and thin film technologies are coming up in one of India's first renewable SEZ's in Greater Noida.

Snapshot of Enterprises in India: Outlook & Key Events 07 & Prospects of randomly selected companies in Pharmaceuticals products, heavy engineering, Power industries, electronics, metal sector, Auto sector, Telecommunication, Information technology (IT) sector, Energy, Oil and Petrol Sector, Mines, Shipbuilding and dredging, Biometric Sector, infrastructure, Bioethanol and ethanol, chemicals, 3-dimensional video technology device that lets you virtually teleport a person across continents, educational solutions, engineering and industrial equipment, medical equipment, precision instruments, textile machinery, financial services and textiles.

Pharmaceuticals Products: Dr. Reddy, Cipla, Pfizer, Merck, SunPharma are other notables. Dr. Reddy's, Nicholas Piramal, Jubilant Organosys, Dishman Pharma Indian companies are bidding to acquire Pfizer's Ireland-based manufacturing unit, which may be valued in the range of USD 60-80 million.

Pfizer has put its unit up for sale, as part of its global manufacturing rationalization plan. Pfizer's Irish plant is said to be manufacturing raw materials for high-value cytotoxic substances, which goes into several key life saving oncology drugs.

India's present pharmaceutical market was estimated at $6.3 billion in 2005. It is expected to touch $20 billion by 2015, with a compounded annual growth rate of 12.3 per cent, the study said. Between 2000 and 2005, the pharma market witnessed a growth rate of 9 per cent. Similarly, in terms of scale, Indian pharmaceutical market, which is ranked 14th in the world, would be among top 10 by 2015 in the world overtaking Brazil, Mexico, South Korea and Turkey, the study noted. The incremental growth of USD 14 billion over the next decade is likely to be the third largest among all markets. The money is paltry when compared to that of the US, which is expected to add $200 billion, it said.

Ranbaxy India

Outlook & Key Events 2007 & Prospects

It may rank just no. 14 in the $28 billion US market for prescription generic drugs. But it is a leader in nations like Nigeria and Brazil. It has earned goodwill by being one of the biggest suppliers of $1-a-day generic AIDS treatments to Africa at cost, and hopes to have its own new malaria drug on the market by 2008. It has also acquired smaller generic drug makers in Belgium, Italy, and Romania.

Ranbaxy hopes this R&D base will enable it to spring into the top five in the US by 2012 and to No. 1 globally, passing Israel's Teva Pharmaceutical Industries Ltd. It has 58 generic medicines pending at US Food & Drug Administration approval, including a version of the anti-cholesterol drug Lipitor. Its pipeline is the second-biggest in the generic industry. Ranbaxy Laboratories said it was prepared to provide oseltamivir phosphate capsules (generic version of Tami flu) to the US healthcare system to ward off threat from avian flu (2007).

The company intends focusing on European markets for pharma biosimilars. It acquired Zenotech in Oct. 2007 and valued acquiring Zenotech Company on the basis of biosimilars and the oncology pipeline. It will launch oncology products in 2009. The valuation for Zenotech is not as much in the business that it has today; but in the pipeline and the potential it provides for the next decade, in terms of giving a very significant opportunity in biosimilars, oncology and in specialized injectibles.

The pipeline that Zenotech has is probably unmatched globally and it provides Ranbaxy with a very significant opportunity to be a very strong global player in the emerging markets and in the developed markets for biosimilars, injectibles and especially for oncology, over the next 10-15 years.

Wockhardt's India

Outlook & Key Events 2007 & Prospects

It acquired three international companies in 07. Morton Grove Pharmaceuticals is latest. It had acquired Pinewood, the largest generic company in Ireland and the largest supplier of liquid generic products in the UK, in early October 2007, and Negma, the fourth largest independent pharmaceutical company in France, in May 2007. These acquisitions propelled the company to become the largest Indian pharmaceutical company in Europe.

Wockhardt, manufacturer and trader of pharmaceutical products, has presence in different drug segments like inflammation and pain, anti-infective, cough syrups, corticosteroids and medical nutrition.

Heavy Industries and electronics, Power and Industries. Notables in this area are:

BHEL (Bharat Heavy Electrical Ltd.)

Spurred by the buoyancy in the power and industry sector, the company has embarked on an ambitious and aggressive capital expenditure (capex) plan whereby it seeks to enhance manufacturing capacity to 15,000 MW for the XI Plan with a total investment of around Rs. 32 billions, from the planned 10,000 MW by the end of 2007. The Company's move to enter into technical collaborations and take minority stakes in various state utilities to get super critical orders will open new avenues for growth and also help to face competition from Chinese manufacturers. BHEL is also pursuing the inorganic route to broaden its operational horizon.

Outlook & Key Events 2007 & Prospects

- BHEL entered into a MoU with Toshiba of Japan for know-how in higher horsepower locomotives, from design to producing a prototype and putting it on trial with the Indian Railways.
- It has won orders valued at over Rs. 29 bn. for the supply and installation of the Main Plant Package at the upcoming Jhajjar Super Thermal Power Project in Haryana, involving three units of 500 MW each.
- It has won contracts for setting up two units of 500 MW each at Koderma Thermal Power Station (TPS) in Jharkhand and two units of 500 MW each at Durgapur

Steel TPS in West Bengal, both on turnkey basis. Valued at over Rs. 65 bn., the orders have been placed by Damodar Valley Corporation.

- BHEL and MMTC Ltd. signed a MoU to cooperate with each other to promote the export of BHEL equipment in overseas markets.
- The company signed a MoU with NTPC Ltd. to form a 50:50 JV to carry out EPC activities in the power sector on mutually beneficial terms.
- The company is negotiating to set up a joint venture (JV) in the country to manufacture nuclear power plant equipment with global power equipment firms Siemens, Areva, and General Electric (GE). The proposed JV will give BHEL a head start in the competition after the nuclear power market in India opens up when the upcoming Indo-US nuclear deal is put into operation.
- It is considering taking equity in the Koradi Thermal Power Station near Nagpur. The plant would undergo a 1,600 MW expansion in the generation capacity based on super-critical technology and would involve a capital outlay of Rs. 8,000 crore.
- It expects capacity and capability enhancement with increased emphasis on innovation and R&D to leverage its efforts in core area of operations.

The key risks could be increased competition especially from Chinese manufacturers, delays in execution of projects, fluctuations in prices of raw materials, and failure of projects involving super critical technology (considering BHEL's relative inexperience in this field) are the potential risks.

Electronics

Bharat Electronics Ltd. (BEL)

Outlook & Key Events 2007 & Prospects

- BEL has taken some major steps in the last few quarters in terms of expanding its product range into new but related products and systems. In order to cease the opportunity arising out of the mandatory offset clause in the Indian Defense Procurement Procedure-2006, BEL has signed MoUs with major aerospace companies like Lockheed Martin, Northrop Grumman, Boeing, European Aeronautics Defense, and Space.

- The company is looking ahead to set up a state of the art facility for Rapid Proto-typing, Rapid Tooling and Rapid Manufacturing, which will cut down development cycle time by 30% and provide customers with better products.
- BEL is in discussions with various technology partners to expand its business operations through JVs in various growth areas such as thermal imaging, avionics, etc. Besides, increased government emphasis on defense products is also likely to boost the Company's growth in the near future.

Key risks to its growth are attrition of trained and skilled manpower and increased competition from the private sector for defense contracts.

Larsen & Toubro (L&T)

Outlook & Key Events in 2007 & Prospects

- Raytheon and L&T sign MoU for Medium Multi Role Combat Aircraft Program (MMRCA) on 20th November. This strategic alignment is intended to help develop superior defense technology for India's military forces.
- L&T has been awarded an order worth around US $60 million from Methanol Chemical Company (CHEMANOL) in Saudi Arabia. This E&P (engineering & procurement) order involves setting up high technology methyl amines and dimethyl formamide plants. Chemanol (Saudi Formaldehyde Chemical Company) is a private sector enterprise, operating grassroots, second-generation petrochemical complex located in the Al Jubail industry city, Saudi Arabia, manufacturing formaldehyde and its derivative products.
- Davy process technology, UK (DPT), has provided the process technology for the 50,000 MTPA methyl amines and 60,000 MTPA dimethyl formamide plants

incorporating advance design elements and elaborate environment control measures.

The company's scope of work comprises residual process design, detailed engineering, project management and procurement of the equipment and materials for the plant. The company will also provide the technical services for the erection and commissioning of the plant.

- L&T acquires Switchgear Company in Malaysia. It has entered into a share sale agreement with Malaysia-based Tamco Corporate Holdings Bhd towards the acquisition of the latter's de-merged switchgear business, Tamco Switchgear Malaysia Sdn Bhd.
- The two parties propose to enter into three other share sale agreements for acquisition of three of Tamco's switchgear manufacturing subsidiaries—Tamco Shanghai Switchgear Co. in China, Tamco Electrical Industries Australia Pty in Australia and PT Tamco Indonesia in Indonesia. The deal was signed on 11 October 2007 in Kuala Lumpur.
- With this acquisition; the company will have access to the fast growing MV Switchgear markets like the Middle East and the EPC contractors that have approved use of Tamco's products. This synergistic acquisition will enhance L&T's capability in both LV with MV categories, and will allow it to offer turnkey solutions to customers.
- The national focus on the fast tracked incremental power generation program will provide a strong impetus to spur the demand for MV switchgear leading to an increase in the growth rate of these products.
- The company is one of the leading global manufacturers of low voltage switchgear, with the scale, sophistication and product range that meet international standards. It has a track record that includes the supply of intelligent switchboards, systems and service to major industrial projects.
- In addition to its leadership position in the Indian market, the company has a growing presence in overseas

markets. It has four manufacturing facilities for switchgear operations in India and one each in China and Saudi Arabia.

- L&T announced the signing of a USD 95 million shipbuilding contract with Netherlands-based Big Lift. The production of ships is scheduled to commence in June 2008.
- The company secured Rs. 1,140 million order from SAIL for the turnkey construction of 220/132 kV gas insulated substation and associated transmission network.

ONGC awarded a Rs. 8,770 million turnkey project order for the NQ Reconstruction (NQRC) project in Mumbai High North fields.

L&T signed a MoU with Japan's Toshiba Corporation to jointly manufacture power plant equipment in India with an investment of Rs. 3,000 million.

L&T and Tatas are in the race to set up the rail wheel factory in Chhapra on a public-private partnership basis with the Indian Railways.

L&T, Mitsubishi Heavy Industries (MHI), and Mitsubishi Electric Corporation (Mitsubishi Electric) signed a technology licensing and technical assistance agreement for manufacture of supercritical turbine and generators.

With presence in various infrastructure development sectors through its subsidiaries, the company will be able to capture the surge in demand and realize better margins due to economies of scale and faster execution of orders. Currently, L&T has planned various capacity additions that are likely to support its growth plan. The company has also made plans to foray into power generation business that offer higher margins. Hence, given the strong economic fundamentals, we expect the company's earnings to improve due to superior realizations, cost efficiencies, and faster execution of orders.

Aditya Nuveau (ABNL) business focus is Telecom, Insurance, BPO, Garments, Textiles, Rayon, Insulators, Carbon, Fertilizers, IT Services and Financial Services. The booming economy has driven demand for value as well as high growth products sold by ABNL. This has given a growth momentum to its broad based segments.

Outlook & Key Events 2007 & Prospects

- In high growth businesses, revenue from the Telecom segment is likely to increase significantly after Idea's entry into Mumbai and Bihar circle by Jan. '08.
- In the BPO segment, after acquisition of Minacs, ABNL will add 4 more centers to its business that will increase operating seats by 2,576. The company also won 10 contracts during the quarter along with 3 new clients.
- Revenue from Life insurance business is expected to grow after the expansion of low cost branches and improvement in the distribution network.
- The Company's Fertilizer and Insulator segment products are expected to realize better sales volume driven by acute deficit of fertilizers in India, favorable government policy and increased thrust on development of energy sector.
- ABNL also has plans to build leadership position in branded garments for youth segment and leisure clothing considering the upsurge in consumer demand in this segment and has subsequently added new stores to its retail space along with better distribution network.

Metals Sector. Driven by a continued growth in developing and emerging economies, global steel demand is likely to remain robust. The International Iron and Steel Institute (IISI) forecasts global steel consumption to grow by 5.9% in 2007 and 6.1% in 2008, driven by strong demand from Asia, Africa and South America.

Domestic demand for steel is expected to grow at 10.2% for the year 2007.

Besides this, per capita consumption of steel in India is less than 50 kg, whereas it is 150 kg in the world and 350 kg in the developed world. This per capita consumption is estimated to reach levels of 165 kg by 2019-20. Keeping in view the